SANDRA GUSTAFSON'S

GREAT EATS ITALY

FLORENCE · ROME · VENICE
FIFTH EDITION

CHRONICLE BOOKS
SAN FRANCISCO

Manufactured in the United States of America

FIFTH EDITION

ISBN: 0-8118-4555-9
ISSN: 1074-5084

Cover design: Ayako Akazawa
Book design: Words & Deeds
Typesetting: Jack Lanning
Series Editor: Jeff Campbell
Author photograph: Marv Summers

Distributed in Canada by
Raincoast Books
9050 Shaughnessy Street
Vancouver, B.C. V6P 6E5

10 9 8 7 6 5 4 3 2 1

Chronicle Books LLC
85 Second Street
San Francisco, CA 94105

www.chroniclebooks.com
www.greateatsandsleeps.com

For Michael, a great friend

Contents

To the Reader

In Florence you think, in Rome you pray, and in Venice you love. In all three, you eat.
—Italian proverb

Italians tend to think of themselves first as Romans, Venetians, Florentines, and Sicilians, and only secondarily as Italians. But what unites them all is their love of and appreciation for food—whether the simple cooking of Tuscany, the seafood in Venice, the garlic, aromatic herbs, spices, and meats in Rome, or the Parma ham and robust pastas of Bologna. Italians have been trendsetters at the table ever since the Middle Ages. They were the first to use a fork, the first to wash their hands before a meal, and among the first to make a point of preparing food using the freshest ingredients. When it comes to cuisine, few countries in the Western world have given so much to so many. Just think of all the foods you love, and no doubt a majority will be Italian: pasta, pizza, balsamic vinegar, Parmesan cheese, sun-dried tomatoes, porcini mushrooms, polenta, osso buco, prosciutto, minestrone—the list is endless. When we want satisfaction, comfort, or pure enjoyment, we eat Italian.

To Italians, life is meant to be lived fully, and much of everyday life in Italy revolves around eating. Food is not considered mere sustenance but rather a work of art to be enjoyed and relished at every meal, and meals are meant to be shared with company. In fact, the word *company* is derived from two Italian words: *con,* meaning "with," and *pane,* for "bread"—which means "breaking bread in friendship." But a meal only starts with the bread. From there you move on to the appetizer, a first and second course, vegetables, salad, cheese, fruit, dessert, coffee, and, finally, a digestive, which you will need after a lengthy meal. If you seriously overindulge, a shot of the strong herbal mix Fernet-Branca, available in most bars, will set you straight in no time.

In the last fifty years, Italy has gone through a complete economic transformation. It is now the world's fifth-largest industrial power. As a result, prices have skyrocketed, the dollar goes up and down like a yo-yo against the euro, and inflation is rampant. *Nothing* is cheap in Italy—certainly not the food. Today it costs more than $2 to buy and send a postcard back to the States, many restaurants charge $30 to $40 for a meal, and you can easily spend too much on a mediocre sandwich and a glass of rough house wine if you don't know where to eat.

Eating well takes planning, and this is where *Great Eats Italy* comes to your rescue: it is your reliable dining guide to the best quality food at the best prices. My commitment in *Great Eats Italy* is to help you find the best dining value in all price ranges, so whatever your budget may be, you know you will be getting a good meal—whether it's a romantic Big Splurge or a simple picnic on the piazza. Just as important, you will dine where the natives dine, not where the tour buses stop.

When it comes to research, other guidebooks may send a questionnaire, or have someone stop by a random selection of restaurants. I do not do that. I am personally responsible for every entry in this book, and I visit every address, new or old, for every edition. Updates are frequent. In doing the research for this edition of *Great Eats Italy,* which includes more than three hundred dining selections, I spent months in Italy, plotting maps, walking hundreds of miles in every type of weather, checking on countless addresses, and eating food that ranged from terrible and indifferent to delightful and gourmet. In the write-ups, I describe the atmosphere and decor, and tell you about the history of the restaurant and the family who runs it, even mentioning any children or pets who may greet you when you arrive. I describe the other diners; how the food is prepared, presented, and tastes; and what it all costs. I recommend dishes to give you an idea of what the restaurant does best, and I warn you about any dishes to avoid. Because most menus in Florence, Rome, and Venice reflect the four seasons of the year and very often change on a daily basis, many of the foods I describe may not be served when you visit, but the quality and value will still be firmly in place. One subject I do not cover is that of Italy's many fine wines . . . that would necessitate another book, and many excellent ones have already been written on it. However, I do comment on some of the house wines and tell you if they are drinkable.

In the back of the book is a "Readers' Comments" page for your notes, suggestions, and comments. I hope you agree with my selections, and let me know when you do, but it is just as important to me to know about changes you may find, and any Great Eating discoveries you have made that you would like me to know about for the next edition. Please take a few minutes to drop me a note telling me about your experiences. As the countless readers who have written to me know, your letters are very important to me, and I read them all and answer as many as possible.

Whether you are traveling to Italy for business or pleasure, I urge you to go with an open mind. When you leave home, don't expect to encounter your way of life, or your favorite comfort foods. Enjoy the moment wherever you are—the people, the sights, the sounds, and even the smells. Sample a wide variety of foods, and roll with the punches, since travel is rarely trouble free. If you can see the humor in a difficult situation, you will come home a more knowledgeable person, with a lifetime of happy memories.

By using this edition of *Great Eats Italy,* I hope you will return with some of the best memories of all: those of delicious meals in wonderful settings, enjoyed all the more because they were affordable. If I have been able to help you do this, I will consider my job well done. *Buon viaggio,* and especially . . . *buon appetito!*

Tips for Great Eats in Italy

The President could solve all the country's problems by having a big plate of spaghetti once a week. Congress can supply the meatballs.
—*Will Rogers*

1. If you want to eat dinner with the tourists, eat early. If you want to eat with the locals, eat late. Most places do not require men to wear a tie, but Italians always dress with casual elegance when they eat out. You will never see a well-dressed Italian man or woman dining out in shorts and athletic shoes . . . except at beach resorts.

2. If you see a headwaiter or chef standing in the doorway, tour buses parked outside, or an empty restaurant during prime time, keep going.

3. When dining out, remember to order appropriately according to the place and the chef's abilities. Do not expect gourmet fare in a snack bar, and do not go to a fancy restaurant and order only a bowl of soup. You do not have to order something from every course, but you should have at least two courses in better restaurants.

4. Italians make a big fuss over children; therefore, taking children to restaurants in Italy is not the problem it can be in France. You can ask for a high chair (*seggiola* or *sediolina*) and for half portions (*mezze portione*).

5. By law, all eating establishments must post a menu outside. *Always* read it before going in. This prevents you from being seated before finding out that you do not like what is being served or, worse, that the prices are too high. Generally, it is best to avoid places that have long, laminated menus printed in four or five languages.

6. Pay attention to the daily specials and the house specialties. You can be sure these will be the best the chef has to offer and will usually consist of seasonally fresh foods. If they are not on your menu, look for them on a chalkboard, or ask your server.

7. Try to include a trip to a daily outdoor market. This is not only a colorful look at local life, but a window on what your plate may contain at your next meal.

8. If your budget is tight, consider the fixed-price menu, sometimes referred to as the *menù turistico* or *prezzo fisso*. Even though the choices may be boring and limited, it is usually a good buy because it includes at least two courses and often the cover and service charges. Some also include dessert and/or a beverage.

9. To keep the tab lower on an à la carte meal, skip the antipasto course and head straight for the pastas and entrées. Keep in mind that main courses on an à la carte menu are usually not garnished, and orders of vegetables and salads will be extra.

10. Restaurants in Italy must indicate when frozen food is used by adding an asterisk (*) by any such menu items. Most often you will find that if anything is frozen (*congelato* or *surgelato*), it will be the fish, sometimes the potatoes. Most Italians would never order anything frozen, and neither should you. Make sure what you are ordering is *fresco* (fresh).

11. Don't sit down in a bar! Drink your morning cappuccino and eat your snack or sandwich for lunch while standing. If you sit down in a bar, you risk being charged up to twice as much for the privilege of occupying a chair. If you sit at an outside table, the tab could be even more. The benefit of sitting is that you acquire something akin to "squatter's rights" and can linger at your table for the price of a coffee for hours without being bothered.

12. The cover charge (*coperto*) is per person; so is the bread (*pane*) charge, which replaces the cover charge in Rome. The service charge (*servizio*) is a percentage of the total bill. The good news is that the service charge *is* the tip. You do not have to pay one euro more unless you feel the service has been out of the ordinary. (For more information on cover and service charges, see page 14.)

13. Every restaurant in Italy is required to give you a formal bill, which you are legally required to take with you when you leave. Before leaving, compare the bill with the prices on the menu and add up the figures. Do not hesitate to question anything you do not understand. Mistakes are all too common. Separate checks are not common—please try to avoid asking for them.

14. A new law in Italy bans smoking in public places, which includes restaurants. Laws in Italy are one thing . . . Italians willing to obey them are another. However, most places do have at least a few tables set aside for nonsmokers.

15. If you have enjoyed a place recommended in *Great Eats Italy*, tell the owner or manager where you found out about them. They are always very appreciative.

How to Use *Great Eats Italy*

Each listing in *Great Eats Italy* includes the following information: the name and address of the establishment, the area of the city in which it is located, the telephone number (plus email and Internet if available), the days and hours it is open and closed, annual closing dates, whether reservations are necessary, whether and which credit cards are accepted, the average price of a three-course à la carte meal without beverages, the price of the fixed-price meal, the cover and service charges, and whether or not English is spoken. Most listings include a map key number in parentheses to the right of the restaurant name; an entry without a number means it is located beyond the parameters of the map. A dollar sign ($) to the right of the name means that it is a Big Splurge; a cent sign (¢) means it is a Cheap Eat.

At the end of the restaurant listings, you will find a glossary of Italian menu and restaurant terms; an index of all restaurants including indexes by category; and finally, a "Readers' Comments" page.

Big Splurges and Cheap Eats

Most of the restaurants in this guide are in the midrange category, but a few are more expensive and labeled as "Big Splurges," and a few are bargain finds and labeled as "Cheap Eats." Restaurants in the Big Splurge category are included for those who have more flexible budgets, or for special-occasion dining to celebrate a birthday, anniversary, or any other memorable event, such as being in Italy. In many cases these restaurants also offer a fixed-price menu for lunch, and sometimes dinner, that is well within the budget of most diners. They become Big Splurges when you order à la carte. These restaurants are marked by a dollar sign ($). See the index for a complete list of Big Splurges in Florence, Rome, and Venice.

Being labeled a Cheap Eat does not mean a restaurant lacks quality or is somehow inferior. On the contrary, these establishments offer exceptional value for money and constitute some of the great bargain eats in Florence, Rome, and Venice. Note that this designation is used only for restaurants, not bakeries, ice cream shops, and other places that don't, as a rule, serve meals. In the text, Cheap Eats are marked with a cents sign (¢) and are listed in the index under each city.

Holidays

Very few restaurants in Italy are open 365 days a year. Most are closed at least one day a week and for an annual vacation of up to one month. Many close on some or all of the holidays listed below, and those closings depend on the economy at the moment as well as the whims of the owner. You can also count on many places being closed at least a few days between Christmas and New Year's Day. If a holiday falls on a Tuesday or Thursday, many will also take the Monday and/or Friday off. Because of these constantly changing policies, please call ahead to check if your visit falls during these holiday times or in the months of December, January, July, or August.

New Year's Day (*Capo d'Anno*)	January 1
Epiphany (*La Befana*)	varies; early in January
Good Friday	varies; March or April
Easter Sunday (*Pasqua*)	varies; March or April
Easter Monday (*Lunedì Pasqua*)	varies; March or April
Liberation Day (*Venticinque Aprile* or *Festa della liberazione*)	April 25
Labor Day (*Primo Maggio* or *Festa del Lavoro*)	May 1
National Day	June 2
Assumption of the Virgin (*Ferragósto*)	August 15
All Saints' Day (*Tutti Santi*)	November 1
Feast of the Immaculate Conception (*Festa dell'Immacolata*)	December 8
Christmas Day (*Natale*)	December 25
Day after Christmas (*Santo Stefano*)	December 26
Patron Saints' Days:	
Florence: St. John the Baptist's Day	June 24
Rome: St. Peter's Day	June 29
Venice: St. Mark's Day	April 25

Hours and Days Closed

Nearly every eating and drinking establishment has a regular *giorno de chiusura:* the one or two days a week they are closed (*chiuso*). That doesn't mean much. Due to holidays, local customs, government red tape, the ever-present threat of *scioperi* (strikes), yearly vacations, restoration and remodeling, the weather, and much more than the non-Italian can ever fathom, the one place you really want to try may be closed. A few places maintain that they "never" close for holidays (and are so noted in the text), but in reality they may close for certain holidays when they feel like it; they just don't want to be pinned down. Though *Great Eats Italy* lists each establishment's days and hours of operations, be sure to call ahead to double-check, especially if you do not have a backup choice nearby or your heart is set on a particular place.

Bakeries, fruit and vegetable shops, and other food stores are closed all day Sunday and usually one afternoon per week. Pastry shops are often open on Sundays until early afternoon, and some large supermarkets are staying open for a few hours on Sunday. Food shopping hours are generally 8:30 A.M. to 1 P.M. and 3:30 to 7:30 P.M. Open-air markets are open Monday through Saturday from 8 A.M. to 1 P.M.

Maps

Great Eats Italy has an accompanying map and restaurant key for each city, and in the text, these map key numbers appear in parentheses to the right of the restaurant's name. If a restaurant does not have a number, it is located beyond the boundaries of the map.

Please note that the maps in *Great Eats Italy* are designed to help the reader locate the restaurant listings; they are not meant to replace fully detailed street maps. Italian cities can be very confusing to get around in, so no matter what your length of stay is, I strongly recommend that you buy a locally produced city map. These are generally available at any news kiosk or bookstore. See the introductions to Florence and Venice for more information on negotiating these notoriously convoluted cities.

Smoking

I am happy to report that Italians are smoking less than ever before. To encourage a smoke-free environment, a new law slated to take effect in 2005 prohibits smoking in any public area, and that includes bars, restaurants, and trattorias. However, just because there is a law does not mean an Italian is going to obey it. Many laws of this type are considered mere "suggestions," and I am sure that the no-smoking ban will be one "suggestion" ignored with great frequency. On the plus side, most restaurants do have a few tables set aside for nonsmokers. To ensure that you are seated at one of them, request yours when reserving.

Paying the Bill

Italian restaurant bills can be confusing. With the following information, you will be better able to avoid the pitfalls of overcharging or confusion when *il conto* (the bill) is presented.

Issuing separate checks is not popular; in fact, management often flat-out refuses to do this. Please try to avoid this practice. In many small places, especially bars, *pasticcerias, tavola caldas,* or *rosticcerias,* cash is king; plastic money is reluctantly accepted and only with a minimum order. Most restaurants, though, take credit cards. Every listing in *Great Eats Italy* states the restaurant's credit-card policy. The following abbreviations indicate which credit cards are accepted:

American Express	AE
Diners Club	DC
MasterCard	MC
Visa	V

Italian law requires that all establishments give a bill to the customer and that the customer carry the bill out of the restaurant. Who knows if anyone ever checks, but it is a protection for the consumer—you must get a proper bill for your money spent. And don't waste the protection: always add up the bill yourself and question any discrepancies. There are often mistakes.

Prices

All *Great Eats Italy* listings give the prices for à la carte meals and the fixed-price meal (sometimes referred to as the *menù turistico*) if one is available. All printed menus are required to list whether there is a *coperto* (cover charge), a bread (*pane*) charge (Rome only), and/or a *servizio* (service charge) and the amount. The à la carte prices quoted in this book represent the average cost of a three-course meal only; they do not include the cover or service charge if there is one or any beverages (unless otherwise noted). In determining the average price of a meal, the cheapest and the most expensive foods were avoided. Thus, you could spend more or less, depending on what you decide to eat and drink. In using *Great Eats Italy,* you should expect prices to increase each year based on the margin of labor costs, inflation, and most important . . . the owner's view of the economy.

Cover Charge (*Coperto*)

The cover charge is levied per person and is not to be confused with the service charge. In Rome, the cover charge has been theoretically banned, but Roman restaurateurs don't give up easily, so there is now a bread charge, called *pane,* to take its place; in establishments you will see it noted as *pane, pane e coperto,* or still just *coperto.* Supposedly it is not applicable if you do not touch the basket of bread, but theory and fact do not always agree. In Florence and Venice the cover charge is intact and is referred to as such. No matter what it is called or in which city, the cover charge includes the table settings, flowers, and everything else the owner wants to toss into this catch-all charge, plus the bread, whether or not you want it or eat it. All menus *must* clearly state the cost of the bread/cover charge, which is listed separately on the bill and added to the total on which you will pay service. Usually, if you order the fixed-price menu, and always if you eat or drink standing at a bar counter, you will avoid the cover and service charges. In *Great Eats Italy,* each establishment's cover and service charges are noted.

Service Charge (*Servizio*)

Just as menus must state the cover charge, they must also state the service charge, or lack of it. *Servizio incluso* and *servizio compreso* mean the service charge is included in the price of the meal, and no further tip is necessary (nor will there be another charge added to your bill). *Servizio non-incluso* or *servizio non-compreso* means that the service charge has not been added; it is technically discretionary, but you will be expected to pay an additional 10 to 15 percent of the total bill. "Servizio 15%" means that the restaurant will automatically add 15 percent to your bill, and this will appear as a separate charge. All of the listings in *Great Eats Italy* describe how the service charge is handled: either "service included," "service discretionary," "10% service added" (the percentage will vary), or "no service charged."

Italians are not known as big tippers. Please remember that the service charge is the tip, and you are not required to leave anything more unless the service has been especially good and you are feeling generous, in which case you can round off the total. For service above and beyond, consider the ultimate tip: informing the person's employer by writing a letter of praise.

Reservations

Every *Great Eats Italy* listing states the reservation policy. If reservations are advised, please make them. If you want a nonsmoking table, consider them mandatory. It is always better to arrive with reservations than to wish you had. If you feel uncomfortable calling, ask your hotel to do it for you. They may even be able to get you a better table. Only a few places that are very busy do not honor their reservation times. However, you should arrive on time, call if you will be late, and definitely call to cancel if you will be unable to keep your reservation.

Italian telephone numbers are not as crazy as they once were, but the improvement is slight. In Rome, some phone numbers have only five or six digits, while newer numbers have seven digits. The area codes for Florence, Rome, and Venice, including the beginning zero, are part of the number you dial. For example, in Florence you dial 055 plus the restaurant number; in Rome, dial 06 plus the number, and in Venice, 041 and the number. All telephone numbers in this book include the entire number you are required to dial, for example, 055 123 456. If you have difficulties, try calling the operator (dial 12). Operator assistance offers no guarantees, but it is worth a try.

Transportation

It is beyond the scope of *Great Eats Italy* to note all of the public transportation options in the three Italian cities covered in this book. Of the three, only Rome has a metro system, and it consists of two lines, which are designed to take people through or across the city, not around it. Since the system is only marginally useful as a way to travel to the restaurants listed in this guide, metro stops are not mentioned. Rome's buses are a more comprehensive way to get around, though the city is small enough that you can walk comfortably to many places.

Florence and especially Venice are cities where walking is not just the most convenient but the preferred way to travel. Otherwise, Florence has a public bus system, and in Venice one travels on foot or by canal, whether in a vaporetto, an expensive private water taxi, or a very expensive gondola.

General Information about Italian Dining

Everything you see I owe to spaghetti.
—*Sophia Loren*

No man is lonely while eating spaghetti; it requires too much attention.
—*Christopher Morley*

When to Eat

Breakfast (*La Prima Colazione*)

Hotels and pensiones usually serve at least a Continental breakfast (normally served between 7:30 and 10 A.M.) that consists of coffee, tea, or hot chocolate, fresh rolls, butter, and preserves. In the last few years, many hotels have expanded their breakfast into a buffet where guests help themselves to a full range of breakfast foods—from fruit and fruit juice, cereals, and assorted pastries to cheese, cold meats, yogurt, eggs, and all the coffee, tea, or hot chocolate you can drink. While this may seem like a great idea, it is seldom in your best fiscal interests. Hotels make up to 200 percent on these buffets, but you never see the cost because hotel rates are quoted including breakfast. Savvy, budget-minded Great Eaters should try to get their hotel to deduct this cost—which can be as much as $15 per person—from their bill and eat their breakfast at a bar or *caffè*. Doing so will cost a fraction of what the hotel charges. The coffee will be better, the pastry fresher, and the local scene far more interesting. However, if you do partake of your hotel's breakfast buffet, please do not load your pockets and bags with enough food to see you through lunch and afternoon snacks. Hoteliers take a very dim view of this cheap trick.

Lunch (*La Colazione*)

Lunch usually starts at noon or 12:30 P.M. and lasts anywhere from thirty minutes (standing up) to three hours (sitting down). Last order is supposed to be the time the restaurant says it is closing, but more often the last order will be taken about thirty minutes *before* closing. Lunch can be anything from a quick sandwich eaten standing at the corner bar to a full-blown four- or five-course meal ending with a strong coffee under the umbrellas on a busy piazza . . . which has to be one of the true pleasures of eating in *Bella Italia*. Time, cost, calories, location, and hunger are the factors that go into deciding what to do for lunch. Sandwiches are available in a *paninoteca,* a bar selling sandwiches either made to order or ready-made and displayed under napkins in a case. In most trattorias and restaurants, the à la carte menus for lunch and dinner are the same, and there is no price break offered at lunch. There is, however, often a fixed-price menu available only for lunch.

Dinner (*La Cena*)

If you want to eat with other foreigners, reserve a table for 7:30 P.M. If you want a more Italian experience, dine at 9 P.M. or later; dinner is usually served until 10:30 P.M. Solo diners, especially women, may be relegated to poor table locations. To avoid this as much as possible, reserve a table for two. Upon arrival, say your dining companion had to cancel at the last minute and tell the waiter how sad this makes you. It is amazing how well this works, and how much the service improves.

Where to Eat

At one time there was a distinct difference between a trattoria and a *ristorante,* based on the type of clientele and the prices charged. Now they are virtually interchangeable. A trattoria is generally a family affair, with Mama or Papa in the kitchen, and the children helping out as needed. The decor and the menu are simple and the prices only slightly less than in a *ristorante.*

Fast-food *italiano* is a boon to all Great Eaters, and I am not talking McDonald's, where a burger, fries, and shake can cost upward of $15. Besides, who wants a Big Mac in Italy? Bars offer some of the best food, from an early-morning *cornetto,* the Italian croissant (either plain or filled with custard or jam), to *tramezzini,* sandwiches made with sliced white bread, and *cicchetti,* bite-sized tapas served in Venice. Inexpensive meals can also be found in stand-up snack bars that feature a *tavola calda,* which means "hot table." Usually frequented for lunch, these places feature a buffet of hot and cold dishes either to eat there or take out. A *rosticceria* also offers hot and cold dishes to eat in or take out. At either the *tavola calda* or *rosticceria,* items are priced by the portion. You choose your food, pay the cashier, get a receipt, and give that to the person behind the counter, who will dish up your food. You will also encounter pizzerias (very often open only in the evening, especially in Rome and Florence) and places called *pizza al taglio* or *pizza rustica.* These hole-in-the-wall shops sell slices of ready-made pizza sold by weight. It is fun to try several small pieces. Alcoholic beverages are not served, but you can get soft drinks and bottled mineral water. Seating is virtually nonexistent.

Other places for a quick bite or a simple meal include a *latteria,* which sells cheese, yogurt, and other dairy products; a *gelateria,* which serves ice cream; and a *pasticceria,* which sells fresh pastries all morning and in the afternoon. At *il forno* you can buy bread, and at an *alimentari,* which is a combination grocery and deli, you can order a custom-made sandwich on a roll. In a *salumeria,* or *gastronomia,* you can buy cold cuts, cheese, wine, bread, mineral water, and other foods to put together a picnic in the piazza or back in your hotel room. For a glass or two of wine and a light meal or upmarket snack, go to an *enoteca,* or wine bar. *Osterias* were wine bars years ago, but now they are more restaurant than wine bar and feature old-fashioned homestyle cooking.

The Italian Menu

One cannot think well, love well, or sleep well, if one has not dined well.
—*Virginia Woolf*

The most important thing about eating in Italy is to not let the length of the menu frighten you, and to order according to the establishment. If you are in a simple trattoria, you probably will not be expected to order every course, and the overworked waiters won't have much time to go into detail about the dishes they are serving. In restaurants, the pace is not as frantic, and waiters should explain the dishes and help you select a wine. Portions tend to be smaller, and thus you will be expected to order more.

Bread is served with all Italian meals and is part of the *coperto.* Butter is not served, but if you ask for it, you will probably get it.

Salad is generally eaten after the main course, even if you are ordering only a pasta or a pizza.

Don't order fish on Sunday, when the markets are closed: the fish will be at least one day old. In Venice, extend this to Monday, since the Rialto fish market is closed then as well.

Most Italian menus follow this order:

antipasti, or appetizer—which can be as simple as a few olives brought to your table or as lavish as a serve-yourself buffet, whereby you can almost make a meal from this course alone

I primi, or *primo*—the first course, a choice of pasta, risotto, soup, or a light vegetable dish

I secondi, or *secondo*—second or main course of meat, fish, or game

contórni—vegetables and salads

formaggi—cheese

dolci—dessert

caffè—espresso only

digestivo—after-dinner liqueur (*grappa* or *limoncello*)

Some restaurants and trattorias offer a *menù turistico,* at an all-inclusive price. Do not let the name turn you off . . . it is only a fixed-price menu that at the very least includes a pasta or soup, main course, and either a vegetable or a salad. It may also include dessert, beverage, *coperto* (cover charge per person), and *servizio* (service charge), in which case there will be no additional expenses tacked onto your final bill. While this can be the best budget way to go, the quantity and selection might not be up to the standard of an à la carte meal. You cannot expect the finest beef, soft-shell crabs, or the chef's best dishes. You can expect a filling if unsurprising meal.

If you are handed the English menu, it may not list the daily specials. Always ask to see the Italian menu along with the English one, otherwise you may miss out on the best dishes at the best prices. If you are a woman dining with a man in a better restaurant, you may be handed a menu without prices; this chauvinistic practice will probably fade in time, but for now, simply insist on seeing a menu with the prices clearly marked.

For a complete list of menu terms, and for phrases to help you while ordering, please see the Glossary, page 253.

Finally, it cannot be said enough: Double-check your bill before you pay, and ask questions if you think something is incorrect. Mistakes, unfortunately, happen with great regularity.

How to Drink Italian Style

A wine is like a man; it can have flaws and still be pleasing.
—Italian village salami-maker

An Italian bar is much more than a place to drink coffee or alcoholic beverages. Here you can eat breakfast, have a snack, sandwich, or hot lunch, make phone calls, use the toilet, read the newspaper, listen to or watch sporting events, meet your neighbor or lover, and argue over politics. If there is a black-and-white "T" (for tobacco) displayed outside, you can also buy cigarettes, matches, some toiletries, stamps, lottery tickets, and bus tickets. No wonder there are more than five thousand such places in central Rome alone. In most bars, you pay for what you want at the *cassa* (cash desk) before you order it at the bar. Then take your receipt and put it on the bar for the barman to see. Remember, standing costs less. If you sit at a table, you will be charged more, but you can stay at your table as long as you like for the price of a cup of coffee or glass of beer.

What kind of coffee or drink should you order? The possibilities can be confusing to many Americans. This is a list of the most popular caffeine-laden drinks:

caffè/caffè espresso	A small cup of very strong coffee, i.e., espresso
caffè Americano	American-style coffee
caffè corretto	Coffee "corrected" with a shot of grappa, cognac, or other spirit
caffè doppio	Double espresso
caffè freddo	Iced coffee
caffè Hag/decaffeniato	Decaffeinated coffee
caffè latte	Hot milk mixed with espresso and served in a glass for breakfast
caffè lungo	More water added, similar to *caffè Americano*
caffè macchiato	Espresso "stained" with a drop of steamed milk—a small version of a *cappuccino*
caffè moka	Equal mix of espresso, chocolate, and hot milk
caffè ristretto	Short, very strong espresso

cappuccino	Espresso infused with steamed milk and consumed in the morning but never, ever after lunch or dinner
cappuccino senza schiuma	Cappuccino without the froth
granita di caffè con panne	Iced coffee with whipped cream
latte macchiato	hot milk with a shot of espresso
tè	tea
tè detèinato	decaffeinated tea

Like the French, Italians never drink coffee or tea with any meal except breakfast, although coffee (*caffè espresso*) is often ordered after a meal. Tea is considered a morning or between-meal beverage, or one to be used for medicinal purposes. Only unknowing tourists order a cappuccino in a restaurant after lunch or dinner.

Coffee accounts for almost 80 percent of a bar's earnings, but there are other things to drink, starting with *birra* (beer). Beer is either *alla spina* (on tap) or *alla bottiglia* (in the bottle). If you order it *alla spina*, ask for it as *una birra piccola* (small), *media* (medium), or *grande* (large). Wine is always available by the glass, but unless you are in an *enoteca* (wine bar), chances are it will be of low quality. Every bar has *grappa*, but be careful; it can be lethal. The most popular *apéritivi* (apéritifs) are *Spritz*, a traditional Venetian drink (made with white wine, selzer, a twist of lemon rind, and Campari soda), Martini *rosso* or *bianco*, and the everpresent *prosecco* (dry sparkling white wine). Finally, there is water, either from the tap, called *acqua naturale*, or bottled, which comes *non gassata* (still or plain) or *gassata* (with gas).

Cooking Classes

Cooking classes for tourists are becoming more popular in Italy, and a good one can be the highlight of any trip. In Florence I've included two highly recommended cooking classes—by Apicius and Divina Cucina (see pages 22–23)—and in Venice I couldn't heap more praise on Samantha Durell (see page 180) and her *Art of Eating Well* tour.

FLORENCE

Their smiles and laughter are due to their habit of thinking pleasurably about the pleasures of life.
> —*Peter Nichols,* Italia, Italia, *1973*

Whichever way you turn, you are struck with picturesque beauty and faded splendors.
> —*William Hazlitt,* Notes of a Journey through France and Italy, *1826*

For nearly three centuries, from Giotto's time to Michelangelo's, Florence was the cultural center of Europe, producing countless art treasures and generating ideas that formed the cornerstone of twentieth-century thought. Five centuries after the Renaissance was born here, Florence has become a victim of her own beauty and is in danger of being consumed by traffic, pollution, and crowds from the four corners of the planet. Streets designed to accommodate horse-drawn carriages and pedestrians now cope with cars, trucks, Vespas, and hundreds of smog-inducing tour buses. Despite this, visitors continue to flock to this beautiful city to immerse themselves in the art, the literature, and the soft Tuscan light. The home of Dante and David, Machiavelli, the Medicis, and the Guccis, Florence is still the perfect place to fall in love, for the first time or all over again.

The food in Florence is simple and hearty, without rich sauces or elaborate spices. The cuisine reflects the Tuscan emphasis on bread, beans, deep-green extra-virgin olive oil, wild game, free-range poultry, and grilled and roasted meats. Most of Florence's restaurants are not gourmet, but many regional dishes are prepared so well that the food is considered some of the best in Italy. Because of the influx of more than a million visitors a year, the good-value restaurants are known to visitors and natives alike.

In Florence you will probably consume more bread than you will pasta. Most of the bread is baked without salt, which seems odd at first, but once you develop a taste for it, the plain unsalted bread is almost addictive. Stale bread goes into some of the best dishes. *Crostini* (toasted bread spread with pâté) is a delicious antipasto or light snack. *Ribollita,* a hearty vegetable soup with beans and black cabbage, reheated and poured over a thick slice of bread, is a favorite first course. In summer, *panzanella,* a salad of torn bread tossed with tomatoes and onion in red wine and virgin olive oil, is a light and refreshing lunch. Not to be forgotten is *bruschetta,* made with thick slices of bread toasted on the grill, rubbed with garlic and sprinkled with olive oil, and usually topped with chopped tomatoes. A pasta staple on every menu is pappardelle, wide, flat pasta strips served with hearty meat and sauces laced with red wine. The meat courses are a delight to all carnivores, especially the *bistecca alla Fiorentina*, a two- to three-inch slab of Chianti beef salted and coated with olive oil and served juicy rare. Tuscan beans are another favorite dish, especially the white cannellini beans that are served with meat or plain with extra-virgin olive oil. Olive oil is synonymous with Italy, and in Florence you will find the best to be a murky, dark green with a robust edge to it. Chianti wine is always a fit accompaniment to any meal, but it can have a very rough taste. For the best Chianti, look for Chianti Classico, with the DOCG guarantee of quality and the *gallo nero,* or black rooster, label on the neck.

Dessert usually consists of a piece of fresh fruit or a glass of *vin santo,* a sweet wine made from dried grapes. *Cantuccini di Prato* (also called *biscotti di Prato*) are hard almond cookies that are usually dipped in the wine—a nice finish to any Tuscan meal.

Street Addresses in Florence

In Florence, the street numbers of commercial establishments (stores, restaurants, and businesses) are indicated by a red "r" following the number of the address (i.e., 34r). A blue or black "b" means the address is a private residence or a hotel. To add to the fun, addresses seldom follow a strict numerical sequence, as we might expect them to. Instead, they are in sequence according to the "r" or the "b" numbers, but they are not necessarily next to one another, which can create confusion for the unknowing visitor.

Cooking Classes

Apicius, The Culinary Institute of Florence—Gabriella Ganugi

In 1997, after many years as a successful architect, Gabriella Ganugi changed courses and careers and opened Apicius. With thirty-five teachers and twenty chefs, it is now recognized as one of the foremost cooking schools in Italy. As the brochure states, "Apicius is a cooking school which associates cooking with the historic and artistic background of Italy." The school is divided into two teaching sections: one for professionals and one for nonprofessionals, all of whom want to increase their knowledge of the preparation of Italian dishes. The programs for nonprofessionals range from a one-day hands-on experience for one person to weekly, monthly, and yearly programs. In addition to participating in cooking classes and pasta workshops, individuals may request tours of gourmet shops, famous food markets, and cooking supply shops, and attend special events such as olive-oil tastings, dinner in a Tuscan home, a field trip to Chianti, and a wine class focusing on Tuscan and Italian wines. All-inclusive customized programs for two to twenty participants, lasting up to ten days, include not only daily cooking classes but also visits to famous Florentine restaurants and lectures on Renaissance Florence. All nonprofessional classes are conducted in English. For details on the professional classes and all prices, please consult the Website.

Contact information: Apicius, The Culinary Institute of Florence, Via Guelfa, 85, 50129, Firenze, Italia; Tel: 055 265 8135; Fax: 055 265 6689; Email: info@apicius.it; Internet: www.apicius.it. Credit cards: AE, DC, MC, V.

Divina Cucina—Judy Witts Francini

If you love good food and long to be Italian, even for only a day, treat yourself to one of Judy Witts Francini's wonderful Divina Cucina cooking classes. Judy is an enthusiastic, dynamic American with an extensive food background who came to Florence, met and married her Italian husband, and never looked back. A marvelous cook and teacher, Judy's classes are always fun and interesting, providing great insight into the food culture of Florence and the Tuscan region. Programs range from one to five days, and classes are small (six students maximum). The one-day class takes you on a guided shopping trip to the Mercato Centrale, followed by preparation of the meal in Judy's colorful kitchen, and lastly, the chance to savor the fruits of your labor. To help re-create at home the dishes you prepare under Judy's tutelage, everyone gets to take home one of her recipe books as well as a Divina Cucina apron.

Judy also has a kitchen in Chianti where she conducts classes. Please see her Website for more about this venture. If you have more time, by all means consider the five-day program, which includes a full-day trip to Chianti, three days of cooking classes, and shopping and walking tours of Florence. Judy can also arrange for housing and assist in tour planning.

Contact information: Tel & Fax: 055 29 25 78; Email: diva@divinacucina .com; Internet: www.divinacucina.com. Credit Cards: MC, V.

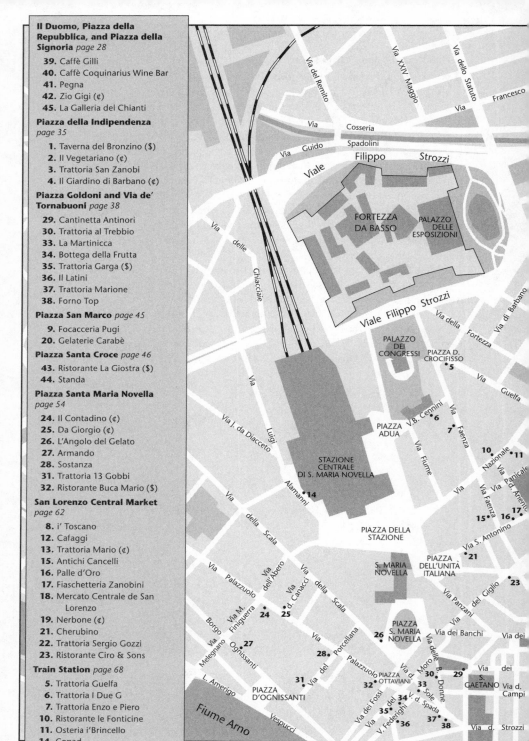

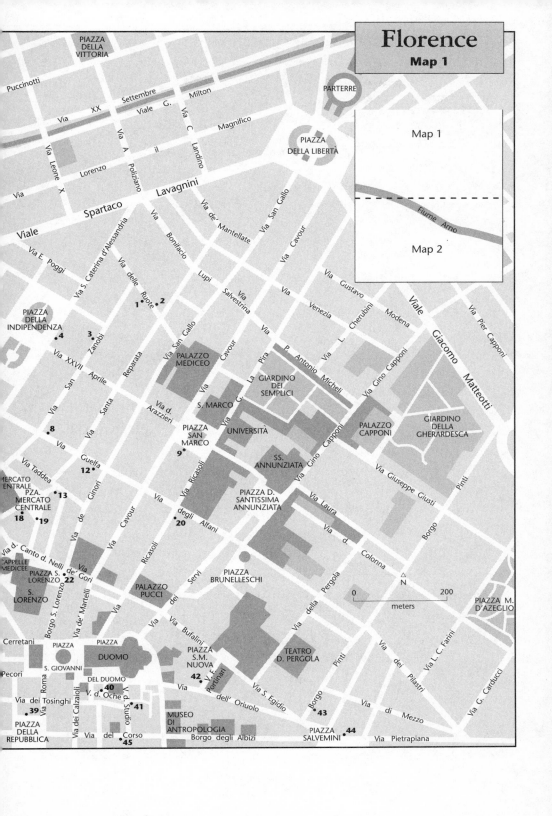

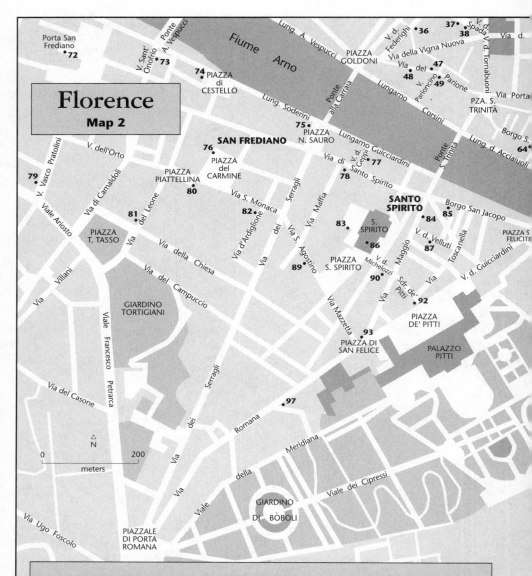

Florence
Map 2

Porta San
Frediano
•72

V. Sant'
Onofrio •73

Ponte
A. Vespucci

Fiume Arno

Lung. A. Vespucci

V. d.
Federighi •36   37•
38•

Via d.
Spada V. d. Tornabuoni

Via d.

PIAZZA
GOLDONI

Via della Vigna Nuova

74• PIAZZA
di
CESTELLO

Lung. Soderini

Lungarno

Via, del
48•   47•

Via, V. de
Parioncino
49•
Parione

Corsini

PZA. S.
TRINITÀ

Via Porta

Borgo S.

64•

V. dell'Orto

79•

V. Vasco Pratolini

75• PIAZZA
N. SAURO

SAN FREDIANO

76•

PIAZZA
del
CARMINE

Lungarno Guicciardini

Via di
Serragli
V. d.
Geppi
77•

Ponte
S. Trinità

Lung. d. Acciaiuoli

78•
di
Santo Spirito

Lung. Soderini

Ponte
alla Carraia

PIAZZA
PIATTELLINA

80•

Via di Camaldoli

PIAZZA
T. TASSO

81•
del Leone

Via della Chiesa

Via S. Monaca

82•

Via d'Ardiglione

Via

Via S. Agostino

Serragli

Via Maffia

83•
S.
SPIRITO

•86

SANTO
SPIRITO

Borgo San Jacopo

•84   85•

V. d. Velluti
87•

Toscanella

PIAZZA S
FELICITE

PIAZZA S.
SPIRITO

89•

V. d.
Michelozzi

90•

Via Maggio

Sdr. de'
Pitti

Via

•92

V. d. Guicciardini

Via del Campuccio

GIARDINO
TORTIGIANI

Viale
Francesco
Petrarca

Serragli

Via
dei

93•
PIAZZA DI
SAN FELICE

PIAZZA
DE' PITTI

PALAZZO
PITTI

Via
Villani

Via del Casone

Viale Ariosto

0   200
meters

△
N

•97

Romana

Meridiana

della

Via dei Cipressi

GIARDINO
DI BÒBOLI

Via
Via Ugo Foscolo

PIAZZALE
DI PORTA
ROMANA

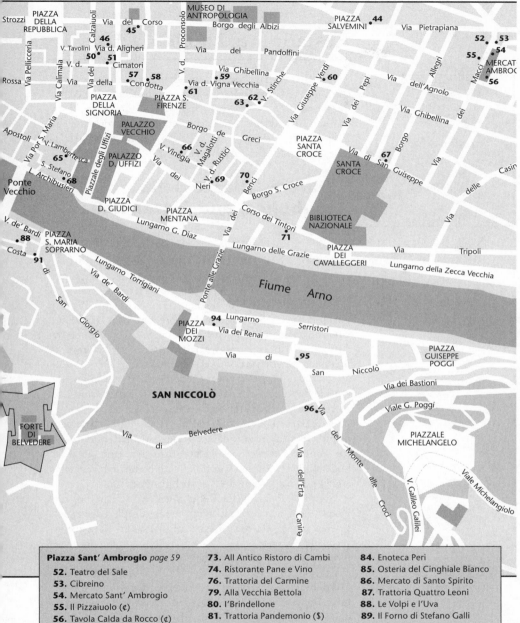

Restaurants *Di Qua d'Arno*

The listings have been organized into two main sections: those on the Uffizi Gallery and Il Duomo side of the Arno, known as *Di Qua d'Arno* (which literally means "this side of the Arno"), and those across the Ponte Vecchio on the Pitti Palace side of the Arno, *Di La d'Arno,* or *Oltrarno* (literally, "the other side of the Arno").

Il Duomo, Piazza della Repubblica, and Piazza della Signoria

Florence is a city-museum whose art treasures are unparalleled anywhere in the world. This city of refinement and elegance gave Italy its national language and was the birthplace of the Renaissance. The city symbol is the gothic cathedral Santa Maria del Fiore, known as Il Duomo. The thirteenth-century cathedral, crowned by a dome by Brunelleschi and covered with distinctive pink, white, and green marble inlays, dominates the Piazza del Duomo and all around it. Opposite the cathedral is the green and white marble Baptistery of San Giovanni (1128), a masterpiece of Florentine Romanesque architecture.

Ringed by *caffès* and with countless shops lining the streets leading into the large square, the Piazza della Repubblica is the commercial heart of Florence. In ancient times it was a huge marketplace that was filled with merchants, farmers, and beggars all doing a successful business.

South of Piazza della Repubblica and Il Duomo, the Piazza della Signoria, although never completed, is considered one of the most beautiful piazzas in Italy and is certainly Florence's civic showplace. The square, once the forum of the Republic and the center of secular life during the rule of the Medici family, is dominated by the magnificent Palazzo Vecchio and a series of magnificent statues including a copy of Michelangelo's *David* (the original is housed in the Galleria dell'Accademia on Via Ricasoli), an equestrian bronze of Cosimo I by Giambologna, and the *Fountain of Neptune* by Ammanati.

Also here is the Uffizi Gallery, which contains some of the best Renaissance art in the world. To avoid spending hours standing in line with literally hundreds of hapless tourists, you can book a morning or afternoon time in advance. There is a small surcharge, but when you see the line, you will be happy to pay it. The booking number for the Uffizi, as well as other major museums, is 055 294 883. This office is open Mon–Fri 8:30 A.M.–6:30 P.M., Sat 9 A.M.–noon. There are also two Websites: www.weekendafirenze.com and musa.uffizi.firenze.it.

RESTAURANTS

GELATERIAS

GOURMET FOOD AND WINE SHOPS

GROCERY STORES AND SUPERMARKETS

(¢) indicates a Cheap Eat

Restaurants

ANTICO FATTORE (65)
Via Lambertesca, 1/3r

Founded in 1929, Antico Fattore quickly became popular with artists and writers who met here to discuss art, literature, and politics in a lively atmosphere of good food and plenty of wine. In 1931, the restaurant helped to define a particular time in twentieth-century Italian literature when it offered the annual Antico Fattore literary prize. The philosophy of the restaurant has always been to nourish both body and soul by recognizing and celebrating the noble origins of traditionally prepared Tuscan dishes accompanied by Chianti Classico wine. Always on the menu are such Florentine stalwarts as *ribollita* (Tuscan bread soup), *pappa al pomodoro* (tomato soup with bread),

TELEPHONE
055 288 975

OPEN
Mon–Sat: lunch 12:15–2:45 P.M., dinner 7:15–9:15 P.M.

CLOSED
Sun; 15–20 days in Aug (dates vary)

RESERVATIONS
Advised for lunch, essential for dinner

CREDIT CARDS
AE, DC, MC, V

À LA CARTE	*pasta e fagioli* (pasta and bean soup), *bistecca alla Fiorentina*
25–30€	(a huge Florentine beefsteak cooked very rare), *trippa alla*
FIXED-PRICE MENU	*Fiorentina* (a dish reportedly predating the Uffizi Gallery),
None	*picccione saltato alle olive* (sautéed pigeon with olives), *fagioli*
COVER & SERVICE CHARGES	*all'olio* (beans in olive oil), *panna cotta* (vanilla cream pud-
Cover 1.30€, 12% service added	ding), and *biscottini di prato* (hard almond cookies dipped
ENGLISH	in sweet dessert wine).
Yes, and menu in English	

Locals and visitors appreciate the reliable food, and as a result reservations are essential, especially for dinner, when all the tables are filled by 8:30 P.M.

CAFFÈ COQUINARIUS WINE BAR (40)
Via delle Oche, 15r

Susan Rushton and her daughter Tania run this very friendly wine bar near Il Duomo. On the menu you will find *crostini* (toasted bread with assorted toppings), bean and barley soup (during the winter), and ravioli with cheese and pears in a butter sauce (as rich as it sounds), as well as various salads, cheese and cold meat plates, vegetarian quiches, and homemade desserts including cheesecake and dark chocolate cake. Each week, different wines are featured and sold by the glass; prices range from 2.70 to 10€. The well-prepared food is nicely presented and served continuously throughout the day, making this a Great Eat to remember at times when most other restaurants have locked their doors.

TELEPHONE
055 23 02 153
EMAIL
coquinarius@tin.it
OPEN
Daily: 9 A.M.–11:30 P.M., continuous service
CLOSED
Sun in summer; Aug
RESERVATIONS
Not necessary
CREDIT CARDS
MC, V
À LA CARTE
15–25€, includes a glass of wine
FIXED-PRICE MENU
None
COVER & SERVICE CHARGES
None
ENGLISH
Yes

CAFFÈ GILLI (39)
Piazza della Repubblica, 36/39r

Caffè Gilli has been serving coffee, picture-perfect pastries, wonderful chocolates, and light meals in this original Belle Epoque setting since 1910. Go early and have a warm fruit pastry with your first cappuccino of the day. Come back around noon and treat yourself to lunch on the terrace, which while costing more than eating a sandwich at the bar, gives you a great vantage point for unparalleled people-watching. The whole experience is very Florentine, and by far the most glamorous on the piazza.

TELEPHONE
055 213 896

INTERNET
www.gilli.it

OPEN
Daily: 8 A.M.–midnight, continuous service

CLOSED
Never

RESERVATIONS
Not necessary

CREDIT CARDS
AE, DC, MC, V

À LA CARTE
From 2.65€ for coffee and pastry at the bar, 15–18€ for light lunch on the terrace, 12€ for ice cream

FIXED-PRICE MENU
None

COVER & SERVICE CHARGES
Cover: none at bar; 3€ inside or on terrace; service included

ENGLISH
Yes, and menu in English

CANTINETTA DEI VERRAZZANO (¢, 46)
Via dei Tavolini, 18/20r

On one of my early morning walks, I found this elegant *caffè*, which is also a bakery, wine bar, wonderful lunch stop, and elegant teatime rendezvous. Starting at 8 A.M., the bakers send out heaping trays of breakfast goodies along with loaves of brown, white, olive, and wine-flavored breads. After discovering it I would regularly stop in after my walk, order a glass of freshly squeezed orange juice, a *cornetto,* and a double cappuccino to enjoy while glancing through the morning paper. The gleaming glass display cases are filled with a colorful assortment of individual tarts, marvelous cakes sold whole or by the slice, beautiful piles of *biscotti,* and sandwiches made with salmon, cucumber, thinly sliced beef, or ham. By noon, the wood-burning oven along the back is in full force, turning out individual pizzas or focaccia bread split in half while hot and then layered with your choice of fillings. I love the assorted open-faced sandwiches garnished with a slice of hard-boiled egg, a sprinkle of chives, and a splash of olive oil. Later in the day, it is a good choice for getting a glorious Italian pastry treat to either eat here or have packaged to go, and between noon and 8 P.M., it is a nice place to sip a glass of wine while contemplating your next shopping,

TELEPHONE
055 268 590

INTERNET
www.verrazzano.com

OPEN
Mon–Sat: 8 A.M.–9 P.M.; in Aug until 4 P.M., continuous service

CLOSED
Sun

RESERVATIONS
Not accepted

CREDIT CARDS
AE, DC, MC, V

À LA CARTE
3.20–10€

FIXED-PRICE MENU
None

COVER & SERVICE CHARGES
Both included

ENGLISH
Yes

sightseeing, or walking destination. The wine bar is part of the Castello da Verrazzano in Chianti, and it offers the best vintages by the glass or bottle.

I FRATELLINI (¢, 51)
Via dei Cimatori, 38r

TELEPHONE
055 239 6096
OPEN
Mon–Sat: 8 A.M.–8 P.M.,
continuous service; also Sun in
Jan, March–May, Sept–Oct,
and Dec
CLOSED
Sun in Feb, June–Aug, Nov;
1 week in Feb (dates vary),
2 weeks mid-Aug, 10 days
mid-Nov
RESERVATIONS
Not accepted
CREDIT CARDS
None
À LA CARTE
Sandwiches from 2.15€, wines
from 1.80€
FIXED-PRICE MENU
None
COVER & SERVICE CHARGES
None
ENGLISH
Yes

One of the best ways to cut food costs and have a Great Eat in the bargain is to have lunch at a snack bar. Here you will be joined by savvy Italians who know they can order the blue-plate special or a meaty sandwich and a glass of wine for a mere fraction of the cost of a restaurant meal. Further savings are possible if the meal is eaten while standing rather than seated at a table. Only you can decide how far you want to pinch your euros on that score.

This brings me to I Fratellini, a stand-up wine bar and sandwich counter that has been going strong since 1875 and is now run by two friendly, hardworking brothers. You can order your freshly made sandwiches to eat here or to go. They serve twenty to twenty-seven sandwiches, specializing in those piled with *prosciutto crudo* (air-dried, salt-cured ham) and homemade chicken liver pâté spread on thinly sliced bread. To round out your repast, order a glass of their Chianti Classico, but be careful. If you ask for the large, it will be served in a tall water tumbler. There are no tables; you are expected to stand. If you can't manage holding both your big sandwich and glass of wine at the same time, look for a spot along the little shelves on each side of the stand. That's where you can place your wineglass between sips.

OSTERIA VINI E VECCHI SAPORI (¢, 58)
Via del Magazzini, 3r

TELEPHONE
055 293 045
OPEN
Tues–Sat: lunch noon–2:30 P.M.,
dinner 7–10:30 P.M.; Sun: lunch
noon–2:30 P.M.
CLOSED
Sun dinner, Mon; Aug
RESERVATIONS
Advised
CREDIT CARDS
AE, MC, V
À LA CARTE
10–14€
FIXED-PRICE MENU
None
COVER & SERVICE CHARGES
None
ENGLISH
Yes

Look for the Chianti bottle sitting on a wine barrel and the green plants hanging in front of this great little Florentine *osteria* around the corner from Piazza della Signoria. *Little* is the operative word here: there are only a handful of tables inside, and they are always full of Great Eaters who know that size means nothing . . . the quality of food and service says it all. For both lunch and dinner, plates of *crostini* (toasted bread with assorted toppings) and tempting homemade desserts are spread along the bar. If you are not too hungry, you could easily make a meal of a plate of liver-, sausage-, mushroom-, fresh tomato-, or pesto-topped *crostini* and a slice of their very special barley cheesecake, a Sicilian specialty. *Pappa al pomodoro, ribollita,* tripe, sausage and beans, roast pork with potatoes, and roast lamb make regular appearances, and in the spring and summer there is always a main course salad.

TRATTORIA ANITA (¢, 66)
Via Vinegia, 16r (angle Via del Parlascio, 2r)

The Cheap Eats at Trattoria Anita are limited to lunch, but all budgeteers should take advantage of them. Because of this, I have two words of warning: go early. Otherwise, there won't be an empty seat, and worse still, they could be out of the dish you want. The unpretentious pan-Italian cooking leaves little to the imagination, but the ingredients are fresh and the servings generous when you consider the philanthropic price for the two fixed-price lunches served Monday through Friday. What do you get for your outlay of 5.50€? Your choice of both a first and second course plus a vegetable from the *menù del giorno*. Admittedly pasta with butter or tomato sauce isn't going to inspire gourmet yearnings, but you might also be able to select one laced with salmon or tuna, or a bowl of hearty *ribollita*. Seconds could include chicken cordon bleu, boiled meats, roasted rabbit, or pork stew. Veggies are limited to roast potatoes or baked eggplant. Dishing out an extra 2.50€ buys you a grilled veal chop or beefsteak served with a salad. What about dinner? Frankly, due to the price, I would keep this Florence restaurant firmly in the lunch column.

TELEPHONE
055 218 698

OPEN
Mon–Sat: lunch noon–3:30 P.M., dinner 7–10 P.M.

CLOSED
Sun; 15 days in Aug (dates vary)

RESERVATIONS
Not accepted for lunch

CREDIT CARDS
MC, V

À LA CARTE
18–25€

FIXED-PRICE MENU
Lunch only Mon–Fri: 5.50€, 2 courses plus vegetable, or just one first or second course; 8€, grilled meat and salad, beverages; cover and service extra for both menus

COVER & SERVICE CHARGES
Cover 1€; 10% service added

ENGLISH
Yes

TRATTORIA GABRIELLO (57)
Via Condotta, 54r

The three dining areas in Trattoria Gabriello have a country look created by the red-and-white or green-and-white tablecloths and sturdy blue-and-white Tuscan pottery. The simple menu of Tuscan classics draws a local lunch crowd, as does the reasonable fixed-price menu, which offers two courses and includes the cover and service charges. Ordering only a pasta and a salad, or one main course, is perfectly acceptable and will definitely keep prices well within a budget.

Start with a *crostini* topped with *funghi porcini* (mushrooms) and melted *scamorza* cheese, then maybe a bowl of rich *ribollita* soup or spaghetti with fresh clams. The beef stew is a popular cold-weather dish, and so is the rich osso buco. Desserts aren't the strong suit here; treat yourself to a gelato later instead.

TELEPHONE
055 21 20 98

OPEN
Daily: lunch noon–3 P.M., dinner 7–10:30 P.M.

CLOSED
Never

RESERVATIONS
Not necessary

CREDIT CARDS
AE, DC, MC, V

À LA CARTE
22–28€

FIXED-PRICE MENU
Lunch or dinner, 13€, 2 courses, includes cover and service charges, beverages extra

COVER & SERVICE CHARGES
Cover 1.50€, 10% service added

ENGLISH
Yes, and menu in English

ZIO GIGI (¢, 42)
Via F. Portinari, 7r

TELEPHONE
055 215 584

OPEN
Mon–Sat: lunch noon–2:30 P.M.,
dinner 7–11 P.M.

CLOSED
Sun; Aug (dates vary)

RESERVATIONS
Not necessary

CREDIT CARDS
MC, V

À LA CARTE
20€

FIXED-PRICE MENU
Lunch only, 6.50€, 2 courses;
beverage, cover, and service
extra

COVER & SERVICE CHARGES
Cover 1€, service included

ENGLISH
Yes

Great Eaters in Florence who are looking for decent budget fare near Il Duomo should jot down the name Zio Gigi. The fixed-price menu in this knotty-pine trattoria is amazing, considering the quality of the offerings. When you arrive, sit in the front room, unless you want to watch a blaring television set that competes with the boisterous diners in the back room. No wonder they are all so happy. Just look at what they are paying for a lunch that starts with a choice of four pastas or *ribollita* for the *primi,* and for the *secondo* chicken, veal, tripe, or beef carpaccio, along with a choice of fried potatoes, beans in olive oil, or *insalata misto.* For a few cents more, you can have a choice of pizza and a beverage.

À la carte ordering ups the ante somewhat, but it is still possible to enjoy a nice meal and a glass or two of the house wine for around 20€ and change. A big bowl of steamed mussels gets things off to a filling start. So does gnocchi Zio Gigi–style, which is served with a ham, mushroom, cheese, and tomato sauce. The gnocchi will leave out Atkins dieters, who can have the beef fillet Zio Gigi, which is a rare fillet topped with porcini mushrooms and an umbrella of rocket salad.

Gelaterias

PERCHÈ NÒ! (50)
Via dei Tavolini, 19r (near Via dei Calzaiuoli)

TELEPHONE
055 239 8969

OPEN
Daily in summer: 11 A.M.–
midnight; Mon, Wed–Sun in
winter: noon–7:30 P.M.

CLOSED
Tues in winter; Nov 5–25

CREDIT CARDS
None

PRICES
Cones and cups from 2.10€

ENGLISH
Limited

Perchè Nò! opened its doors in 1939 and is recognized today as the oldest *gelateria* in Florence. Along with its longevity, it has an impressive history. During World War II it supplied the American troops stationed in Florence with ice cream. When the city's electrical supply was shut off, officers ordered soldiers to reconnect the electrical supply that serviced Perchè Nò! and the surrounding area. After the war, the owners installed the first counter showcase for ice cream, which became a model for all others.

From the beginning, Perchè Nò! was known for its varieties of *semifreddo,* that illegally rich and creamy ice cream that has untold fat grams and tastes like a gift from heaven. Be sure you also sample the white chocolate, rum crunch, hazelnut mousse, or coffee mousse. In summer, the green apple *sorbetto* is a refreshing change of pace. The yogurt ice cream is a big seller, as is the brioche filled with whipped cream. You can have your gelato in a cone or cup, and dipped in a flurry of chocolate pieces and nuts if you've tossed aside all thoughts of dieting.

Piazza della Indipendenza

Piazza della Indipendenza is a large green space near the train station. On the third Saturday and Sunday of the month an antique/flea market is held here.

RESTAURANTS

Il Giardino di Barbano (¢)	**35**
Il Vegetariano (¢)	**36**
Taverna del Bronzino ($)	**36**
Trattoria San Zanobi	**37**

($) indicates a Big Splurge
(¢) indicates a Cheap Eat

Restaurants

IL GIARDINO DI BARBANO (¢, 4)
Piazza della Indipendenza, 3/4r

Handsome Giancarlo and his pretty wife, Tosca, have been running this successful restaurant for almost twenty years, and they are now joined by their son Marco. Giancarlo told me, "I was born in Florence, my entire family lives here, and I will die here." He has definitely captured the essence of being Florentine. From noon to 3 P.M. and 6 P.M. to midnight every night but Wednesday, most of the restaurant's 120 seats are filled with a happy crowd that ranges from tourists and tradesmen to locals. In summer, request a table in either the glassed-in or outdoor garden; in winter, ask for a booth in front. The specialties include *pappardelle al cinghiale* (wide, flat noodles sauced with wild boar meat), fusilli with sausage and porcini mushrooms, Florentine beefsteak, and grilled veal chop with potatoes. If those don't speak to you, perhaps one of the thirty other pastas and risottos will. Still not enticed? Then order one of the thirty or so wood-fired pizzas made with *fior di latte mozzarella* and extra-virgin olive oil. There are also large salads, appetizers, and a host of desserts, including the house version of *panna cotta* with raspberries or chocolate, tiramisù, and crème caramel—all are guaranteed to keep you fully contented for some time.

TELEPHONE
055 486 752

INTERNET
www.giardinodibarbano.com

OPEN
Mon–Tues, Thur–Sun: lunch noon–3 P.M., dinner 6 P.M.–midnight

CLOSED
Wed; 2 weeks in winter, 2 weeks in summer (dates vary)

RESERVATIONS
Not necessary

CREDIT CARDS
AE, MC, V

À LA CARTE
Salads from 6€, pastas from 5.50€, pizzas from 5€, 2-course meal 15–17€

FIXED-PRICE MENU
None

COVER & SERVICE CHARGES
Cover 1€, service included

ENGLISH
Yes, and menu in English

IL VEGETARIANO (¢, 2)
Via delle Ruote, 30r

TELEPHONE
055 475 030

OPEN
Tues–Fri: lunch 12:30–2:30 P.M.,
dinner 7:30–10:30 P.M.; Sat–
Sun: dinner 7:30–10:30 P.M.

CLOSED
Sat–Sun for lunch, Mon; Aug

RESERVATIONS
Not accepted

CREDIT CARDS
None

À LA CARTE
14–20€

FIXED-PRICE MENU
None

COVER & SERVICE CHARGES
None

ENGLISH
Yes

Exceptional vegetarian food, served in a warm, friendly atmosphere, is dished out cafeteria-style here to faithful diners, who return with great regularity. Murals of Tuscany, fresh flowers on the tables, and a summer garden create an appealing natural setting.

The menu changes daily and varies with the seasons. It is executed by a team of Italians and one Irish woman, Brenda, who has been making the desserts for twenty years. Once you enter the restaurant, check the printed blackboard, decide what you want, write it down on the form provided, and take it to the cashier to pay. The dishes for each course are priced the same, allowing you to add up your total easily. The wine is organic and served either in a carafe or by the bottle. After paying, take your menu form to the cafeteria counter to be served. The varied selection of food usually includes soup, rice and pastas, casseroles made from beans and legumes, quiches, soufflés, vegan and macrobiotic choices, salads, and for dessert, anything from pumpkin pie and fruit crumble to vegan cake or brownies.

NOTE: There is no sign outside the restaurant. Look for the round sign with a red telephone receiver hanging above the entrance at Via della Ruote, 30r.

TAVERNA DEL BRONZINO ($, 1)
Via delle Ruote, 25r

TELEPHONE
055 495 220

OPEN
Mon–Sat: lunch 12:30–2 P.M.,
dinner 7:30–10 P.M.

CLOSED
Sun; last 3 weeks of Aug

RESERVATIONS
Advised for dinner

CREDIT CARDS
AE, DC, MC, V

À LA CARTE
45–60€

FIXED-PRICE MENU
None

COVER & SERVICE CHARGES
Cover 5€, service included

ENGLISH
Yes

Eating at the Taverna del Bronzino is always a great pleasure. It is the perfect place for Big Splurge–occasion dining, be it a birthday, anniversary, or romantic evening with the love of your life. The understated and elegant interior is done in muted colors with flattering lighting. Seating is comfortable, and the nicely appointed tables have crisp linens, heavy silver, and fresh flowers. Formal waiters offer gracious and unobtrusive service that is always one step ahead of what you need.

You are bound to be as impressed with the food as you are with the surroundings. First you are given a free glass of the house apéritif to enjoy while you decide what to order. If you ask, your waiter will make knowledgeable suggestions to help you plan your meal. The imaginative dishes are inspired by the seasonal best of the Italian harvest, and each is cooked to order. The appetizers lean toward fresh seafood and smoked fish. The fresh pastas are blanketed with robust sauces of seafood, *funghi porcini,* or black truffles; the creamy risottos are filled with delicate artichokes or perhaps morelles lightly seasoned with fresh mint. The meat, poultry, and fresh fish are perfectly cooked, gently perfumed with wines and herbs, and attractively served. Even a plate of springtime asparagus is beautifully executed. Sublime desserts and a distinguished wine list round out a meal you will favorably recall long after you have forgotten many others.

TRATTORIA SAN ZANOBI (3)
Via San Zanobi, 33A/r

This is a simple trattoria, with red-tile floors, original brick archways, wood-framed windows, and a Liberty-style bar brought from the north of Italy. It is run by two sisters, Mariangela and Delia, one of whom is always on board to welcome guests. Each room takes its design cue from a famous Florentine landmark: Il Duomo, the Palazzo Vecchio, and the Palazzo da Vanzati. The printed à la carte menu covers the bases, but, as usual, prime plates are those the chef recommends that day. These are neatly written on a small sheet of paper fastened to the inside of the menu, and represent uncomplicated interpretations of *ribollita, pasta e fagioli,* risotto, tagliatelle with duck, roast lamb with potatoes, grilled salmon, and roast beef with arugula salad. Dessert gives you a choice of several ice cream flavors, fresh fruit, and of course *cantuccini di prato con vin santo* (almond cookies dipped in sweet wine).

The Pasta Lunch Break, available Monday to Friday, offers one-plate meals—a fast-food value for those seeking a quick meal without sacrificing quality. You can have either your choice of pasta (choose among fifteen different toppings); two salads; eggplant Parmesan; or a big bowl of vegetable soup.

TELEPHONE
055 475 286

OPEN
Mon–Sat: lunch noon–2:30 P.M., dinner 7–10:30 P.M.

CLOSED
Sun; 1 week in Aug

RESERVATIONS
Advised for dinner

CREDIT CARDS
AE, MC, V

À LA CARTE
20–25€

FIXED-PRICE MENU
Pasta Lunch Break (Mon–Fri): 4.20–10€, includes cover and service charges; beverages extra

COVER & SERVICE CHARGES
Cover 2.10€, service discretionary

ENGLISH
Yes, and menu in English

Piazza Goldoni and Via de' Tornabuoni

The Piazza Goldoni serves as a crossroads joining the Ponte alle Carraia with Via del Fossi leading to the Piazza Santa Maria Novella, the train station, and Lungaro Amerigo Vespucci and Lungaro Corsini following the Arno.

Completing a rough triangle with these streets northeast of the piazza is Via de' Tornabuoni, which leads from Piazza Santa Trinità up to Piazza Antinori. Florence is justly famous for its wealth of shopping opportunities, and none are more elegant or expensive than those along Via de' Tornabuoni and the surrounding streets.

($) indicates a Big Splurge
(¢) indicates a Cheap Eat

Restaurants

CANTINETTA ANTINORI (29)
Piazza Antinori, 3r

Many years ago, owners of large estates around Florence kept small cellars in their palaces and sold products from little windows on the street. Following this long-standing tradition, the Antinori family has established the Cantinetta in their fifteenth-century Renaissance Palazzo Antinori in the heart of Florence. Without question, this is a show-place for the vintages of the oldest and most distinguished wine producer in Tuscany, and knowledgeable visitors and beautifully clad Florentines have made this one of the most popular wine bars in the city. Full meals can run into the Big Splurge category and frankly are not worth the price. I think the best way to enjoy the Cantinetta Antinori is to sit at the bar (saving both the cover and service charges) and order an appetizer or plate of assorted cheeses along with a glass or two of their excellent wines.

TELEPHONE
055 292 234

OPEN
Mon–Fri: lunch 12:30–3:30 P.M., dinner 7–11:30 P.M.

CLOSED
Sat–Sun; Aug 4–28, Dec 24–Jan 8

RESERVATIONS
Essential for a table; not accepted at the bar

CREDIT CARDS
AE, DC, MC, V

À LA CARTE
35–45€ (3 courses); appetizers and cheese plates 9–12€

FIXED-PRICE MENU
None

COVER & SERVICE CHARGES
None at the bar; at a table: cover 1.60€, 10% service added

ENGLISH
Yes, and menu in English

COCO LEZZONE (49)
Via Parioncino, 26r

There is no sign outside, but that does not mean that this beloved spot has not been found by everyone from Florentine workers and blue bloods to Prince Charles and Luciano Pavarotti. The inside has barely changed since it opened a century ago. It still has plain white-tile walls and elbow-to-elbow seating along narrow tables. The hearty, traditional cooking is prepared with high-quality, fresh ingredients. The only nod to modern times is the note printed on the menu, *il trillo dei telefoni cellulari disturba la cottura della ribollita* ("the ringing of your cellular telephone disturbs the cooking of the *ribollita*").

There is a weekly menu, but not all of the dishes are available every day. Listen to what the waiter says about the daily specials, and remember that you can always depend on osso buco on Monday, beef stew on Tuesday, veal scaloppine or *involtini* (stewed rolls of meat) on Wednesday and Saturday, tripe for your Thursday main course, and *baccalà* on Friday. Diners are expected to order full meals, to eat them with zeal, and to drink plenty of wine in the

TELEPHONE
055 287 178

OPEN
Mon, Wed–Sat: lunch noon–2:30 P.M., dinner 7–10:30 P.M.; Tues: lunch noon–2:30 P.M.

CLOSED
Tues dinner, Sun; July–Aug (5 weeks), Dec 22–Jan 7

RESERVATIONS
Not accepted for tables, but must call ahead to order Florentine beefsteak

CREDIT CARDS
None: "We accept any foreign currency, eurochecques and traveler's checks, but we don't accept any credit cards."

À LA CARTE
30–35€ (50–60€ for Florentine beefsteak)

FIXED-PRICE MENU
None

process. That is very easy to do, especially if you start out with a light *primo piatto* (first plate) of *pappa al pomodoro,* their famous *ribollita,* or the seasonally available *farfalle con piselli* or *tartufo* (pasta with peas or truffles). For the *secondo piatto,* go with the daily special, or if you have been working up the courage to try tripe, here is your chance. Served in a tomato sauce with freshly ground Parmesan cheese, it is perfectly tender and delicious. Beef eaters can dig into one of the Florentine steaks, cooked rare and literally overflowing the plate. But, be forewarned, even though you cannot make a table reservation, you must call ahead to reserve your steak. The desserts are all made here and reflect the season and mood of the chef, but don't expect an after-dinner coffee, because it is not served. Bring cash. Credit cards are not accepted.

IL LATINI (36)
Via dei Palchetti, 6r

Il Latini enjoys a lingering, widespread reputation it no longer deserves, and this is a rare case where I feel I must warn readers. Angelo Latini opened Il Latini in the early 1900s as a *fiachetteria,* or wine shop. In the fifties, his nephew took over, expanded, and began to serve sandwiches and hot food prepared by his wife, first in her own kitchen at home and later in the restaurant. For most of us, this popular trattoria became synonymous with good food, good wine, and good cheer. It was everything one expected and hoped for, and guide books from around the world touted Il Latini's virtues. Unfortunately, as a result things have changed drastically, and not for the better. Il Latini is now overrated, overpriced, and impossibly crowded with *only* unsuspecting tourists (the Florentines have long since sworn off it). The service is rude, the food mediocre and unappetizingly presented, and the prices are ridiculous. It is extremely disappointing when an old standby fails to live up to its long-held reputation, but Il Latini is no longer a recommended choice. In fact, it is better avoided until, hopefully, it improves in the future.

I' PARIONE (47)
Via del Parione, 74/76r

The crowd is a buzzy mix of attractive locals and savvy visitors; the atmosphere is slightly chaotic when things get going; and the food is deliciously inventive but not fussy. The entrance from the street opens directly onto the kitchen, with two distinct dining areas on each side. To

COVER & SERVICE CHARGES
Cover 2€, 10% service added
ENGLISH
Yes

TELEPHONE
055 210 916
OPEN
Tues–Sun: lunch 12:30–2:30 P.M., dinner 7:30–10:30 P.M.
CLOSED
Mon; Aug (dates vary)
RESERVATIONS
Accepted, but largely ignored
CREDIT CARDS
AE, DC, MC, V
À LA CARTE
30–35€, includes house wine
FIXED-PRICE MENU
None
COVER & SERVICE CHARGE
None
ENGLISH
Yes

TELEPHONE
055 214 005
OPEN
Daily: lunch 12:30–2:30 P.M., dinner 7:30–10:30 P.M.
CLOSED
Never

the left is a small space set with country tables and chairs, brightly colored Tuscan-style painted pottery, and linen napkins. To the right is a slightly larger room completely enveloped in massive paintings in the style of Picasso, Diego Rivera, or (some say) Michelangelo . . . you decide. The same furniture and table settings prevail. Downstairs in the old wine cellar another six tables can be found. While the paintings may be a source of speculation, all will agree that the food is consistently good and fairly priced. Start with a plate of seasonal vegetables, lightly grilled and dusted with shavings of fresh Parmesan, an arugula salad laced with slices of raw baby artichokes, or a plate of Tuscan salami and ham. The asparagus risotto is soul food at its best, and so is the ravioli stuffed with eggplant and buffalo mozzarella. The fresh fish selection depends on the chef's trip to market, and might include fat, lightly grilled shrimp or a moist swordfish in a Mediterranean tomato sauce. The grilled chicken or the seared tuna steak, both served with seasonal vegetables, are wonderful main courses. A side order of rosemary-seasoned potatoes and fresh spinach drizzled with olive oil can easily be shared. Not so the chocolate cake with orange sauce. I thought I was too full to even think of finishing it, but it was just the right ending to a very nice Great Eat in Florence.

RESERVATIONS
Essential for dinner, advised for lunch
CREDIT CARDS
AE, MC, V
À LA CARTE
35–45€
FIXED-PRICE MENU
None
COVER & SERVICE CHARGES
Cover 3€, 10% service added
ENGLISH
Yes, and menu in English

LA MARTINICCA (33)
Via del Sole, 27r

A meal at La Martinicca is pleasant and unhurried, featuring hearty Tuscan food and wine to match. The interior is typical trattoria style, with assorted artwork in three small rooms and tables set with pink linens. Arrive early and you will be surrounded by other foreigners or neighborhood guests with children in tow. Go around 9 P.M., when the service and noise level are better and the one waiter is not so overworked. I must say, however, that if I ever open a restaurant, I want this man to work for me. He is precision personified, a good example of grace under pressure as he trots—not walks—between the tables, never missing a beat or an order. The all à la carte seasonal menu covers the important bases, including a tempting list of homemade pastas. The cheese-dressed gnocchi is a rich choice, and so is the *tagliatelle genovese*, loaded with fresh basil, garlic, and Parmesan cheese. As always, pay attention to the daily specials, watching for grilled baby lamb chops, roast chicken, veal scaloppine with asparagus, or a satisfying osso buco with spinach. A

TELEPHONE
055 218 928
OPEN
Mon–Fri: lunch noon–2:30 P.M., dinner 7–10:30 P.M.; Sat: dinner 7–10:30 P.M.
CLOSED
Sat lunch, Sun; Aug
RESERVATIONS
Preferred
CREDIT CARDS
MC, V
À LA CARTE
25–35€
FIXED-PRICE MENU
13€, 2 courses, vegetable, dessert, and wine or mineral water, cover and service included
COVER & SERVICE CHARGES
Included
ENGLISH
Yes, and menu in English

dessert cart is wheeled around at the appropriate time, and their version of *torta della nonna* is good, as well as their chocolate-doused profiteroles.

MARIANO (¢, 48)
Via del Parione, 19r

TELEPHONE
055 214 067
OPEN
Mon–Fri: 8 A.M.–8 P.M., continuous service
CLOSED
Sat–Sun; 2 weeks in Aug (dates vary)
RESERVATIONS
Not accepted
CREDIT CARDS
AE, MC, V
À LA CARTE
2.50–6€
FIXED-PRICE MENU
None
COVER & SERVICE CHARGES
None
ENGLISH
Limited, but it doesn't really matter

As you walk by, look for the sign *"Alimentari"* written over the door. This little dugout-style deli is easy to miss, but if you see a lunchtime crowd inside, that's it. The first room is dominated by a large glass case that has all the fixings for made-to-order sandwiches, which you can get wrapped to go or take into the next room and eat sitting on one of the wicker bar stools. Two sandwich masters man this operation as hungry office workers stand six deep waiting their turn.

You name it in sandwiches and they can undoubtedly put it together from a raft of ingredients, which includes anchovies, five types of ham, countless sausages, marinated vegetables, smoked salmon, cheese . . . even a hot dog. Wash it all down with a glass of their daily wine, which costs only 2€. What you save by becoming a regular at this Great Eat in Florence can be applied to the beautiful shops that define this luxurious part of Florence.

TRATTORIA AL TREBBIO (30)
Via delle Belle Donne, 47/49r

TELEPHONE
055 287 089
OPEN
Mon, Wed–Sun: lunch noon–2:30 P.M., dinner 7–10:30 P.M.; Tues: dinner 7–10:30 P.M.
CLOSED
Tues lunch
RESERVATIONS
Essential for dinner, advised for lunch
CREDIT CARDS
AE, DC, MC, V
À LA CARTE
20–28€
FIXED-PRICE MENU
None
COVER & SERVICE CHARGES
Cover 1€, 10% service added
ENGLISH
Yes, and menu in English

Noisy, rushed or snail-paced service, sometimes with attitude . . . why is this trattoria packed night after night? Because the food is good, the surroundings are appealing, and the final bill is one most anyone can live with. The inside has the popular shabby-chic look with wall lights over each table, and in the evening a little candle is added. In the summer, tables spill out onto the small square in front. House wine is served in colorful Tuscan pottery pitchers, and the menu is short—always a good indicator that frozen foods will not be part of your dining experience. In the early spring, I like to start with the rocket salad showered with tender, raw artichoke hearts and long slivers of Parmesan cheese. Pappardelle with rabbit or duck sauce is a heavy pasta, but if you are not going on to a waist-expanding main course and dessert, then it is a satisfying choice. I loved the risotto bursting with tender green asparagus tips, followed by moist fried chicken and rabbit served with assorted vegetables. Fortunately I had enough room for the pear and chocolate cake and a taste of my companion's velvety tiramisù. Along with the bill, guests are presented with a miniature Tuscan dish and, depending on your waitperson, the announcement that, "Even though there is a 10 percent service charge added to the bill, this is not my *tip!*" Obviously I am not Italian, because the waiter would *never* dare to make such a statement if I were. Italians are not known for their tipping largess and, at best, round off the bill.

TRATTORIA GARGA ($, 35)
Via del Moro, 48r

Trattoria Garga is one of the most sought-after dining destinations in Florence, and rightfully so. Once you get used to the wild, brightly colored interior—which my dining companion dubbed "tastefully hideous"—and settle in for an evening of good wine and food, you too will be making plans for your next visit. I have one—no, make that two—words to say about the food . . . *absolutely wonderful.* On several visits, every dish ordered displayed high quality, not only in the ingredients but in their execution and presentation.

Portions are generous, so my advice is to share an antipasto and pasta and save room for a main course and dessert. Start with the *insalata del Garga,* a colorful mix of baby greens, avocados, fresh tomatoes, and maybe a handful of fresh anchovies in olive oil marinade. The risotto with fresh asparagus is delicious, and so is the tagliatelle tossed with the season's best vegetables, or rich *funghi porcini.* For a main course, the thick, moist piece of swordfish with a Sicilian tomato sauce or veal scaloppine with lemon, avocado, chantal mushrooms, or artichokes in season are unbeatable choices. The bowl of fresh strawberries is a cool finish, but chocoholics will not want to miss the illegally rich chocolate tart.

La Cucina del Garga is a cooking school associated with the restaurant. As the brochure aptly says, "the only prerequisite one needs is a love of food and Italy." Classes are for a minimum of four to a maximum of twelve people and are held Monday to Saturday from noon until after everyone has finished eating the meal they've prepared.

Further details can be found on their Website.

TELEPHONE
055 239 8898
OPEN
Daily: dinner 7:30–11 P.M.
CLOSED
Lunch
RESERVATIONS
Essential, at least a day in advance
CREDIT CARDS
AE, MC, V
À LA CARTE
50–60€
FIXED-PRICE MENU
None
COVER & SERVICE CHARGES
No cover, 12% service added
ENGLISH
Yes

LA CUCINA DEL GARGA COOKING SCHOOL
TELEPHONE
055 211 396
INTERNET
www.garga.it

TRATTORIA MARIONE (37)
Via della Spada, 27r

Trattoria Marione is a crowded place where Sergio and his extended family prove their Italian pedigree with their version of *cucina casalinga* (homestyle cooking). The typical decor consists of rows of wine bottles, assorted paintings,

TELEPHONE
055 214 756
OPEN
Daily: lunch noon–3 P.M., dinner 7–10:30 P.M.

CLOSED
1 week in Aug

RESERVATIONS
For 4 or more

CREDIT CARDS
AE, MC, V

À LA CARTE
18–20€ (minimum charge 10€)

FIXED-PRICE MENU
13€, 2 courses, fruit, wine or mineral water, cover and service included

COVER & SERVICE CHARGES
Cover 1€, 10% service added

ENGLISH
Yes, and menu in English (but not daily specials)

and rush-seated chairs positioned around tightly packed tables. Especially appealing for some is their fixed-price menu, which includes two courses, fruit for dessert, wine or water, and the cover and service charges. While this menu has several choices for first and second courses, it offers few surprises. Loosening the money belt a bit and going à la carte with the daily specials will not put your budget in peril, and will allow for a more interesting dining experience, including their famous award-winning *ribollita* soup, a dense vegetable soup thickened with bread and left a day before reheating and eating (*ribollita* means "reboiled"). The restaurant's *ribollita* was voted one of the best in Florence by the Academy of Italian Cooking. Other selections include gnocchi with salmon, pappardelle with wild boar sauce, fresh grilled fish, roast lamb or veal served with creamy potatoes, and a moist roast chicken. Dessert? Not here, thank you, unless you want fruit or *biscottini con vin santo*.

Pastry Shops and Bakeries

FORNO TOP (38)
Via della Spada, 23r

TELEPHONE
055 219 854

OPEN
Mon–Sat: 7:30 A.M.–2:30 P.M., 5–7:30 P.M.

CLOSED
Sun

CREDIT CARDS
None

PRICES
0.80€ for a roll, 1.50€ for a 100 g pizza, sandwiches around 2.50€, sweets from 1.50€

ENGLISH
Very limited, depends on server

Mmmm . . . I can still smell the wonderful breads and pastries from this popular bakery and pastry shop that used to be just down the street from my apartment—and a source of endless temptation. If you go by in the morning, you'd think they couldn't possibly sell everything they have on display: breads, cookies, cakes, tarts, pizzas, and more. However, if you arrive in the late afternoon, crumbs may be all that are left. So come as early as possible, grab a number, and try to make your deliciously difficult decisions by the time they call you to the counter. Forno Top has several locations throughout Florence, but this one is the best.

Piazza San Marco

The magnificent fifteenth-century frescoes by Fra Angelico are displayed in the Museo di San Marco. The Accademia, where the statue of David is seen by virtually everyone coming to Florence, is nearby. The piazza also serves as a crossroads for fleets of city buses.

GELATERIAS
Gelaterie Carabè   **45**

PASTRY SHOPS AND BAKERIES
Focacceria Pugi   **45**

Gelaterias

GELATERIE CARABÈ (20)
Via Ricasoli, 60/r

Every *gelateria* in Florence has its devotees, but none more than Carabè, a Sicilian emporium of the fabulous ice creams this part of Italy is so famous for. It is a little place, not far from the Accademia, but just look at the hours and you will see that ice cream is scooped here in a big way. I think their almond ice cream served in a chocolate-dipped cone with nuts is a gift from heaven. Others swear by the butterscotch with chocolate swirls, or the plain dark chocolate. Can't decide? Have several flavors. You can, because you only pay for the size of the cone or cup, not the number of flavors that are piled on.

TELEPHONE
055 289 476
OPEN
Daily: winter 11 A.M.–8:30 P.M., summer 8 A.M.–2 A.M.
CLOSED
Never
CREDIT CARDS
None
PRICES
Cones 2.20–8.50€, cups 1.70–7.30€
ENGLISH
Limited

Pastry Shops and Bakeries

FOCACCERIA PUGI (9)
Piazza San Marco, 10r

Go in, look, point, pay, and eat one of the best slices of *schiacciata* (Tuscan focaccia) in Florence. Also on display are slices of pizza, fruit *crostini*, bread, and cookies. It is a good address to remember if you need sustenance before tackling the Museum of San Marco with its lovely Fra Angelico frescoes, or the endless lines waiting to get in to see the *David* at the Accademia (if you are standing in line, you didn't make a reservation; see page 28 to avoid the queue).

TELEPHONE
Not available
OPEN
Mon–Sat: 8 A.M.–8 P.M.
CLOSED
Sun; 3 weeks in Aug (dates vary)
CREDIT CARDS
MC, V
PRICES
0.30€ for a small *schiacciata*, 1.80€ for pizza
ENGLISH
Very limited, depends on server

Piazza Santa Croce

Santa Croce Church, founded by Franciscans in 1228, is considered the richest medieval church in Florence. It is also the pantheon of Italy's great men: Michelangelo, Machiavelli, Galileo, Rossini, and Foscolo are buried here. Inside are frescoes by Giotto. To the right of the church stands Brunelleschi's beautiful Pazzi Chapel. The Piazza Santa Croce is anchored by the church and ringed with lovely medieval palazzos and scores of tourist hawker stalls. In the back of the piazza is one of the most interesting working areas of Florence and the bustling Sant' Ambrogio Market (see page 94).

($) indicates a Big Splurge
(¢) indicates a Cheap Eat

Restaurants

ACQUA AL 2 (59)
Via della Vigna Vecchia, 40r (at Via dell'Acqua)

TELEPHONE
055 284 170
INTERNET
www.acquaal2.it
OPEN
Daily: 7:30 P.M.–1 A.M.,
continuous service

Almost everyone loves Acqua al 2, one of the most firmly established and well-known casual restaurants in Florence. It consists of three rooms with stone walls, arched brick ceilings, wooden banquettes, hard wooden chairs and benches, and tables set with fresh flowers, candles, and paper place mats. The animated diners come from all walks of life and every corner of the globe to enjoy the hearty food. The menu doesn't leave much to chance, with twenty-six pastas (many of which are vegetarian), chicken prepared five ways, a few omelettes, and several variations of veal and beef. You can order just one course, go whole hog and have the works, or land somewhere in between and share. The house specialties offer some particular treats that lend themselves to sharing. Start with the *assaggio di primi,* your choice of any five pastas; then the *assaggio di secondi,* a choice of three or four meat or main dishes; follow that with the *assaggio di insalate,* which gives you several salad selections; and then the *assaggio di formaggi* or *assaggio di dolci,* which offers an assortment of cheeses or desserts of the day. Follow this with a trip to a diet spa! The house wine is good and priced to flow . . . which it does in large quantities.

NOTE: The restaurant has a second location in the Gaslamp quarter of San Diego: 322 Fifth Avenue, San Diego, CA 92101; Tel: 619-230-0382.

CLOSED
1 week mid-Aug
RESERVATIONS
Advised
CREDIT CARDS
AE, DC, MC, V
À LA CARTE
18–25€, includes house wine
FIXED-PRICE MENU
None
COVER & SERVICE CHARGES
Cover 1€, 10% service added
ENGLISH
Yes

ENOTECA BALDOVINO (67)
Via San Guiseppe, 18r

Enoteca Baldovino, run by the same owners as Trattoria Baldovino nearby (see page 52) and Beccofino on the other side of the Arno (see page 80), is an informal place, serving lighter dishes geared to go well with the weekly featured wines (twenty of which are available by the glass) and other drinks poured here from morning until night. In the summer, the action expands to coveted seats on the terrace. For lunch, I like to have the *gran piatto misto,* an assortment of four of the daily specials: perhaps a spinach and pecorino torte, a chicken salad spiked with stilton cheese, a spicy chicken curry served over rice and potato, and tuna salad tossed with fresh green beans. I also love the endless varieties of *crostini* and carpaccio, made with everything from wild boar to smoked salmon, eggplant, and zucchini. Salads, cheeses, and foie gras served on toast round out the menu. In the evening, the lively bar lists dozens of cocktails in addition to the full range of wines. Enoteca Baldovino also has a selection of Italian wines, extra-virgin Tuscan olive oil, and balsamic vinegar that can be shipped tax-free anywhere in the world.

TELEPHONE
055 234 7220
INTERNET
www.baldovino.com
OPEN
Daily: noon–3:30 P.M.,
6 P.M.–1 A.M.
CLOSED
Christmas Eve and Christmas Day
RESERVATIONS
Advised, and essential for terrace tables
CREDIT CARDS
MC, V
À LA CARTE
10–18€
FIXED-PRICE MENU
None
COVER & SERVICE CHARGES
Cover 1€, 10% service suggested
ENGLISH
Yes

IL BARROCCIO (61)
Via della Vigna Vecchia, 31r

TELEPHONE
055 211 503

OPEN
Mon–Tues, Thur–Sun: lunch
12:15–2:30 P.M., dinner 7:15–
10:30 P.M.

CLOSED
Wed; 3–4 weeks in Jan

RESERVATIONS
Advised for weekends

CREDIT CARDS
AE, DC, MC, V

À LA CARTE
20–23€

FIXED-PRICE MENU
Vegetariano: 14€, 3 courses;
Menù Speciale: 15€, 2 courses
and vegetable or salad; for both,
beverages, cover, and service
extra

COVER & SERVICE CHARGES
Cover 1€, 10% service added

ENGLISH
Yes

For Sunday lunch, Il Barroccio is a full house, with a mix of Italian families, area regulars, and tourists visiting the Santa Croce Church. The closely spaced tables are set with white-and-red linen cloths, polished silver, china, and fresh flowers. Tuscan watercolors crowd almost every inch of space on the sponged-yellow walls.

The menu has all the Tuscan standbys—plenty for the vegetarian in your party—plus a fixed-price menu and a selection of seasonal and daily specials. All the pastas, sauces, and desserts are made here and are free of preservatives and additives. You can actually taste the potatoes in the gnocchi, with its fresh basil and tomato sauce. The *ravioli alle noci* (ravioli with nuts in a cream sauce) is a very interesting first course. Main courses to rely on include the *carpaccio Parmigiano e rucola*—thin slices of raw beef served with fresh Parmesan and bitter greens. Veal is fixed several different ways, and there are always grilled meats and vegetables. The desserts consist of *panna cotta,* tiramisù, *biscotti con vin santo, sorbetto,* and fresh fruit. A nice alternative is the plate of assorted Italian cheeses paired with a glass of wine.

NOTE: If you are the host for a small group, the restaurant can provide a set menu with wines if notified in advance.

OSTERIA DEI BENCI (70)
Via de' Benci, 13r

TELEPHONE
055 234 4923

OPEN
Daily: lunch 1–2:45 P.M., dinner
7:15–10:45 P.M.

CLOSED
Most major holidays, call to
check

RESERVATIONS
Essential, and on weekends, a
day in advance

CREDIT CARDS
AE, DC, MC, V

À LA CARTE
25–40€

FIXED-PRICE MENU
None

COVER & SERVICE CHARGES
Cover 1.50€, 10% service added

ENGLISH
Yes

The three rooms with arched brick ceilings are informal. Colorful pottery adds zip to the bare wooden tables covered in paper place mats and matching napkins. In warm weather, the action moves to the sidewalk terrace. House wine and water are served in glass tumblers, but if you upgrade your wine, they will pour it into a proper wine glass. The monthly changing menu at this popular Santa Croce *osteria* keeps the young, hip food cognoscenti always interested and coming back for more. The kitchen owes its success to an imaginative use of fresh ingredients and its ability to offer more than the obvious Tuscan staples. Admittedly, the full menu takes some study, not only to decide but to decipher. However, if you stick to the one-page monthly offering, you will have not only an easier time ordering but a better meal into the bargain. In late winter, you might start with fresh anchovy *crostini* or a bracing tagliolini in a rich pork sausage sauce made with balsamic vinegar and topped with Parmesan cheese.

A lighter alternative is the spaghetti laced with fresh artichokes and plenty of fresh garlic. Only Sumo wrestlers could finish the Florentine beefsteak, which literally falls off the platter onto the table. The roast beef *di filetto di Chianina,* served with a creamy potato purée, is a more manageable choice, especially if accompanied by an array of seasonal vegetables drizzled with thick Tuscan olive oil. Weight-watchers will be happy with one of their large salads, the best of which is the *andromeda,* laden with arugula, pear, nuts, and pecorino cheese. For dessert, try an assortment of cheeses and another glass of bracing red wine, or the heavenly cheesecake.

Light one-dish meals, sandwiches, and bar snacks are served between 8:30 A.M. and midnight in their corner café on the corner of Via de'Benci and Via dei Neri.

PALLOTTINO (62)
Via Isola delle Stinche, 1r

Ask the natives living around the Santa Croce Church where they eat, and the unanimous reply is: "Pallottino! Where else?" I have had the opportunity to try this restaurant several times, and I certainly share the Florentines' enthusiasm, especially for the two fixed-price menus, served only at lunch Tuesday to Saturday and never on holidays. These are Great Eats to behold. To keep the regulars interested and coming back in droves, the two-course menu changes daily and offers several choices for each course. Whole-wheat bread comes with the meal, but cover and service do not. You can also order just one first course, or one main course, but what for, when for 0.50 to 3€ more you can have two courses? The house wine is cheap and drinkable.

What about dinner? This menu is replaced by seasonal à la carte choices, which provide enough of a variety of the usual Tuscan favorites to keep everyone well fed and content. Naturally, the offerings are a little more sophisticated, but the prices are still reasonable enough not to ruin the budget. There is a two-course minimum order at night.

TELEPHONE
055 289 573
OPEN
Tues–Sun: lunch 12:45–2:30 P.M., dinner 7:30–10:15 P.M.
CLOSED
Mon; 15 days in Aug (dates vary)
RESERVATIONS
Accepted for dinner only
CREDIT CARDS
AE, DC, MC, V
À LA CARTE
Lunch: 3.50–8.50€; dinner & holidays: 20–28€
FIXED-PRICE MENU
Tues–Fri: 5.50€, 2 courses, beverages, cover and service extra; Tues–Sat: 7.50€, 2 courses, includes water, cover, and service
COVER & SERVICE CHARGES
Cover 1.50€, 10% service added
ENGLISH
Yes, and fixed-price menus in English

RISTORANTE DEL FAGIOLI (71)
Corso dei Tintori, 47r

During one research trip to Florence, I stayed in a beautiful penthouse apartment facing the Piazza Santa Croce. My neighbors were a delightful couple who were celebrating their retirement by spending six months in Florence and another six months in a villa in the Tuscan countryside. What a way to start retirement! As part of

TELEPHONE
055 244 285
OPEN
Mon–Fri: lunch 12:30–2:30 P.M., dinner 7:30–10:30 P.M.
CLOSED
Sat–Sun; 1 week at Easter and Christmas, Aug

RESERVATIONS
Advised
CREDIT CARDS
None
À LA CARTE
22–28€
FIXED-PRICE MENU
None
COVER & SERVICE CHARGES
Cover 1€, service discretionary
ENGLISH
Yes

their immersion into Italian life in Florence, they ate out at least once a day and would often report their findings to me. One of their standbys was this family-owned and -run trattoria right around the corner from our flats.

The restaurant has been here since 1966, and I can assure you that not one thing has changed in either its two rooms or in the Tuscan food, prepared by Luigi, the father, and leisurely served by his two sons, Antonio and Simone. While contemplating what to have, ask for the *pinzimonio misto di stagione,* a plate or bowl of raw seasonal vegetables to dip in olive oil, a light and refreshing way to start your meal. The portions are more than generous, especially the *ribollita,* brought to you in a big bowl so you can help yourself to as much as you want. It would be easy to make a meal out of this rich, twice-cooked bean and bread soup highlighted with vegetables, garlic, oil, and herbs, but save room for the comforting dishes that follow, such as osso buco, *baccalà* with tomato, and spicy sausages. The owners make all of their own desserts, but frankly, I never had room for more than a few of their homemade *biscotti* dipped in *vin santo.*

RISTORANTE LA GIOSTRA ($, 43)
Borgo Pinti, 10r

TELEPHONE
055 241 341
EMAIL
lagiostra@iol.it
OPEN
Mon–Fri: lunch 1–2:30 P.M.,
dinner 7:30 P.M.–midnight; Sat–
Sun: dinner 7:30 P.M.–midnight
CLOSED
Sat–Sun lunch
RESERVATIONS
Advised for dinner
CREDIT CARDS
AE, DC, MC, V
À LA CARTE
45–55€
FIXED-PRICE MENU
None
COVER & SERVICE CHARGES
Cover 2€, 10% service added
ENGLISH
Yes

The motto of Ristorante La Giostra is "In Food We Trust." Judging from its popularity, it is obvious that Florentines have come to trust the food and fall in love with La Giostra.

You will recognize Dimitri, the Russian owner of this very "in" place, when he comes out of the kitchen in full chef's garb and goes from table to table greeting his guests. He is a dignified and well-educated man, with doctorates in both chemistry and biology. Always a lover of fine food and cooking, he was told for years by his friends, "You are such a good cook—why don't you open your own restaurant?" Several years ago he came out of retirement and opened La Giostra with the help of his twin sons and daughter. The restaurant was an instant hit and remains full seven days a week. The name means "carousel," and there is a picture of one to the right of the entry.

Lunchtime does not seem to be a drawn-out affair, though dinner can be. If you go when the restaurant opens, chances are the service will be more attentive. As the evening progresses, the waiters are stretched beyond their limits, resulting in long delays between courses. Almost the minute you are seated, you are served a flute of champagne and a plate of assorted *crostini;* toast with various toppings. This helps with the long lag until the waiter comes back to take your order, and again until the appearance of the first course. All of the *primi piatti* (first courses) are good, especially their own ravioli with pecorino cheese and pears, the pappardelle with a gamey wild boar sauce, and the tagliatelle with a flavorful sauce of wild asparagus. One of the most popular main courses is the *spinata,* finely sliced beef flavored with sage, bay leaves, rosemary, salt, and pepper, and baked only two minutes in the oven. It is brought to your table on a sizzling hot plate. The *gran frittura de verdure alla Fiorentina* (a plate of assorted deep-fried vegetables) and the *scamorza,* slices of ham covered with cheese that has been browned and bubbled under the broiler just before it arrives at your table, are two side dishes large enough to share. For dessert, forget the *tart Tatin di mele,* a dreary apple tart, and opt instead for a cool lemon *sorbetto* or the wickedly fattening tiramisù. The wine list is not cheap in general, but there are a dozen or so bottles priced between 16–25€, and a few vintages are also served by the glass.

SALUMERIA/GASTRONOMIA VERDI (¢, 60)
Via Guiseppe Verdi, 36r

Glorious picnics, terrific takeout, and Great Eater-friendly lunches all begin at Pino's Salumeria/Gastronomia Verdi, a few short blocks from Piazza Santa Croce. Walking by, you can smell the good things awaiting you inside, where the artistically presented food is as delightful to the palate as it is to the eye. Pino gets up with the chickens so he can be at the market when it opens to find the best ingredients, which are skillfully prepared into wonderful dishes by Antonella, a sweet French cook who grew up in Monte Carlo. With these two virtuosos in my neighborhood, I never needed to go near the kitchen to cook again! They work long hours six days a week, dishing out a fabulous selection of pastas, sweet and savory crêpes, tortes, salads galore, and a host of sandwiches. The latter are made with the best cold meats and cheeses—or any other ingredient you can think of to put between two slices of freshly baked bread. A nice variety of Italian wines are also available to complement your repast.

Everything can be packaged to go or consumed in the small side room dedicated to what Pino calls "speed lunches." You must ask for these meals, which are put together from the deli counter and consist of a first and

TELEPHONE
055 244 517

OPEN
Mon–Sat: 8 A.M.–3 P.M., 5–8 P.M.

CLOSED
Sun; 2–3 weeks mid-Aug

CREDIT CARDS
MC, V

À LA CARTE
Sandwiches from 2–2.50€, all other food sold by weight

FIXED-PRICE MENU
8€, 2 courses, vegetable, and mineral water

COVER & SERVICE CHARGES
None

ENGLISH
Yes, and French

second course with vegetable garnish and a half bottle of mineral water for less than a hamburger, shake, and fries would cost you in a Stateside fast-food joint.

TRATTORIA BALDOVINO (67)
Via San Giuseppe, 22r

TELEPHONE
055 241 773
INTERNET
www.baldovino.com
OPEN
Nov–Mar, Tues–Sun; April–Oct, daily: lunch 11:30 A.M.–2:30 P.M., dinner 7–11:30 P.M.
CLOSED
Mon from Nov–Mar; last week of Nov and first week of Dec
RESERVATIONS
Recommended for lunch, essential for dinner
CREDIT CARDS
MC, V
À LA CARTE
Pizza from 5.50€, 3-course meal 20–30€
FIXED-PRICE MENU
None
COVER & SERVICE CHARGES
Cover 1.50€, 10% service suggested
ENGLISH
Yes, and menu in English

Follow the *bel mondo* to Baldovino, one of the best—and definitely most popular—trattorias in Florence. Opened a few years ago on a shoestring by David and Catherine Gardner, a delightful Scottish pair, it hit the ground running and became a favorite among Florentines and tourists alike. Success allowed them to expand up the street, and there you will find Enoteca Baldovino, their wine bar and outdoor terrace (see page 47). Across the Arno is Beccofino (see page 80), another of their very successful ventures.

Trattoria Baldovino has several rooms, painted in wild color combinations of orange and purple, or just plain green. Once you are inside the front door, wend your way through the first room and the exhibition kitchen to the more desirable back rooms, which have less waiter and patron traffic. The inventive menu puts an imaginative twist on the bounty of Tuscany. Appetizers to whet your appetite include grilled vegetables marinated in olive oil and served with a hunk of fresh mozzarella, and the plate of smoked fish, which gets star billing, as do several types of rosemary-flavored focaccia seasoned with olive oil and topped with either chopped tomatoes, garlic, and basil; Parmesan and oregano; or smoked salmon, arugula, and Parmesan. Six meal-in-one salads begin with the Baldovino—featuring chicken breast, grapes, walnuts, and celery—and end with a raw vegetable combination dusted with shavings of pecorino cheese. The soups, pastas, wood-fired pizzas, *calzoni,* main courses of oven-baked rabbit seasoned with marjoram, char-grilled chicken shish kebab, or roast lamb with juniper berries all prove winners in the eyes of the trendsetters who fill the restaurant on a daily basis. The tempting homemade desserts—guaranteed to keep you on the treadmill an extra twenty minutes per day for the next week—include apple pie with pinenuts and raisins, topped with warm custard, double-chocolate torte served with vanilla ice cream, and cheesecake with strawberry salsa.

NOTE: David and Catherine, along with their young daughter Jemima, have opened a country villa in Greve in Chianti. Please consult their Website for details.

Gelaterias

GELATERIA DEI NERI (69)
Via dei Neri, 20/22r

How do you know the gelato here is made from fresh ingredients? One look through the streetside window into the kitchen presided over by Mauricio, the hardworking owner, tells it all. This ice cream maestro works six days a week from 1 P.M. until midnight churning out some of the best gelato I have ever tasted. If you are lactose intolerant, not to worry; he has developed a sugarless, vegetarian soya ice cream that belies all notions that anything healthy can't possibly taste good. His chocolate mousse *semifreddo* alone is worth a trip to his shop, as is the lemon cream yogurt ice cream and the *profiterole semifreddo* laced with dark chocolate syrup that is beyond rich . . . and wonderful. Not content to rest on his laurels, Mauricio also makes ice cream cakes to order. Clearly he has orders, and lots of them, because I have never passed his shop without admiring his masterpieces displayed in the front window, waiting to be picked up.

TELEPHONE
055 210 034

OPEN
Oct–Mar, Mon–Tues, Thur–Sun; April–Sept, daily: 11:30 A.M.– 11:30 P.M.

CLOSED
Wed from Oct–Mar

CREDIT CARDS
None

PRICES
Tasting cone 0.50€, cones 1.40–3.30€, cups 1.40–5€, cakes from 15€

ENGLISH
Limited

VIVOLI (63)
Via Isola delle Stinche, 7r

Since 1930, the largest and creamiest selections of ice cream have been scooped out at Vivoli. It is most active in the evening, when young Florentines strut their stuff, and on Sundays, when it becomes a family affair. These are the times you will be able to witness the Italian phenomenon of the *passeggiata,* the see-and-be-seen stroll all Italians love.

Baskets of fresh berries, cases of bananas, and crates of oranges go into the thousand-plus quarts of all-natural ice cream made and consumed here each day. The revolving list of thirty-eight flavors follows the seasons. For my gelato euro, the absolute best flavor, and one of their specialties, is the orange-chocolate cream, a cloudlike mixture of chocolate, cream orange liqueur, and pieces of fresh orange. Another specialty is *zabaione,* always made from the same recipe used by the founder of this ice cream dynasty. Any of the *semifreddo* choices are fabulous, provided you can stand the fat-gram blowout from the whipped cream–based ice cream. Dieters need not feel left out: the fruit flavors are fat-free, with the exception of the banana. The gelato is served only in cups, and you pay for the size of the cup, not the number of flavors you want in it. Avoid the strange rice cream flavor,

TELEPHONE
055 292 334

INTERNET
www.vivoli.it

OPEN
Tues–Sun: 7:30 A.M.–midnight, until 1 A.M. in summer

CLOSED
Mon; last 3 weeks in Aug

CREDIT CARDS
None

PRICES
Cups from 1.50–10€

ENGLISH
Usually

a bland-tasting vanilla with hard pieces of almost raw rice sprinkled throughout. Also available are drinks at the full bar and homemade morning pastries and sandwiches.

Piazza Santa Maria Novella

The Gothic Renaissance church of Santa Maria Novella was the Florentine seat of the Dominicans. Inside the church is *The Trinity* by Masaccio, frescoes by Filippino Lippi, and the wooden crucifix by Giotto. The piazza outside, one of the largest in the city, is frequented by backpackers coming and going from the train stations and assorted other foreigners just hanging out.

RESTAURANTS

GELATERIAS

($) indicates a Big Splurge
(¢) indicates a Cheap Eat

Restaurants

ARMANDO (27)
Borgo Ognissanti, 140r

TELEPHONE
055 216 219
INTERNET
www.trattoria-armando.com
OPEN
Mon: dinner 7:30–10:30 P.M.;
Tues–Sat: lunch 12:30–3 P.M.,
dinner 7:30–10:30 P.M.
CLOSED
Mon lunch, Sun; holidays, Aug
(dates vary)
RESERVATIONS
Advised, especially for dinner

Everyone loves dining at Armando, and I certainly do, too. The restaurant has remained on my short list of best-value restaurants in Florence because it offers consistently fine cooking that is not only pleasing but nourishing. Handed down from father to son, and now mother to daughter, this typically Tuscan trattoria is as authentic as the cuisine, with friendly service provided by the family and long-term staff in an ever-crowded and cheerful atmosphere. Keep in mind that Italians dine late; in fact, at 9:30 P.M. they are still arriving and often waiting for a table to clear.

If it is on the menu, one of the best ways to start is with the green salad of *pecorino di Pienza* and pears. The beautiful presentation has slices of fresh pears circling a salad of pecorino cheese and walnuts, and it is served with honey for drizzling over it along with a splash or two of extra-virgin olive oil. The Oscar for the best pasta dish goes to their *ravioli al burro e salvia,* homemade ravioli stuffed with ricotta cheese and sage and lightly covered in a buttery sauce. Throw cholesterol and fat counting to the wind just once and treat yourself to this. Another hands-down favorite in the pasta category goes to the *spaghetti alla carriettiera,* pasta topped with a spicy sauce made from garlic, fresh basil, tomato, and red pepper. This dish will wake up your taste buds in a hurry. In the early spring, order the tagliatelle with zucchini flowers, which is a light homemade pasta tossed with zucchini flowers and cherry tomatoes and served topped with a few slices of zucchini and a bouquet of fresh basil. Even if you have spent a lifetime turning up your nose at liver, please consider it here and try the *fegato alla salvia,* calves' livers broiled just to the tender pink stage. In the dessert department, look seriously at their homemade offerings, especially the decadently rich bitter chocolate cake.

DA GIORGIO (¢, 25)
Via Palazzuolo, 100r

If the line is too long down the street at Il Contadino (see page 56), walk up to Da Giorgio, another cheap eat with a bargain set-price menu. If I had to choose between the two, I would give the edge to Da Giorgio. In spite of the shared tables with plastic-covered linen, there are cloth napkins, green plants, a few pictures scattered on the walls, and a larger selection of dishes.

Of course, there is no printed menu; you must depend on the waiter to tell you what is available that day. For starters, there might be macaroni with a spicy sauce; *pasta al pesto;* risotto with peas, tomatoes, and meat; or tortellini. On Thursday, there is always gnocchi, and fresh fish on Friday. Your second course of meat, chicken, or fish is garnished with vegetables, salad, or potatoes. Wine or mineral water is included, but coffee is extra. The only dessert option is a piece of fresh fruit, which costs extra and is not worth it.

CREDIT CARDS
AE, DC, MC, V
À LA CARTE
35–45€
FIXED-PRICE MENU
Lunch only: 15–20€, 2 courses, vegetable and coffee; cover and service extra
COVER & SERVICE CHARGES
Cover 2.50€, service included
ENGLISH
Yes, and menu in English

TELEPHONE
055 284 302
OPEN
Mon–Sat: lunch noon–2:30 P.M., dinner 6–10 P.M.
CLOSED
Sun; Aug
RESERVATIONS
Not accepted
CREDIT CARDS
MC, V
À LA CARTE
First and second courses 8€, vegetables 4€, fruit or coffee 1€
FIXED-PRICE MENU
Lunch, 9.50€, dinner 10.50€: 2 courses, vegetable, wine, cover and service
COVER & SERVICE CHARGES
Included
ENGLISH
Yes

IL CONTADINO (¢, 24)
Via Palazzuolo, 69/71r

TELEPHONE
055 238 2673

OPEN
Mon–Sat: lunch noon–2:30 P.M.,
dinner 6 P.M.–midnight

CLOSED
Sun; 3 weeks in Aug (dates vary)

RESERVATIONS
Not accepted

CREDIT CARDS
MC, V

À LA CARTE
None

FIXED-PRICE MENU
Lunch, 9:50€; dinner, 10€:
2 courses, wine or mineral water

COVER & SERVICE CHARGES
Included

ENGLISH
Yes

You will probably have to wait in line with the Italians at lunch and the tourists at dinner if you want one of the cheapest eats in Florence. Il Contadino is across the street from the area's other bargain eat, Da Giorgio (see page 55), and they both serve just about the same food and appeal to the same type of thrifty eater.

Except for a few old photos of Florence, interior decor is almost nonexistent in the two white-tiled rooms, which are filled instead with eager eaters, sleeves rolled up and ties loosened. The food is unimaginative but filling, and there is plenty of it. House wine or mineral water is included. For both courses, there are usually at least five selections, such as ravioli, minestrone, lasagne, *pasta e fagioli,* pork, beef, chicken, and frozen fish on Wednesday and Friday. The main courses are garnished with either a salad, vegetable, fries, or beans. Coffee and fresh fruit each cost 1€ extra.

RISTORANTE BUCA MARIO ($, 32)
Piazza Ottaviani, 16r

TELEPHONE
055 214 179

OPEN
Mon–Tues, Fri–Sun: lunch
12:30–3:30 P.M., dinner 7:30–
12:30 P.M.; Wed–Thur: dinner
7:30–12:30 P.M.

CLOSED
Wed–Thur lunch; Aug
(dates vary)

RESERVATIONS
Advised at night

CREDIT CARDS
AE, DC, MC, V

À LA CARTE
40–55€

FIXED-PRICE MENU
None

COVER & SERVICE CHARGES
Cover 3€, service included

ENGLISH
Yes

To best appreciate a meal at Buca Mario, avoid the front dining area, which serves as a passageway, and request a table in one of the other rooms in this large, meandering restaurant. Slightly on the formal side, with career waiters in black pants and burgundy bow ties, it is hardly in the fast track of hot Florentine dining spots. However, it has courteous and correct service and, above all, reliable food. In the spring, I like to start with a salad of designer greens mixed with tender raw baby artichoke slices and shavings of Parmesan cheese, splashed with fresh lemon and extra virgin olive oil. Another favorite is fragrant melon served with prosciutto, or milky *mozzarella de bufala* sandwiched between bright-red tomatoes and accented with fresh sprigs of basil. For the *primo piatto,* look for *taglierini* with salmon, pappardelle with wild boar, or a classic *ribollita*. If you are ordering a *secondo piatto* of either meat or fish, I'd suggest you go easy on the pastas and head straight for their roast lamb flavored with rosemary and garlic or one of the veal scallopini renditions. Most fried foods are on everyone's no-no list, but here they are worth a special indulgence, especially if you order the zucchini, cauliflower, and *melanzane* mix or the fried calamari and shrimp served with a soothing tartar sauce. Desserts? Frankly, besides the fresh fruit tart or the *torta della nona,* they are uninspired. Perhaps have a grappa or *limoncello* instead.

SOSTANZA (28)
Via del Porcellana, 25r

Sostanza is one of the city's oldest and best-loved trattorias, frequented by the great, the near-great, and just plain folks. On the day I was here, Siliano and Fosco, the two friendly bosses, were celebrating forty-nine years here. As always, forty places are crammed into a long room that, despite its pristine plainness, becomes hectic as the meal progresses and the diners crowd in together. The waiters wear jackets, but the formality ends there. The wine is served in tumblers, the bread is handed to you, and the plates are passed. Lots of hugging, kissing, and waving goes on among the regulars. Reservations are essential for both lunch and dinner.

The handwritten menu is easy to read and usually states at the top, *Si serve solo pranzo completo*. That generally translates as, "Don't come here if you are only going to order a pasta and a salad." Dishes to remember are the *tortino di carciofi* (artichoke omelette), the *bistecca alla Fiorentino*—a 600-gram T-bone steak geared toward lumberjacks but ordered, and finished, by wafer-thin models—and the *bollito di manzo con salsa verde:* boiled beef with a green sauce of chopped parsley, capers, anchovies, dill pickles, breadcrumbs, garlic, onion, vinegar, and olive oil. The only dessert made here, a meringue cake, is a must—you will think you don't have room, but will end up enjoying every bite.

NOTE: Via del Porcellana is winkingly known in Florence as the home of the aging hookers, some of whom look as though they have been standing in these doorways for decades. They are harmless but do add a note of local color.

TELEPHONE
055 212 691
OPEN
Mon–Fri: lunch 12:30–2:10 P.M., dinner 7:30–10:45 P.M
CLOSED
Sat–Sun; last 2 weeks of Dec, Aug
RESERVATIONS
Essential
CREDIT CARDS
None
À LA CARTE
25–30€
FIXED-PRICE MENU
None
COVER & SERVICE CHARGES
Cover 2.50€, service included
ENGLISH
Enough

TRATTORIA 13 GOBBI (31)
Via del Porcellana, 9r

"Artistically rustic" are the words that come to mind when asked to describe the interior of this popular trattoria not far from Piazza Goldoni and Piazza Santa Maria Novella. Bare wooden tables are covered with linen place mats and painted Tuscan pottery. The back room overlooks the summer patio and some apartments next door, where you can often see the occupants' laundry lazily flapping in the breeze. The menu offers a good, but not overwhelming, selection of seasonal local dishes; the excellent house wine is served in big pitchers. On Friday the focus is on fresh fish. On other days, I like to start with the *antipasti della casa,* an assortment of *crostini* topped with various cured meats and pâtés, or share one of their huge salads, especially the

TELEPHONE
055 284 015
OPEN
Mon: dinner 7:30–10:30 P.M.; Tues–Sun: lunch 12:30–2:30 P.M., dinner 7:30–10:30 P.M.
CLOSED
Mon lunch
RESERVATIONS
Advised for lunch, essential for dinner
CREDIT CARDS
AE, MC, V
À LA CARTE
28–38€

FIXED-PRICE MENU
None
COVER & SERVICE CHARGES
Cover 1€, 10% service added
ENGLISH
Yes, and menu in English

pear and pecorino, or raw zucchini tossed with gorgonzola and pine nuts. For a first course, I follow the suggestion on the menu and "ask what's boiling in the pan." Sometimes it might be a simple but soothing bowl of spaghetti mixed with double butter, a bubbling eggplant parmigiana, or a pasta tossed with garlic, peppers, bacon, and olive oil. The roast lamb is wonderfully tender, and so is the liver flavored with sage. I can't say this about any of the veal dishes, all of which suffered from overcooking and oversaucing. The *dolci* (desserts) are worth the guilt trip, especially the chocolate pear tart and the cheesecake. Some of the waiters have an attitude problem and actively discourage lingering on crowded weekends, when the tables are turned at least twice in the hopes of getting more tips.

Gelaterias

L'ANGOLO DEL GELATO (26)
Via della Scala, 2r

TELEPHONE
055 210 526
OPEN
Summer: daily 10 A.M.–1 A.M.;
winter: daily 11 A.M.–midnight
CLOSED
Never
CREDIT CARDS
None
PRICES
Cones from 1.50€, cups from
2.10€, *panna* (whipped
cream) 0.30€
ENGLISH
Limited

Italians are addicted to gelato, and nowhere is this more evident than in Florence, where *gelaterias* seem to be a dime a dozen. For the best ice cream near Santa Maria Novella, drop by L'Angolo del Gelato, a corner store owned by Lidia and Filippo. Everything they serve is made here from fresh ingredients and seasonal fruits. The gelato is sold by the size of the cup, and you can have as many flavors as you want in whatever cup size you select. The most popular flavors are chocolate and banana/nutella. In summer you can indulge to your waistline's content with their fat-free fruit *sorbettos* or fruit-based yogurt ice cream. The servings are generous. Those in the know always ask for their gelato with some *panna montata* on top . . . freshly whipped cream.

Piazza Sant' Ambrogio

This is an interesting working-class neighborhood and features the most local Florence market. The best time to experience all the fauna and flora is on a Saturday morning.

RESTAURANTS

Cibreino	59
Il Pizzaiuolo (¢)	60
Tavola Calda da Rocco (¢)	60
Teatro del Sale	61

INDOOR/OUTDOOR MARKETS

Mercato Sant' Ambrogio	94

(¢) indicates a Cheap Eat

Restaurants

CIBREINO (53)
Via dei Macci, 122r

Confirmed reservations and a healthy bank account are absolute necessities before embarking on a trip to the well-known Trattoria Cibrèo restaurant, whose fame has now spread to Japan, where it has opened up a branch. However, if you don't like planning far in advance and shudder at spending upwards of 65 to 70€ for a meal, then Cibreino, their trattoria spin-off around the corner, is your answer. And why not—the food is prepared in the same kitchen (admittedly in a more simple manner), the mood is buzzy and fun, and while standing in the queue (because reservations are not accepted) you will probably meet some interesting people. Lunch is from 12:50 to 2:30 P.M., and dinner from 7 to 11:15 P.M. The best game plan is to arrive very early, very late, or at about two-hour intervals, when the tables are turned. What will you eat? For openers, the famous tomato flan and the equally touted herb polenta get things going. There is no pasta, so you can comfortably move on to Cibrèo's famous chicken neck, stuffed with chicken mousse and served head intact. (I promise you this is much better than it sounds.) Other mains may include a squid stew, some version of *baccalà,* or a veal dish. There are several desserts, but the one to walk ten miles for is their fabulous chocolate *budino* ringed with caramel sauce.

TELEPHONE
055 234 1100

EMAIL
cibreo.fi@tin.it

OPEN
Tues–Sat: lunch 12:50–2:30 P.M., dinner 7–11:15 P.M.

CLOSED
Sun, Mon; Aug (dates vary)

RESERVATIONS
Not accepted

CREDIT CARDS
Not accepted

À LA CARTE
Appetizer, first course, vegetables, dessert and cheese 5€ each; second course 15€

FIXED-PRICE MENU
None

COVER & SERVICE CHARGES
None

ENGLISH
Yes

Figuring the bill is simple: all dishes are priced the same for each course, and even if you order all the courses, the bottom line should be at least half of what the big spenders around the corner are being charged.

Cibrèo also runs the Cibrèo Caffè (on Via Andrea del Verrocchio, 5r), where coffee, pastries, light lunches, and drinks are served Tuesday through Saturday from 8 A.M. to 1 A.M. The newest feather in the Cibrèo cap is the Teatro del Sale (see page 61).

NOTE: If you are coming for lunch, please allow some time to browse the Sant' Ambrogio market and peek into the windows of the shops lining the surrounding streets, which will give you a good idea of where the locals do business.

IL PIZZAIUOLO (¢, 55)
Via dei Macci, 113r

TELEPHONE
055 241 171

OPEN
Mon–Sat: noon–3 P.M., dinner 7:30 P.M–midnight

CLOSED
Sun; 4 days at Easter and Christmas, Aug

RESERVATIONS
Required for dinner

CREDIT CARDS
V

À LA CARTE
Pizza 4.50–9.50€, salads & antipasti 4–9€, desserts 4.50–6.50€

FIXED-PRICE MENU
None

COVER & SERVICE CHARGES
Cover 1.50€, service included

ENGLISH
Yes

Pizza pundits debate who has the best pizza in town, but all of them would agree on one thing: if you like Neapolitan pizza, this place has the best in Florence. It is a casual spot, across the square from the busy market at Piazza Sant' Ambrogio. You can arrive for lunch without a reservation, but forget it if you arrive for dinner without one. In the evening, reservations are taken for 8, 9, 10, or 11 P.M., and without your name in the book for one of these times, you will not get in. The twenty-five or so pizzas range from a simple *Napoli*—with tomatoes, mozzarella, anchovies, capers, and oregano—to the *pizza bomba ripena,* which has the usual tomato and mozzarella, plus *prosciutto cotto* (cooked prosciutto), ricotta, mushrooms, and salami. If you don't see the combination you want, they will create it for you. Also on board are a half-dozen pastas, as well as the usual meats and fish, but bypass these for another meal. If you are eating here, you eat pizza and perhaps share a salad or antipasti.

TAVOLA CALDA DA ROCCO (¢, 56)
Mercato di Sant' Ambrogio

TELEPHONE
339 838 4555 (cell phone)

OPEN
Mon–Sat: lunch noon–2:30 P.M.

CLOSED
Sun

RESERVATIONS
Not accepted

CREDIT CARDS
None

Here you know everything is fresh: The Rocco family shops at the market daily for the food they prepare in their open kitchen in the center hall of this wonderful Florentine dining landmark. The hot dishes are ready by noon and are served to seriously hungry market workers and regulars, who lap it up while sitting on stools closely spaced at Formica tables. The menu, which always includes sturdy soups and stews, hearty pastas, and in winter, baked pears in red wine for dessert, changes daily and advises *Le mezze porzioni non saranno servite,* which means "Half portions are not served." Yet even if you ordered every course, you would have trouble spending $14, and that would include a generous plastic cup filled with the rough-and-ready house *vino.* After your meal, saunter across the aisle to the Bar-Jolly Caffè–La Caffetteria del Vecchio Mercato, and have one of the cheapest espressos in town.

TEATRO DEL SALE (52)
Via dei Macci, 111r

The Teatro del Sale is a work in progress being developed by the powers that be at Cibrèo (see page 59). The brochure says loftily, "'Our aim is to create business and nourish the economy; that is why we will be selling the most valuable and precious product in the world: 'The search for quality of life.'" That's quite a mouthful, and a lot to live up to. And what does it mean? Quite simply it means you pay a yearly 5€ membership fee for the privilege of eating a buffet breakfast, lunch, or dinner in a theater space, in full view of an open kitchen staffed by Cibrèo chefs and line workers. In the evening, various entertainment workshops are held, ranging from cooking to singing, acting, set design, stage lighting, and more. A weekly list of these events is available at the *teatro* or on their Website. Reservations are required for dinner, but it's come one, come all for breakfast and lunch. At no time are more than ninety-nine members allowed in.

For the breakfast buffet, members may choose from a small selection consisting of cake, two types of bread (which can be toasted), three jams, orange juice, yogurt, cereal, and strong coffee. Only if you have your bread toasted will the kitchen serve you a warm slice of focaccia with ham. A bowl of fresh fruit would be a welcome addition to this very starchy way to start the day. The lunch and dinner buffets (at 13€ and 20€ per person, respectively) are run according to the same drill: go to the buffet, get your food and wine, and take it to a comfortable tufted leather armchair or to a table in the "auditorium." For both lunch and dinner, my advice is to go early, before all the dishes get picked over. After dinner, at 9:30 P.M., the entertainment workshops begin.

One has to hand it to the Cibrèo marketing team for never missing a sales opportunity. As you enter the *teatro,* there is a small selection of grocery products for sale, including anchovies, honey, wine, olive oil, salt, cheeses, and (they admit) "not much more."

À LA CARTE
First courses 2.70€, main courses 3.80€, vegetables 2.20€, fruit and dessert 1.20–2.20€

FIXED-PRICE MENU
None

COVER & SERVICE CHARGES
Cover 0.70€, service 0.70€

ENGLISH
Enough

TELEPHONE
055 200 1492

INTERNET
www.teatrodelsale.com

OPEN
Tues–Sat: breakfast 9–11 A.M., lunch noon–2 P.M., dinner 7–9 P.M.

CLOSED
Sun–Mon; first week of Jan, Aug

RESERVATIONS
Not accepted for breakfast or lunch; required for dinner

À LA CARTE
None

FIXED-PRICE MENU
Buffet breakfast 5€, lunch 13€, dinner 20€, includes wine, cover, and service charges

COVER & SERVICE CHARGES
Included

MEMBERSHIP FEE
5€ yearly fee per person; membership card must be shown at each meal

ENGLISH
Yes

Ponte Vecchio

The famous Ponte Vecchio, dating from 1345, is lined with small shops displaying an awe-inspiring collection of magnificent gold and jewels. It is thronged with tourists on their way to and from the Pitti Palace, window shopping and posing for countless photos.

BUCA DELL' ORAFO (68)
Volta dei Girolami, 28r

TELEPHONE
055 213 619
OPEN
Tues–Sat: lunch 12:30–2:30 P.M.,
dinner 7:30–10 P.M.
CLOSED
Sun, Mon; Aug
RESERVATIONS
Essential, at least a day in advance
CREDIT CARDS
None
À LA CARTE
30–35€
FIXED-PRICE MENU
None
COVER & SERVICE CHARGES
Cover 2.50€, service included
ENGLISH
Yes

Hidden under an archway near the Ponte Vecchio is the tiny Buca dell' Orafo, a favorite for years of Florentines and visitors alike for its good value and authentic cuisine. The two owners are on tap every day, running the kitchen and serving their guests. Everyone seems to know one another, particularly at lunch, when lots of laughing and talking goes on between the tables. If you go for lunch or after 9 P.M., you will likely share your dining experience with Italians. If you go for an early dinner, you will hear mostly English spoken and probably run into your cousin's neighbor from Detroit.

The regulars know to come on the specific days their favorite dishes are served. Friday is always fresh codfish. On Thursday, Friday, and Saturday, *ribollita* is the headlining opener. And every day you can count on finding a special, such as *stracotto e fagioli al' uccelletto,* braised beef with beans in a sauce with garlic, onions, and sage. Two spring favorites are the *tortino di carciofi,* an artichoke omelette that will change your mind about what can be done with an artichoke, and the deliciously simple *taglierini* pasta with fresh peas. The dessert to melt your heart and your willpower is the house special *dolce,* a sponge cake with layers of cream and meringue and almonds on top. It will be one of the best desserts you will have on your entire trip.

San Lorenzo Central Market

The Piazza Mercato Centrale, which celebrates the glories of Tuscan food, is a nineteenth-century cast-iron landmark housing one of the largest and most interesting markets in Europe. It is a must-see in Florence for all food lovers. Crowding the surrounding streets are countless stalls with sellers hawking more than enough goods to fill up an extra suitcase. For even the least committed Great Chic shopper, it is definitely worth a look, though the stalls sell basically the same things: polyester scarf copies of the real Guccis or Fendis, leather bags, belts, jackets, T-shirts, Florentine paper goods, souvenirs, and accessories. Despite what the setting suggests, bargains are rare, because the competition is so intense that the prices are almost fixed. Therefore, look around and buy from the vendor who treats you the best.

RESTAURANTS

Restaurants

ANTICHI CANCELLI (15)
Via Faenza, 73r

At Antichi Cancelli, which means "the old gate," it does not take newcomers long to blend in and quickly catch the mood of the place. With its hanging peppers and garlic braids, potted plants, brick ceiling, and tiny paper-covered, marble-topped tables, it looks like the quintessential movie set for an Italian film. The difference, of course, is that the food and jovial ambience are real, and so is its popularity. Do not even *think* of arriving without reservations, and even then you can count on having to wedge yourself into the crowd and wait for a table.

It is important that you come prepared to eat. Managers Romeo and Enzo take a dim view of dieters or anyone else not ordering at least a pasta, main course, and dessert. The daily menu is based on what is best at the market during each season and is handwritten on a scrap of paper stapled to the regular menu. The dishes of Tuscany are well prepared,

TELEPHONE
055 218 927

OPEN
Tues–Sun: lunch noon–2:45 P.M., dinner 6–10:45 P.M.

CLOSED
Mon

RESERVATIONS
Essential

CREDIT CARDS
AE, DC, MC, V

À LA CARTE
18–25€

FIXED-PRICE MENU
12€, 2 courses, salad, dessert, wine or mineral water included, cover extra

COVER & SERVICE CHARGES
Cover 1€, no service charge

ENGLISH
Yes, and fixed-price menu in
English

and everything from the antipasti and pasta to the sauces and desserts is made here. As always, the best dishes will be on the daily menu. The filling portions promise that no one will be thinking about their next meal for a long time.

NOTE: Especially appealing to many Great Eaters are the restaurant's hours. Dinner is available at the unheard-of hour of 6 P.M.

CAFAGGI (12)
Via Guelfa, 35r

TELEPHONE
055 294 989
OPEN
Mon–Sat: lunch noon–2:30 P.M.,
dinner 7–10 P.M.
CLOSED
Sun; 1 week in Jan, 4 weeks
July–Aug (dates vary)
RESERVATIONS
Advised, especially weekends
and holidays
CREDIT CARDS
AE, MC, V
À LA CARTE
25–35€
FIXED-PRICE MENU
16.50€, 2 courses, includes
bread, cover, and service
charges; beverages extra
COVER & SERVICE CHARGES
Cover 2.80€, service included
ENGLISH
Yes

One of the best ways to discover good places to eat is to ask the natives where they go. The top contender on Via Guelfa, between Piazza della Indipendenza and Piazza San Marco off Via Cavour, is Cafaggi. This plain-Jane restaurant has been in the Cafaggi family for decades and consists of two rather large rooms. The second room off the kitchen is slightly more appealing, owing to a few plants scattered about. Smart Great Eaters will join the well-dressed businesspeople at lunch and the attractive neighborhood crowd in the evening, all of whom come prepared to dine well, not to lounge in magnificent surroundings. After you have had your first glass of wine and have tasted the fine food, you will quickly forget about the dull atmosphere. Some Great Eaters will want to stay with the set-price menu, which includes a first and second course. However, with a bit of careful ordering, à la carte will not be prohibitively expensive.

The real boss in the kitchen is Sra. Cafaggi, who oversees it all, including her son Leonardo, who is the chef and prides himself on turning out carefully prepared dishes using the freshest seasonal ingredients. In fact, the front window has a vivid display of the types of fresh fish, meat, and produce you can expect to see on your plate. They are wizards with fresh fish and veal, especially the veal and artichokes, and they always prepare a special vegetarian main dish. The desserts are all made here; try the lovely apple and pear *torta*. The house wine is adequate, so there is no need to splurge on anything else. The service by brothers Lorenzo and Andrea is friendly yet professional.

I' TOSCANO (8)
Via Guelfa, 70r

TELEPHONE
055 215 475
INTERNET
www.itoscano.it

The chef at i' Toscano displays his varied skills with dishes of fresh, flavorful food attractively presented in two rather formal rooms—formal by Florence standards, that is. A collection of black-and-white pictures of Florence adds the only point of interest in the brightly lit, stark-white surroundings. Yet the properly set tables are spaced wide enough to prevent your being a part of your neighbor's conversation, and the waiters are friendly and make an effort to explain any dish you are not sure about.

The food is just creative and imaginative enough to lift it out of the ordinary. Depending on the season, you might start with a plate of cold slices of wild boar, deer, and other game meats, or something typically Florentine, such as toasted bread topped with black cabbage, garlic, and olive oil. The porcini mushroom ravioli in a butter and thyme sauce is a satisfying first-course pasta, as is the *bucatini* with Italian bacon and tomato sauce. For the main dish, if you are here on a Friday, by all means order the *baccalà*—cod served with a fresh tomato sauce. On other days, it is a toss-up between the lamb with artichokes in a white wine sauce and the savory beef stew. For your vegetable, if it is on the menu, the *gobbi alla Fiorentina* (*gobbi* is a thistlelike plant with leaves and stalks that are eaten like celery), served here lightly braised in a butter sauce, is an interesting selection you seldom see. Otherwise, there is a choice of fried artichokes, fresh green peas, or spinach sautéed with garlic and olive oil. Saving room for dessert takes some willpower, but at least share a slice of the lemon cake or order an assortment of local cheeses served with apple jam.

OPEN
Mon, Wed–Sun: lunch noon–2:30 P.M.; dinner 7:30–10:30 P.M.

CLOSED
Tues; 1st week of Aug

RESERVATIONS
Advised for dinner

CREDIT CARDS
AE, DC, MC, V

À LA CARTE
25–35€

FIXED-PRICE MENU
None

COVER & SERVICE CHARGES
Cover 2€, service included

ENGLISH
Yes, and menu in English

NERBONE (¢, 19)
Stand #292, Piazza del Mercato Centrale (next to the San Lorenzo Church)

The Mercato di San Lorenzo, Florence's huge indoor market, is the main source of food for a region that takes food very seriously, and it is without peer for its wide variety and enormous selection. Be sure you allow yourself enough time to appreciate the displays of food, which provide a quick course in the art and ingredients of Italian cooking. While here you will see several Italian-style fast-food stalls, the most famous, and unquestionably the best, is Nerbone, Stand #292, where hot meat sandwiches have been the major draw since 1872.

Nerbone, which is under the same ownership as Alla Vecchia Bettola (see page 74), appeals to those with hearty appetites who don't mind a noisy, no-frills setting. The menu lists bowls of beans, mashed potatoes, tripe, roast chicken, pork, and pastas. Never mind any of these. The standard order here from 7 A.M. until the kitchen runs

TELEPHONE
055 219 949

OPEN
Mon–Sat: 7 A.M.–2 P.M., continuous service

CLOSED
Sun; Aug (dates vary)

RESERVATIONS
Not accepted

CREDIT CARDS
None

À LA CARTE
Sandwiches 2.50€, 2-course meal with vegetable 12€

FIXED-PRICE MENU
None

COVER & SERVICE CHARGES
None

ENGLISH
Depends on server, but generally none

out is a sandwich of boiled beef (*bollito*) or *lampredotto* (cow intestines), sliced onto a crusty roll and then dipped into the meat juices (*bagnato*). After you are handed your food, take it to the tables across the aisle or stand at the bar with a beer or a glass of rough *vino rosso,* and enjoy!

PALLE D'ORO (16)
Via Sant' Antonino 43/45r

TELEPHONE
055 288 383
OPEN
Mon–Sat: lunch noon–3:30 P.M., dinner 6:30–10 P.M.
CLOSED
Sun; Aug
RESERVATIONS
Not necessary
CREDIT CARDS
AE, DC, MC, V
À LA CARTE
Sandwiches from 2.50€, lunch 15€, dinner 18–22€
FIXED-PRICE MENU
14€, 3 courses, includes mineral water, cover and service
COVER & SERVICE
1.30€, service included
ENGLISH
Yes, and menu in English

Sooner or later, all cost-conscious eaters in Florence learn about Palle d'Oro, which sits on a crowded shopping street leading to the big Mercato Centrale. For more than a hundred years this fourth-generation family-run jewel has provided dependable and good fast food *alla italiano.* It is so crowded at noon you probably won't be able to see the walls, which means you will miss the interesting black-and-white family photos showing Lorenzo, the great-grandfather (whose nickname was Palle d'Oro), bringing the country wine to Florence piled high on a horse-drawn two-wheeled cart.

At lunchtime, you will be joining Florentines ordering freshly crafted sandwiches up front or quick and easy hot dishes in the back. In the evening when the sandwich counter is closed, take a seat in back, where candles are added to the wooden tables. Order a brimming bowl of soup or pasta, a fragrantly roasted chicken with a green salad, veal simmered in red wine, or a piece of grilled fish seasoned with fresh lemon and a splash of olive oil, along with a carafe of the house red.

RISTORANTE CIRO & SONS (23)
Via del Giglio, 28r

TELEPHONE
055 289 694
INTERNET
www.ciroandsons.com
OPEN
Mon–Sat: lunch noon–3 P.M., dinner 6–10:30 P.M.
CLOSED
Sun
RESERVATIONS
Advised, especially for the terrace
CREDIT CARDS
MC, V
À LA CARTE
20–25€, includes a glass of wine

If you order a wood-fired pizza, a big salad, the home-made ravioli, or *schiaffoni principe di Napoli* (pasta with juicy meatballs), you will do just fine at this large restaurant with a covered terrace only fifty meters from the Medici Chapel and the stalls of the huge San Lorenzo Marketplace.

As the name implies, this is a Napolitani family-run show, headed by father Ciro, his wife, Palma (the *real* boss), and their four sons: Salvatore in the kitchen; Guiseppe taking care of guests; Vincenzo, the wine expert; and Antonio, who mans the wood-fired pizza ovens that turn out marvelous *vero pizza napolitana* for both lunch and dinner. The inside is rather formal, with gold cloths, silver candlesticks, and giant wineglasses adorning the tables. Photos of the famous and not so famous crowd the walls in competition with pictures of Ciro family members.

I think this is an all-purpose Great Eat to remember for several reasons. First, the pizzas are served for both lunch and dinner, and so is the beautiful selection of antipasti. It is open early for dinner, a great boon if you are traveling with children or just cannot face another heavy dinner right before going to bed. Finally, if pizza, pasta, or salads don't appeal, you can dig into platters of steaks or seafood.

FIXED-PRICE MENU
None
COVER & SERVICE CHARGES
No cover, 15% service added
ENGLISH
Yes

TRATTORIA MARIO (¢, 13)
Via Rosina, 2r

Mario's boasts many avid, loud, and local regulars, all of whom seem to be on a first-name basis. Consequently, there is a great deal of good cheer and camaraderie, with everyone swapping tall tales and telling jokes. They all know to arrive early and order a glass or two of the house red while waiting for the lunch service to begin. Latecomers will have to wait, or worse yet, they won't get their favorite dish, since the kitchen often runs out early.

The daily menu is posted on a board by the open kitchen. On Friday, fresh fish is served, and on Thursday gnocchi is the dish to order. On any day smart choices include the vegetable soup, pasta with meat or tomato sauce, or a slab of roast veal or beef garnished with their own fresh fries cooked in olive oil. Everything is market fresh . . . no frozen food allowed. You don't need to save room for dessert because all they serve is fresh fruit or a glass of sweet wine with wonderful, hard, almond-flavored biscotti. No coffee is served either, but there are dozens of bars around the market that are fun places to stand for an after-lunch espresso that will recharge your batteries for more afternoon market browsing. You will know you are a regular when the waiter doesn't write down your order. After finishing lunch, go to the cash register and tell Fabio what you have eaten, and he will tally up your bill.

TELEPHONE
055 218 550
INTERNET
www.trattoriamario.com
OPEN
Mon–Sat: lunch noon–3:30 P.M.
CLOSED
Sun; Aug (dates vary)
RESERVATIONS
Not accepted
CREDIT CARDS
None
À LA CARTE
10–14€
FIXED-PRICE MENU
None
COVER & SERVICE CHARGES
Cover 0.50€, service included
ENGLISH
Yes, and menu in English

TRATTORIA SERGIO GOZZI (22)
Piazza San Lorenzo, 8r

There are many places to eat around the Mercato Centrale de San Lorenzo, some very good and others appallingly bad. One of the most authentic and tourist-free places is this trattoria, a true worker's hangout where you can enjoy hearty Tuscan food (for lunch only) with burly market men and women. The only menu is posted outside. When you are seated, the waiter will tell you what's cooking. You are expected to order a full meal—just a salad and a glass of wine is out. You can count on chunky minestrone and bean soups, roasted meats, a strapping boiled brisket, and always fresh

TELEPHONE
055 281 941
OPEN
Mon–Sat: lunch noon–3 P.M.; also on Fri: dinner 8–10:30 P.M.
CLOSED
Dinner Sat-Thur, Sun; major holidays, Aug
RESERVATIONS
Not necessary
CREDIT CARDS
DC, MC, V

À LA CARTE
18–20€
FIXED-PRICE MENU
None
COVER & SERVICE CHARGES
Cover 1.05€, service
discretionary
ENGLISH
Yes

fish on Friday. Follow the lead of fellow diners and order a bottle of the house Chianti while enjoying the friendly service and a lunch that will leave some money in your pocket to spend shopping at the San Lorenzo Market stalls.

Train Station

All long-distance trains arrive at the Santa Maria Novella railway terminal, which joins Piazza di Santa Maria Novella and the great church of the same name. The station is a comfortable ten- or fifteen-minute walk from the center. Almost all buses in and out of Florence stop nearby, as do taxis and pickpockets, who work the area on a twenty-four-hour basis. Attached to the station underground are a series of typical mall shops and, in one corner, a handy mini-supermarket with so much stock that two people cannot get down the aisles at the same time.

RESTAURANTS

GROCERY STORES AND RESTAURANTS

Restaurants

OSTERIA I'BRINCELLO (11)
Via Nazionale, 110r

TELEPHONE
055 282 645
OPEN
Daily: lunch noon–3 P.M.,
dinner 7–10:30 P.M.
CLOSED
Never
RESERVATIONS
Essential

Fredi and Claudia's Osteria i'Brincello is deservedly popular with everyone who lives in or visits Florence. It is therefore always packed to the walls, so if you arrive without a reservation, especially during prime time, you will need a shoehorn and good luck to get a table. During the crunch, be prepared to wait; if you are alone or a couple, definitely share one of the wooden picnic-style tables. Naturally in such a busy beehive, service is fast and furious by the fleet of muscled waiters sporting black T-shirts with their names boldly written in white. Wine is poured from straw-wrapped Chianti bottles, and the food is served on colorful Tuscan pottery plates. If there are two or more of you, by all means begin by ordering the *brincello,* which is a huge selection of Tuscan cold meats and cheese served on a turkey platter. The pastas are all wonderful, especially the spicy *spaghetti alla carrettiera,* bursting with tomatoes, garlic, and chili peppers. For something more subdued but just as pleasing, the ravioli in a butter and sage sauce or *taglierini al pesto* fill the bill. Still to come are huge portions of pork chops, grilled sausage or chicken, veal and beefsteaks, or a large plate of grilled veggies and brie cheese, which is another dish successfully shared. Never mind saving room for dessert, unless you like *panna cotta,* dubbed by one food humorist as "jello for adults."

CREDIT CARDS
MC, V

À LA CARTE
15–25€

FIXED-PRICE MENU
None

COVER & SERVICE CHARGES
Cover 1€, service included

ENGLISH
Yes

RISTORANTE LE FONTICINE (10)
Via Nazionale, 79r

This restaurant is named after the sixteenth-century fountain by Luca della Robbia on the street in front. Originally a convent, the building has become one of Florence's best-loved dining addresses. The food honors the best of both Tuscan cuisine and the robust dishes from Emilia-Romagna, combined over fifty years ago by founder Silvano Bruci and his wife, Gianna. Today their strong traditions are being carried on by family members, and nothing has really changed. Patrons still walk by the open kitchen and the tempting displays of fresh pasta and antipasti. Seating is in a large, wood-beamed room with blue-and-white-checked tables where every inch of wall space is covered with a portion of Silvano's vast collection of artwork. At the far end, behind wrought-iron gates, is the impressive wine collection. Service is carried out by no-nonsense career waiters. The menu is long and more than covers all the bases. I like to start with a typical Tuscan appetizer of assorted *crostini* and always order the founding grandmother's Bolognese recipe of *tortelloni nostra moda,* a melt-in-your mouth homemade ravioli stuffed with ricotta cheese and covered with a cream and tomato sauce. Tuscany is well represented with such standards as *bistecca alla Fiorentina,* osso buco in tomato sauce, wild boar with onions, and grilled porcini mushrooms. In early spring, watch for fat asparagus dressed simply with olive oil, salt, and pepper, and for dessert, a divine *crema di mascarpone con frutti di bosco*—mascarpone with wild fruits.

TELEPHONE
055 282 106

INTERNET
www.lefonticine.com

OPEN
Tues–Sat: lunch noon–2:30 P.M., dinner 7–10 P.M.

CLOSED
Sun, Mon; 7–10 days at Christmas, end of July–end of Aug

RESERVATIONS
Advised for dinner

CREDIT CARDS
AE, DC, MC, V

À LA CARTE
35–45€

FIXED-PRICE MENU
None

COVER & SERVICE CHARGES
Cover 2.60€, 12% service added

ENGLISH
Yes, and menu in English

TRATTORIA ENZO E PIERO (7)
Via Faenza, 105r

TELEPHONE
055 214 901

OPEN
Mon–Sat: lunch noon–3 P.M.,
dinner 7–10 P.M.

CLOSED
Sun; 10 days at Christmas,
3 weeks in Aug (dates vary)

RESERVATIONS
Advised for dinner

CREDIT CARDS
AE, DC, MC, V

À LA CARTE
20–22€

FIXED-PRICE MENU
12€, 3 courses, cover and
service included

COVER & SERVICE CHARGES
Cover 1.55€, service included

ENGLISH
Yes

Enzo and Piero's trattoria is very simple, with rough stuccoed walls and lots of well-fed habitués sitting at the linen-clad tables. Enzo's son, Massimo, is on hand each day to ensure that all runs well. He greets his guests with sincere respect, suggests what is best to order, and checks back periodically to see that everyone has everything necessary for a fine meal. He also keeps an eagle eye on the kitchen, where his son Aldo is the chef, and in front, where his daughter Francesca is behind the bar. Whenever you come, be sure to ask for the daily specials, which sometimes are not given with the regular menu. If you are here on a Friday, try the *baccalà alla livornese*, salt cod cooked in a nippy red sauce with liberal doses of garlic; on Wednesday, order the osso buco cooked in a tomato sauce. Flavorful pasta options are the *taglierini* with truffles, sprinkled with arugula, and one of the better *pasta al pomodoro* renditions in Florence. Bottles of Chianti wine vinegar and good olive oil are brought to your table so you can dress your own salad or, as the Italians do, sprinkle olive oil on just about everything but dessert. For dessert you want the *panna cotta,* a cooked custard surrounded by fresh strawberries and chocolate. The fixed-price menu is a Great Eat buy if there ever was one, even though it does not include a beverage. For a little more, you can add a quarter or half carafe of wine and still walk away for under 22€ per person.

TRATTORIA GUELFA (5)
Via Guelfa, 103r

TELEPHONE
055 213 306

OPEN
Mon–Tues, Fri–Sun: lunch
noon–2:30 P.M., dinner
7–10:30 P.M.; Wed: dinner
7–10:30 P.M.

CLOSED
Wed lunch, Thur; Aug

RESERVATIONS
Advised for dinner

CREDIT CARDS
AE, DC, MC, V

À LA CARTE
25–30€

FIXED-PRICE MENU
9€, 2 courses, dessert, wine or
mineral water, cover and service
included

The Trattoria Guelfa has its regulars filling it every day for lunch and dinner. Reservations are crucial, but even with them, be prepared to wait up to half an hour, especially on weekends. Service can be slow, but when you consider that only two waiters, including hardworking Claudio (the owner), are on duty to serve the congenial crowd, it is amazing anyone gets anything, let alone gets it piping hot.

The key to success here is the wonderful back-to-basics Italian homecooking. If you stay with the chef's specialties, or the daily offerings scribbled on a two-by-two-inch piece of white paper, you cannot go wrong. Depending on the day and time of year, expect to find lots of asparagus-based specials, such as the risotto, covered with Parmesan cheese or mixed with beef. The fat green-and-white tortellini filled with ham and mushrooms will inspire frequent trips to your local gym, and so will the pappardelle with wild boar sauce or the *cappellacci,* three big pasta tubes stuffed with cheese and spinach and served in a white mushroom cream sauce. Second courses to note include roast pork and grilled veal chops served with rosemary-roasted potatoes. All the desserts remind me of home, especially the *panna cotta con cioccolato,* a cold pudding with hot chocolate poured over it, and the *budino di castagne,* a rich chestnut pudding.

TRATTORIA I DUE G (6)
Via B. Cennini, 6r

A big basket of fresh focaccia bread and the house wine will keep you occupied while you wait for your first course at this typical Florentine trattoria that takes its name from the two owners named Luigi, nicknamed the "two G's." When the jolly, red-faced waiter brought my carafe of wine, I said, "Oh, that's too much wine!" "Nonsense," he replied. "Water makes your stomach rusty. Wine keeps it clean!" I am sure he followed his own drinking advice, and ate rich food to ensure he never felt a hunger pang. Besides plenty of good wine, you can expect wonderful risottos, plump ricotta-filled ravioli, lamb stuffed with artichokes, cooked-to-order roast chicken (a thirty-minute wait), fried rabbit (only a ten-minute wait), beautiful seasonal vegetables, plump beans with sage and a ring of olive oil, and flavorful summer strawberries drizzled with raspberry vinegar and a dusting of sugar. To say that visitors have not found this place would be dead wrong. All the hotels along Via Fiume and Via Faenza recommend I Due G, but this has not inflated the trattoria's sense of self; it still takes pride in serving good food and wine at sensible prices.

COVER & SERVICE CHARGE
Cover 1.55€, service included
ENGLISH
Yes

TELEPHONE
055 218 623
OPEN
Mon–Sat: lunch 12:15–2:30 P.M., dinner 7:30–10 P.M.
CLOSED
Sun; holidays, Aug
RESERVATIONS
Advised
CREDIT CARDS
AE, DC, MC, V
À LA CARTE
25–30€
FIXED-PRICE MENU
None
COVER & SERVICE CHARGE
Cover 1.50€, 10% service added
ENGLISH
Yes

Restaurants *Di La d'Arno,* or *Oltrarno*

Di La d'Arno, or *Oltrarno,* means "the other side of the Arno." Crossing the Ponte Vecchio from the central part of the city, visitors usually walk and shop along Via Guicciardini until they reach the enormous Pitti Palace, the Medici family showcase that is now an art gallery with works by Titian, Tintoretto, Rubens, and Raphael. Shops and restaurants around the palace are naturally geared toward the tourist trade, but if you get a few blocks away from this, you will find fascinating enclaves of artisans and art galleries, as well as beautiful antique shops. Restaurants on the Piazza Santo Spirito are some of the most popular in the city, and on the second Sunday of every month, crowds browse through a flea market that flows from the piazza in front of the church onto the neighboring side streets. Also on the *Oltrarno* are the hilly Boboli Gardens, Forte Belvedere, San Miniato al Monte (a thousand-year-old church with an unparalleled view of the city), and the Piazzale Michelangelo, built in 1869 by Guiseppe Poggi, also with a magnificent view of Florence.

Boboli Gardens

Behind the Pitti Palace are eleven rolling acres of gardens known as the Giardinia di Boboli, which was the playground of the Medicis when they lived here. Laid out by the great landscape architect Triboli, the gardens are popular today for quiet walks and include a long expanse of cypress trees, lovely plantings, statuary, fountains, and L'Isolotto, a miniature island in the middle of a lake.

TRATTORIA BOBOLI (97)
Via Romana, 45r

TELEPHONE
055 233 6404
EMAIL
trattoriaboboli@infinito.it
OPEN
Mon–Tues, Thur–Sun: lunch noon–3 P.M., dinner 7:30–10 P.M.
CLOSED
Wed; Aug
RESERVATIONS
Advised

Do you remember your mother or a sympathetic friend ever telling you, "Keep your eyes and ears open, and never give up. You never know what good thing is awaiting you around the next corner"? Well, I can tell you it's true. Such was the case for me one rainy day in Florence near the Boboli Gardens. I had just reinspected a hotel nearby that unfortunately had to be dropped from *Great Sleeps Italy* because management had become complacent, favoring deferred maintenance over conscientious upkeep. I was tired and hungry when I noticed this friendly-looking trattoria across the street. Any port in a storm, I thought, as I hung up my dripping raincoat and settled into a cozy corner table. The room itself was typical: crowded with wine bottles; posters, paintings, and plates on the walls; mini-lights along the back; a few plants here and there; and a ceiling fan.

The rather limited à la carte menu offered good value, but better still was the two-course (no choices) *menù degustazione*, which includes a bottle of excellent Chianti wine. I started with *crepes à la Florentine,* a duet of crêpes filled with spinach and ricotta and covered with a cream sauce and cheese gratinée. Next I had a grilled steak topped with arugula and a side of potatoes. My dessert was a plate of *biscotti* for dipping into a glass of *vin santo,* followed by coffee. I was graciously served by Gilberto and his wife, who have been taking care of their loyal patrons for almost four decades. While I hadn't stumbled upon an undiscovered gem of destination dining, Trattoria Boboli is much more than a mere port in a storm. If you are near the Boboli Gardens, it is the perfect place for a nice, simple meal.

CREDIT CARDS
AE, DC, MC, V

À LA CARTE
25–30€

FIXED-PRICE MENU
Menù degustazione: 28€, 2 courses, dessert, wine, mineral water, coffee, cover and service charges included

COVER & SERVICE CHARGES
Cover 1.50€, no service charge

ENGLISH
Yes

Piazza del Carmine and San Frediano

Santa Maria del Carmine and the Brancacci Chapel is a Baroque church with restored frescoes by Masaccio and Masolino; viewing times are limited to a mere quarter of an hour. The square is a popular gathering place. West of here is San Frediano, a working-class area that is rapidly becoming gentrified.

RESTAURANTS

All Antico Ristoro di Cambi	**74**
Alla Vecchia Bettola	**74**
Cavolo Nero ($)	**75**
l'Brindellone	**76**
Ristorante Pane e Vino	**76**
Trattoria del Carmine	**77**
Trattoria Pandemonio ($)	**77**
Trattoria Sabatino (¢)	**78**

($) indicates a Big Splurge
(¢) indicates a Cheap Eat

Restaurants

ALL ANTICO RISTORO DI CAMBI (73)
Via Sant' Onofrio, 1r

TELEPHONE
055 217 134
INTERNET
www.anticoristorodicambi.it
OPEN
Mon–Sat: noon–2:30 P.M.,
dinner 7:30–10:30 P.M.
CLOSED
Sun; Aug 10–20
RESERVATIONS
Advised for dinner
CREDIT CARDS
MC, V
À LA CARTE
25€; or 40–50€ for 3 courses
including *bistecca alla Fiorentina*
FIXED-PRICE MENU
None
COVER & SERVICE CHARGES
Cover 1€, service discretionary
ENGLISH
Yes

All Antico Ristoro di Cambi offers its guests a winning mix of atmosphere and hearty, meat-based Tuscan food. No vegetarians need apply. This is the place for followers of the Atkins diet, or anyone else who thinks no meal is complete without meat, and plenty of it. Owners Stefano and Fabio Cambi are known for their antipasti plates featuring a variety of pork and wild boar salami, strapping dishes of meat-sauced pastas, and their famous (1 kilo) 2.2-pound *bistecca alla Fiorentina*. The brick-arched room is festooned with hanging sausages and hams, bunches of corn, and braids of garlic and red peppers. The dishes are served with dispatch to a hungry clientele sitting on backless stools placed around wooden tables set with paper place mats and napkins. Impossible as it may sound, don't skip their best dessert—*sfogliatina di mele e crema calda*—an unusual apple cake made of flaky pastry and ricotta cheese that is served with warm cream . . . mm-mm good, even after that steak!

ALLA VECCHIA BETTOLA (79)
Viale Vasco Pratolini, 3/9b

TELEPHONE
055 224 158
OPEN
Tues–Sat: lunch noon–2:30 P.M.,
dinner 7:30–10:30 P.M.
CLOSED
Sun–Mon; Dec 23–Jan 2, Aug
RESERVATIONS
Essential for dinner
CREDIT CARDS
None
À LA CARTE
30–35€
FIXED-PRICE MENU
None
COVER & SERVICE CHARGES
Cover 1.60€, service included
ENGLISH
Yes

Tuscany's simplest foods tend to be its most successful, and nowhere is this more evident than at Alla Vecchia Bettola, a picturesque trattoria specializing in the region's native cuisine. On my last visit, I was happy to see that the only thing different was the address and the renaming of the street.

The handwritten but legible menu changes almost daily. A bottle of house wine is on the table for you to pour into green glasses, and you pay for only as much as you drink. Seating is at marble-topped row tables on benches along the wall or on four-legged, backless stools. Despite the rather rustic decor, the atmosphere is upscale and so are the diners, arriving when the doors open and standing in line as the night goes on. While management does not put much value on creature comforts, it definitely values good food offered at fair prices.

If it is available, start with the *pecorino con baccelli,* a basket of raw, unshelled fava beans (similar to limas) with two slabs of smoky pecorino cheese. You shell the beans and pop them into your mouth with a piece of the cheese and a chunk of country bread. It is different and good, not heavy as one might expect. Move on to *topini al pomodoro,* a light gnocchi bathed in tomato sauce, or *risotto alle zucchine,* followed by a second course of roast veal, spicy sausage and beans, or paper-thin slices of raw beef served with arugula. The salads can be disappointing. The desserts, on the other hand, won't let you down. Try the house tiramisù or the plate of assorted *biscotti* consisting of macaroons and almond cookies for you to dip into a glass of sweet *vin santo.*

NOTE: Alla Vecchia Bettola is under the same ownership as Nerbone (see page 65).

CAVOLO NERO ($, 82)
Via dell'Ardiglione, 22

Book in advance, dress up, and treat yourself to a memorable meal at Cavolo Nero. Everything about this upscale pick is right, from the sleek, white slipcovered chairs and soft orange sorbet–colored walls (hung with photos of every type of cabbage imaginable and wonderful black-and-white prints of Italian vegetables) to the romantic jasmine-scented candlelit patio in back. The restaurant owes its success to its imaginative use of fresh ingredients, highlighting a monthly menu of updated Tuscan classics. Of course everything is made in-house, including the breads and the seductive desserts. In early spring, you might start with a creamy goat cheese served with an interesting olive oil and honey sauce, or a zucchini timbale with pesto sauce. Next, try the absolutely amazing artichoke parmigiana, which is available only in the spring, when baby artichokes are at their prime. Otherwise, pillows of eggplant ravioli with zucchini and sweet tomatoes, gnocchi with tuna and dried fennel, or the fusilli with fava beans, fresh onion, and salted ricotta cheese make excellent first courses. Wonderful main courses include pigeon filled with rich foie gras, grilled lamb ribs with roasted tomatoes, or steamed salt cod (*baccalà*) served with a horseradish sauce and garnished with buttered spinach. Desserts are to die for, especially the pear tart Tatin with thick cream, the warm apple cake, and the heavenly chocolate cake. The fine food, coupled with fair wine prices and excellent service in a very pleasing atmosphere, adds up to a Great Eat in Florence.

TELEPHONE
055 294 744

INTERNET
www.cavolonero.it

OPEN
Mon–Sat: dinner 7:30–11 P.M.

CLOSED
Sun; last 3 weeks in Aug

RESERVATIONS
Essential

CREDIT CARDS
AE, MC, V

À LA CARTE
40–45€

FIXED-PRICE MENU
None

COVER & SERVICE CHARGES
None

ENGLISH
Yes, and menu in English

I'BRINDELLONE (80)
Piazza Piatellina, 10/11r

TELEPHONE
055 217 879
OPEN
Tues–Sun: lunch noon–2:30 P.M.,
dinner 7–11 P.M.
CLOSED
Mon
RESERVATIONS
Not necessary
CREDIT CARDS
MC, V
À LA CARTE
20–25€
FIXED-PRICE MENU
Lunch only: 15€, 2 courses,
vegetable, wine or mineral
water, and coffee; cover and
service extra
COVER & SERVICE CHARGES
Cover 1€, no service charge
ENGLISH
Yes

You can't judge a book by its cover, and this is certainly the case at I'Brindellone. From the street it looks tiny, but once inside this plain place, you will count about fifty place settings spread over three small rooms. The menu is equally small in its selections, but high in quality—which is what counts, and obviously why it is so popular with the neighbors in this corner of San Frediano. I like it, especially for lunch during the week, when the two-course fixed-price menu is offered. I can eat a satisfying meal, have a glass of wine, and be out the door for well under 20€. Even if you don't opt for the lunch special, there are ten pastas priced under 7€, and for the carnivore a good selection of grilled meats. No, it is not destination dining, but it is a good place to jot down and remember if you are nearby and it is time to eat.

RISTORANTE PANE E VINO (74)
Piazza di Cestello, 3r

TELEPHONE
055 247 6956
EMAIL
panevino@yahoo.it
OPEN
Mon–Sat: dinner 7:30 P.M.–
midnight
CLOSED
Sun
RESERVATIONS
Essential
CREDIT CARDS
DC, MC, V
À LA CARTE
35–40€
FIXED-PRICE MENU
Menù degustazione (must be
ordered by table, two-person
minimum): 30€, 2 appetizers,
2 first courses, 1 main course
with two vegetables; dessert and
beverages extra
COVER & SERVICE CHARGES
Cover 2€ if only one dish is
ordered, service included
ENGLISH
Limited, but menu in English

Dining at Pane e Vino puts you in stylish surroundings where you will enjoy dishes that creatively straddle the line between contemporary Italian and international. When ordering, you might start with a leek flan colorfully surrounded with tomato mousse, or an artichoke puff pastry with gorgonzola sauce. Both are rich but served in just the right portions. The buckwheat tagliatelle with rabbit or the fresh pea soup are both winning first courses. So is the fat asparagus dumpling drizzled with melted butter and dotted with tender asparagus tips. Follow this with grilled duck breast served with pears cooked in red wine or a very tender roast kid. Vegetarians are catered to with a soft eggplant pudding with a mozzarella cheese soufflé and tomato sauce. Desserts are different and don't always work. One that does is the hazelnut custard covered in a hot chocolate sauce with a side of ricotta cream. The bland pear bavarian with a too-sweet strawberry sauce definitely didn't make the grade.

TRATTORIA DEL CARMINE (76)
Piazza del Carmine, 18r

The pretty Trattoria del Carmine lures a loyal base of locals who know the quality of food is consistently reliable. They also know to ignore the regular menu and try to decipher the daily specials handwritten on a lined piece of paper. I like to go on a balmy summer evening and sit at a table on the umbrella-shaded terrace, separated from the square by green shrubs. It is a good idea to exert some willpower and order a light starter, thus saving room for a flavorful risotto loaded with green asparagus and fresh chives or the lusty *pappardelle al cinghiale* (fat noodles in a wild boar sauce). Main courses could include fresh tuna served with broad beans, eggplant cooked to order, or, for the committed red meat eater, *bistecca alla Fiorentina*—a huge T-bone steak coated with salt and olive oil and charcoal-broiled until barely warm in the middle. To finish, ask for *torta della nona,* the famous Florentine custard cake.

TELEPHONE
055 281 601

OPEN
Mon–Sat: lunch 12:30–2:30 P.M., dinner 7:30–10:30 P.M.

CLOSED
Sun; Aug

RESERVATIONS
Advised for dinner

CREDIT CARDS
DC, MC, V

À LA CARTE
25–30€

FIXED-PRICE MENU
None

COVER & SERVICE CHARGES
Cover 1.50€, service discretionary

ENGLISH
Yes, and menu in English

TRATTORIA PANDEMONIO ($, 81)
Via del Leone, 50r

Whatever your evening dining mood, be it festive, romantic, or just plain starved, Pandemonio always fills the bill, from the first sip of champagne to the complimentary grappa or frosty *limoncello* finale. In between apéritif and *digestif,* you will sample creative Tuscan cuisine good enough to pack the attractive, flower-filled dining rooms night after night. The service, headed by the owner, Giovanna—called "Mama" by all who know her—is especially warm and welcoming.

Trying to decide what to order takes time because everything looks, and *is,* special. If it is on the menu, please consider the fresh baby artichoke salad, which is the absolute best I have ever had. It is served on an oval dish ringed with artichoke leaves. In the center is a mound of paper-thin, sliced raw hearts dressed with a spritz of lemon and a dose of olive oil, and covered with long slices of Parmesan cheese. So simple, so good . . . I could eat it every night. If you are considering a pasta course, look for pasta stuffed with potatoes and asparagus in a gorgonzola cheese sauce, *pappa al pomodoro,* or the flavorful *straccetti al pesto e pomodoro* (torn egg noodles with pesto and fresh tomatoes). Grilled meat and fish dominate the *secondi piatti,* but there are also all-star portions of succulent chicken and veal rolled with zucchini and cooked in a broth of garlic and parsley, or a slowly simmered beef stew served with silky mashed potatoes. Even though you may have had the

TELEPHONE
055 224 002

EMAIL
pandemonio.fi@tiscali.it

OPEN
Mon–Sat: dinner 7:30–10:30 P.M.

CLOSED
Sun; middle 2 weeks in Aug

RESERVATIONS
Absolutely essential

CREDIT CARDS
AE, DC, MC, V

À LA CARTE
40–50€

FIXED-PRICE MENU
None

COVER & SERVICE CHARGES
Cover 3€, 10% service added

ENGLISH
Yes, and menu in English

artichoke salad to start, if the fried artichokes make a menu appearance, don't miss these tender morsels. Neither should you overlook the fresh fruit tarts or sweet wild strawberries, if you are lucky enough to be here during the few weeks in the spring when they are in season. Otherwise, treat yourself to Mama's cheesecake, which many of her guests think is the best in the world. The recipe is her state secret, and nothing will entice her to divulge it.

TRATTORIA SABATINO (¢, 72)
Via Pisana, 2r (Porta San Frediano)

If you are willing to venture off the well-worn tourist trail on the Pitti Palace side of the Arno, want to see where regular folks eat, and will be satisfied with plain *casalinga* (homecooking), then look no further than this barnlike trattoria just beyond the Porta San Frediano, run by the Buccioni family for decades. The menu is changed and mimeographed daily, and it seems to please those patrons who come every day, occupy the same table, and are served without ordering. Take one look at the menu and you will see that originality is not the kitchen's strong suit. There are four starters, three of which are variations of salami; the fourth is prosciutto. Seven first courses include two soups and five pasta types covered with meat and tomato sauce, or plain tomato sauce. Pork, chicken, tripe, veal, and fresh fish every Friday sum up the mains. Veggies include a rarely seen cucumber salad plus the usual beans in oil, potatoes, and *insalatas*. Dessert is either fresh fruit, some mighty fattening desserts brought in every day from a nearby bakery, or the everpresent *biscotti di prato e vin santo*.

TELEPHONE
055 225 955

OPEN
Mon–Fri: lunch noon–2:30 P.M., dinner 7:20–10 P.M.

CLOSED
Sat–Sun; Aug

RESERVATIONS
Advised for 4 or more

CREDIT CARDS
AE, DC, MC, V

À LA CARTE
10–15€

FIXED-PRICE MENU
None

COVER & SERVICE CHARGES
Cover 1.50€, service included

ENGLISH
Limited

Pitti Palace and Piazza Santo Spirito

The Palazzo Pitti, a fifteenth-century palace designed by Brunelleschi as a residence for Luca Pitti and later occupied by the powerful Medicis, is across the Arno on Florence's "Left Bank." Only a ten-minute stroll from the Ponte Vecchio, the fortress palace holds one of Europe's greatest art collections, scattered through several museums. The most famous is the Galleria del Palatina, with masterpiece paintings by Rubens, Titian, and Raphael hung four or five feet high on damask-covered walls. In addition to the galleries, there is the Museo del Costume and the Appartamenti Reali, royal apartments. The Boboli Gardens, designed by Tribolo in 1549, extend between the Pitti Palace and Fort Belvedere.

The Augustinian church of Santo Spirito was designed by Brunelleschi in 1444. Its austere exterior houses numerous works of art, including a *Madonna and Child* by Filippo Lippi. The piazza has a small morning farmer's market during the week, and on the second Sunday of the month a flea market is held. On the third Sunday of the month, an organic market sets up, mixed in with hippie kitsch. The neighborhood is full of craftsmen, restorers, and antique dealers.

RESTAURANTS

PASTRY SHOPS AND BAKERIES

GOURMET FOOD AND WINE SHOPS

INDOOR/OUTDOOR MARKETS

($) indicates a Big Splurge
(¢) indicates a Cheap Eat

Restaurants

BECCOFINO ($, 77)
Piazza degli Scarlatti, 1r, off Lungarno Guicciardini

TELEPHONE
055 290 076 (for both restaurant and wine bar)
INTERNET
www.beccofino.com
OPEN
Tues–Sat: dinner 7–11:30 P.M.;
Sun: brunch 12:30–2:30 P.M.,
dinner 7–11:30 P.M
CLOSED
Mon
RESERVATIONS
Essential, as far in advance as possible
CREDIT CARDS
MC, V
À LA CARTE
Restaurant 40–50€; wine bar 8–20€; Sunday brunch 25–30€
FIXED-PRICE MENU
None
COVER & SERVICE CHARGES
Cover 2€, service discretionary
ENGLISH
Yes, and menu in English

Beccofino puts the "T" in trendy as one of Florence's hottest restaurants and wine bars. The sufficiently hip clientele makes it as much of a people-watching place as a watering hole and dining destination. In warm weather, the action takes place on the covered terrace overlooking the banks of the Arno River. Inside, the exhibition kitchen and the big, open, loud dining room with banquette seating wrapped around bare wooden tables could be anywhere in Manhattan or Los Angeles. But in traditional Florence it has caused a stir and serves as the benchmark and point of comparison for all new modern restaurants. With the winning combination of the restaurant and wine know-how of David Gardner (see Trattoria Baldovino, page 52) and the exceptional cooking skills displayed in the kitchen, it is no wonder that reservations for dinner tables are required days in advance.

Beccofino means "good taste and good palate," and you will definitely satisfy both with whatever is on your oversized plate. Everyone is tended to by a buffed, bronzed, and buzz-cut staff dressed in black Armani and speaking Italian-accented English. The menu changes monthly, but if you are here in early spring, I can assure you that the poached egg on a bed of braised onions with white truffles will be an antipasto you will never forget. Also memorable is the deceptively simple fresh pea soup with fresh ricotta and mint, or the hot asparagus in a balsamic vinaigrette served with a pecorino cheese mousse. The risotto with Italian bacon, fresh herbs, and celeriac gives this often dull dish a new kick. If you are pacing yourself, the warm vegetable plate seasoned with basil-infused olive oil is the perfect choice for sharing. If there are two of you who love lamb, the pink, herbed leg of lamb is required eating. Otherwise, consider the roasted pigeon with prunes and red cabbage, or any fresh fish offering. Don't overlook the nearly perfect desserts, especially the lemon tart with kiwi sauce or the light pistachio mousse with chocolate sauce. The wine list is exceptional, with vintages priced for everyone.

If a full meal stretched out over the entire evening seems too much, then book a table for the wine bar, which serves lighter meals featuring salads, cold meat and cheese plates, daily soups, and main courses in addition to irresistible desserts, such as pears in red wine with a cinnamon *zabaione* sauce or a prune and armagnac parfait. Featured wines are listed on a blackboard, and more than forty wines are poured by the glass, enabling guests to sample several types before deciding on a favorite.

LA MANGIATOIA (¢, 93)
Piazza San Felice, 8/10r

You can always count on a budget Great Eat at La Mangiatoia, a pizzeria, trattoria, *rosticceria,* and *tavola caldo* not far from the Pitti Palace. Be it a wood-fired pizza consumed at the lunch counter in front (or packed to go), the daily special, a quarter of a roast chicken, or a simple bowl of pasta with a fresh garden salad eaten in the downstairs dining room, La Mangiatoia always fills the bill. While you are here, take time to visit the Casa Guidi at Piazza San Felice, 8b: a suite of rooms on the first floor of the Palazzo Guidi, which was the home of poets Elizabeth and Robert Browning from 1847 to 1861. The palazzo is open to visitors from April to November on Monday, Wednesday, and Friday afternoons from 3 to 6 P.M. It is also available for short-term rentals through the Landmark Trust in England. Please see *Great Sleeps Italy* for more information.

NOTE: The restaurant states: *Non si effettuano conti separati.* Or, "We don't do separate bills."

TELEPHONE
055 224 060
OPEN
Tues–Sun: lunch noon–3 P.M., dinner 7–10 P.M.
CLOSED
Mon
RESERVATIONS
Not accepted
CREDIT CARDS
AE, MC, V
À LA CARTE
11–14€, pizza 4–7.50€
FIXED-PRICE MENU
None
COVER & SERVICE CHARGES
Cover 1€, service discretionary
ENGLISH
Yes

LE VOLPI E L'UVA (88)
Piazza de' Rossi, 1r

The motto of this outstanding wine bar is attributed to Luigi Pulci (1432–1484), a Florentine poet during the time of Lorenzo Il Magnifico: "Above all I believe in good wines, and I think whoever believes in this will be saved."

Everything is small at Le Volpi e l'Uva, except the quality, which is tremendous. The six friendly owners strive to give good wine at civilized prices, and judging from their smart-looking group of devotees, they have succeeded brilliantly. French and a smattering of other wines are available, but the specialty here is wines from small producers throughout Italy. More than forty varieties are sold by the glass, and many more by the bottle. A glass of prosecco will run around 2.30€, and a vintage brunello from 7.50€. The only foods served are small sandwiches and platters of cheese and cold meat. The regulars know to stand at the marble bar, because if you sit at one of the tables—either inside or on the tiny terrace sandwiched in between parked cars and vespas—you will add 25 percent to your bill.

TELEPHONE
055 239 8132
OPEN
Mon–Sat: 11 A.M.–8 P.M., continuous service
CLOSED
Sun
RESERVATIONS
Not necessary
CREDIT CARDS
AE, MC, V
À LA CARTE
Sandwiches from 1.70€, cold meat and cheese plate 5€
FIXED-PRICE MENU
None
COVER & SERVICE CHARGES
None
ENGLISH
Yes

OSTERIA DEL CINGHIALE BIANCO (85)
Borgo Sant' Jacopo, 43r

TELEPHONE
055 215 706
INTERNET
www.cinghialebianco.it
OPEN
Mon–Tues, Thur–Fri: dinner
6:30–11:30 P.M.; Sat–Sun: lunch
noon–3 P.M., dinner 6:30–
11:30 P.M.
CLOSED
Lunch Mon–Tues, Thur–Fri;
Wed; 3 weeks in July
(dates vary)
RESERVATIONS
Essential
CREDIT CARDS
MC, V (5% discount for cash)
À LA CARTE
25–38€
FIXED-PRICE MENU
None
COVER & SERVICE CHARGES
Cover 1.50€, service
discretionary
ENGLISH
Yes, and menu in English

Massimo Masselli represents the third generation of this well-known Florentine family of restaurateurs. Their popular establishment, set in a fourteenth-century tower, specializes in wild boar, a delicacy best made into sausage, salami, or ham and served as an antipasto, or stewed with red wine and vegetables and served with polenta as a main course.

There is a bargain Great Eat fixed-price menu, served only for lunch. Choices for this two-course meal include a large salad, but no wild boar. Headlining the Tuscan dishes on both this and the à la carte menus are *pappa al pomodoro* (a filling bread soup made with tomatoes, garlic, and olive oil) and *ribollita* (a hearty, long-simmered soup made with beans, vegetables, and bread). These age-old recipes date back to the times when peasants did not have much to eat and had to make do with what few ingredients they could find. Homemade pappardelle with hare is a warming winter dish, as is tripe with tomato sauce. Another choice with admittedly more appeal for many is the *strozzapreti al burro,* boiled spinach pasta dumplings filled with cheese and drizzled with butter. The popular *crema di mascarpone con lingue di gatto* (mascarpone cream with cookies) is usually available, but if not, the house tiramisù made with ricotta cheese is lighter and less sweet than the regular, heavier versions.

Please keep in mind that reservations are essential for lunch and dinner, and that the romantic mezzanine table must be booked several days in advance.

PITTI GOLA E CANTINA (92)
Piazza Pitti, 16r

TELEPHONE
055 212 704
EMAIL
pigola@tin.it
OPEN
Tues–Sun: 11 A.M.–9 P.M., until
midnight in the summer
CLOSED
Mon
RESERVATIONS
Not necessary
CREDIT CARDS
AE, MC, V
À LA CARTE
5–12€; wine from 4€ a glass
FIXED-PRICE MENU
None

The Pitti Gola e Cantina wine bar occupies a primo location directly across from the Pitti Palace. Open Tuesday through Sunday, it offers Tuscan wines, light lunches, and bar snacks from 11 A.M. until 9 P.M. It is a small spot, easy to stop in after a day traipsing through the Boboli Gardens or admiring the museums of the Pitti Palace. Also, it is handy to remember if you have missed the regular lunch hour and want something light to tide you over until dinner. When this happens, I like to order the mixed vegetable plate dressed with Tuscan extra-virgin olive oil, or if it is a hot day, the *mozzarella di bufala* layered with red, ripe tomatoes. The house specialty is *tonno del Chianti,* pork marinated in white wine and bay leaf until it becomes almost flaky. All the Tuscan wines, olive oils, and vinegars you see here can be shipped worldwide. Remember, when shipping you will pay the shipping costs but not the VAT.

Pitti Gola e Cantina is owned by a dynamic wife-and-husband team, Sabina and Giancarlo, who also own two wonderful hotels in Florence—the Hotel Torre Guelfa and the Palazzo Castiglioni—as well as Villa Rosa in the Chianti countryside (see *Great Sleeps Italy*).

COVER & SERVICE CHARGES
None

ENGLISH
Yes

RICCHI CAFFÈ (¢, 83)
Piazza Santo Spirito, 8/9r

What a pleasant Great Eat destination the Ricchi Caffè continues to be. I dashed into the *caffè* one day several years ago to avoid being drenched by a sudden rainstorm. I had planned to have a quick sandwich and regroup for the rest of the afternoon, but when I saw the lunch plates being served to the eager patrons, I quickly changed my order.

Each time I have visited the Ricchi Caffè since, I have found the food to be beautifully prepared and delicious. When you go in winter, sit in the room next to the stand-up bar and settle into a soft, tufted banquette seat before a tiny marble-topped café table. Covering the walls here and in the bar is a fascinating display of framed photographs of the Santo Spirito Church. On warm days, enjoy your lunch outside on the terrace with its commanding view of the church.

The person behind the success of the kitchen is Alfonsina, the wife of the owner, who usually positions himself behind the cash register. Her menu selections are limited, but change every day—with the exception of the roast beef and creamy mashed potatoes, the lasagne, and the big one-plate salads. On my last visit, in addition to these three staples, she had *pasta al pesto* tossed with beans and potato (much lighter than it sounds), liver with oven-roasted tomatoes, and eggplant parmigiana. This is not the place to skip dessert. Treat yourself and indulge in one of Alfonsina's almost illegally rich pastries, a tiramisù made with wild fruits, a slice of chocolate or apple cake, or a serving of their homemade ice cream. As with most insider Great Eats, the best dishes go quickly, so plan to arrive early for lunch. If you are in the neighborhood between 6 and 9 P.M., drop by for "happy hour," where the nibbles at the bar are included in the price of the drinks.

NOTE: Ricchi Caffè is open for lunch on the second Sunday of every month (except August), when there is a flea market on Piazza Santo Spirito.

TELEPHONE
055 215 864

OPEN
Mon–Sat: 7 A.M.–9 P.M. (till 1 A.M. in summer); lunch noon–3 P.M., happy hour 6–9 P.M.

CLOSED
Sun; last 2 weeks in Aug

RESERVATIONS
Not accepted

CREDIT CARDS
MC, V

À LA CARTE
5–12€

FIXED-PRICE MENU
None

COVER & SERVICE CHARGES
Cover 1.10€, service included

ENGLISH
Yes

RISTORANTE RICCHI ($, 83)
Piazza Santo Spirito, 8/9r

TELEPHONE
055 215 864
OPEN
Mon–Sat: dinner 7:30–11 P.M.
CLOSED
Sun; last 2 weeks in Aug
RESERVATIONS
Essential
CREDIT CARDS
MC, V
À LA CARTE
40–50€
FIXED-PRICE MENU
Menù degustazione: 35€,
2 appetizers, 2 pastas, 1 main
course, dessert, wine; cover and
service extra
COVER & SERVICE CHARGES
Cover 2.60€, service included
ENGLISH
Yes

Not content to rest on their laurels, the owners of the Ricchi Caffè (see page 83) have opened a small but very select and upscale fish restaurant next door. Here the damask-covered tables are set with fresh flowers. While you wait for your order, a basket of the chef's homemade bread and a plate of tidbits—perhaps a bite of tuna on a tomato slice or a *baccalà* mousse on a tiny square of whole-meal bread—is brought to you. Between courses, a light *sorbetto* is served, and before dessert, a plate with heavenly chocolate truffles and chocolate-dipped citrus puts you in the mood for the sweet ending ahead.

Because the fish is fresh daily, the choices are seldom the same for any length of time and are limited to four or five selections for each course. However, the chef has added two outstanding meat or vegetarian options for each course. The zucchini flowers stuffed with crab and ricotta cheese in a fresh tomato coulis is a perfect beginning. The *antipasto misto del giorno* for two is another wonderful starter, providing samples of whatever is best that day. Here, the usual ravioli with spinach and ricotta cheese is lifted way out of the ordinary, and my dinner companion claimed it to be the best she ever tasted. This filling dish consists of four ravioli pillows in a delicate eggplant and red pepper sauce garnished with fresh basil and served on an oversized square plate. If you are going to do fish for every course, the homemade *tagliolini* with asparagus and scampi is a wonderful first course. For a second course, the lightly grilled tuna is light and not too filling, because you must save room for desserts, and hope they are serving *sfogliata de mele con crema calda*—flaky pastry layers with apples and cream. If not, share the plate with three selections, including a fabulous ricotta cheesecake with a kumquat salsa and Tuscan chocolate crust, crème brûlée with apple compote, and *millefoglie con mousse di banane,* a flaky pastry layered with banana mousse and custard and topped with caramel sauce.

TRATTORIA ANGIOLINO (78)
Via Santo Spirito, 36r

TELEPHONE
055 239 8976
OPEN
Daily April–Sept; Tues–Sat
Oct–March: lunch 12:30–
2:30 P.M., dinner 7:30–11 P.M.
CLOSED
Mon Oct–March

Trattoria Angiolino certainly gets an A for authenticity, with an interior filled with hanging copper pots, garlic braids, bunches of dried herbs, and in the center of it all, a potbellied stove. You enter along a big marble bar in the first room, and sit at the red-and-white linen–draped tables that line the wall. The food matches the setting:

it's strictly Tuscan in scope and presentation. The menu is a textbook for the region's favorites of *ribollita, pappa al pomodoro,* and *trippa,* and it also offers grilled steaks and a handful of chef's specialties. It is a good place to remember if you want a leisurely lunch or dinner any time you are on this side of the Arno, prowling around Piazza Santo Spirito, checking out the outrageously priced antiques along Via Maggio, or walking in the Boboli Gardens.

RESERVATIONS
Advised

CREDIT CARDS
MC, V

À LA CARTE
25–30€

FIXED-PRICE MENU
None

COVER & SERVICE CHARGES
Cover 1.55€, 10% service added

ENGLISH
Yes

TRATTORIA BORDINO (91)
Via Stracciatella, 9r (on a little square off Via Guicciardini)

Bordino's two rooms have closely spaced tables and are outfitted with an amazing collection of flea-market finds—ranging from horns, cowbells, farm implements, and fencing masks to a map of Scottish clans, ears of dried corn, gourd rattles, and black-and-white sketches of a beguiling dog with long silky ears. There's just no accounting for taste, even at a Florentine trattoria; at least this one serves decent food at decent prices. While it is in the general tourist area that leads across the Ponte Vecchio to the Pitti Palace, Bordino is just far enough off the well-trodden path to escape the madding crowds and attract a local audience. As always, the smart diners are zeroing in on the daily specials and perhaps upgrading the house red to a better Chianti Classico. You can also order a pasta and a salad and not incur the wrath of the waiter. If you do this, remember that the risotto with gorgonzola or the ravioli with butter and sage are better than the heavy tortellini with *funghi porcini.* Desserts are impossible to resist, especially anything with strawberries. Service is honest and genuine, but there is a lag between courses. Never mind; have another glass of wine and remember no one is in a hurry to go someplace else.

TELEPHONE
055 213 048

OPEN
Mon–Sat: lunch noon–2:30 P.M., dinner 7:30–11 P.M.

CLOSED
Sun

RESERVATIONS
Advised for dinner

CREDIT CARDS
AE, DC, MC, V

À LA CARTE
20–30€

FIXED-PRICE MENU
Lunch: 6€, 2 courses; 9€, *bistecca alla Fiorentina* and salad; both include beverages; cover and service extra

COVER & SERVICE CHARGES
Cover 1€, 10% service added

ENGLISH
Yes

TRATTORIA LA CASALINGA (90)
Via dei Michelozzi, 9r

If you are a collector or just an admirer of fine furniture and antiques, be sure to walk down Via Maggio and browse the many beautiful shops and boutiques selling one-of-a-kind items with prices to match. Try to time your visit to include a meal at this typical Florentine trattoria, which is extremely popular with everyone from this writer to students, families, toothless pensioners, Japanese tourists, and ladies who lunch.

TELEPHONE
055 218 624

OPEN
Mon–Sat: lunch noon–2:30 P.M., dinner 7–9:30 P.M.

CLOSED
Sun; 2 days at Easter, 3 weeks in Aug (dates vary)

RESERVATIONS
Advised for 4 or more

CREDIT CARDS
DC, MC, V
À LA CARTE
15–22€
FIXED-PRICE MENU
None
COVER & SERVICE CHARGES
Cover 2€, no service charge
ENGLISH
Yes

The two rooms with knotty-pine wainscoting and high ceilings have closely spaced white linen–covered tables. The trattoria is run by the Bartarelli family: The father is the cook and the mother gives him a hand, while out in front an uncle and a sister named Andrea handle the service, which is bright and friendly. The basic menu of pastas, grilled meats, roasts, and vegetables remains the same, and these are dished out in heaping proportions. The daily specials are handwritten, and as usual, these are the dishes to pay attention to. Because the tables are turned at least twice during each meal, service is quick, so you can count on being in and out in an hour or so—a real accomplishment in Italy.

TRATTORIA QUATTRO LEONI (87)
Piazza della Passera, Via dei Vellutini, 1r

TELEPHONE
055 218 562
INTERNET
www.4leoni.com
OPEN
Daily: lunch 12:20–2:30 P.M.,
dinner 7:30–10:30 P.M.
CLOSED
Never
RESERVATIONS
Essential, at least 1–2 days
ahead
CREDIT CARDS
AE, DC, MC, V
À LA CARTE
30–35€
FIXED-PRICE MENU
None
COVER & SERVICE CHARGES
Cover 1.50€, 10% service added
ENGLISH
Yes

Florentines hope you won't discover one of their favorite places between the Pitti Palace and Santo Spirito Church. Arriving without a reservation is a big mistake: the place is filled from the minute it opens with dining hopefuls standing in the bar waiting for a miracle. Despite the crunch, the chef and staff pay attention to important details, and no one ever makes you feel rushed.

A wider than usual selection of antipasti adds variety to the meal. On cold days, you could start with the *crostini misti* (mixed toasts), grilled vegetables, or *mozzarella di bufala* with either tiny tomatoes or prosciutto. In summer, try the *tegamino di zucchine,* with smoked, dried beef, creamy white cheese, zucchini, and *tartufo* (truffle) oil, or *cuore di carciofo,* a tempting dish composed of smoked meat, small artichokes, gorgonzola cheese, and *tartufo* oil, with pine nuts sprinkled on top. The pasta list is short, offering six or seven choices, the best and definitely most interesting of which is *fiocchetti di pere con salsa di taleggio e asparagi,* which is similar to ravioli. The fried chicken and rabbit is a typical Florentine main-course bet, as is the liver with fresh sage or the tender beef stew spiked with balsamic vinegar. For garnishes, you could order deep-fried vegetables, sautéed greens, fat white beans topped with extra-virgin olive oil, oven-roasted potatoes, or a pedestrian *insalata mista* (mixed salad). Desserts allow you multiple choices: *biscotti con vin santo,* the house sweet of the day, cheesecake, a chocolate torte, or fresh fruit.

Pastry Shops and Bakeries

IL FORNO DI STEFANO GALLI (89)
Via Sant' Agostino, 8r

Bread and pastry lovers come from across the river for the privilege of taking a number and waiting elbow to elbow for their turn to buy their favorite baked goodies at this heavenly palace of carbohydrates and calories.

The ovens are fired up all day long, turning out an endless supply of *crostini,* wonderful breads (sold by weight), pizza slices, and sandwiches on a nonstop basis from Monday to Saturday without interruption. How many loaves of bread are baked here daily? More than a thousand, and they are sold by a crew of smiling girls who are on their feet from the moment the doors open until 7 P.M., when only a few crumbs remain.

TELEPHONE
055 21 97 03
OPEN
Mon–Sat: 7:30 A.M.–7:30 P.M.,
Sun & holidays: 8 A.M.–7 P.M.
CLOSED
Never
CREDIT CARDS
None
PRICES
Everything is sold by weight
ENGLISH
Not much

PASTICCERIA MARINO (75)
Piazza Nazario Sauro, 19r

For some of the best croissants (called *cornetti* or *brioche*) in Florence, the name to remember is Pasticceria Marino, a bar and pastry shop on the Piazza N. Sauro at the end of the Ponte alla Carraia. Dozens of other pastries are also made here, but the best are these buttery croissants that come fresh out of the oven all morning long.

The croissants are available plain, filled with chocolate or vanilla custard (called *crema*), or filled with marmalade. If they are temporarily out when you arrive, be patient— another batch is undoubtedly baking in the back. Order a cappuccino to consume with your treat, and either stand with the crowd around the bar or sit at one of the little table stools placed along one wall.

TELEPHONE
055 212 657
OPEN
Tues–Sun: 6:30 A.M.–8 P.M.
CLOSED
Mon; 15 days in Aug (dates vary)
CREDIT CARDS
None
PRICES
Pastries from 1€
ENGLISH
Limited

San Niccolò

The Piazzale Michelangelo and the magnificent Romanesque church of San Miniato al Monte provide sweeping views of Florence that you will never forget. The winding road leads you through the old city gates to Via di San Niccolò and the church of the same name with its fifteenth-century frescoes.

RESTAURANTS

Restaurants

FUORI PORTA (96)
Via del Monte alle Croci, 10r

TELEPHONE
055 234 2483

INTERNET
www.fuoriporta.it

OPEN
Mon–Sat: 12:30 P.M.–12:30 A.M., continuous service; hot food served 12:30–3 P.M. and 7 P.M.–midnight

CLOSED
Sun (except in Dec); holidays, Aug 7–20 (dates vary)

RESERVATIONS
Advised on weekends

CREDIT CARDS
AE, DC, MC, V

À LA CARTE
15–25€

FIXED-PRICE MENU
None

COVER & SERVICE CHARGES
Cover 1€, service charge included

ENGLISH
Yes

Fuori Porta romances patrons with attentive service, good food, and an impressive selection of wines from around the world, with the emphasis on vintages from Tuscany. Located just beyond the city walls, off Via di San Niccolò and Via San Miniato and below Piazzale Michelangelo, this wine bar, run by knowledgeable wine connoisseur Andrea Conti, is considered one of the best in Florence. While it is known for its fine wines, which are shipped worldwide from their wine shop next door, you need not experience fiscal trauma to enjoy an evening spent sampling some of the thirty-five weekly and monthly featured superior wines (which sell from 3.50€ to 9€ a glass).

Patrons also come for the kitchen's simple take on regional foods, which pair well with any of the six hundred–plus wines available at any one time. Lunch and dinner both feature a daily menu of assorted pastas, fresh fish at night, *carpaccio,* sandwiches, and cheese and meat plates, plus every *crostino* and *bruschetta* you can possibly imagine. If you are a serious wine buff, visit their Website for a list of wines that can be shipped to your doorstep.

I TAROCCHI (¢, 94)
Via dei Renai, 12/14r

Wood-fired pizzas served in laid-back surroundings with bench seating and bare tables outside tells you this is a young place. The throng at night tells you it is also popular and obviously well priced. While probably not worth a long hike from your hotel, it is a worthy neighborhood choice if you are in the mood for a really good pizza. Pastas also share the menu, and are also good, especially the *tagliatelle alla certosina,* loaded with shrimp, fresh tomatoes, and arugula, a bitter green that gives the dish a bite. However, the main event is pizza. If you are looking for something light, try the *stracchinella,* made with two soft cheeses—mozzarella and *stracchino,* a delicate soft cheese from Lombardy—or one of the house specialties, a thick-crust affair called *bella napoli,* topped with *mozzarella di bufala* and fresh tomatoes. For a pizza with a punch, there is the *capricciosa,* loaded with tomato, mozzarella, prosciutto, mushrooms, pepperoni, olives, and *wurstels* (German sausage). Nothing light about that! Don't discount desserts, especially the cheesecake, which is made by the owner's mother from a recipe sent to her by a friend in America.

TELEPHONE
055 234 4373
INTERNET
www.pizzeriatarocchi.it
OPEN
Tues–Fri: lunch 12:30–2:30 P.M., dinner 7 P.M.–1 A.M.; Sat–Sun: dinner 7 P.M.–1 A.M.
CLOSED
Sat–Sun lunch, Mon; lunch in Aug
RESERVATIONS
Advised for dinner on weekends in summer
CREDIT CARDS
AE, MC, V
À LA CARTE
Pizza 5–8€, 2-course pasta meal 9€
FIXED-PRICE MENU
None
COVER & SERVICE CHARGES
Cover included for lunch, 1€ for dinner; service charge included
ENGLISH
Yes

OSTERIA ANTICA MESCITA (95)
Via di San Niccolò, 60r

Bench seating along exposed stone walls in what was once the crypt of the San Niccolò church sets the rough-hewn tone of this pleasant *osteria* in a quiet, non-tourist-plagued section of the *Oltrarno.* For lunch you will be served by members of the Prosperi family; at dinner, other waiters help out. Curious carnivores will be happy with wild boar sausage, a plate of smoked meats, rabbit, or roast pork. Others will be content with vegetable couscous, salad, a plate of assorted local meats or cheeses, or fresh fish, which appears on Friday. For dessert there is no contest. Everyone orders either the chocolate torte—a thin wedge of short-bread crust topped with dark chocolate, or fruit cooked with sugar, cinnamon, and red wine. The house wines are adequate, the prices fair, and the service friendly, which adds up to a nice meal just far enough from the tourist hub of Florence to keep it local and appreciated.

TELEPHONE
055 234 2836
OPEN
Mon–Sat: lunch noon–3 P.M., dinner 7:30 P.M.–midnight
CLOSED
Sun; Aug
RESERVATIONS
Advised for dinner
CREDIT CARDS
AE, MC, V
À LA CARTE
20–28€
FIXED-PRICE MENU
None
COVER & SERVICE CHARGES
Cover 0.70€, service included
ENGLISH
Yes

Food Shopping in Florence

Probably one of your favorite Great Eats in Florence will be the one you prepare yourself. It may be an ambitious three-course meal cooked in your apartment kitchen or a snack purchased from the market and eaten on the run or on a bench in a pretty piazza. Whether or not you are buying, strolling through an Italian outdoor market or cruising the aisles of a supermarket gives you a window into the everyday Italian way of life. In Florence, here are the places where I like to shop for food and wine.

Gourmet Food and Wine Shops

BOTTEGA DELLA FRUTTA (34)
Via dei Federighi, 31r (Piazza Goldoni)

TELEPHONE
055 239 8500

OPEN
Mon–Tues, Thur–Sat: 8 A.M.–7:30 P.M.; Wed: 8 A.M.–1:30 P.M.

CLOSED
Sun; Aug

CREDIT CARDS
MC, V

ENGLISH
Yes

The Bottega della Frutta is sheer heaven if you appreciate fine fruits and vegetables. It is run by a friendly, outgoing husband and wife, Francesco and Elizabetta, who offer the bounty of Tuscany—and of the world—in their two-room shop piled high with the freshest, highest-quality produce you are likely to see anywhere. Wines, olive oils, balsamic vinegar, cheese, Tuscan herbs, seasonings, and condiments . . . you name it, they have it. After two visits, you will feel like a regular. More important, you will be treated like one. On top of this, their prices are very fair, and Elizabetta speaks wonderful English, offers easy-to-follow recipes using their magnificent products, and rightfully says, "If we don't have what you want, it is 'to be discovered.'"

CHERUBINO (21)
Via Sant'Antonino, 4r (Piazza del Mercato Centrale)

Why is Cherubino better than scores like it in Florence? The hospitable owner, Maris, is the reason I shop here for fresh ravioli and her array of dried pastas in all shapes, sizes, and flavors. She also sells good olive oil, balsamic vinegar, local wines, *limoncello* and *biscotti* and *vin santo*.

TELEPHONE
055 210 901

OPEN
Mon, Thur–Sun: 10 A.M.–8 P.M.; Tues–Wed: 3–8 P.M.

CLOSED
July 10–Aug 10

CREDIT CARDS
MC, V

ENGLISH
Yes

ENOTECA PERI (84)
Via Maggio, 5r (Pitti Palace)

At this forty-year-old shop you will find fair prices for local wines and a friendly owner who knows his stuff. He also carries a good line of Tuscan olive oils.

TELEPHONE
055 21 26 74

OPEN
Mon–Sat: 8 A.M.–1 P.M., 3:30–8 P.M.

CLOSED
Sun; Aug 8–22

CREDIT CARDS
DC, MC, V

ENGLISH
Limited

FIASCHETTERIA ZANOBINI (17)
Via Sant'Antonino, 47r (San Lorenzo Market)

If you are a wine buff, this is a required stop in Florence. The mind-boggling selection of wines includes those from their own vineyards, such as a fine Chianti Classico. The owner is very knowledgeable and will spend time with each customer. Also available are grappas, old Italian liqueurs, and *limoncello*.

TELEPHONE
055 239 6850

EMAIL
zanobini@tin.it

OPEN
Mon–Sat: 8:15 A.M.–2 P.M., 3:30–8 P.M.

CLOSED
Sun

CREDIT CARDS
AE, MC, V

ENGLISH
Yes

LA BOTTEGA DELL'OLIO (64)
Piazza del Limbo, 2r (Piazza Goldoni and Via de' Tornabuoni)

La Bottega dell'Olio is located on a tiny square next to the SS Apostoli Church, which is one of the oldest places of worship in Florence and the starting point of the famous Easter Day parade. A visit to the shop is a very pleasant education in the joys of olive oil consumption.

TELEPHONE
055 267 0468

INTERNET
www.labottegadellolio.it

OPEN
Mon–Sat: 10 A.M.–7 P.M.

Almost everything here has something to do with olives or olive oil, and the owner, Andrea, will patiently explain the virtues of his large stock of extra-virgin olive oils or let you browse to your heart's content. I like the olive-motif kitchen linens, his olive oil–based skin-care products and soaps, the olive-wood cooking and serving implements, and the wonderful array of flavored vinegars, including carob, honey, fig, and, of course, raspberry. Best of all, you can taste before you buy.

LA GALLERIA DEL CHIANTI (45)
Via del Corso, 41r (Il Duomo)

TELEPHONE
055 291 440
INTERNET
www.galleriadelchianti.com
OPEN
Daily: 9:30 A.M.–8:30 P.M.
CLOSED
Never
CREDIT CARDS
AE, DC, MC, V
ENGLISH
Yes

As the name implies, this store offers food and wines from Tuscany, including a good selection of flavored oils, eighty-year-old balsamic vinegar (almost 170€ per bottle), and bags of *cantuccini* for dipping in *vin santo*. Shipping via Fedex is available.

CLOSED
Sun
CREDIT CARDS
DC, MC, V
ENGLISH
Yes

Grocery Stores and Supermarkets

CONAD (14)
Via L. Alamanni 2/20r (Train Station)

TELEPHONE
Not available
OPEN
Mon–Sat: 8 A.M.–7 P.M.
CLOSED
Sun; holidays
CREDIT CARDS
MC, V
ENGLISH
Limited

Conad is a handy but expensive all-purpose pit stop if you are out of consumables. The cheese section in back is exceptional, as are the lines that jam the narrow aisles. Also on the same block is a flower shop and a branch post office.

PEGNA (41)
Via dello Studio, 8r (Il Duomo)

TELEPHONE
055 282 701
OPEN
Mon–Tues, Thur–Sat: 9 A.M.–
1 P.M., 3:30–7:30 P.M.; Wed:
9 A.M.–1 P.M.
CLOSED
Sun
CREDIT CARDS
AE, DC, MC, V
ENGLISH
Limited

Skip the mops and cat food in front and head for the back of this snazzy grocery store, which sells everything you could possibly want, except produce.

STANDA (44)
Via Pietrapiana, 42/44 (Piazza Santa Croce)

This is the Safeway of Italy, with food, bakery, deli, meat, and liquor sections. It is centrally located, not far from Piazza Santa Croce and across the street from a main post office.

TELEPHONE
Unavailable

OPEN
Mon–Sat: 8 A.M.–9 P.M.; Sun: 9 A.M.–9 P.M.

CLOSED
Never

CREDIT CARDS
MC, V

ENGLISH
Limited

Indoor/Outdoor Markets

MERCATO CENTRALE DE SAN LORENZO (18)
Piazza del Mercato Centrale

The San Lorenzo Central Market is a must for all visitors to Florence. Inside, stalls on two levels sell every sort of meat, fish, cheese, fruit, and vegetable imaginable. Outside are hundreds of stalls with hawkers selling a variety of fake Gucci scarves and bags, plus T-shirts for everyone on your list, Florentine paper products, questionable leather goods, and more. No one has a monopoly on any item . . . it's just dozens of sellers all selling the same things at the same prices. Consequently, there's not much bargaining, so pick the seller with the best attitude. Very touristy, but fun and worth at least an hour or so.

OPEN
Indoor food market: Mon–Sat 7 A.M.–1 P.M. Some stalls stay open Saturday afternoon from 2–5 P.M.; outdoor stalls: in winter Tues–Sat 9 A.M.–6 P.M., in summer, daily 9 A.M.–9 P.M.

MERCATO DELLA CASCINE
Cascine Park (past Lungarno Amerigo Vespucci at the western edge of Florence)

If you can eat it, wear it, water it, feed it, or dust it, chances are it is for sale at the Mercato della Cascine. This weekly outdoor market on Viale Lincoln along the Arno River includes an outdoor food market and endless clothing and houseware stalls pitching everything from aprons to underwear. It is very local, since most tourists don't venture out this far. Go early for the best selection. Watch your wallets and purses, and take your own shopping bags. The English spoken here is very limited. If you don't feel like walking, hop on bus number 1, 9, or 12. Most stalls don't really get going until 8 A.M.

On the three Sundays before Easter, the market is open with literally hundreds of stalls selling clothing and housewares. Look for the signs saying "vintage" or "stock." With a little digging, I found Façonable, Ann Taylor, and Land's End shirts for 5€ and cashmere sweaters for 20€. Look carefully; some have big flaws.

OPEN
Weekly market 7 A.M.–1 P.M., three Sundays before Easter 9 A.M.–7 P.M.

MERCATO DI SANTO SPIRITO (86)
Piazza Santo Spirito

OPEN
Mon–Sat: 8 A.M.–1 P.M.; Sun: organic market 9 A.M.–4 P.M.

A morning market is held here from Monday to Saturday. Most of the stalls are devoted to clothing, but there are several farmers selling their produce from carts near the church end of the square. On the third Sunday of each month, there is an organic market.

MERCATO SANT' AMBROGIO (54)
Piazza Sant' Ambrogio at Piazza Ghiberti

OPEN
Mon–Sat: 7 A.M.–1 P.M.

This is a lively indoor/outdoor neighborhood market selling to the locals. If you patronize a stall three or four times, you will be treated just like one of the natives. Here you will find all the same meats, fish, dairy products, fruits, and vegetables found at the Mercato Centrale, but at slightly better prices. Tavola Calda da Rocco (see page 60) is a great place for lunch. The dry-goods stalls outside have some worthwhile buys in cotton underwear and socks. Best day to go: Saturday.

ROME

Every road does not lead to Rome, but every road in Rome
leads to eternity.
        —Arthur Symons, Cities, 1903

There are more than forty McDonald's in Rome, it's true, but
there are four hundred Italian restaurants in New York City.
        —U.S. Ambassador Thomas Foglietta, in an
        interview with Turin daily, La Stampa

In the eternal city of Rome, antiquity and history are taken for granted
as part of everyday life. This city, teeming with humanity and choked
with traffic jams and crazy drivers, happily thrives amid some of Western
civilization's greatest monuments, piazzas, and landmarks.

Romans originated the first developed cuisine in the Western world and
remain famous to this day for their passion for eating. While Rome cannot claim to be the gastronomic capital of Italy, it is the city where food is
most pleasurably consumed. The cooking is rich in flavors and aromas, but
there is nothing fancy about it. In fact, some people may think it almost
primitive, because many famous meat dishes, such as *coda alla vaccinara*
(oxtail stew with vegetables), *trippa alla romana* (tripe cooked with meat
sauce, mint, and pecorino cheese), and *cervella fritta* (fried calves' brains),
are based on the head, tail, and innards of the animal. The Jewish community in Rome favors deep-frying and has raised this cooking method to a
delicate art form. Consider *carciofi alla giudia* (artichokes flattened and fried
until brown and crisp) and zucchini blossoms stuffed with ricotta cheese
and anchovies and quickly deep-fried. Other vegetables have a starring
role, especially green leafy vegetables cooked in water and served *all'agro,*
with lemon juice and olive oil. *Puntarella,* an interesting light-green leafy
vegetable, is served as a salad with an unforgettable dressing made from
pounded garlic and anchovies.

In Rome there are literally thousands of dining choices, from the elegant
citadels of fine cuisine to the rapidly vanishing little family-owned and -run
trattorias. As in every major world capital, fast-food chains have invaded.
The good news is that serious chefs are sticking with regional standbys
and the basic cuisine everyone wishes Mama still had the time and desire
to prepare. Roman restaurants of all types are noted for serving the same
specialties on the same days of the week. On Tuesday and Friday, look for
fresh fish. On Thursday, gnocchi is served, and on Saturday, tripe. For a
traditional Sunday lunch with the extended family, plan on rich lasagne.
Pizza is the light meal of choice in the evening. You will find mouthwatering displays of vegetables, meat, and seafood antipasti laid out with the
precision of a fine jeweler. Favorite pastas are *penne all'amatriciana* (pasta

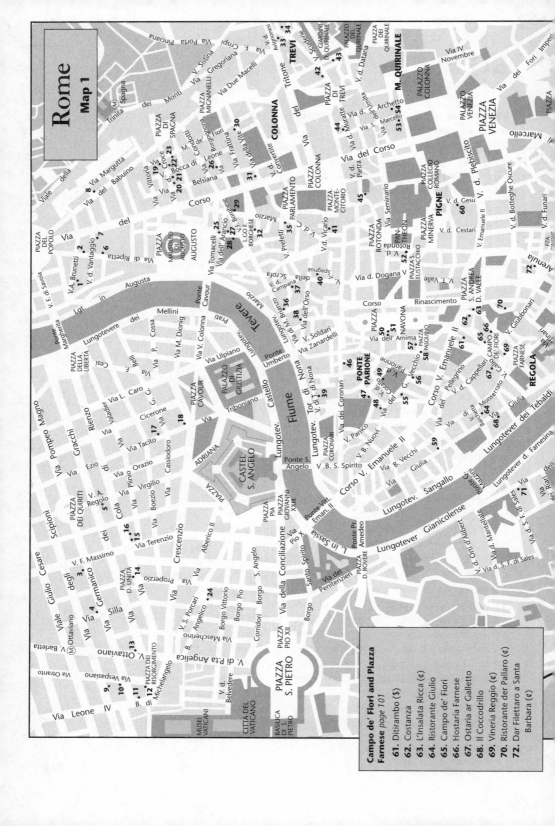

Rome
Map 1

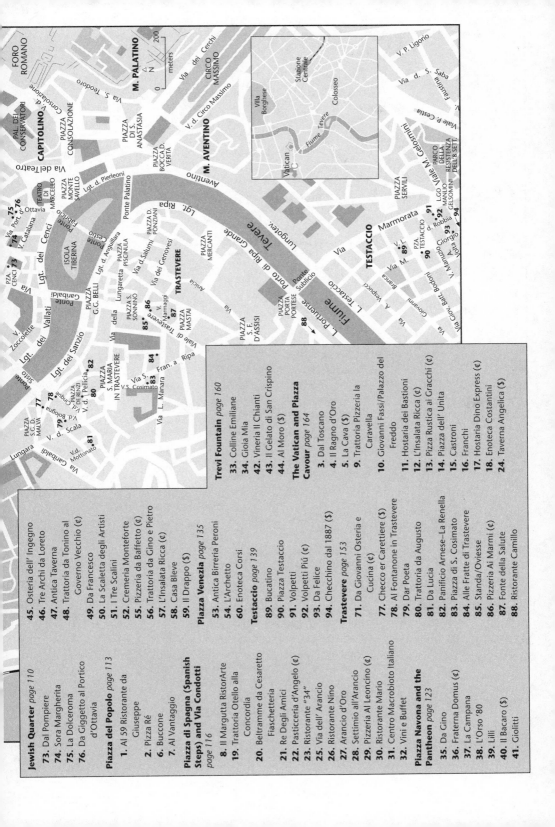

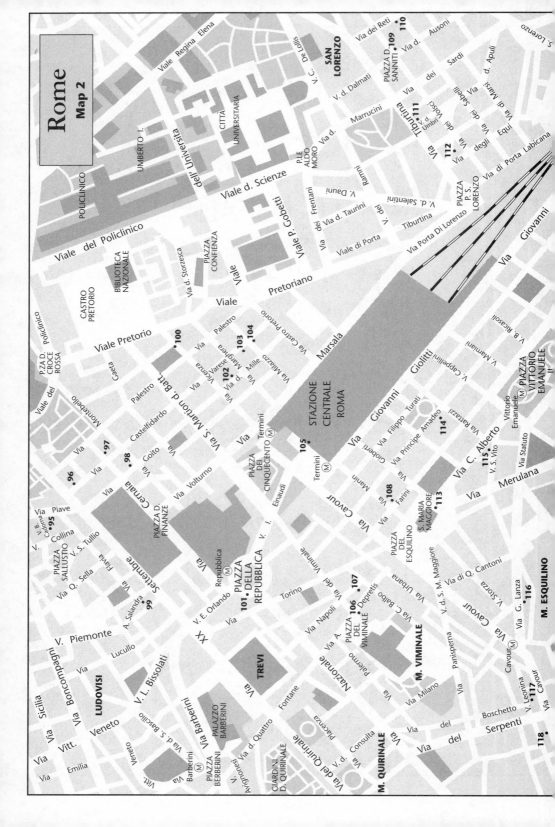

Rome
Map 2

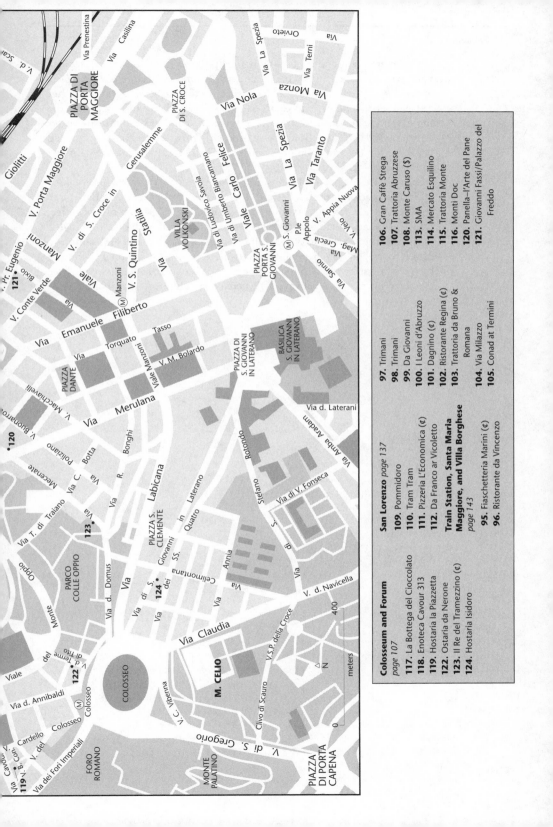

Colosseum and Forum
page 107

117. La Bottega del Cioccolato
118. Enoteca Cavour 313
119. Hostaria la Piazzetta
122. Ostaria da Nerone
123. Il Re del Tramezzino (¢)
124. Hostaria Isidoro

San Lorenzo *page 137*

109. Pommidoro
110. Tram Tram
111. Pizzeria L'Economica (¢)
112. Da Franco ar Vicoletto

Train Station, Santa Maria Maggiore, and Villa Borghese *page 143*

95. Fiaschetteria Marini (¢)
96. Ristorante da Vincenzo
97. Trimani
98. Trimani
99. Da Giovanni
100. I Leoni d'Abruzzo
101. Dagnino (¢)
102. Ristorante Regina (¢)
103. Trattoria da Bruno & Romana
104. Via Milazzo
105. Conad at Termini
106. Gran Caffè Strega
107. Trattoria Abruzzese
108. Monte Caruso ($)
113. SMA
114. Mercato Esquilino
115. Trattoria Monte
116. Monti Doc
120. Panella–l'Arte del Pane
121. Giovanni Fassi/Palazzo del Freddo

with tomatoes, onions, bacon, and hot pepper), *spaghetti alla carbonara* (pasta with bacon, onion, eggs, cheese, and wine), and *spaghetti con aglio, olio, e prezzemolo* or *peperoncini,* spaghetti with olive oil, garlic, and parsley or hot red peppers. Popular entrées are *saltimbocca* (which means "hop into the mouth" and consists of thin slices of prosciutto and veal sautéed in butter and wine), *abbacchio* (milk-fed baby lamb either roasted, or the chops grilled to perfection over an open fire), and *baccalà* (dried salt cod, usually dipped in butter and fried in olive oil).

Desserts are kept simple—usually a single piece of fruit or a dish of fresh fruit. If something more is desired, there is the ever-present *dolce* darling of the past decade, tiramisù (which means "pick me up"), a rich mix of coffee, cake, chocolate, and mascarpone cheese liberally laced with liqueur. Finally, no trip to the Eternal City would be complete without a liberal sampling of gelato, the favorite Roman between-meal treat. Cones and cups are sold by the size not by the number of scoops, so it is easy to sample two or three flavors at a time—and always *con panna* (with whipped cream) on top.

Restaurants in Rome

Campo de' Fiori and Piazza Farnese

The name *Campo de' Fiori* means "field of flowers." The original flower market has moved to the outskirts of Rome (see page 175), and now there are only a few flower stalls open during the morning market, which is one of the most colorful in Rome. Around the market can be found a maze of cobblestone alleys, fading *palazzos,* crumbling churches, bubbling fountains, and restaurants and bars of all types. Not far from Campo de' Fiori is the serenely elegant Piazza Farnese, with its Michelangelo-designed Palazzo Farnese, now site of the French Embassy.

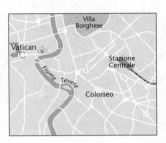

($) indicates a Big Splurge
(¢) indicates a Cheap Eat

Restaurants

COSTANZA (62)
Piazza del Paradiso, 63/65

Costanza is almost buried in a hidden corner of this tiny piazza a minute or two away from Campo de' Fiori. The rather anonymous exterior masks the warmth of this multiroom *hostaria,* which sits on part of the ruins of the Theater de Pompeo, sections of which are displayed behind

TELEPHONE
06 686 1717, 6880 1002
OPEN
Mon–Sat: lunch 12:30–3 P.M., dinner 7:30–11:30 P.M.
CLOSED
Sun; Aug

RESERVATIONS	Essential
CREDIT CARDS	AE, DC, MC, V
À LA CARTE	25–40 €
FIXED-PRICE MENU	None
BREAD & SERVICE CHARGES	Bread 2€, service included
ENGLISH	Yes

glass. The attractive interior is a mix of stuccoed walls, low ceilings, and long beams, with the expected roundup of wine bottles, paintings, candles, and other bric-a-brac. Its dark, cozy atmosphere makes it the perfect place for a romantic meal with a special person.

The wide-ranging menu holds few disappointments, but it is admittedly for diners with more flexible budgets. On the pasta front, the *pasta e fagioli Costanza* is delicious—a carbohydrate festival of white beans and pasta in a broth with onions, bacon, and tomato sprinkled with grated cheese. Also delicious are any of the risottos, the seasonal ravioli with artichokes, crêpes with spinach and cheese, or the *tagliolini* with salmon and radicchio. From here, you move on to a number of main-course dishes, ranging from steak tartare, grilled or roasted veal, pork, baby kid, and beef to fresh fish and vegetable side dishes. The ever-present *dolce,* tiramisù, is featured and is especially rich, as are most of the other homemade desserts.

DAR FILETTARO A SANTA BARBARA (¢, 72)
Largo dei Librari, 88

TELEPHONE	06 686 4018
OPEN	Mon–Sat: dinner 5–10:40 P.M.
CLOSED	Sun; Aug, Dec 24–Jan 3
RESERVATIONS	Not accepted
CREDIT CARDS	None
À LA CARTE	6–9€
FIXED-PRICE MENU	None
BREAD & SERVICE CHARGES	Bread 0.80€ (eat-in only); service included
ENGLISH	Limited

All the fast-food fish fanciers in this section of Rome flock to Dar Filettaro. When you arrive, you need only remember one thing about this bargain Great Eat hidden on a tiny side street off Via dei Giubbonari: *filleto di baccalà,* or deep-fried codfish, the house specialty. Their version is batter dipped and quickly deep-fried, leaving the inside moist and the outside crisp. Add a glass of wine and maybe a salad, and you should be ready for the next round of sightseeing. Everything on the menu can be packaged to take away.

DITIRAMBO ($, 61)
Piazza dell Cancelleria, 74/75

TELEPHONE	06 687 1626
INTERNET	www.ristoranteditirambo.com
OPEN	Mon: dinner 8–11 P.M.; Tues–Thur: lunch 1–3:30 P.M., dinner 8–11 P.M.; Fri–Sun: lunch 1–3:30 P.M, dinner 7:30–11:30 P.M.

Ditirambo, named after an ancient Greek god of wine and food, is a casual place with beams and planked floors, wines displayed on tiered shelves, and servers wearing green aprons that match the green-and-white tablecloths. The quality and freshness of the seasonal ingredients form the base for the food, an innovative take on traditional Italian recipes. All bread, pasta, and desserts are made here by two women who do nothing else. If you look in before lunch or in the afternoon, you will probably see them working in the front room, rolling and cutting the pasta, or putting the finishing touches on a sublime dessert. The menu changes often, and almost everything on it works—with the notable exception of the bread pasta with a pecorino and pesto sauce. The rubbery pasta tastes like uncooked dough balls and lands like wet laundry in your stomach, but the sauce is sensational. A better choice is red chicory ravioli or the *malfatti* pasta, made with walnut and almond flour and sauced with squash blossoms. For a second course, skip the odd cabbage and cuttlefish rolls and choose instead the venison stew with prunes or the *pollo alla marengo,* chicken cooked with white wine, tomatoes, and mushrooms. Vegetarians are offered three or four main courses that might include a shallot flan with pumpkin sauce or a carrot flan with a cheese fondue. The best salad is the spinach with walnuts, fresh pears, and *moliterno* cheese.

You cannot possibly consider leaving without dessert . . . remember those two hardworking ladies I mentioned? Their sweet finales will not let you down, especially their rich and unusual apple tart with a dark chocolate sauce swirl, the wild cherry and ricotta cake, or the flaky *millefoglie* layered with wine-infused *zabaione.* More than forty wines are available by the glass, as are weekly featured vintages. Locals place Ditirambo high on their list of favorites, so arrive with reservations or be prepared to go elsewhere.

CLOSED
Mon lunch; Aug
RESERVATIONS
Essential
CREDIT CARDS
MC, V
À LA CARTE
40–50€
FIXED-PRICE MENU
None
BREAD & SERVICE CHARGES
Bread 1.50€, service included
ENGLISH
Yes, and menu in English

HOSTARIA FARNESE (66)
Via dei Baullari, 109

At the Hostaria Farnese, you will enjoy homemade food served in the pleasant atmosphere of the Contini family. The interior hasn't much froufrous, just black bentwood chairs, tables with green tablecloths, and a few outside tables during the summer months.

Everyone gets into the act with the food and service: Mama cooks while Papa and the three daughters and one son serve. The menu is one of utmost simplicity, featuring healthy minestrone, spinach ravioli, *pasta e ceci,* eggplant Parmesan, roast lamb, grilled meats, veal scaloppine, pizza for lunch and dinner, and a few homemade desserts. The portions will not overwhelm you, and neither will your bill.

TELEPHONE
06 6880 1595
OPEN
Mon–Wed, Fri–Sun: lunch noon–3 P.M., dinner 7–11:30 P.M.
CLOSED
Thur; Aug
RESERVATIONS
Advised
CREDIT CARDS
AE, DC, MC, V
À LA CARTE
25–30€
FIXED-PRICE MENU
None
BREAD & SERVICE CHARGES
Bread 1.50€, 10% service added
ENGLISH
Yes

IL COCCODRILLO (68)
Via Giulia, 14

TELEPHONE
06 6819 2650

OPEN
Mon–Tues, Thurs–Sun: lunch
1–2:30 P.M., dinner 7:30–
11:30 P.M.; wine bar 1–2:30 P.M.,
6:30 P.M.–2 A.M.

CLOSED
Wed; Jan or Feb

RESERVATIONS
Advised for dinner

CREDIT CARDS
MC, V

À LA CARTE
20–40€

FIXED-PRICE MENU
None

BREAD & SERVICE CHARGES
Bread 2€, service included

ENGLISH
Yes, and menu in English

Sasha and Christopher Matthews run the front part of Il Coccodrillo while talented chef Angela Zincone oversees the kitchen in this wine bar/restaurant not far from Piazza Farnese. You enter through the casual wine bar, where you can sample a few wines and order a light meal. The next room blends into a lovely garden in the back and is reserved for more leisurely dining. In addition to a seasonal menu, Angela offers daily specials (each with appropriate wines) that clearly reflect her inventive takes on the usual Roman fare. As a starter, perhaps she will offer deep-fried, golden swordfish cubes or a Sicilian broccoli flan served with a pecorino cheese sauce. Follow this with her homemade *fettuccelle* tossed with spinach, duck breast, and truffles, guinea hen with pomegranate, or a tender veal osso buco made with mushrooms and fresh peas and complemented by a glass of *rosso di Montefalco*. For dessert, I love her coffee *semifreddo* with sambuca sauce, or the fresh baked pears in a tangy orange sauce. The interesting food and wines have made an impression on the well-dressed lunch and dinner patrons, who know to book at least a day ahead for a garden table.

L'INSALATA RICCA (¢, 63)
Largo del Chiavari, 85/86, at Corso V. Emanuele II

TELEPHONE
06 6880 3656

INTERNET
www.linsalataricca.it

OPEN
Daily: lunch 12:30–3:30 P.M.,
dinner 6:45–11:45 P.M.

CLOSED
Christmas

RESERVATIONS
Advised for 4 or more

CREDIT CARDS
AE, DC, MV, V

À LA CARTE
10–15€

FIXED-PRICE MENU
None

BREAD & SERVICE CHARGES
Bread 1.10€, service included

ENGLISH
Yes, and menu in English

L'Insalata Ricca is a small chain of popular, almost-fast-food trattorias strategically located around Rome. Several are in the tourist boonies and are not listed here, but in addition to this one, which was the first to open, you will find another not far away, near Piazza Navona (see page 131), and another close to the Vatican (see page 168). All are bustling with Italian families and foreign residents, as they offer great value and variety, admirably conforming to the budget and quality concerns of Great Eaters. For both lunch and dinner, plan to arrive early, because within ten minutes of the trattoria's opening, there will be a crowd standing outside waiting for a seat. Once in, everyone sits at closely packed tables or on the outside terraces, delighting in the mammoth helpings of their specialties: antipasti, pastas, pizzas (but not at this location), and huge salads that are meals in themselves. Fresh fish is served Thursday through Sunday. The trattoria's own dense chocolate cake, fruit tarts, mousses, and *tartufo* will round out your successful meal. The house wines—including organic varieties—are good. Other pluses included an English menu and a nonsmoking policy that is enforced.

OSTARIA AR GALLETTO (67)
Vicolo del Gallo, 1 at Piazza Farnese, 102

Ostaria ar Galletto is a perennial favorite because it is a family-owned place where every member plays a part. Mama, a.k.a. the boss, runs the kitchen. Papa holds court in the dining room while seating and serving guests, who swap stories about their favorite soccer teams. One of the sons-in-law, a colonel in the Italian army, jokes that he ate here as a young man and loved the restaurant so much he married the owner's youngest daughter. After one meal you will understand his enthusiasm. The inside is charming, featuring a wood-beamed ceiling festooned with hanging hams, hunting murals, and bright orange linens on well-spaced tables. On warm days, reserve a table outside on the Piazza Farnese, a beautiful Baroque square that is an ideal place to forget everything but what is on your plate and who is across the table.

A full meal can creep into the Big Splurge category if you are not watchful, but with a little care and a liter of the house wine you should be fine. I recommend going easy on the appetizers, thus saving room for a bowl of Mama's homemade ravioli, gnocchi, or fettuccine noodles tossed with zucchini. If you like fish, be sure to order the special *fritto misto Italiano* when you reserve your table. Meat eaters lean toward the *saltimbocca alla romana,* thin slices of veal seasoned with fresh sage, covered with ham, and sautéed in butter with a splash of white wine. The beef, slowly cooked in red wine with carrots and fresh mushrooms, and the osso buco with mushrooms are other favorites. The desserts are all homemade, but I have never had any room for more than the *fragole con gelato,* fresh strawberries spooned over vanilla ice cream.

TELEPHONE
06 686 1714

OPEN
Mon–Sat: lunch 12:30–3 P.M., dinner 7–11:30 P.M.

CLOSED
Sun; 1 week mid-Aug (dates vary), Dec 23–Jan 14

RESERVATIONS
Advised, especially for outside tables

CREDIT CARDS
AE, DC, MC, V

À LA CARTE
30–35€

FIXED-PRICE MENU
None

BREAD & SERVICE CHARGES
Bread 1.50€, service included

ENGLISH
Yes

RISTORANTE DER PALLARO (¢, 70)
Largo del Pallaro, 15

Ristorante der Pallaro will not wow you with a glitzy location, a snappy interior design, or gourmet vittles on your plate. The cast of characters in this knotty-pine *ristorante* usually includes a lively mix of families, spry senior citizens, a yuppie or two, and anyone else on the prowl for a satisfying budget Great Eat in Rome.

When you arrive, look a little to the right of the beaded curtains covering the entry to see Paolo Fazi busily working in her tiny kitchen. Her husband, Mario, and Carlo, the waiter (who has been here more than a decade and is considered "almost a son"), help out front. They offer no à la carte menu—whatever Paolo cooks is what you eat, and

TELEPHONE
06 6880 1488

OPEN
Tues–Sun: lunch 12:30–3:15 P.M., dinner 7 P.M.–midnight

CLOSED
Mon; Aug 10–15

RESERVATIONS
Advised, especially on Sun and holidays

CREDIT CARDS
None, cash only

À LA CARTE
None

the portions are so large that even a veteran coal miner after a ten-hour shift would be daunted. You will start with an antipasto, then be served the pasta of the day, which is usually rigatoni with tomato sauce and cheese. Next comes the main course, which varies between beef or veal served with homemade fried potatoes. Finally, there is eggplant, a piece of cheese, and the house sweet—homemade peach marmalade cake—all washed down with water and wine. Coffee is not available.

RISTORANTE GIULIO (64)
Via della Barchetta, 19

Ristorante Giulio is in a wonderful old building that dates back to the early 1400s. Fiorella and Giulio, the friendly owners, are into their fourth decade of serving and pleasing their guests. The small dining room has arched ceilings, a beautifully tiled floor, and stone walls lined with black-and-white prints of old Rome and an interesting collection of Sicilian and provincial plates. The twenty-two tables are covered with light yellow linens and bouquets of fresh flowers. During the steamy summertime, be sure to reserve one of the tables on the sought-after streetside terrace.

The menu features a parade of seasonal dishes. Depending on when you visit, you will find good renditions of homemade ravioli filled with spinach and ricotta cheese, fettuccine either with a garlicky pesto or topped with truffles in a white sauce, and *orecchiette* (ear-shaped semolina pasta) tossed with broccoli in winter and with fresh tomatoes and mozzarella cheese in summer. The gnocchi is homemade and is served daily with a choice of sauces: gorgonzola, pesto, meat and tomato, or truffle (*tartufo*). Veal and fresh fish are always on the menu, along with vegetables, assorted cheeses, and the usual desserts, including wild strawberries in season. In the end, you will not have spent much more than 25 or 30€ per person, including a glass or two of the drinkable house wine.

VINERIA REGGIO (¢, 69)
Campo dè Fiori, 15

Vineria Reggio not only is the oldest wine bar on Campo dè Fiori but also pours one of the cheapest glasses of house plonk within a two-block radius (1.30€ at the bar, 2.30€ at a table). A glass of Frescobaldi will set you back less than 3€, and a modest Brunello rings up at just under 8€. If these don't appeal, you have forty-three other choices, ranging in price from 2.50–20€ per glass. The cozy interior is lined with wine bottles and set with ten tables, but this is not the place to sit. The best seating is on the shaded terrace in front facing the busy *campo*, where regulars and visitors alike seem to stay almost forever to people-watch, not only when the big market is bustling but throughout the day and into the evening, when the square draws people of all persuasions. The only meal served is lunch, and my advice is to stick with the daily specials. Later on, sandwiches as well as cold meat and cheese plates are served. Do your waistline a favor and skip the tired desserts.

CREDIT CARDS
MC, V

À LA CARTE
9–15€, glass of wine included

FIXED-PRICE MENU
None

BREAD & SERVICE CHARGES
Bread 1.50€, service discretionary

ENGLISH
Yes

Colosseum and Forum

The main archaeological ruins are concentrated south of Piazza Venezia, down Via dei Fori Imperiali to the Forum, around the Colosseum to the Circus Maximus, and south toward the Baths of Caracalla.

Restaurants

ENOTECA CAVOUR 313 (118)
Via Cavour, 313

For a light lunch or dinner accompanied by a few glasses of fine wine, it would be hard to beat the Enoteca Cavour 313, one of the most complete wine bars in Rome. This appealing location features more than six hundred different wines and champagnes from every wine-growing region in Italy, as well as wines from France, California, and Australia. The casual atmosphere with its wooden tables and booths draws everyone from construction workers in dusty shoes on their way home from a job site to socialites dressed to the nines. Angelo, one of the owners, speaks English and knows his wines. He and his partner, Marco, will be happy to make suggestions about what to drink or to discuss whatever special wines are being featured at

TELEPHONE
06 678 5496

EMAIL
cavour313@libero.it

OPEN
Mon–Sat: lunch 12:30–2:30 P.M., dinner 7:30 P.M.–12:30 A.M.; Sun: dinner 7:30 P.M.–midnight

CLOSED
Sun lunch; Sun in Aug

RESERVATIONS
Advised in the evening

CREDIT CARDS
AE, DC, MC, V

À LA CARTE
Lunch 10–20€, includes a glass
of wine; dinner 18–25€
FIXED-PRICE MENU
None
BREAD & SERVICE CHARGES
Bread 2€, service included
ENGLISH
Yes, and menu in English

the moment. They are also known for their selection of whiskey and grappas. Lingering is encouraged, and you are free to order as much or as little as you want to eat. Don't expect pizza, pasta, or three-course meals. Instead, for lunch they serve cold food: tempting salads, smoked fish, cold meats, cheeses, and pâtés. For dinner, in addition to cold food, they offer a select choice of hot soups, fresh fish, and meat dishes. At any time, rich desserts are never far away.

HOSTARIA ISIDORO (124)
Via di San Giovanni in Laterano, 59/a-61-63 (Colosseo)

TELEPHONE
06 700 8266
OPEN
Mon–Fri, Sun: lunch 12:30–
2:30 P.M., dinner 7:30–11 P.M.;
Sat: dinner 7:30–11 P.M.
CLOSED
Sat lunch
RESERVATIONS
Advised, especially for dinner
CREDIT CARDS
MC, V
À LA CARTE
15–20€
FIXED-PRICE MENU
None
BREAD & SERVICE CHARGES
Bread 1.50€, service included
ENGLISH
Yes, and menu in English

Hostaria Isidoro is a happy, crowded place within walking distance of the Colosseum and Forum. Murals of old Rome and brick archways connecting the rooms set the stage for the simple tables covered in white cloths and accented with red napkins. The kitchen is known for its huge selection of pastas (twenty-three at last count), ranging from a simple tagliatelle with asparagus or mushrooms to penne with walnuts and vodka to an unusual risotto with fresh strawberries. On Fridays, there are five special pastas featuring either mussels, clams, salmon, scampi, or anchovies. On any given day, if you can't decide which of the pastas to have, no problem. Order the house special, the *assaggino,* an endless stream of different pasta plates to try. There is a two-person minimum for this carbohydrate fest, and by the time you have been served the last one, you will have had more than your fill. In addition to the multitude of pastas, the menu lists pizzas for lunch and dinner and a handful of the usual meat dishes and desserts. But when you are at Isidoro's, pasta should be the order of choice, along with a glass or two of the decent house red.

HOSTARIA LA PIAZZETTA (119)
Vicolo del Buon Consiglio, 23/a (at the Forum end of Via Cavour)

TELEPHONE
06 699 1640
OPEN
Mon–Sat: lunch 12–3 P.M.,
dinner 7–11 P.M.
CLOSED
Sun; 2 weeks in Aug (dates
vary)
RESERVATIONS
Advised for dinner
CREDIT CARDS
MC, V

Quietly hidden on a little street mere minutes from the Forum and Colosseum is Hostaria la Piazzetta, a charming respite from the usual tourist-clogged choices in the heart of historic Rome. At the entrance is an inviting display of the house antipasti and lovely desserts. The small off-white dining room is decorated with formally set tables and presided over by Franco Bartolini, the owner, and one or two waitpersons. Because the restaurant is so secluded, on warm days or evenings you can enjoy alfresco dining on the shaded terrace, blissfully free of automobile fumes and sidewalk crowds. Service is not hurried—all the more reason to order a nice bottle of wine and settle in for a relaxed Roman meal that is pleasing from beginning to end. I like to start with an assortment of the chef's antipasti, accompanied by a basket of herbed focaccia bread. Because the antipasti buffet is so generous and tempting, I usually skip the pasta course in favor of grilled fish or a hearty *saltimbocca a la romana*—slices of tender veal with ham and sage cooked in butter and white wine. Another favorite is Franco's own *polpette,* meatballs flavored with pine nuts and raisins and served with a fresh tomato-herb sauce (trust me—you will ask him for the recipe). The only problem with dessert is the number of choices: fresh fruit tarts, creamy custards, a dense chocolate slice . . . and these are just for openers. Just let your eyes and your appetite be your guides.

À LA CARTE
25–30€

FIXED-PRICE MENU
None

BREAD & SERVICE CHARGES
No bread charge, 10% service added

ENGLISH
Franco does not speak English, but one of his waitstaff does

IL RE DEL TRAMEZZINO (¢, 123)
Via Mecenate, 18A

Management does not stand on ceremony at this residential neighborhood bar within walking distance of the Colosseum and Forum. They only care about providing good food, and lots of it, to hungry diners searching for a decent value. When you go, check the hot food menu written on a board either by the bar or in the front window. You can sit at the bar, which wraps around an antipasti display, or in summer nab one of the few sidewalk tables.

The typical lunch-only menu should put you in fine spirits; it contains such dependable standbys as gnocchi, eggplant *alla parmigiana,* and *pasta all'amatriciana* (bacon, garlic, tomatoes, hot red peppers, and onion). In addition to the daily hot specials, they offer various salads, cold meat plates, great sandwiches, and a homemade dessert, served throughout the day. Because it is a bargain eat in a pricey area, this is a very popular destination at any time of day. If you are aimed here for lunch, it is best to time your visit to beat the rush, as they often run out of the best dishes early.

TELEPHONE
06 487 2360

OPEN
Mon–Fri: bar 7 A.M.–7:30 P.M., lunch 12:30–3 P.M.; Sat: bar 7 A.M.–3:30 P.M., no hot food

CLOSED
Sun; Aug

CREDIT CARDS
AE, V

À LA CARTE
Sandwiches from 1.50–3€, lunches 8–11€

FIXED-PRICE MENU
None

BREAD & SERVICE CHARGES
No bread charge at bar, 0.30€ per roll at a table; service included at bar and indoor tables; 10% service added at tables outside

ENGLISH
Minimal

OSTARIA DA NERONE (122)
Via delle Terme di Tito, 96

This classic restaurant is a smart choice for a leisurely lunch between sightseeing rounds near the Colosseum and the Forum. The emphasis is firmly on old-fashioned value, as is evidenced by its many longtime patrons, some of whom have been eating here for decades. In addition, I have had readers tell me that once they found this restaurant, they didn't eat anyplace else during their stay in Rome. I think

TELEPHONE
06 481 7952

OPEN
Mon–Sat: lunch 12–3 P.M., dinner 7–11 P.M.

CLOSED
Sun; Aug

RESERVATIONS
Advised

CREDIT CARDS
AE, DC, MC, V
À LA CARTE
25–30€
FIXED-PRICE MENU
None
BREAD & SERVICE CHARGES
Bread 1.50€, 10% service added
ENGLISH
Enough, and menu in English

that is because no matter who you are or how many times you visit, you receive the same genuinely friendly service. The interior is mighty basic: whitewashed walls with a picture or two, white linens on the tables, uniformed waiters (who came with the building), hard chairs, and a pay phone by the front door. In warm weather, tables are set up outside so you can dine in view of the Colosseum.

Before ordering, be sure to take a long look at the beautiful antipasti display and the lovely desserts, and plan the rest of your meal accordingly. For lunch, you may want to concentrate solely on these two courses. Otherwise, for the first course, hope that the homemade ravioli stuffed with ricotta cheese and sage in a butter sauce is on the menu. On Thursday, you can depend on gnocchi, and every day you can order their specialty, *fettuccine alla Nerone,* a creamy dish with salami, ham, peas, mushrooms, and eggs. As your main course, try the chicken with tomatoes and peppers in a wine sauce or the roast rabbit. The desserts are worth every calorie. To ease your pangs of guilt, remember that you can always walk back to your hotel or spend the afternoon strolling around Rome's ancient sites.

Jewish Quarter

It is said that when St. Peter came to Rome, he stayed in the Jewish Quarter in Trastevere, where there were some thirty thousand fellow Greek-speaking Jews and fifteen synagogues. Europe's oldest surviving Jewish community was moved in 1555 to its present location by Pope Paul IV, who ruled that the Jewish Quarter was the only place where all Rome's Jews could live and work. During World War II, two thousand Jews were deported from here to the death camps, and only two dozen returned. Today, the Jewish population in Italy is what it was in Nero's time, and the Roman community is the largest. The Via del Portico di Ottavia, behind the synagogue, is the Jewish Quarter's main street and naturally has the best Jewish restaurants in Rome.

RESTAURANTS

PASTRY SHOPS AND BAKERIES

Restaurants

DA GIGGETTO AL PORTICO D'OTTAVIA (76)
Via del Portico d'Ottavia, 21/a

Any trip to Rome would be incomplete without sampling Roman-Jewish cuisine. Nowhere will it be more authentic than in this family-owned trattoria next to the ruins of the Theater of Marcellus. Out front is a large seating area shaded by umbrellas. Inside are four rooms done in the usual rustic style, with terra-cotta floors and ropes of garlic and dried herbs hanging from the ceiling. Thankfully the ambitious menu is translated into English.

For your appetizer course, you must try one of their specialties: crisp and tender fried artichokes, fried zucchini flowers filled with mozzarella and anchovies, fried codfish fillets, rice balls filled with mozzarella and covered with tomato sauce, or potato croquettes. If I order meat, I usually like to stay light on the *primo* course, selecting a simple spaghetti with butter and Parmesan cheese. When I skip the meat and fish dishes, I order something more substantial, say, the *spaghetti carbonara* or the *spaghetti con vongole veraci* (with fresh clams). If you are having meat, the osso buco with mushrooms and peas is a filling choice, as is the roast lamb or veal. True to Roman tradition, many unusual cuts of meat are featured. If you're not careful, the beef tongue in parsley sauce, the lamb sweetbreads, or the fried brains with mushrooms, artichokes, and zucchini will make a convert out of you. The pace doesn't let up with dessert, which includes fresh fruit, ice cream, or a sinfully fattening delicacy from La Dolceroma, an American-Austrian bakery next door run by the owner's son (see page 112).

TELEPHONE
06 686 1105

INTERNET
www.giggettoalportico.com

OPEN
Tues–Sun: lunch 12:30–3 P.M., dinner 7:30–11 P.M.

CLOSED
Mon; last week of July, 1st week of Aug

RESERVATIONS
Advised, especially on weekends

CREDIT CARDS
AE, DC, MC, V

À LA CARTE
25–35€

FIXED-PRICE MENU
None

BREAD & SERVICE CHARGES
Bread 1.55€, service included

ENGLISH
Yes, and menu in English

DAL POMPIERE (73)
Via S. Maria del Calderari, 38 (off Via Arenula)

The Jewish Quarter in Rome is a maze of tiny piazzas, cobblestone streets, small shops, restaurants, and ancient ruins. In the heart of this you will find Dal Pompiere, a charming restaurant located on the second floor of the Cenci Bolognetti Palace, which dates from the 1600s. The three simple dining rooms feature dark ceilings, frescoes, rustic wooden tables and chairs, and not much else. The emphasis here is on Roman-Jewish cooking at its best.

For the antipasti, do not miss the *carciofo alla giudia,* a flattened, fried artichoke that looks like a pressed flower. Another must, whenever they are in season, are the *fiori di zucca ripieni,* zucchini blossoms stuffed with mozzarella and anchovies, then deep-fried. Other house specialties include

TELEPHONE
06 686 8377

OPEN
Mon–Sat: lunch 12:30–3 P.M., dinner 7:30–11 P.M.

CLOSED
Sun; July 20–Aug 31

RESERVATIONS
Advised

CREDIT CARDS
AE, MC, V

À LA CARTE
25–35€

FIXED-PRICE MENU
None

daily homemade pastas, succulent roast baby lamb, *baccalà* (salt-dried cod), paella on Thursday and Saturday, and *fritto vegetale,* a plate of crisply fried vegetables. The desserts to order include ricotta cheesecake and three types of *crostata:* cherry-cheese, cherry-almond, and chestnut-cheese.

SORA MARGHERITA (74)
Piazza della Cinque Scole, 30

To the designer-sunglasses and cellular-phone glitterati, Sora Margherita has little appeal. But for Great Eaters searching for good value in unexpected places, this basement hideaway (behind a green door with no sign) is very appealing. The menu is handwritten in red and black felt-tip pen on a piece of grid paper ripped out of a notebook. Wine is served in juice glasses, which are placed on paper overlays covering Formica tables. Despite the humble setting, chef Margherita Tomassini turns out some of the heartiest and best Jewish cooking in the Quarter. She wears slippers to work and stands on tradition, never changing her timeworn menu, which is served for lunch Tuesday to Saturday and for dinner on Friday and Saturday nights.

She always fixes homemade egg fettuccine (which she told me features a hundred eggs per batch!) with cheese, black pepper, and tomatoes or a cream sauce, as well as her specialty, *agnolotti*—a type of meat ravioli. On Thursday she dishes up her own gnocchi with tomato sauce. Grilled fish is the Tuesday and Friday highlight, but before ordering, be sure you check the price: is it sold by the gram or the piece? Meatballs are a daily dish, as are the fried artichokes, beef stew, and the veal chops. For dessert, a slice of her fruit *crostata* should wrap up this filling Great Eat in Rome.

Pastry Shops and Bakeries

LA DOLCEROMA (75)
Via del Portico di' Ottavia, 20/B

Stefano Ceccarelli's family has owned the restaurant next door for generations (Da Giggetto al Portico d'Ottavia, page 111). But Stefano wanted to do something on his own. Since he has always been interested in baking, it was natural for him to open La Dolceroma, which sells American and Austrian delicacies and is now one of Rome's most popular and well-known bakeries.

The tiny place, which has a display case and a table with two chairs, allows you to see directly into the kitchen.

Stefano does all of the baking himself, listing the ingredients so you will know exactly what you are eating. And what will you be eating? The choices are endless: chocolate or blueberry muffins, scones, several types of cookies including chocolate chip and oatmeal raisin, brownies, cheesecake, carrot cake, chestnut cake, and Sacher torte. He has also added several types of whole-grain breads, including rye and black bread. At Christmastime you will find *stollen* and Linzer torte. Once your order has been pulled together, it will be impossible to leave without trying one of his hand-dipped chocolates or ice cream. Everything is sold by weight and packaged to go. From late spring until October, American coffee and cappuccinos are served.

PRICES
From 1.60€ per pastry; bread sold by weight
ENGLISH
Yes

Piazza del Popolo

The Piazza del Popolo, which means the "people's square," is at the northern entrance to the city. Today the piazza serves as a general meeting and assembly place for celebrations, strikes, and political demonstrations. Standing here, you can see the Piazza Venezia at the end of Via del Corso; the Via di Ripetta, which served as a thruway to the Vatican; and Via del Babuino, leading to the Spanish Steps. In the center of the piazza is the 3,200-year-old obelisk of Pharaoh Ramses II, the largest in Rome, brought by Augustus from Egypt around 10 B.C.

RESTAURANTS

Restaurants

AL 59 RISTORANTE DA GIUSEPPE (1)
Via Angelo Brunetti, 59

The food at Al 59 Ristorante da Guiseppe is a triumph of Bolognese cooking and a good reason to make a pilgrimage across Rome. The clean and classic interior is elegant, and so is the superb food, which is passionately prepared according to the guidelines of the late master chef and owner, Guiseppe, who was from Bologna. Everything

TELEPHONE
06 321 9019
OPEN
Mon–Sat: lunch 1–3 P.M., dinner 8–11 P.M.
CLOSED
Sun; Aug

RESERVATIONS
Essential for dinner, advised for
lunch
CREDIT CARDS
AE, MC, V
À LA CARTE
30–35€
FIXED-PRICE MENU
None
BREAD & SERVICE CHARGES
Bread 2€, service included
ENGLISH
Yes, and menu in English

from start to finish is made in-house. If you walk by before lunch, you will see several gray-haired men sitting around a large table hand-rolling tortellini, the trademark pasta of Bologna. The meal could begin with antipasto or soup, but I always start with the tortellini with pumpkin or the heaven-sent spinach ravioli filled with ricotta cheese and lightly sauced with fresh tomatoes. Next, consider the *bolliti misti* (boiled meats), served from a special cart that is rolled to your table, or the fresh fish of the day. With a side of vegetables or a mixed salad, you will have a very filling meal. The sheer culinary bliss continues with the desserts, whether you choose the plump baked apple or the *crostata* filled with jam.

Because this restaurant is so popular with the locals, reservations are absolutely essential, especially for dinner, which is still humming at 10:30 P.M.

AL VANTAGGIO (7)
Via del Vantaggio, 34

TELEPHONE
06 323 6848
INTERNET
www.alvantaggio.it
OPEN
Daily mid-March–Dec;
Wed–Mon otherwise: lunch
12–3 P.M., dinner 7–11 P.M.
CLOSED
Tues Jan–mid-March; 15 days
in Jan (dates vary)
RESERVATIONS
Advised for outside tables
CREDIT CARDS
AE, DC, MC, V
À LA CARTE
Pizza and pasta from 6.50€,
3 courses 23–35€
FIXED-PRICE MENU
3 courses, 16€
BREAD & SERVICE CHARGES
Bread 0.80€, service included
ENGLISH
Yes, and menu in English

An interesting mixture of neighborhood locals and smart Great Eating visitors has been filling this family-run restaurant for more than forty-five years, as it consistently offers good food and good value. During one of my research trips to Rome, my flat was just around the corner, so I grew to know and enjoy this homespun spot, whether I was eating there (again and again) or merely walking by and observing. The tables in the two rooms inside or on the streetside terrace are always busy because the owner, Luigi, keeps everyone well served and well fed.

The fixed-price menu is a dependable Great Eat that includes a choice of two pastas or two meats garnished with vegetables or a salad, and fruit or lemon *sorbetto*. If you are going à la carte, the menu has all the popular icons of Roman cuisine served in generous portions and always includes pizza and a dozen or more pastas. No matter what you order for your meal, be sure to ask for an order of the house pizza bread, which comes to the table in a puffy, hot round (if you are not careful, it will be gone before your first course appears!). The house wine is fine.

BUCCONE (6)
Via di Rippeta, 19/20

TELEPHONE
06 361 2154

The modest business card says, "Buccone sells wine, liquors, champagnes, regional foods, and has tastings"—which is true enough in fact but not in spirit. Inside this noble eighteenth-century family coach house is a fabulous *enoteca* filled with wines and spirits, all clearly organized by region and at prices to fit every pocketbook. In addition, they stock an amazing selection of olive oils and balsamic vinegars and serve lunch daily and dinner on Friday and Saturday nights. The menu always includes soup, two or three pastas, vegetables, salads, cold meats and cheeses, and tortes, strudels, and lemon cake for dessert. Wine is served by the bottle or glass, enabling you to sample as you go, and if all you want is a glass or two of wine, you can stop in at the bar any time during the day. Francesco and Vincenzo Buccone speak English and are very knowledgeable and proud of their wines, which can be shipped only in Italy, not abroad.

OPEN
Mon–Sat: wine shop 9 A.M.–8:30 P.M. (until midnight Fri–Sat), lunch 12:30–3 P.M.; also Fri–Sat: dinner 9 P.M.–midnight

CLOSED
Mon–Thur dinner, Sun; 3 weeks in Aug (dates vary)

RESERVATIONS
Advised for dinner

CREDIT CARDS
AE, DC, MC, V

À LA CARTE
12–20€

FIXED-PRICE MENU
None

BREAD & SERVICE CHARGES
None

ENGLISH
Yes, and menu in English

PIZZA RÉ (2)
Via di Ripetta, 14

Pizza Ré has been a hit from the get-go because it delivers what Romans adore: huge Neapolitan wood-fired pizzas with enough toppings to keep things interesting. The location, a block or so from Piazza del Popolo, is open, airy, and pleasant. The floors are tiled with turquoise and yellow inserts, the yellow walls feature murals and blue light fixtures, the tabletops are plain marble, and the food is served with dispatch. Even though every table is crowded to the point of having to share, and the waiting crowd spills ten deep into the street almost every night, you never feel squeezed in or get the bum's rush. On Sunday you will share your Pizza Ré experience with happy, boisterous families, while on weekends after 10 P.M., the scene gets decidedly trendy—women will feel out of place unless they can fit into a strappy size 2 minidress and move around on stiletto heels; men will only need a dark shirt and a cell phone to feel part of the action.

If you decide to start your meal with a salad, I advise you to share it; they arrive on a platter big enough for three. Two of the best are the *caprese,* made with *mozzarella di bufala,* and the *saporita,* with spinach, mushrooms, nuts, cherry tomatoes, and Parmesan cheese. All of the thirty-six pizzas almost fall off the plate—you will think you can't finish more than a slice or two, but you will be surprised. They are light and oh so easy to eat. You can also get grilled meats, including a hamburger, but for best results, stick with the pizza program.

TELEPHONE
06 321 1468

OPEN
Daily: lunch 12:45–3:30 P.M., dinner 7:30 P.M.–midnight

CLOSED
Never

RESERVATIONS
Essential for dinner

CREDIT CARDS
AE, DC, MC, V

À LA CARTE
Pizzas from 8€, 3-course meal 20–25€

FIXED-PRICE MENU
Lunch only: 7.50€, choose between five pizzas, the daily pasta, any salad, or a hamburger; water, beer, or soda included

BREAD & SERVICE CHARGES
Bread 1.50€ at dinner, service discretionary

ENGLISH
Yes, and menu in English

Piazza di Spagna (Spanish Steps) and Via Condotti

The 138 steps in the Piazza di Spagna were built from 1723 to 1725 to join the piazza with the important places above it, including the Villa Medici and the Church of Santa Trinità dei Monti. In May the steps are banked by potted azaleas, and throughout the year, they serve as resting grounds for an international collection of lounge lizards, who hang out here hoping for some action. The view from the top over the roofs of Rome is worth the climb, but the view from Via Condotti looking up the steps is equally beautiful. The streets leading to the piazza are lined with expensive boutique shops, especially the Via Condotti, one of the city's premier shopping streets.

RESTAURANTS

INDOOR/OUTDOOR MARKETS

(¢) indicates a Cheap Eat

Restaurants

ARANCIO D'ORO (27)
Via Monte d'Oro, 17

TELEPHONE
06 686 5026
OPEN
Mon–Sat: lunch 12:30–3 P.M., dinner 7:30–11:30 P.M.
CLOSED
Sun; July and August

Located near the small daily antiques market on the Piazza Borghese, this typical trattoria is a popular lunchtime rendezvous for the area's many businesspeople. In the evening, when the mood slows down, it is filled with residents and a stray tourist or two. Arancio d'Oro and its cousin, Settimio all'Arancio (see page 122), are owned by the Cialfi family, and both are equally well known for their friendly hospitality and good food at realistic prices. The only time I have seen them fall a little short is on major holidays (such as Christmas or New Year's Day), when other restaurants are closed. The help and the kitchen staff operate on a limited basis during these holiday times, and this is reflected in the food and service, which can be mediocre. At all other times, you will be tempted with pastas in creamy sauces, sizzling platters of grilled meats, fresh fish every day, pizza at night, and a lemon mousse dessert you will wish was twice as big.

BELTRAMME DA CESARETTO FIASCHETTERIA (20)
Via della Croce, 39

I cannot claim to have discovered this uncut gem, because it has been a household name for more than a century. It is now a national monument, and not much has changed since it opened in 1879. There are still just seven tables with forty place settings. In the 1960s, it was the hangout of important painters, actors, and poets, as well as the scriptwriters for *La Dolce Vita,* which was conceived over long lunches at the back tables. The restaurant is located on an interesting shopping street that has everything from fishmongers, flower stalls, and fancy bakeries to luxurious lingerie shops and trendy leather boutiques. It doesn't stand out as a flashy spot; in fact, the only indicators you will see at this address are the word *Fiaschetteria* positioned at the top of the building and the line outside waiting to get in. The present mix of diners figures into the restaurant's continuing success. At lunchtime, regulars sit at shared tables with napkins around their necks, earnestly downing their food and wine. At night, it consists mostly of couples who live nearby and a few smart visitors who have been tipped off to some of the only affordable food in this expensive enclave of Rome. All is presided over by a humorless owner who sits in the back, chain smokes, and gets up only to serve an occasional plate of food.

While it is a national monument, this is no health-food sanctuary for the calorie conscious. So put all Puritan thoughts aside and delve uninhibited into an outrageously rich fettuccine with veal or mushroom sauce, rabbit in white wine, or a filling pork chop. The basic menu stays about the same, but watch for the daily handwritten specials, which reflect seasonally fresh choices. Desserts are entirely forgettable.

RESERVATIONS
Advised for dinner

CREDIT CARDS
AE, DC, MC, V

À LA CARTE
Pizza 6.50–9€, 3-course meals 24–28€

FIXED-PRICE MENU
None

BREAD & SERVICE CHARGES
Bread 1€, service included

ENGLISH
Yes, and menu in English

TELEPHONE
None

OPEN
Mon–Sat: lunch 12:30–3 P.M., dinner 7:30–11 P.M.

CLOSED
Sun; 2 days at Christmas and New Year's

RESERVATIONS
Not accepted

CREDIT CARDS
None

À LA CARTE
28–35€

FIXED-PRICE MENU
None

BREAD & SERVICE CHARGES
Bread 2€ (includes bottle of mineral water), service included, but tips appreciated

ENGLISH
Yes

CENTRO MACROBIOTO ITALIANO (31)
Via della Vite, 14 (Third Floor)

TELEPHONE
06 679 2509

OPEN
Mon–Fri: lunch 12:30–3 P.M.,
dinner 7:30–11 P.M.; Sat: dinner
7:30–11 P.M.

CLOSED
Sat lunch, Sun; Aug

RESERVATIONS
Required for the monthly
international evening, otherwise
advised for dinner

CREDIT CARDS
MC, V

À LA CARTE
Lunch 8–10€, dinner 15–18€
(vegetarian), 25€ (fish)

FIXED-PRICE MENU
Vegetarian: 14€, 2 courses,
water or tea; international
dinner: 26–28€, includes
everything but drinks

BREAD & SERVICE CHARGES
Bread 1.10€, service included;
1€ lunch surcharge for visitors

ENGLISH
Yes

Serious vegetarians in Rome all know about Centro Macrobioto Italiano, the first macrobiotic center in Italy, which is reached via either four long flights of steep stairs or a white-knuckled trip in a creaking elevator. For lunch, you can either eat here or take your meal with you. At dinner, it becomes a fish restaurant, and there is no takeout.

The center is run by Aloma, a dedicated vegetarian who believes that not only what you eat but how you eat is important. She is assisted by her mother, who makes the desserts. All the food is made with organic products and contains no animal fat or eggs. The lunch menu offers something for every type of vegetarian, including vegans. Macrobiotic grain casseroles, steamed veggie plates, and a variety of salads and interesting breads are offered, as well as yogurt shakes, natural ice creams (made here between May and September), fresh fruit, vegetable juices, biologic wines, and organic beer. In the evening, only fresh fish and seasonal vegetable plates are served. Once a month a particular country is honored, with native food, dance, and music (reservations are required; please phone for the next date).

Because the center is a private organization, membership is required. If you are a resident of Rome, it costs 5€ per year to belong. Visitors are allowed to eat here for lunch by paying a 1€ surcharge; however, at dinner this fee is waived.

IL MARGUTTA RISTORARTE (8)
Via Margutta, 118

TELEPHONE
06 3265 0577

INTERNET
www.ilmargutta.it

OPEN
Daily: brunch 12:30–3:30 P.M.,
dinner 7:30–11:30 P.M.

CLOSED
Aug (dates vary)

RESERVATIONS
Advised, especially for Sat and
Sun brunch

CREDIT CARDS
AE, DC, MC, V

À LA CARTE
Dinner only: 30–45€

This popular upmarket vegetarian restaurant has been serving stylishly health-conscious Romans for a quarter century. There is an open, airy feel to the two rooms, with their black leather banquettes and cushioned wicker armchairs and their vivid orange walls showcasing changing exhibitions of contemporary art. Every day for brunch, guests are invited to help themselves from the picturesque selection of salads, pastas, vegetables, and grain dishes, plus one or two soups, and, of course, dessert. The price includes all this plus bread, water, juice, and the service charge. Wine is extra.

In the evening there is only table service. The lights are turned down, the candles are lit, and the mood becomes relaxed and quite romantic. One of the best choices at this time is the *menu degustazione,* which is served only if everyone at the table orders it. For the price it is a Great Eat value, as it includes an apéritif, salad, a choice of three vegetarian main courses, and dessert. Depending on the season, you might start with an artichoke and couscous salad, then a *millefoglie* of vegetables subtly seasoned with ginger and soy, and for dessert, a white chocolate mousse with a fresh strawberry sauce. Otherwise, in late winter look for the grilled vegetable terrine topped with buffalo mozzarella or the delicate eggplant flan highlighted with tahini sauce and mint. Pastas play an important role, as do hearty soups and colorful salads. But save room for the Parmesan crust filled with steamed baby vegetables, the deep-fried vegetables and cheeses served with interesting sauces, or the crispy fried artichokes sitting on a bed of polenta with a mild cream sauce of Jerusalem artichokes. Desserts hold their own, with the brownie topped with vanilla ice cream and chocolate sauce, a pear and almond tart with custard and almond ice cream, and a simple and refreshing orange cream served with sesame cookies and sprinkled with candied orange slivers.

FIXED-PRICE MENU
Brunch: Mon–Sat: "Green Brunch Buffet" 15€, Sun and holidays: "Festivity Brunch Buffet" 25€; dinner: *menù degustazione,* 38€, apéritif, 3 courses, bread and service included

BREAD & SERVICE CHARGES
Bread 3€; service included for brunch, discretionary for dinner

ENGLISH
Yes, and menu in English

PASTICCERIA D'ANGELO (¢, 22)
Via della Croce, 30

For power snacking or lunching, the Pasticceria d'Angelo in the heart of Rome's premier shopping district is a must. It is open from 7:30 A.M. until 9 P.M., with continuous service from the bar and pastry counter and lunch service from 12:30 P.M. until 3 P.M. It's a good place to start the day with a quick cappuccino and warm roll or other tantalizing sugary pastry made in their kitchen. Later on, between shopping sprints, you can order lunch from the cafeteria line, where the daily offerings include assorted antipasti, salads, soups, pastas, and meats. The nice thing about eating here is that you can either have just a bowl of soup or indulge in a four-course blowout if you are stoking up for heavy-duty afternoon shopping. Freshly made sandwiches, pizza slices, and all the usual drinks are also available, but these must be eaten standing at one of the bar tables in front or the price will double because you are sitting down and being served. If you are on the run, ask to have your order wrapped to go: *"Da portare via."*

TELEPHONE
06 678 2556

OPEN
Daily: bar and pastries 7 A.M.– 9 P.M., lunch 12:30–3 P.M.

CLOSED
Never

RESERVATIONS
Not necessary

CREDIT CARDS
AE, DC, MC, V

À LA CARTE
Cafeteria: 7–12€, pastries from 1.25€, sandwiches from 1.85€

FIXED-PRICE MENU
None

BREAD & SERVICE CHARGES
None

ENGLISH
Limited, but ordering is easy

PIZZERIA AL LEONCINO (¢, 29)
Via del Leoncino, 28

TELEPHONE
06 687 6306
OPEN
Mon–Tues, Thur–Fri: lunch
1–2:30 P.M., dinner 7 P.M.–
midnight; Sat–Sun: dinner
7 P.M.–midnight
CLOSED
Sat–Sun for lunch, Wed; Aug
RESERVATIONS
Not necessary
CREDIT CARDS
None
À LA CARTE
6–10€
FIXED-PRICE MENU
None
BREAD & SERVICE CHARGES
None
ENGLISH
Limited, but menu in English

Look for pizza, pizza, and more pizza at Al Leoncino, a knotty-pine pizzeria with Formica tabletops and hooks around the walls to hold winter coats. The service is fast, the pizzas are inexpensive, the ambience is as informal as it gets, and the place is popular. What more can any Great Eater ask? The hardworking pizza chefs, wearing Fruit-of-the-Loom undershirts, cook crisp-crust creations in the wood-fired oven in full view of the diners. Romans know their pizza, so when it is good and cheap, expect to wait, especially here, as few other pizzerias in the area are open for lunch. The drinkable house wine sells for around 6€ a half-liter.

RE DEGLI AMICI (21)
Via della Croce, 33B

TELEPHONE
06 679 5380, 06 678 2555
OPEN
Daily: lunch 12:30–2:30 P.M.,
light meals 3–7 P.M., dinner
7:30–11 P.M.
CLOSED
Never
RESERVATIONS
Advised for dinner
CREDIT CARDS
AE, DC, MC, V
À LA CARTE
28–32€, pizza from 8€, other
light meals 8–10€
FIXED-PRICE MENU
None
BREAD & SERVICE CHARGES
Bread 1.50€, service included
ENGLISH
Yes

This five-room restaurant, run by friendly Luigi for thirty years, is a Roman institution with orange-and-white tablecloths, murals on the ceiling, local artists' works lining the walls, and brash waiters racing about madly. The classic trattoria cooking offers multiple-choice self-service antipasti, a full complement of pastas, succulent grilled meats, and wood-fired pizzas (for both lunch and dinner) to hungry guests. Re Degli Amici also upholds the long-standing Roman tradition of serving a particular dish on certain days of the week. On Tuesday and Friday, fresh fish are the specials. On Thursday, you can count on gnocchi; Saturday is tripe. Sometimes these dishes and other daily specials are not on the menu, so be sure and ask about them. Lasagne is baked daily. A big bonus for many Great Eaters is that you can select your entire meal from the beautiful antipasti buffet, or order just a first or second plate, along with maybe a salad to start or a dessert to finish, and not suffer from a grumpy waiter who expects you to order the works. They are also open in the afternoon for light meals, such as a plate of antipasti, pizza, or lasagne.

RISTORANTE MARIO (30)
Via della Vite, 55

No one ever comes to pick and nibble at Mario's, a typical Tuscan-style trattoria with whitewashed walls, raffia-covered chairs, bottles of Chianti on the tables, and service that ranges from friendly and attentive to rather slow, but with a trusty Chianti at hand, who cares? For almost fifty years it has been run by the Mariani family, and it's a popular eating destination for both Romans and visitors. I think it is fine for lunch but best for dinner, when there is a crowded, happy atmosphere. Because of the crunch during this prime time, always arrive with a dinner reservation.

This is definitely the place to sample classic Tuscan fare, including *ribollita,* a heavy bread-thickened soup, and the famous *bistecca alla Fiorentina,* a big steak rubbed with olive oil and herbs and grilled very rare. Other dishes to consider are the braised beef with polenta, any of the daily specials, and (when in season) the wild boar and pheasant. Your wine, of course, should be a bottle of the house Chianti Classico. For dessert, I recommend zeroing in on the tiramisù, a liqueur-soaked layering of cake, Marsala wine, espresso, and creamy mascarpone cheese.

TELEPHONE
06 678 3818

OPEN
Mon–Sat: lunch 12–3 P.M., dinner 7–11 P.M.

CLOSED
Sun; Aug

RESERVATIONS
Strongly advised

CREDIT CARDS
AE, DC, MC, V

À LA CARTE
35–40€

FIXED-PRICE MENU
None

BREAD & SERVICE CHARGES
Bread 2€, service included

ENGLISH
Yes, and menu in English

RISTORANTE NINO (26)
Via Borgognona, 11

Despite its prime location in boutique central, Nino is a fashion-resistant restaurant that has not changed its interior, staff, or traditional Roman cooking . . . nor, by the looks of things, does it have any intention of ever doing so. You can easily recognize the owner—dressed in a coat and tie and sitting by the cash register reading a newspaper, yet always keeping an eagle eye on the hourly take. Patrons are seated at white-draped tables in a dark wood-paneled room with wrought-iron coat hooks along the walls. If possible, consult the Italian menu, because the one in English leaves out the daily specials, and these are definitely the dishes to order. Here you will find such dishes as risotto loaded with shellfish, fettuccini with truffles or fresh artichokes, *orecchiette* with a light, buttery broccoli sauce, roast chicken with potatoes, wild hare, wild boar, liver with polenta, grilled scampi, and stewed cod with tomatoes and sliced potatoes. The house dessert is *castagnaccio,* a cake made with chestnut flour, pine nuts, almonds, raisins, and candied fruits. The final tally? The service is professional and correct, the food consistently well-prepared, and the bill fair, all vital ingredients for a Great Eat in Rome.

TELEPHONE
06 679 5676

OPEN
Mon–Sat: lunch 12:30–3 P.M., dinner 7:30–11 P.M.

CLOSED
Sun; Aug

RESERVATIONS
Essential

CREDIT CARDS
AE, DC, MC, V

À LA CARTE
35–40€

FIXED-PRICE MENU
None

BREAD & SERVICE CHARGES
Bread 2€, service included

ENGLISH
Yes, and menu in English

RISTORANTE "34" (23)
Via Mario de' Fiori, 34

TELEPHONE
06 679 5091
INTERNET
www.webeco.it/al34
OPEN
Tues–Sun: lunch 12:30–3 P.M.,
dinner 7–11 P.M.
CLOSED
Mon; Aug 6–28
RESERVATIONS
Essential, especially for dinner
CREDIT CARDS
AE, DC, MC, V
À LA CARTE
30–38€
FIXED-PRICE MENU
"Oscar" del Gambero Rosso and
Menu "Roma": 35€, appetizer,
3 courses; Menu "Syrenuse":
40€, fish for every course and
sorbetto; both include salad,
wine, water, coffee, and bread
charge
BREAD & SERVICE CHARGES
Bread 1€, service included
ENGLISH
Yes, and menu in English

Popular, crowded, and romantic, Al 34 was voted "Best Value Trattoria" in its price category by American Express cardholders in Rome. I am not surprised—it is a wonderful restaurant. Reservations are essential for both lunch and dinner; the best time to make them for in the evening is 9 or 9:30 P.M. If you eat much earlier, you will be dining with other tourists, and any later could have you standing in the aisles waiting for your table to clear. The cozy, wood-beamed interior is illuminated at night with ceramic table lights. Both dried and fresh flowers add a nice touch, as does the collection of soup tureens and lids displayed near the entrance to the kitchen. The food is typically Roman, and for variety and sheer elegance of dishes offered, the three fixed-price menus are, without question, the best high-class Great Eating deals in Rome.

Waiters in bow ties and black vests serve guests big bowls of soup, the best spinach salad in the area, pastas with imaginative toppings, well-executed meat dishes (including Argentine Angus beef), and fresh seasonal vegetables. For dessert, any of the homemade cakes are recommended, especially the chocolate almond torte or the tiramisù.

SETTIMIO ALL'ARANCIO (28)
Via dell' Arancio, 50

TELEPHONE
06 687 6119
OPEN
Mon–Sat: lunch 12:30–3 P.M.,
dinner 7–11:30 P.M.
CLOSED
Sun
RESERVATIONS
Advised
CREDIT CARDS
AE, DC, MC, V
À LA CARTE
25–35€
BREAD & SERVICE CHARGES
Bread 1€, service included
ENGLISH
Yes, and menu in English

Settimio all'Arancio is another trattoria run by the Cialfi family. The other is Arancio d'Oro (see page 116). The mood here is exactly right for a neighborhood dining establishment, with wholesome, well-prepared food served in two small whitewashed dining rooms with rustic furnishings. In summer dining moves to one of the tables on the street, shielded from traffic by a wall of planter boxes filled with trees and shrubs.

For your appetizer, go for the *fritto misto Arancio,* an assortment of fried zucchini, olives, and artichokes; for your pasta dish, try the *calamarata con spigola e zucchine* (macaroni with sea bass and zucchini) or the *orecchiette con broccoletti.* On Tuesday and Friday, fresh fish is always available, and anytime you can count on tender roast lamb or a he-man Chianti beefsteak for your main course. Popular desserts include the lemon mousse or tiramisù. The menus at both places are virtually the same, with an impressive number of interesting wines.

TRATTORIA OTELLO ALLA CONCORDIA (19)
Via della Croce, 81

The off-street Otello alla Concordia features a vine-covered garden with a dramatic fruit and vegetable display in an ancient Roman bathtub. A restaurant has existed on this site since 1750, and since 1948 this trattoria has been run by the Caproicci family, who have kept it a neighborhood favorite due to their reliable, good-value food. The wide-ranging menu covers Roman cuisine nicely and includes a series of handwritten seasonal and daily specials. Unfortunately, the person writing the specials on the Italian daily menu flunked penmanship, but you should be able to decipher most of it. In early spring, start with prosciutto and fresh melon or a linguine tossed with shrimp and arugula. The daily main courses include tripe, roast pork, veal, lamb, and sausage, all fixed almost any way you want. Fresh fish is served on Tuesday, Wednesday, Friday, and Saturday, and wines from Castelli Romani and Tuscany are poured with your meal.

TELEPHONE
06 679 1178

OPEN
Mon–Sat: lunch 12:30–3 P.M., dinner 7:30–11:30 P.M.

CLOSED
Sun; 2 weeks in Jan or Feb (dates vary)

RESERVATIONS
Advised

CREDIT CARDS
AE, DC, MC, V

À LA CARTE
24–30€

FIXED-PRICE MENU
22€, 2 courses, potato or salad, fruit or cheese, wine or water

BREAD & SERVICE CHARGES
Bread 1.50€, service included

ENGLISH
Enough, and menu in English

VINI E BUFFET (32)
Piazza della Torretta, 60

"This is a place for people; I am here for the neighborhood," states Victorio, the hospitable owner of this trattoria, and he has indeed been here for his devotees for better than a decade. Inside, the twelve white-tiled tables feature grape-accented centers; prints on the stark-white walls carry the grape theme further. A seasonal menu changes four times a year and lists appetizers, *crostini,* main-course salads, cheeses, and cold plates. Wine is sold by the bottle, and you pay only for what you drink; if you want to experiment with several of Victorio's regional Italian wines, you can order by the glass. This is a good watering hole to keep in mind if you are between the Spanish Steps and Piazza Navona and want to escape from the more touristy wine bars in the area.

TELEPHONE
06 687 1445

OPEN
Mon–Sat: lunch 12:30–3 P.M., dinner 7:30–11 P.M.

CLOSED
Sun; 4–5 days around Aug 15

RESERVATIONS
Accepted for dinner only

CREDIT CARDS
None

À LA CARTE
15–18€ with glass of wine

FIXED-PRICE MENU
None

BREAD & SERVICE CHARGES
Bread 1.50€, service included

ENGLISH
Yes, and menu in English

Piazza Navona and the Pantheon

Piazza Navona is the most theatrical square of Baroque Rome. It is where the aristocracy rubbed shoulders with the populace at the games and where celebrations were held on the site of Roman Domitian's stadium. In the center is Bernini's towering *Fountain of the Four Rivers,* representing four of the world's great rivers: the Nile, the Danube, the Ganges, and the Plata. At the south end is Bernini's fountain depicting a Moor fighting with a dolphin and at the north end is his fountain of Neptune, the Roman god of the seas. On the west side is Borromini's masterpiece, the Church of Sant' Agnese in Agone. Serving as Rome's center stage, the impressive piazza is ringed with *caffés* and is filled night and day with residents, tourists, and hawkers.

The Pantheon, with its majestic marble columns, original bronze doors, and domed interior, is unchanged from two thousand years ago, when it was erected by Hadrian. It is the only perfectly preserved ancient building in Rome and a reminder of the city's glorious past.

RESTAURANTS

GELATERIAS

($) indicates a Big Splurge

(¢) indicates a Cheap Eat

Restaurants

ANTICA TAVERNA (47)
Via Monte Giordano, 12

Antica Taverna is just what you'd expect in a Roman trattoria: mildly uncomfortable seating, closely packed tables, a lively crowd of regulars, and a laid-back wait-staff sporting Levi's and T-shirts. Don't bother with the plasticized menu; concentrate on the two hand-scribbled specials written on white notepaper inside. The mildly robust food is meant to be enjoyed, and you are expected to keep the orders rolling. Start by sharing a plate of *crostini* or a *caprese* salad (tomato, mozzarella, and basil) and a pasta, perhaps penne with salmon or ravioli with ricotta cheese and nuts. This leaves room for a succulent roast chicken or rabbit served with potatoes and a plate of grilled vegetables with razor-thin slices of eggplant, zucchini, peppers, and radicchio. If you can entertain dessert thoughts, think *torta della nonna* (a light cream cake), or walk over to Piazza Navona and indulge in a *tartufo* at I Tre Scalini (see page 129).

TELEPHONE
06 6880 1053

OPEN
Wed–Mon: noon–midnight, continuous service

CLOSED
Tues

RESERVATIONS
Essential for dinner

CREDIT CARDS
AE, DC, MC, V

À LA CARTE
25–30€

FIXED-PRICE MENU
None

BREAD & SERVICE CHARGES
Bread 1€, no service charge

ENGLISH
Enough

CASA BLEVE (58)
Via del Teatro Valle 48/49

Whenever I am in the neighborhood and want a bite to eat, I head for this stylish *enoteca,* where I can depend on having a light meal and a glass or two of excellent wine. It is a handsome place, with a stunning bar in front and a huge room beyond supported by columns, arches, and a stained-glass ceiling. No hot food is served; instead, there is a large lunch and evening buffet, filled with artistically arranged salads, vegetables, assorted Italian cheeses, cold meats, seafood, and rich desserts. At lunch, it attracts a business crowd of men in Brioni suits and women in Prada. In the evening, there doesn't seem to be much schmoozing among the oh-so-stylish thirty- and fortysomethings who have earmarked this as their early evening watering hole.

TELEPHONE
06 686 5970

INTERNET
www.casableve.it

OPEN
Tues–Sat: lunch buffet 10:30 A.M.–3 P.M., evening buffet 6–8 P.M. (Wed–Fri till 10 P.M.)

CLOSED
Sun–Mon

RESERVATIONS
Not necessary

CREDIT CARDS
AE, DC, MC, V

À LA CARTE
25–30€, includes a glass of wine

FIXED-PRICE MENU
None

BREAD & SERVICE CHARGES
No bread charge, service included

ENGLISH
Yes

DA FRANCESCO (49)
Piazza del Fico, 29 (corner of Via della Fossa and Via del Corallo)

TELEPHONE
06 686 4009
OPEN
Mon, Wed–Sun: lunch noon–
3 P.M., dinner 7 P.M.–1 A.M.;
Tues: dinner 7 P.M.–1 A.M.
CLOSED
Tues lunch
RESERVATIONS
Preferred for dinner
CREDIT CARDS
None
À LA CARTE
Pizza 10–12€, 3-course meal
15–20€
FIXED-PRICE MENU
None
BREAD & SERVICE CHARGES
Bread 1€, no service charge
ENGLISH
Usually limited

"What are they giving away?" my friend asked as we strolled by this local favorite across a narrow street from a heavy-duty biker bar where regulars and hangers-on play chess in the late afternoons. At lunchtime Da Francesco boasts wall-to-wall people inside and almost as many milling outside waiting to get in. The chef/owner prepares huge portions of food at fair prices in a lively atmosphere—proving that the public will support a good thing. His food packs a punch, starting with fettuccine covered in a mushroom cream sauce, *penne all'arrabbiata,* or *tonnarelli* with artichokes. Meatballs in tangy tomato sauce, pork stewed in white wine, or ham and beans will keep you going for hours. At night, everyone is back for the antipasti table and the wood-fired pizza bursting with tomatoes, mozzarella, and the usual toppings. It is all very informal, with paper-covered tables and wine poured into drinking glasses by prompt, if inelegant, waiters. Note that pizza is served for dinner only.

DA GINO (35)
Vicolo Rosini, 4 (a narrow alley off of Piazza del Parlamento)

TELEPHONE
06 687 3434
OPEN
Mon–Sat: lunch 1–2:45 P.M.,
dinner 8–10:30 P.M.
CLOSED
Sun; Aug
RESERVATIONS
Not accepted
CREDIT CARDS
Not accepted
À LA CARTE
25–30€, includes house wine
FIXED-PRICE MENU
None
BREAD & SERVICE CHARGES
Bread 1€, service included
ENGLISH
Yes

Da Gino opens for lunch at 1 P.M., and fifteen minutes later, it is SRO for those who don't know to arrive before the doors open. The same mob scene plays again every night with diners streaming in and still packing the two dining rooms at 10 P.M., even on a so-called slow Monday night. There is a very general menu that everyone totally ignores. Instead, they listen intently to the waiter, who rattles off in rapid-fire Italian what's cooking on that particular day. Listen for *zucchine ripiene* (meat-stuffed zucchini), *pasta e ceci* (pasta and chickpea soup), *coniglio al vino bianco* (hearty rabbit in a white wine sauce), osso buco (veal shanks), pastas with rich meat sauces, and delicious fresh fruit *crostini.* Wines are reasonably priced to encourage everyone to drink plenty.

FRATERNA DOMUS (¢, 36)
Via dell' Cancello, 6 (at Via di Monte Brianzo, 62; close to Piazza Nicosia)

TELEPHONE
06 6880 2727
OPEN
Mon–Wed, Fri–Sun: lunch
seating 1 P.M., dinner seating
7:30 P.M.

For an inspiring Great Eat in Rome, consider communal dining, family-style, at Fraterna Domus, a Holy Hotel run by nuns. In addition to providing very nice Great Sleep accommodations (see *Great Sleeps Italy*), the exceptionally friendly and welcoming nuns serve lunch and dinner to both guests and nonguests every day but Thursday. Since each meal has only a single seating, reservations are required. The smells coming from the spotless kitchen are your first signal that the simply prepared food is going to be wonderful, and you can trust me, it is. There is only one set-price menu, so make sure you ask what they are serving if you have dietary restrictions. The menu includes a pasta or soup, main course, garnish, salad, and fruit. Wine is extra. They also offer special student prices.

If you have time, attend mass in their lovely thousand-year-old chapel. Even though the sisters received church funds to expand and improve their bed and breakfast and dining operations for the 2000 Holy Year Jubilee, no money has been forthcoming for the badly needed restoration of this magnificent chapel. The sisters told me they are praying for a miracle . . . maybe you can help.

CLOSED
Thur

RESERVATIONS
Required

CREDIT CARDS
MC, V

À LA CARTE
None

FIXED-PRICE MENU
14€, 3 courses, bread and service included

BREAD & SERVICE CHARGES
Included

ENGLISH
Yes

IL BACARO ($, 40)
Via degli Spagnoli, 27

I am always happy to stumble upon places like Il Bacaro. Hidden on a back street just far enough from tourist central to keep it locally based, it caters to a well-dressed, sophisticated clientele who know and appreciate good food. It is open for lunch and dinner, with two reservation-only seatings for dinner at either 8 or 10 P.M. Inside is a small, understated room with a bar in one corner and rather loud music playing over it all, while outside is an umbrella-shaded terrace with fourteen tables.

No matter what time of the year you are here, or where you sit, you can depend on an imaginative meal, well-executed and politely served. Start with the house salad, a pretty array of thin slices of zucchini and fresh Parmesan on a bed of fancy greens, garnished with finely chopped carrots and fennel and dressed with a light vinaigrette. The pastas are all made here and presented in different combinations. I thought the *orecchiette alle erbe aromatiche con patate, fagiolini e broccoli* (handmade pasta tossed with herbs, potatoes, and string beans) was a surprisingly light mix that worked well, as did the *rigatoncini con funghi, asparagi e ricotta salata* (pasta with mushrooms, fresh asparagus, and salted ricotta cheese). The meat and fish dishes are prepared with simple respect and without sauces that mask the real flavor of the food. Try the *scaloppe di vitella con pomodorini Pachino e ruchetta* (veal escallops with cherry tomatoes and arugula). Also delicious is the *carpaccio caldo di manzo con radicchio, cicorietta e tartufo*

TELEPHONE
06 686 4110

OPEN
Mon–Fri: lunch 12:30–2:45 P.M., dinner two seatings, at 8 and 10 P.M.; Sat: dinner two seatings, at 8 and 10 P.M.

CLOSED
Sat lunch, Sun; Jan 15–1st week Feb, Aug 15–23

RESERVATIONS
Advised for lunch, required for dinner

CREDIT CARDS
DC, MC, V

À LA CARTE
40–45€

BREAD & SERVICE CHARGES
No bread charge, service discretionary

ENGLISH
Yes, and menu in English

(hot, rare beef slices dressed with a mix of red lettuce, chicory and truffles). The fish is as innovatively conceived as the rest of the menu. If you like raw fish, the *carpaccio di marlin affumicato in salsa vinaigrette* (smoked marlin with a viniagrette sauce) is an unusual choice.

And please don't forget dessert! The winner here is the *millefoglie caldo sbriciolato con crema pasticcera*—a hot crumb cake with rich cream that always tops the dessert list, no matter what the season. The house wine is realistically priced by the bottle, or you can order other vintages by the glass.

IL DRAPPO ($, 59)
Vicolo del Malpasso, 9

People often ask me to list my favorite restaurants in the cities that the Great Eats series covers, and it is always a tough call. In Rome, Il Drappo is definitely high on the list because it has everything I am looking for when dining out to celebrate a special occasion. Small, beautifully appointed, and very romantic, Il Drappo offers gracious service and delicious food, which is prepared by the delightful Sardinian owner, Valentina, who has been doing the honors in the kitchen for thirty years. The two-room restaurant is draped from floor to ceiling in a soft, billowing cream-colored fabric, creating the feeling of being in a magical tent. A series of Erte prints (one for every letter of the alphabet) adds a note of whimsy. In back is a secluded garden—an intimate candlelit choice on a summer evening. Each beautifully set table features fresh seasonal flowers and damask linens. Most important, however, is Valentina's generosity of spirit and hospitality, which are reflected in perfectly executed Sardinian specialties that warm your soul.

For the best Sardinian experience, let Valentina prepare her fixed-price dinner menu based on the daily specials, which includes everything from appetizer to dessert (wine is extra). You will start with a basket of warm homemade bread and perhaps one or two of her bite-sized pizzas with tomatoes, a selection of vegetable fritters, or a bowl of Sardinian cream cheese. Next, her gnocchi-like pasta, or spaghetti with either zucchini or asparagus and shrimp, is served in portions that let you later enjoy suckling pig served with black currants, duck with apples, or the most delicious veal meatballs you will ever taste. To end, maybe there will be her apple cake, or almond cookies soaked in a coffee-cream sauce. You will, of course, drink only Sardinian wines with your meal, and end with a welcome *digestif*.

TELEPHONE
06 687 7365
INTERNET
www.ildrappo.com
OPEN
Mon–Sat: lunch 12:30–3 P.M., dinner 7:30–11 P.M.
CLOSED
Sun; Aug
RESERVATIONS
Essential for dinner
CREDIT CARDS
AE, DC, MC, V
À LA CARTE
40–45€
FIXED-PRICE MENU
38€, 4 courses; drinks extra
BREAD & SERVICE CHARGES
No bread charge (it is a menu item), service discretionary
ENGLISH
Yes, and menu in English

I TRE SCALINI (51)
Piazza Navona, 28/32

For a *tartufo* to die for, I Tre Scalini is the place. It is big and barnlike, with a long bar, a dreary tearoom upstairs, and lots of tables on the Piazza Navona. For the uniniti-ated, *tartufo* is a calorie blowout consisting of chocolate ice cream and cherries covered with a bittersweet chocolate casing and swathed in whipped cream. Smart Great Eaters will order theirs standing at the bar, then nab a bench seat on the piazza and people-watch while eating, since it will cost almost double to have it served at a table. If you do sit outside, tell whoever seats you that you are just having a *tartufo,* or you could be seated in the dining section, where ordering just dessert would not be acceptable. Indeed, full lunches and dinners are served, but they are basically high-priced tourist fare that I cannot recommend.

A word of warning: Don't be fooled by imitations and mistakenly go to Al Tre Tartufi next door.

TELEPHONE
06 6880 1996

OPEN
Mon–Tues, Thur–Sun: 9 A.M.–midnight

CLOSED
Wed; Jan, and sometimes in Feb

RESERVATIONS
Not necessary

CREDIT CARDS
None

À LA CARTE
Tartufo at the bar 4€, at a table 6.50€

FIXED-PRICE MENU
Dining here is not recommended

BREAD & SERVICE CHARGES
None for *tartufo* ordered at bar or to go

ENGLISH
Limited

LA CAMPANA (37)
Vicolo della Campana, 18 (at Via della Scrofa and Piazza Nicosia)

It is nice to occasionally enjoy starched-linen table-cloths with proper table settings and polite service by an accomplished Italian waitstaff in rooms filled with well-tailored diners. You will find this, along with meals that are excellent value for the money, at La Campana, one of Rome's oldest restaurants.

The servings are big and the food is robust, so I suggest you follow the lead of the regulars and order as you go along. When ordering, pay attention to the paper menu with its list of daily and seasonal specials, not the plasticized one. Start with either the house red or white to sip with the *antipasti misti,* which is big enough to share. Next, try the spicy *spaghetti alla puttanesca* or the fettuccine with butter and mushrooms, if you plan on ordering a second meat or fish course. Otherwise, the *pappardelle con salsa lepre* (wide noodles with hare sauce) or the Thursday gnocchi special are heavy-duty enough to require only a salad or vegetable accompaniment.

The important thing is to save room for dessert. La Campana wants to make sure you do not miss this course and displays most of its seductive offerings on tables by the entrance, resulting in *oohs* and *aahs* of anticipation.

TELEPHONE
06 687 5273, 06 686 7820

OPEN
Tues–Sun: lunch 12:30–3 P.M., dinner 7:30–11 P.M.

CLOSED
Mon; last 2 weeks in Aug

RESERVATIONS
Advised

CREDIT CARDS
MC, V

À LA CARTE
28–38€

FIXED-PRICE MENU
None

BREAD & SERVICE CHARGES
Bread 2€, service included

ENGLISH
Limited

Their version of tarte Tatin is composed of a spongy base covered with glazed apples. It is not too sweet and is laced with just enough cream to give it an interesting edge. If that does not speak to you, surely one of the cakes, tarts, puddings, abundant fruit creations, or a simple dish of gelato topped with wild strawberries will.

LA SCALETTA DEGLI ARTISTI (50)
Via di Santa Maria dell'Anima, 56

TELEPHONE
06 6880 1872
OPEN
Mon–Tues, Thur–Sun: lunch
noon–3:30 P.M., dinner
7–11:30 P.M.
CLOSED
Wed
RESERVATIONS
Advised for dinner
CREDIT CARDS
AE, MC, V
À LA CARTE
26–30€
FIXED-PRICE MENU
Lunch only: 8€, 2 courses,
includes service but not bread
BREAD & SERVICE CHARGES
Bread 1€, service included
ENGLISH
Limited, but menu in English

Around the corner from the tourist glare surrounding Piazza Navona is La Scaletta degli Artisti, a pretty trattoria where the food is hearty and surprisingly well priced. In typical trattoria style, the rather small interior is decorated with a mix of Roman photos, *trompe l'oeil* paintings, and a mural or two. On warm days, the prime tables are those under big umbrellas on the sidewalk terrace. The fixed-price lunch menu may be a cheap eat, but it's a mighty boring one as well. Instead, try to order from the daily specials taped to the menu. Otherwise, traditional starters of prosciutto and melon or dried beef with arugula lead the way to a choice of sixteen pastas, including gnocchi and lasagne. Skip the tripe and order the homemade meatballs in a tomato and basil cream sauce, along with fresh artichokes or roast potatoes for a filling main course. Desserts are limited in number but not in quality. The tiramisù, crème caramel, and *panna cotta* are all made here and are worthwhile endings to a filling Great Eat in Rome.

LILLI (39)
Via Tor di Nona, 23 (at the corner of Via dell' Arco di Parma)

TELEPHONE
06 686 1916
OPEN
Mon–Sat: lunch 1–3 P.M.,
dinner 8–11 P.M.
CLOSED
Sun; Dec 20–Jan 1, one week
mid-Aug (dates vary)
RESERVATIONS
Advised
CREDIT CARDS
AE, DC, MC, V
À LA CARTE
20–25€
FIXED-PRICE MENU
None
BREAD & SERVICE CHARGES
Bread 1.50€, service
discretionary
ENGLISH
Yes

The Ceramicola family runs this small, modest restaurant nestled alongside the river not too far from Piazza Navona. Lilli caters to locals as well as tourists, and in warm weather everyone wants a seat on their pleasant, umbrella-shaded terrace. The stone-tiled, beamed interior has well-spaced tables draped in brown cloths with white overlays. The homespun food is delicious, there is always more than enough on your plate, and the bottom line is reasonable—all of which make this a compelling Great Eat. Depending on the time of year, the daily menu features pasta laced with clams, *penne all'arrabbiata* (short, thick pasta with a hot red sauce), several meat dishes, and the usual salads and veggies. Anytime, you can count on their signature pasta, *rigatoni alla Lilli,* made with tomatoes, Parmesan cheese, black pepper, basil, and butter . . . oh so rich and good. Thursday, gnocchi heads the pasta list, and on Friday, *baccalà* is the fish order of the day. For dessert, why have an orange or an apple when you can dig into their own *torta di crema e pinogli* (cream cake with pine nuts) or *crostata di ricotta,* their cheesecake version.

L'INSALATA RICCA (¢, 57)
Piazza Pasquino, 72

For a description of this restaurant, see page 104. All other information is the same.

TELEPHONE: 06 6830 7881

L'ORSO '80 (38)
Via dell' Orso, 33

Every year all I want for Christmas, besides world peace and a week at my favorite spa, is another great meal at this wonderful trattoria in the heart of old Rome. The restaurant has been owned for years by brothers Alfredo and Memmo and their longtime friend Antonio, the talented chef. They prepare truly memorable food that is guaranteed to ignite even the most jaded palate, and they serve it with gusto.

The restaurant is justly famous for its fabulous antipasti table, and I agree—it is one of the best I have sampled in Italy. You name it and it is here, from seasonal vegetables prepared six different ways to dozens of bowls of fish and shellfish. If you are not careful, you could make this your entire meal; in fact, many people do just this at lunch. Otherwise please save room for one of the homemade pastas, such as the *papparadelle al salmone,* wide, buttery noodles smothered in a creamy salmon sauce, or the house *amatriciana,* made with bacon, tomato, Parmesan, and pecorino cheese. Grilled meats are another specialty, as is the impressive lineup of fresh fish. In the evenings, the wood-fired pizza oven is roaring, turning out a limited but delicious selection of crisp-crust pizzas. After a meal such as this one, dessert hardly seems possible, but I do recommend a bowl of sweet strawberries as the perfect finish.

TELEPHONE
06 686 4904, 06 686 1710

OPEN
Tues–Sun: lunch 1–3:30 P.M., dinner 7:30–11:30 P.M.

CLOSED
Mon; Aug

RESERVATIONS
Essential for dinner

CREDIT CARDS
AE, DC, MC, V

À LA CARTE
Pizza from 6€, full meals 35–40€

FIXED-PRICE MENU
None

BREAD & COVER CHARGES
Bread 1€, service discretionary

ENGLISH
Yes

OSTERIA DELL' INGEGNO (45)
Piazza di Pietra, 45 (off Piazza Colonna)

The Osteria dell' Ingegno is a happening place from the moment it opens for lunch until it closes at midnight. The draw is its huge selection of Italian wines, accompanied by imaginative, monthly-changing dishes to please the varied palates of its savvy clientele. In addition to the summer terrace, there are forty-five seats scattered throughout two rooms, which are highlighted by a collection of fanciful

TELEPHONE
06 678 0662

OPEN
Mon–Sat: lunch 12:30–3 P.M., apéritifs 3:30–7:30 P.M., dinner 7:30 P.M.–midnight

CLOSED
Sun

paintings of Rome. All is overseen by the owner, Pino, who holds court behind the bar, greeting his guests and discussing his wines.

The lunch menu is quite simple in execution and price yet versatile enough to appeal to all appetites. Main dish salads, antipasti platters, pastas, and a handful of grilled meats and fish sum it up. From 3:30 to 7:30 P.M., regulars are huddled along the bar, grazing through the full range of complimentary snacks that come when you order an apéritif. Soup, grilled vegetables with mozzarella, and cheese plates are also available during this time. After happy hour, the candles are lit, the ambience becomes more intimate, and the prices go up. However, ordering a three-course meal is not the call of the evening; instead, share platters of selected Italian cheeses and meats, sample *crostini* made with polenta and topped with blue cheese and walnut fondue, and enjoy fresh salmon marinated in honey, ginger, and citrus. Depending on the season, other dishes might include a risotto with artichokes, leeks, and Castelmango cheese, or crêpes baked with smoked salmon, goat cheese, and green squash. Seafood couscous, a swordfish roll filled with sundried tomatoes and capers, and buffalo steak in a red wine sauce are other popular dishes. For dessert, I recommend the chocolate walnut torte with a ginger-flavored pear sauce, or the tarte Tatin flavored with honey and Amaretto.

PIZZERIA DA BAFFETTO (¢, 55)
Via del Governo Vecchio, 114

In Rome, Pizzeria da Baffetto is synonymous with good pizza, and the line that forms nightly at the front door of this matchbook-size spot attests to this. Seats are hard, long stays are discouraged, and you can expect to share your table. The tiny room isn't much to look at, either: it is dominated by a pizza oven, a menu board on one wall, and a small cash desk. Besides the sizzling pizzas, the only other things on the menu are *bruschetta,* the traditional preparation of grilled bread covered with garlic, basil, and ripe red tomatoes, and *crostini,* toasted bread with mozzarella cheese and a variety of simple toppings.

RESERVATIONS
Accepted for dinner only
CREDIT CARDS
AE, DC, MC, V
À LA CARTE
Lunch: 16–25€, afternoon light meals 9€, dinner 30–40€
FIXED-PRICE MENU
None
BREAD & SERVICE CHARGES
No bread charge, service included
ENGLISH
Yes, and menu in English

TELEPHONE
06 686 1617
OPEN
Daily: dinner 6:30 P.M.–1 A.M.
CLOSED
2 weeks in Aug (dates vary)
RESERVATIONS
Not necessary
CREDIT CARDS
None
À LA CARTE
7–12€
FIXED-PRICE MENU
None
BREAD & SERVICE CHARGES
Included
ENGLISH
Limited

TRATTORIA DA GINO E PIETRO (56)
Corner of Via del Governo Vecchio, 106, and Vicolo Savelli, 3

Your fellow diners will be a mix of visitors and neighborhood regulars at this venerable trattoria, where the service is welcoming and the food consistently dependable. Good luck on wedging your way in for Sunday lunch if you have not called ahead for your table. At other times, play it safe, make a reservation, and get ready for a meal that never hints at being anything remotely trendy but always epitomizes quality. The eye-popping vegetable antipasti display is a good place to begin your meal planning. Add a pasta, *scamorza al prosciutto* (cheese melted over thin slices of prosciutto), or whatever fresh fish is being served, plus *tiramisù della casa,* and you will have had a fairly priced Great Eat, Roman style.

TELEPHONE
06 686 1576

OPEN
Mon–Wed, Fri–Sun: lunch noon–3 P.M., dinner 6:30–11 P.M.

CLOSED
Thur; Aug 1–15

RESERVATIONS
Advised, especially for Sun lunch

CREDIT CARDS
MC, V

À LA CARTE
20–28€

FIXED-PRICE MENU
None

BREAD & SERVICE CHARGES
Bread 1€, service discretionary

ENGLISH
Yes

TRATTORIA DA TONINO AL GOVERNO VECCHIO (¢, 48)
Via del Governo Vecchio, 16/19

If you are looking for unsung budget dining, you have found it. What you won't find is atmosphere or ambience, unless you count the butcher paper on the tables and the old-fashioned Coke machine standing in the corner. As you walk in, the good smells wafting out of the kitchen tell you that this is going to be good, and the crowd confirms it. All pastas, including an excellent *pasta alla carbonara,* are priced at a mere 5€ a plate. Rabbit, roast veal, and a strapping beef stew will set you back only 6€. Veggies at 2.50€ and creamy tiramisù at 2.50€ a pop should send Cheap Eaters colliding as they try to nab a table at this Great Eat in Rome.

TELEPHONE
333 587 0779 (cell)

OPEN
Mon–Sat: lunch 12–3 P.M., dinner 7 P.M.–midnight

CLOSED
Sun; Aug

RESERVATIONS
Not accepted

CREDIT CARDS
None

À LA CARTE
6–15€

FIXED-PRICE MENU
None

BREAD & SERVICE CHARGES
Bread 1€, no service charge

ENGLISH
Limited

TRE ARCHI DA LORETO (46)
Via dei Coronari, 233

Tre Archi is the sort of folksy place people frequent when no one is in the mood to cook, and as such it provides a glimpse into the life of the average Roman citizen. The clientele ranges from families with noisy children to dealers from the many nearby antique shops to gray-haired couples who have staked out regular tables. The inside is neat and utilitarian, with orange tablecloths, a few green

TELEPHONE
06 686 5890

OPEN
Mon–Sat: lunch 12:15–3 P.M., dinner 7 P.M.–midnight

CLOSED
Sun; Aug

RESERVATIONS
Advised for dinner

plants, and a mural on one wall. The sole waiter is a study in efficiency and grace under pressure. The food is simple, standard fare: minestrone soup, pastas with the familiar *ragù,* daily specials, above-average salads, and desserts in the nevermind column. The *menù turistico* is filling and fattening, the house wine is perfectly adequate, and prices are firmly in the affordable category.

Gelaterias

CREMERIA MONTEFORTE (52)
Via Della Rotunda, 22

No matter what the weather, everyone in Rome eats ice cream, and plenty of it. I would, too, if I lived in the same city as Cremeria Monteforte, which dispenses its delicious, natural flavors every day but Monday from a storefront by the Pantheon. It is owned by Pina, who has been making ice cream for thirty years and scooping in this location for the last two decades. If you can't decide between chocolate or walnut *semifreddo,* white chocolate, caramel, zabaglione, or wine custard mousse, or fresh fruit *sorbetto,* you can order a "tasting cone" with little bites of several flavors to see which one you like best. If you really want to gild the lily, ask to have your cone or cup dipped in dark chocolate or topped with a scoop of real whipped cream.

GIOLITTI (41)
Via Uffici del Vicario, 40

Giolitti is an always-crowded Art Nouveau *gelateria* near the Pantheon where generations of the same family have been selling gelato since 1900. It is admittedly not an easy address to find; the best strategy, once you are within a two-block radius, is to look for people eating ice cream. Head in the direction from which they are coming, and you will soon be there. In the early morning, fifteen flavors of ice cream are available, along with cappuccino and a counter full of waist-expanding pastries. On Tuesday through Saturday, light lunches of salads, omelettes, and a few hot dishes are served in a rather old-fashioned dining room. Standing at the bar, you can order a quick sandwich or more pastries. By 2:30 in the afternoon, there is a three-deep crowd ordering cones or dishes from more than fifty-seven revolving varieties of pure gelato. First you pay for the size you want, then you take your order to the counter. There is no real place to sit while eating your ice cream, but it is fun to join the throng standing outside and indulging in the premier people-watching this place always affords.

Piazza Venezia

The majestic Via dei Fori Imperiali links Piazza Venezia to the Colosseum in a six-way traffic circle that is a supreme spectacle of insane Roman driving. The commanding white Vittoriale was built to honor the first king of the united Italy, and it now houses a permanent museum of tapestries, medieval sculpture, silver, and ceramic works. In the front is an equestrian statue of Vittorio Emanuele, whose moustache is three meters long. This is also the home of the eternal flame, Italy's memorial to the unknown soldier.

Restaurants

ANTICA BIRRERIA PERONI (53)
Via di San Marcello, 19

There is no spa cuisine at Birreria Peroni—only hearty, stick-to-your-ribs plates of sausage and beans, beef, pork, and veal that appeal to strong-hearted souls who have put in a hard day's work. Pasta is relegated to a bit player in this cast. With the unbeatable combination of enormous portions and reliable prices, all washed down with tall mugs of beer or prosecco wine, it is no wonder this restaurant has such a following. Unless you arrive early, or go late and run the risk of your favorite dish being sold out, you can expect to stand and wait for a table during the crowded lunch hour. The service is hectic at best, with waiters shouting orders to a harried cashier who somehow keeps it all straight while ringing up everyone's order. Things calm down somewhat at night, but you can still count on sitting mighty close to your neighbor or sharing a table here in one of Rome's oldest restaurants.

TELEPHONE
06 679 5310
INTERNET
www.anticabirreriaperoni.it
OPEN
Mon–Sat: noon–midnight (Fri–Sat till 1:30 A.M.); lunch noon–3:30 P.M., cold food 4–6:30 P.M., dinner 7 P.M.–midnight
CLOSED
Sun; 2 weeks mid-Aug (dates vary)
CREDIT CARDS
AE, DC, MC, V
À LA CARTE
15–18€
FIXED-PRICE MENU
None
BREAD & SERVICE CHARGES
Bread 0.60€, no service charge
ENGLISH
Yes, and menu in English

ENOTECA CORSI (60)
Via del Gesù, 87/88 (off Via del Plebescito)

TELEPHONE
06 679 0821
OPEN
Mon–Fri: lunch noon–3:30 P.M.
CLOSED
Sat–Sun; Aug
RESERVATIONS
Not accepted
CREDIT CARDS
AE, DC, MC, V
À LA CARTE
16–20€
FIXED-PRICE MENU
None
BREAD & SERVICE CHARGES
Bread 1€, service discretionary
ENGLISH
Yes

Enoteca Corsi is a good roll-up-your-sleeves *enoteca* where patrons have been eating and drinking since 1937. It is packed for lunch, which means if you want a seat, you may have to share a table. The waiter tells you what the specials are, but a daily chalkboard menu is also posted inside the front door. The choices are limited and very traditional. The three starters always include a pasta and a soup; the mains feature meaty dishes of roast pork or veal with potatoes, zucchini flowers stuffed with meat or cheese, and *saltimbocca*. Add a salad or fresh vegetable and a few glasses of the house wine, and you will round out this satisfying good-value meal. For a light ending, everyone orders a glass of icy *limoncello* (lemon liqueur) or *cantucci con vin santo* (hard almond cookies dipped in sweet wine).

L'ARCHETTO (54)
Via dell' Archetto, 26

TELEPHONE
06 678 9064
OPEN
Daily: lunch noon–3 P.M.,
dinner 7 P.M.–midnight (Fri–Sat
till 1 A.M.)
CLOSED
Never
RESERVATIONS
Advised
CREDIT CARDS
AE, DC, MC, V
À LA CARTE
15–22€
FIXED-PRICE MENU
None
BREAD & SERVICE CHARGES
No bread charge, 15% service
added
ENGLISH
Yes, and menu in English

An impressive selection of pastas served in mammoth portions, along with a full complement of pizzas, *crostini, bruschetta,* and meat dishes, make L'Archetto one of the restaurants most frequented by Great Eaters when they are between Piazza Venezia and the Trevi Fountain.

By all means, try not to be seated in the small area upstairs, where there is just too much going on, with waiters zipping around as if they were in training for the next Olympics and diners wandering by en route to better seating downstairs (the best tables are in the second room of the basement).

The only things to consider ordering are the pastas and pizzas; for antipasti, stick to *bruschetta* or *crostini*. Pasta aficionados will have a delicious meal with any of the 130 varieties. There is everything from a simple rendition of spaghetti with garlic, olive oil, and parsley to fresh seafood (Tuesday and Friday only) and the "Chanel," topped with tomato, garlic, lobster, brandy, cream, and pepper. Pizza eaters have thirty or more choices. If you can make it to dessert, the temptations include homemade cakes, tortes, gelato, tiramisù, or *panna cotta*.

San Lorenzo

Located in the center of the sprawling University of Rome, San Lorenzo is about a ten-minute bus ride east of the train station. The streets, named for the ancient tribes of the Italian peninsula, are being rejuvenated, and the area, once entirely blue-collar, is now considered a contemporary place to live. The restaurants here cater mostly to students and are heavy on the pizza, but there are some notable Great Eat exceptions.

RESTAURANTS

(¢) indicates a Cheap Eat

Restaurants

DA FRANCO AR VICOLETTO (112)
Via dei Falisci, 1A

Da Franco ar Vicoletto is destination dining if you love fresh fish, because that is all that is served for every course from appetizer through main. Start by ordering the fish *antipasto misto*. My pick for pasta goes to the fettuccine with shrimp and artichokes or to the spaghetti with fresh mussels and clams. For the second course, order the mixed grilled seafood platter or whatever is touted on the daily special list. Fresh fish has a well-deserved reputation for being very expensive in Rome. To get around having your bill dip into the Big Splurge category, order one of the four fixed-price menus. The only drawback is that they are served for a minimum of two persons. The desserts are mundane, so there's no need to save room for the end.

NOTE: If you arrive around noon, take a few minutes to check out the local outdoor market at the corner of Via dei Falisci and Via dei Latini.

TELEPHONE
06 495 7675, 06 4470 4958

OPEN
Tues–Sun: lunch 12:30–3:30 P.M., dinner 7:30–11:30 P.M.

CLOSED
Mon; last 3 weeks of Aug

CREDIT CARDS
MC, V

À LA CARTE
25–40€

FIXED-PRICE MENU
Four menus (prices per person): 16€, 19€, 20€, 25€; all include 2–3 fish courses, salad, wine, and mineral water

BREAD & SERVICE CHARGES
Bread 1€, service included

ENGLISH
Yes, and menu in English

PIZZERIA L'ECONOMICA (¢, 111)
Via Tiburtina, 46

The name says it all. Pizzeria L'Economica is a barebones place with zero decor. Its wide-ranging claim to fame is that it serves the least expensive (and, according to its fans, the best variety of) pizzas in the San Lorenzo

TELEPHONE
06 445 6669

OPEN
Mon–Sat: dinner 7 P.M.–midnight

CLOSED
Sun; Aug
RESERVATIONS
Not accepted
CREDIT CARDS
None
À LA CARTE
6–10€
FIXED-PRICE MENU
None
BREAD & SERVICE CHARGES
No bread charge, 10% service added
ENGLISH
Yes

area of Rome. The giant wood-burning pizza fires are lit only in the evening, from 7 P.M. to midnight. If you don't want one of their super pizzas, the only other options are *crostini, bruschetta,* or selections from the antipasti. The desserts are definitely in the ho-hum category, so pass them up for another time and place.

POMMIDORO (109)
Piazza dei Sanniti, 44

TELEPHONE
06 445 2692
OPEN
Mon–Sat: lunch 12:30–3 P.M., dinner 7:30 P.M.–midnight
CLOSED
Sun; Aug
RESERVATIONS
Advised
CREDIT CARDS
AE, DC, MC, V
À LA CARTE
25–40€
FIXED-PRICE MENU
None
BREAD & SERVICE CHARGES
Included
ENGLISH
Yes, and menu in English

Anna and Aldo Bravi run a remarkable trattoria here in the university district of San Lorenzo. Opened first as a wine shop by Aldo's grandmother, Clementinona, it was expanded into a restaurant by his father. Aldo has been on the payroll since he was seven, and now his sons and daughters and their spouses all work here. The wonderful food is the creation of his wife, Anna. The clientele comprises a wide sampling of locals—professors and students, intellectuals and artists, workers in overalls, ladies draped in mink, businessmen making deals—and all are welcomed by Aldo with the same degree of warmth and friendliness.

In the main room, with its arched brick ceilings, is a large open-fire oven and grill where seasonal game and other meats are cooked to perfection. Tables set with yellow linens are crowded into several rooms, as well as outside on a glass-enclosed raised terrace that is used year-round. The value-packed menu is astonishing in its versatility, offering the kind of quality that inspires repeat visits. Order a liter of the house wine and a plate of the thinly sliced prosciutto with figs. Don't miss Anna's own fettuccini tossed with wild mushrooms or her pappardelle with wild boar sauce. If you appreciate wild game, nowhere in Rome is it prepared with more skill. The culinary curious can try another of their specialties, offal cooked over the open fire, which they claim removes most of the fat and "gamey" taste. Otherwise, the mutton stew is a tasty alternative, as are any of the grilled chops or fresh fish selections. The delicious desserts are all by Anna, who has a large repertoire. Just ask what she has made that day, and whatever you pick will be sweet and perfect.

TRAM TRAM (110)
Via dei Reti, 44/46

Named after the tram that goes by on Via dei Reti, this popular San Lorenzo trattoria is filled with tram memorabilia. The banquettes are tram seats, and the wine racks above were once coatracks. In the bathroom the soap dispenser is a tram original, as is the collection of old photos, taken from a book on the history of trams in Rome. It is all happily presided over by the Divittorio sisters, Antonella and Fabiola, and their mother, Rosanna. The family makes their own organic bread, and their pastas are a leap above the mundane, especially the *pappardelle tram tram,* a large egg fettuccini sauced with lamb, peppers, and tomatoes; the *orecchiette* with clams and cauliflower; and *cavatelli alla siciliana,* short pasta with swordfish, eggplant, and tomato sauce. It is always acceptable to order just a main course, perhaps the *alici dorate e fritte* (deep-fried anchovies), or, for another anchovy experience, a torte made with anchovies, endive, tomatoes, and cheese, topped with pine nuts. I always keep an eye out for the meat or fish *involtini*—rolls of veal, bread, ham, cheese, and walnuts, or with swordfish, olives, cheese, and pine nuts. Desserts are made by Mama, so you can depend on a wonderful *zabaione,* chocolate mousse, or lemon cream with fresh strawberries. The wines are excellent, with a choice of 250 bottles ranging from a simple house wine to a mighty Brunello.

TELEPHONE
06 490 416

OPEN
Tues–Sun: lunch 12:30–3:30 P.M., dinner 7:30–11:30 P.M.

CLOSED
Mon; Aug 15–22

RESERVATIONS
Advised for dinner

CREDIT CARDS
AE, DC, MC, V

À LA CARTE
25–30€

FIXED-PRICE MENU
None

BREAD & SERVICE CHARGES
Bread 1€, service discretionary

ENGLISH
Usually limited

Testaccio

An area that takes its name from Monte Testaccio (mountain of pottery), a mountain of old, broken Roman oil and wine containers located between Via di Monte Testaccio and Via Zabaglia, Testaccio is not known for its designer boutiques, dainty tearooms, or matrons who lunch. This was once the slaughterhouse district of Rome, and many butcher shops are still in full swing. As you can imagine, food was, and still is, geared toward burly workers who do not worry about cholesterol or their waistlines, but it is well worth a meal foray, especially for those eager to add another unusual culinary experience to their roster. The area has also risen higher on the trendy nightlife index. The morning market in Piazza Testaccio is one of Rome's best and provides a good view of what the locals are eating at any time of year.

Restaurants

BUCATINO (89)
Via Luca della Robbia, 84/86

Bucatino is a popular tavern with three main dining areas: two upstairs and one large one downstairs. I like to sit in the big room upstairs because it is more central to the interesting action and not as claustrophobic or stuffy as the downstairs room. Avoid at all costs the closet-size anteroom to your left as you walk in the door.

The most inexpensive meal, pizza, is served only in the evening, with the usual rundown of toppings. However, this really is not the place to order a pizza and a salad. This is a place to really dig into *cucina alla romana*. On Friday, the *pasta e ceci*—pasta with garbanzo beans in an onion, garlic, and tomato sauce—is a wonderful choice, as is the gnocchi with tomato sauce, served only on Thursday. At any time you can order a heaping plate of *bucatini all'amatriciana,* spaghetti covered in a thick tomato, pecorino cheese, and bacon sauce. Main-course standbys are the *trippa alla romana, coda alla vaccinara* (oxtail stew), roast veal with potatoes, or fresh fish. Those eager to engage in offbeat dining should be satisfied for a long time with the *coratella alla Veneta:* lamb's heart, lung, liver, and spleen cooked in olive oil and seasoned with lots of pepper and onion. If you are still able at this point to think of dessert, the best choice is the house specialty, *millefoglie*—a cream-filled puff pastry. You will need a strong red wine to get you through this lusty meal, so if you go for lunch and have it, plan your afternoon accordingly.

TELEPHONE
06 574 6886

OPEN
Tues–Sun: lunch 12:30–3:30 P.M., dinner 7:30–11:30 P.M.

CLOSED
Mon; end of July–Aug 20

RESERVATIONS
Advised

CREDIT CARDS
AE, DC, MC

À LA CARTE
Pizza 6–10€, 3-course meal 25–35€

FIXED-PRICE MENU
None

BREAD & SERVICE CHARGES
Bread 1.50€, service discretionary

ENGLISH
Yes, and menu in English

CHECCHINO DAL 1887 ($, 94)
Via Monte Testaccio, 30

Please do not be turned off by the location or the many unusual specialty dishes this restaurant is famous for. One of Rome's most elegant and sophisticated dining establishments, Checchino dal 1887 was opened in 1887 as a place to drink wine, and today the original wine license hangs on the wall next to a photo of the great-great-grandfather and -grandmother of the current owners, brothers Elio and Francesco Mariani. In addition to its fine food, the restaurant is known for its diversity of wines, with more than five hundred varieties housed in a naturally temperature-controlled underground cave that dates back to 75 B.C. You can pay up to 420€ for a museum-quality wine, but there are also scores of wines available for 15€ to 25€, as well as monthly featured wines affordably priced by both the glass and the bottle.

The dining room is beautiful, with original marble tables covered with linen cloths, embroidered napkins, and fresh yellow roses, the favorite flower of the Mariani brothers' mother, who ran the restaurant with them until her recent death. During warm weather, tables are placed outside on the front terrace.

Not only is the menu translated into English, but each dish is explained so you will know exactly what you are eating— very important here. The restaurant's Testaccio location means there is an emphasis on meats of all kinds, especially entrails, which most Americans never even consider trying. Even though you think you would never taste, let alone *like,* veal kidneys, lamb's brains, oxtail stew, or pig's trotters, here they are raised to a gourmet level and are quite delicious. Wary at first, I was impressed after one meal and eager to return. Starters include head cheese, macaroni with calf's intestines, rendered pig's cheeks in ewe's milk cheese, and veal foot, the latter boiled, boned, and served in a salad with carrots, beans, celery, and dressing. Any one of these is wonderful, I promise you. To follow, there is the restaurant's signature dish: *la coda alla vaccinara* (oxtail stew), which is cooked for five hours with tomato sauce, celery, pine nuts, raisins, and bitter chocolate; the recipe originated here in the 1890s. There is also tripe, stewed or grilled veal intestines, and the jackpot offal entrée: *arrosto misto,* a sampling of roasted sweetbreads, calf's small intestines, and marrow. Tamer tastes will find many safe but satisfying choices, including *bue garofolato*—beef studded with cloves, garlic, and pancetta, then seared and

TELEPHONE
06 574 6318

INTERNET
www.checchino-dal-1887.com

OPEN
Tues–Sat: lunch 12:30–3 P.M., dinner 8 P.M.–midnight

CLOSED
Sun–Mon; Aug, 1 week at Christmas

RESERVATIONS
Required

À LA CARTE
45–55€

FIXED-PRICE MENU
None

BREAD & SERVICE CHARGES
Included

ENGLISH
Yes, and menu in English

braised in a light tomato sauce—and their specialty lamb dish: *abbacchio alla cacciatora,* bite-size pieces of leg and shoulder of lamb sautéed with garlic, vinegar, olive oil, anchovies, and chili.

To finish your meal, you can order from a long list of interesting cheeses or homemade sweets, each served with an appropriate glass of wine. From beginning to end, the service is impeccable, the food delicious, and the time memorable. Please do yourself a favor and try it as a special Big Splurge.

NOTE: At night especially, the best way to arrive is by taxi.

DA FELICE (93)
Via Mastro Giorgio, 29

TELEPHONE
06 574 6800
OPEN
Mon–Sat: lunch 12:30–
2:30 P.M., dinner 8–11:30 P.M.
CLOSED
Sun; Aug
RESERVATIONS
Not necessary
CREDIT CARDS
MC, V
À LA CARTE
20–25€ (includes house wine)
FIXED-PRICE MENU
None
BREAD & SERVICE CHARGES
Bread 1€, service included
ENGLISH
Some, and most of the menu is
in English

What a change! This used to be a charmless, unfriendly insider cheap eat with the menu either rattled off in rapid-fire Italian (and not repeated) or written in Italian hieroglyphics on a piece of graph paper if the tight-fisted owner felt so inclined. The gruff, eighty-five-year-old boss kept a *riservato* sign on all the tables—not that anyone had booked them; it was his way of looking patrons over and deciding if he wanted to bother with them. You will still see him lurking in the background, but the reins have been handed over to his daughter, son, and grandson, who fluffed, dusted, and painted the gloomy room and continually do their best to be welcoming and courteous. Now they pass out a handsome eight-page menu on thick cream-colored stock, illustrated with both color and black-and-white graphics, which my dining companion pronounced suitable for framing. The four or five daily specials for Monday through Saturday are listed in Italian only, but the selections for the staple Roman *primi, secondi, contorni,* and *dolci* are translated into English. There is still nothing dainty about the recipes or the servings, which are all he-man fare guaranteed to put hair on your chest regardless of your gender. Prices have naturally increased, but when you are through, you will have wined and dined for around 25€.

VOLPETTI PIÚ (¢, 92)
Via Alessandro Volta, 8

Volpetti Piú is a wonderful deli and self-service restaurant around the corner from the gourmet shop, bakery, and cheese shop of the same name (see "Food Shopping in Rome," page 173). At the restaurant, the service is swift and simple, as in most cafeterias: You look, select, pay, have your dish warmed if necessary, and then take it to your seat. The *pizza bianca* is divine, and so are the daily dishes featuring the foods and fabulous cheeses from the gourmet shop. Everything you see can be packaged to go. Smoking is not allowed.

TELEPHONE
06 574 4306

INTERNET
www.volpetti.com;
www.fooditaly.com

OPEN
Mon–Sat: 10 A.M.–9:30 P.M.,
continuous service

CLOSED
Sun

RESERVATIONS
Not necessary

CREDIT CARDS
AE, MC, V

À LA CARTE
Most dishes sold by 100 g;
3-course meal 10–14€

FIXED-PRICE MENU
None

BREAD & SERVICE CHARGES
None

ENGLISH
Limited, but you won't need it

Train Station, Santa Maria Maggiore, and Villa Borghese

From a Great Eating standpoint, most of the immediate area around the train station (Termini Station) should be considered Tourist Trap Central. There are, however, always exceptions, and of course *Great Eats* has found them, though some entail a moderate walk from the train station itself, which had a complete makeover in anticipation of the multitudes arriving for the 2000 Holy Year Jubilee. In addition to the usual news kiosks and greasy pizza joints, there are bars, restaurants including two McDonald's, countless mid-line clothing stores, and a twenty-four-hour supermarket. It is a virtual city unto itself.

Four blocks southwest of the railroad station on top of the Esquilino, one of the seven hills of Rome, is the Basilica of Santa Maria Maggiore, one of the major basilicas of Rome and officially part of Vatican City. The bell tower, built in 1377, is Rome's highest *campanile*. This area is home to Rome's largest immigrant population, which is concentrated around Piazza Vittorio Emanuele II, the city's largest square.

North of the train station is Villa Borghese, a magnificent Baroque park featuring walking and jogging trails; a children's cinema; the city zoo; beautiful, romantic views of Rome; and three important art museums: Galleria Borghese, Galleria Nazionale d'Arte Moderna e Contemporanea, and Villa Giulia. A number of Great Eat selections are about halfway between the train station and the park.

(¢) indicates a Cheap Eat
($) indicates a Big Splurge

Restaurants

DA GIOVANNI (99)
Via Antonio Salandra, 1 (off Via XX Settembre)

Da Giovanni was founded more than forty years ago by the Vittucci family, which continues to run it today. Seating is downstairs in two pine-paneled rooms lined with coat hooks; the entrance is graced with hanging meats, and fresh flowers accent the dessert and appetizer table. Sunny yellow damask linens complete the picture.

The chef really struts his stuff when it comes to the pastas. One of his best is the *fettuccine alla Giovanni,* a combination of butter, cheese, mushrooms, tomatoes, and peas; this dish will go directly to your arteries, but what a delicious journey. Another one in the same category is their homemade *agnelotti*—egg ravioli filled with ground meat and vegetables and served with a meat sauce. The main-course plates range from *abbacchio alla cacciatora con funghi* (lamb served with a dressing of olive oil, vinegar, sage, rosemary, garlic, anchovies, and mushrooms) to grilled veal chops, roast chicken, fresh fish, and eggplant Parmesan. In addition to these regulars, there are several *piatti del giorno* (daily plates) offering pastas, main courses, and a vegetable special. For a finale, the top choices are a heady version of tiramisù or whole baked pears (in season). A very light alternative is the *frutta secca,* a serving of dried fruit and nuts that goes well with an after-dinner espresso.

TELEPHONE
06 485 950
OPEN
Mon–Sat: lunch noon–3 P.M., dinner 7–10 P.M.
CLOSED
Sun; Aug
RESERVATIONS
Not necessary
CREDIT CARDS
MC, V
À LA CARTE
15–20€
FIXED–PRICE MENU
Lunch only: 14€, 3 courses
BREAD & SERVICE CHARGES
Bread 1€, service included
ENGLISH
Yes

DAGNINO (¢, 101)
Galleria Esedra, Via Vittorio Emanuele Orlando, 75

When I first looked for this cafeteria/pastry shop in the Galleria Esedra arcade (near Piazza della Repubblica and the train station), I was pessimistic. Most restaurants in this area are simply terrible: either overpriced greasy spoons, dirty ethnic joints, or total tourist traps serving lousy food to the unsuspecting. What a surprise I had when I reached Dagnino, which bills itself, in alphabetical order, as a "bar, cafeteria, *gelateria, pasticceria, ristorante,* snack bar, and tea room" specializing in Sicilian pastries and ice cream.

Time stopped somewhere in the fifties in this two-level monument to mirrors, marble, fat grams, and sweets. You can stop in during the early-morning cappuccino and *cornetto* rush; hit the cafeteria line around noon before the hot choices get too picked over; or drop by later in the day for a snack. I like to go in the late afternoon, look over the

TELEPHONE
06 481 6660
OPEN
Daily: 7 A.M.–10 P.M., hot food noon–10 P.M., continuous service
CLOSED
1 week mid-Aug
RESERVATIONS
Not accepted
CREDIT CARDS
AE, MC, V
À LA CARTE
Pastries 1.60–3.50€, ice cream 2.75–4.50€, hot food 5.50–6.50€ per dish, teatime 3.10–7€
FIXED–PRICE MENU
16€, 3 courses, includes water and coffee

magnificent pastries displayed along one wall, pick several, and retire to a quiet table with a pot of tea. I always think I will take a few of the pastries home with me, but I usually end up devouring them all right on the spot. If you have children in tow, the ice creams are wonderful, and the *granita di limone* (lemonade) is the best I have tasted.

FIASCHETTERIA MARINI (¢, 95)
Via Rafaele Cadorna, 9 (north of Termini Station off Via Piave)

In its heyday, the Fiaschetteria Marini was an *enoteca,* or wine bar. Today it is a Great Eat that is simply too cheap to ignore. From Monday through Friday, it serves lunch to a packed house of office workers on tight budgets. In the afternoon you can always drop in for a ham and cheese sandwich and eavesdrop on the neighborhood ladies clustered at a table by the door, dishing the dirt on the local scandals and gossip.

The setting is casual, with paper covers on tiny marble-topped tables set inside and, when weather permits, outside on the sidewalk. The menu hangs on a hook by the cash register. The daily-changing choices are limited, but all are filling, especially the *pasta e fagioli* or any of the special German dishes that appear when the owner's mother (who is Austrian) gets busy in the kitchen.

GRAN CAFFÈ STREGA (106)
Piazza del Viminale, 27/31

Huge, brightly lit, and packed with animated Italians, Gran Caffè Strega is a combination cafeteria, restaurant, and pizzeria catering to Ministry of the Interior workers and tourists at lunch and an eclectic crowd in the evening who drop in before or after performances at the Opera or the Teatro Nazionale, both close by.

At lunch, skip the ready-made sandwiches and head straight for the self-service cafeteria counter. Also bypass the diet-destroying display of desserts and concentrate on one of the twenty salads and ten to twelve hot daily specials. Seating is either in a room with the pizza ovens or on a large outdoor lighted terrace shielded from traffic and street noise by a ring of bushes and trees.

If you want to avoid the sometimes frustratingly long cafeteria line, you can opt for a pizza, which is served for both lunch and dinner. The thirty or more wood-fired varieties start with a simple topping of tomato and cheese

---

BREAD & SERVICE CHARGES
None
ENGLISH
Yes

TELEPHONE
06 474 5534
OPEN
Mon–Sat: bar 9 A.M.–8 P.M., lunch 12:15–2:45 P.M.
CLOSED
Sun; 10 days at Christmas, last 3 weeks of Aug
RESERVATIONS
Not necessary
CREDIT CARDS
None
À LA CARTE
10–15€
FIXED-PRICE MENU
None
BREAD & SERVICE CHARGES
Bread 0.75€, service included
ENGLISH
Yes, and German

TELEPHONE
06 485 670
INTERNET
www.grancaffestrega.it
OPEN
Daily: bar 7 A.M.–midnight, lunch noon–3:30 P.M., dinner 7 P.M.–midnight
CLOSED
Never
RESERVATIONS
Not necessary
CREDIT CARDS
AE, DC, MC, V
À LA CARTE
Cafeteria 10–15€ (lunch only), pizza 5–12€, 3-course meal 25–35€
FIXED-PRICE MENU
None

and finish with "the works," with a fried egg on top. In the evening, a waitstaff and a wide-ranging menu geared to every possible taste replaces the cafeteria line.

BREAD & SERVICE CHARGES
Bread 1€, 10% service added at dinner
ENGLISH
Yes, and menu in English

I LEONI D'ABRUZZO (100)
Via Vicenza, 44

Whether you go early and mingle with the other hotel guests, or are more Roman and arrive for the second seating, say around 9 P.M., you will be graciously welcomed by the longtime owner of this basement dining room. The restaurant serves the usual weekly lineup, and after a few days of eating out in Rome, you will know this food drill by heart: fresh fish on Tuesday and Friday, gnocchi on Thursday, lasagne always on Sunday, and pizza at night. In addition, you will always find a vegetable antipasti display, pasta tossed with garlic, olive oil, and hot red pepper, roast lamb, *saltimbocca*, warm almond cake, and drinkable house red or white wine.

TELEPHONE
06 4470 0272
OPEN
Mon–Sat: lunch noon–3 P.M., dinner 6:30–11 P.M.
CLOSED
Sun; 3 weeks in Aug (dates vary)
RESERVATIONS
Not necessary
CREDIT CARDS
AE, DC, MC, V
À LA CARTE
16–22€
FIXED-PRICE MENU
16€, 2 course, fruit, wine, and mineral water
BREAD & SERVICE CHARGES
Bread 2€ for small basket, 3€ for large; service included
ENGLISH
Yes

MONTE CARUSO ($, 108)
Via Farini, 12 (near Santa Maria Maggiore)

The menu states that the chef obeys orders and does everything with love, and it will take only one meal at Monte Caruso to convince you this is true. Reservations for dinner are required, not just for a table but to get in: the front door is always locked, and you will not be admitted unless you have a reservation. The restaurant's several dining areas have well-spaced tables set with Richard Ginori china and attractive glassware; a display of your grand dessert finale is to the right of the entrance.

The atmosphere is pleasant and unhurried, allowing you to relax and enjoy all courses, which lean heavily on the food from Lucana, in the south of Italy. A glass of prosecco, a bowl of black olives, and a plate of bite-sized *crostini* will keep you occupied while you order and wait for your first course. If everyone at your table can agree (since all must order them), the two tasting menus offer a good sampling of the chef's specialties. One offers an assortment

TELEPHONE
06 483 549
OPEN
Mon: dinner 7:30 P.M.–midnight; Tues–Sat: lunch noon–3 P.M., dinner 7:30 P.M.–midnight
CLOSED
Mon lunch, Sun; Aug
RESERVATIONS
Required
CREDIT CARDS
AE, DC, MC, V
À LA CARTE
40–45€
FIXED-PRICE MENU
Two tasting menus (price per person): *menù dell' Amicizia*, 35€, 3 courses; *gran menu degustazione*, 45€, 4 courses

of first and second courses, plus dessert; the other covers four courses. Neither one includes drinks. From the special à la carte menu, I loved both the *orecchiette* (small, home-made ear-shaped pasta served with meat sauce and grated Parmesan cheese) and *cautarogni* (a hot mix of broccoli, olive oil, garlic, and chili peppers); both are accompanied by a basket of fresh bread from the kitchen's oven. If there are two of you and you can't decide on just one pasta, the chef will prepare a plate for you with his choice of four special ones. The same holds true for main courses, but this round only offers two special second courses and three side dishes, chosen by the chef. I found *glu'glu'*, which is a second course with white turkey in an orange sauce, to be an overpowering, cloyingly sweet main course, especially after a hearty first course of pasta. Better choices for this course would be *babette,* roast veal with truffle cream; zucchini flowers stuffed with mozzarella cheese and stewed in a fragrant tomato sauce; or a simple lemon veal escallop. Dessert is important: plan on either the *profitterol fatto al momento*—cream puffs with warm chocolate sauce and whipped cream—or a plate of *frappé,* quickly fried pieces of pastry dough dusted with powdered sugar, which are melt-in-your-mouth wonderful.

MONTI DOC (116)
Via Giovanni Lanza, 95

The Monti Doc wine bar has a loyal base of customers who appreciate its high-quality light lunches and dinners and the chance to sample wines from smaller vineyards. The small interior has only a baker's dozen of tables and a few seats at the bar, so if you are arriving without reservations, it is smart to go early or late to avoid waiting. The menu, which is written in hard-to-read-script on a blackboard, tends to be vegetarian, leaning heavily on fresh, seasonal produce in soups, salads, risottos, lasagne, and fruit-based desserts. Full meal orders are not mandatory, so this is a good address to remember if you are around Santa Maria Maggiore and in need of a stylish bite to go with a glass or two of interesting wine.

BREAD & SERVICE CHARGES
Included

ENGLISH
Yes, and menu in English

TELEPHONE
06 487 2696

OPEN
Tues–Fri: lunch noon–4 P.M., dinner 7 P.M.–1 A.M.; Sat–Sun: dinner 7 P.M.–1 A.M.

CLOSED
Sat–Sun lunch, Mon; 2 weeks mid-Aug (dates vary)

RESERVATIONS
Advised

CREDIT CARDS
MC, V

À LA CARTE
16–20€

FIXED-PRICE MENU
None

BREAD & SERVICE CHARGES
Bread 1€, service included

ENGLISH
Yes

RISTORANTE DA VINCENZO (96)
Via Castelfidardo, 4/6 (off Via XX Settembre)

Even though the menu is translated into English, German, French, and Japanese, the clientele at lunch, and especially after 9 P.M., is usually local. The setting is simple, the service friendly yet professional, the plates warmed when they should be, and the food delicious. From appetizers to dessert, there are fifty-six possibilities. Still, if you do not see what you want, just ask, and chances are it can be prepared for you. Fresh fish is the kitchen's strong suit and is cooked and served with pride. My dinner guests all agreed that it was one of the best fish meals they had had in Rome.

If you are going all the way with fish, the sautéed clams or mussels and the smoked swordfish are nice starters. The spaghetti with clams and prawns or the rice with seafood are well-executed first courses. Besides the fish and seafood pastas, the *penne all'arrabbiata* (a hot combination of peppers, tomatoes, and garlic) is a reliable first course. A fresh lobster salad with the addition of tomatoes, onions, and potatoes makes a filling main course, especially in the summer. The baked sea bass or flounder are served with potatoes and can be topped with a zesty tomato sauce. The *saltimbocca alla romana* (veal and ham cooked in a wine sauce), grilled pork chops, or roast chicken will keep the carnivores in your party happy. Fresh fruit tarts, gelatos, and lemon-flavored *sorbetto* splashed with vodka will not lead you too far astray from your dieting resolutions, but the house specialty, *millefoglie*—thin sheets of pastry layered with cream, chocolate cream, and chocolate—will break them down every time. A shot of Sambuca, served after you order a full meal, will add to your desire to dine again at this wonderful Roman restaurant.

TELEPHONE
06 484 596

OPEN
Mon–Sat: lunch 12:30–3 P.M., dinner 7–11 P.M.

CLOSED
Sun; Aug

RESERVATIONS
Advised

À LA CARTE
30–40€

FIXED-PRICE MENU
None

BREAD & SERVICE CHARGES
Bread 1€, service included

ENGLISH
Yes, and menu in English

RISTORANTE REGINA (¢, 102)
Via de Mille, 46

On a recent trip to Rome, my apartment was just around the corner from Regina's. In a short time, this family-run spot became a dependable standby, where I could always count on a freshly prepared plate of pasta and a warm smile. Nothing about the pine-paneled and stucco-walled room says fancy, but everything about the simple cooking says homemade and delicious. For both lunch and dinner, the tables are filled with students, rotund men mopping their plates with gusto, locals wanting a night off from KP, and visitors glad to have found a decent Cheap Eat in this enclave of Rome. Service is dispatched by two career

TELEPHONE
06 445 3834, 06 491 806

OPEN
Mon–Fri: lunch noon–3 P.M., dinner 6:30–10:30 P.M.; Sat: dinner 6:30–10:30 P.M.

CLOSED
Sat lunch, Sun; Aug 1–23

RESERVATIONS
For 4 or more

CREDIT CARDS
AE, DC, MC, V

À LA CARTE
12–18€

FIXED-PRICE MENU
Lunch only: 15€, 2 courses, includes mineral water, wine, bread, and service

BREAD & SERVICE CHARGES
Bread 1€, service included

ENGLISH
Yes, and menu in English

waiters: Pietro and Khaled. Daily specials reflect shopping trips to the morning market on Via Malazzo (see page 176) and include the required gnocchi on Thursday and fresh fish on Tuesday and Friday. The regular menu is textbook Roman, from pastas sauced with tomato or meat *ragù* to grilled meats, artichokes, sautéed or boiled spinach flavored with garlic and lemon, and desserts no one has room for. If you arrive with a big appetite for lunch, the fixed-price menu is a buy, as it is all-inclusive.

TRATTORIA ABRUZZESE (107)
Via Napoli, 4

The generous cooking at this two-room trattoria, located in the shadow of the opera and near an interesting morning produce market (at the end of Via Napoli), is more likely to please a hungry gourmand than a finicky gourmet. Still, the food is prepared with the best ingredients, and the red-coated waiters in black pants and bow ties serve a reliable crew of regular locals.

The best wallet-watching meal is certainly the fixed-price menu, which includes everything from soup to service. The choices for each course are varied and include daily specials. The meat dishes are better than the fish ones, especially the soul-soothing osso buco or the roast lamb. The typical Roman specialty of tripe offers a different choice you probably can't get back home. If you stray from the set-price meal, you will pay more, but you will be able to indulge in the house pastas—*rigatoni bohème,* a cholesterol indulgence of cream cheese and sausage blanketed with Parmesan cheese, or *tonnarelli alla chitarra,* another outrageously rich pasta with tomatoes, mushrooms, bacon, and peas. For dessert, skip the prunes and the baked pears and go for the *mont blanc,* a meringue of cream, whipped cream, and custard that's covered with even more cream. Oh well, you won't have it every day!

TELEPHONE
06 488 5505

OPEN
Mon–Sat: lunch noon–2:30 P.M., dinner 7–10:30 P.M.

CLOSED
Sun; last 3 weeks of Aug

RESERVATIONS
Recommended on weekends

CREDIT CARDS
AE, DC, MC, V

À LA CARTE
25–35€

FIXED-PRICE MENU
19€, 2 courses, vegetable, dessert, mineral water, wine, bread, and service charge

BREAD & SERVICE CHARGES
Bread 1€, service included

ENGLISH
Yes, and fixed-price menu in English

TRATTORIA DA BRUNO & ROMANA (103)
Via Varese, 29

Well thought of by locals, Trattoria da Bruno & Romana is a safe bet for back-burner home cooking if you are in this neck of the woods, which is not known for gourmet anything. The Santarelli family has been in this spot for half a century, when Bruno's parents operated it as an *osteria;* then, the regulars ate on one side, and on the other, folks drank *vino,* played cards, and caught up on the local gossip. The food is plain but fresh. I know because on my

TELEPHONE
06 490 403

OPEN
Mon–Sat: lunch noon–2:30 P.M., dinner 7–10:30 P.M.

CLOSED
Sun; Aug

RESERVATIONS
Advised for 4 or more

last research trip my flat in Rome was nearby, and I would often see Bruno or Romana shopping at the morning market on Via Milazzo for the food prepared and served that day. That is why you don't need to consult the menu. Just ask Bruno what he would recommend.

I was also interested to learn that Bruno is quite an artist, known for his wood-carved nativity scenes, which he displays at Christmastime and has had reproduced in color on the menu. Look carefully along the back wall of the restaurant and you will see a framed photo of Bruno with Pope John Paul II admiring one of his nativity scenes. If you are interested in seeing his complete masterpiece collection, ask him to take you to the wine cellar. I know you will be as amazed and impressed as I was.

CREDIT CARDS
AE, MC, V
À LA CARTE
25–28€
FIXED-PRICE MENU
None
BREAD & SERVICE CHARGES
None
ENGLISH
Limited, but menu in English

TRATTORIA MONTE (115)
Via San Vito, 13a (near Santa Maria Maggiore)

Everyone who eats here returns. I know I did, despite a few dishes that missed their mark. The three dining areas are defined by brick arches and bright, modern versions of Tiffany lamps. The best seats are somewhere in the middle, away from the kitchen in the back and the door traffic at the entrance. Vegetarians will be in seventh heaven trying to decide between several seasonal vegetable flans (similar to a silky quiche). Carnivores will be curious about the olives stuffed with artichokes and sausage, and then fried. Let's just say it is an acquired taste. Everyone loves the *tortello* (large, stuffed egg ravioli with a sharp tomato sauce), the risotto with artichokes and pumpkin, or the pasta with white truffles, which are only some of the delicious first-course choices. The braised pork and sweet onions was a soothing, wintry second plate, and so was the roasted rabbit, served with sautéed potatoes. I think the most successful ending is either the apple torte with zabaglione or amaretto ice cream covered in hot chocolate. There is no house red wine, but reasonably priced glasses and bottles are available.

TELEPHONE
06 446 6573
OPEN
Tues–Sat: lunch 12:30–3 P.M., dinner 7:30–11 P.M.; Sun: lunch 12:30–3 P.M
CLOSED
Sun dinner, Mon
RESERVATIONS
Essential
CREDIT CARDS
DC, MC, V
À LA CARTE
25–30€
FIXED-PRICE MENU
None
BREAD & SERVICE CHARGES
Bread 1€, service included
ENGLISH
Enough, and menu in English

TRIMANI (97)
Via Cernaia, 37b (between Termini Station and Villa Borghese)

The name *Trimani* is synonymous in Rome with fine wines, which are sold in their shop around the corner on Via Goito (see page 173). In their wine bar, more than six hundred labels are available, fifty or more by the glass. As you can imagine, the wine list looks and feels like a telephone book, but don't feel intimidated—the knowledgeable staff

TELEPHONE
06 446 9630
OPEN
Mon–Sat: lunch 11:30 A.M.–3 P.M., cold plates 3–8 P.M., happy hour 4–6 P.M., dinner 8 P.M.–midnight
CLOSED
Sun; middle 2 weeks in Aug

RESERVATIONS
Advised
CREDIT CARDS
AE, DC, MC, V
À LA CARTE
26–30€, includes 1 glass of wine
FIXED-PRICE MENU
None
BREAD & SERVICE CHARGES
No bread charge, service included
ENGLISH
Yes, and menu in English

is patient with neophytes. From Monday to Saturday, the dining room is filled with an attractive mix of Romans who are dressed for success and enjoying the well-prepared food. The *piatti del giorno* always includes a pasta, cheese plate, something fishy, and a hot meat dish. Quiches, crêpes, *crostini,* salads, assorted cured and smoked meat plates as well as four or five main meat courses (including a horse meat salad) and a handful of fresh and smoked fish plates complete the all-encompassing menu. The chocolate mousse is definitely the dessert of choice.

Gelaterias

TELEPHONE
06 446 4740
EMAIL
giovannifassi@tiscali.it
OPEN
Tues–Sun: noon–midnight (till 1 A.M. Sat, from 10 A.M. Sun)
CLOSED
Mon (unless a holiday)
CREDIT CARDS
None
PRICES
Cones and cups from 1.50€; packed to go 6–14€
ENGLISH
Depends on server

GIOVANNI FASSI/PALAZZO DEL FREDDO (121)
Via Principe Eugenio, 65-67/A (south of Termini Station, two blocks south of Piazza Vittorio Emanuele II)

It is said that modern-day Romans hold the nation's gelato consumption record at more than five gallons per person per year. Judging from the amount I saw consumed at this century-old *gelateria* near the train station, I think that is an extremely low estimate. Giovanni Fassi began in 1816 as a little shop in Piazza Navona, and in 1880 it moved to its present location. It has been run by the same family from the beginning and is considered one of Rome's gelato meccas.

The ice cream is displayed in glass cases, with flavor signs in English. Decide what size *cono* (cone) or *coppa* (cup) you want, pay the cashier, and give your receipt to a server. You can take your treat to one of the tables scattered around the cavernous room or eat it on the run. Prices start at around 1.50€ and climb according to how elaborate and involved your order gets. Ice cream for four or six can be packed to go in dry ice.

NOTE: There is a second location not too far from the Vatican (see page 170).

Pastry Shops and Bakeries

TELEPHONE
Not available

PANELLA–L'ARTE DEL PANE (120)
Via Merulana, 54, at Largo Leopardi (Santa Maria Maggiore)

The locals line up here several times a day. In the morning they come in for a cappuccino and a favorite pastry, and later on for a loaf of their fabulous breads. At lunch, you will see them milling around, enjoying a plate of bite-sized goodies or a slice of pizza, and maybe a glass of wine or a fruit smoothie. In the late afternoon, they are back for more bread for dinner. In addition to great breads and pastries, Panella stocks a large selection of cereals, pastas, herbs, spices, wines, and other gourmet grocery items.

OPEN
Mon–Fri: 8 A.M.–2 P.M., 5–8 P.M.;
Sat: 8 A.M.–2 P.M., 4:30–8 P.M.;
Sun: 8:30 A.M.–2 P.M.
CLOSED
Never
CREDIT CARDS
None
ENGLISH
Very limited

Trastevere

Trastevere means "across the Tiber," and this colorful and vibrant neighborhood is on the other side of the Ponte Sisto from the Jewish Quarter. It is famous for its nightlife, authentic neighborhood atmosphere, and many late-night restaurants, bars, and most especially, pizza palaces. Purists insist that one has not been to Rome until one has had a baptism by pizza in Trastevere.

($) indicates a Big Splurge
(¢) indicates a Cheap Eat

Restaurants

AL FONTANONE IN TRASTEVERE (78)
Piazza Trilussa, 46 (as you cross Ponte Sisto)

TELEPHONE
06 581 7312
OPEN
Mon, Thur–Sun: lunch 12:30–
2:45 P.M., dinner 7:15–11 P.M.;
Wed: dinner 7:15–11:15 P.M.
CLOSED
Wed lunch, Tues; Aug 20–
Sep 18, 1 week at Christmas
RESERVATIONS
Advised
CREDIT CARDS
AE, MC, V
À LA CARTE
20–25€
FIXED-PRICE MENU
None
BREAD & SERVICE CHARGES
Bread 1€, service included
ENGLISH
Yes, and menu in English

Naturally, I recommend every entry in this book. I have been to them all, and in many cases, more than a few times. Still, some stand out more than others, and Al Fontanone in Trastevere remains one of my favorites in Rome. I am not alone; the locals swear by it, and many readers have told me that when in Rome, this is their virtual canteen.

Joseph Pino (or Pino, as everyone calls him), his wife, Marisa, her sister Mariela, and her husband, Luciano, have been greeting guests at their popular restaurant for more than thirty years, treating everyone who arrives as a friend, whether they are here for the first time or the fiftieth. The family's heartfelt hospitality is truly exemplified by the well-loved, gregarious Pino, who, in an effort to cut back a bit, now comes to the restaurant only in the evenings. The good food is nicely complemented by the rustic interior, which features dried herbs and flowers hanging from wooden beams, comfortable chairs, well-spaced green-and-white-covered tables, and a gaily lit summer terrace.

I like to start my meal with a small sampling from the antipasti table or with the *fritto all'italiana,* a plate of vegetables quickly deep-fried, or a perfectly fried artichoke, one of the staples of Roman cuisine. Then I move on to the specialty of the house, *fettuccine alla Fontanone,* a rich pasta with mushrooms, tuna, garlic, tomato, and fresh parsley. The simple fettuccine with *funghi porcini* (wild mushrooms) and a liberal lacing of garlic, fresh parsley, and extra-virgin olive oil is another simple yet very satisfying first course (served only from May through November, when the mushrooms are fresh). The noodles in all the pastas are made here, and the ingredients for most of the dishes come from the family's own vegetable gardens or from local producers near their country home outside Rome. If you are going for a meat course, stellar choices are the *abbacchio al forno* (pink-roasted baby lamb), the strapping *coda alla vaccinara* (oxtail stew cooked with celery, tomatoes, onion, and carrots), and on a cold day, polenta served with spicy sausage or pork ribs with pecorino cheese and tomato. In late spring through summer, try *vignarole,* a dish made with new potatoes, artichokes, fava beans, and green peas cooked with ham, butter, and onion. Demand for this preparation is so high that it is offered for both lunch and dinner. In addition to the regular menu, wood-fired pizzas, *crostini,* and *bruschetta* are available each evening. For dessert order Marisa's tiramisù or a plate of her nut-filled *cantucci* to dip in a glass of *vin santo*.

ALLE FRATTE DI TRASTEVERE (84)
Via delle Fratte di Trastevere, 49-50 (corner of Via dei Fienardi)

Trastevere has more eating and drinking destinations that almost any other part of Rome. Many open and close in a hurry, fire chefs, and develop attitudes that are off-putting at best. Not so at this typical Trastevere trattoria, owned for twelve years by Maria, a painter from New York, who is ably assisted by her daughter Savannah. The first room of the cheerful, bright interior features a painting of Maria wearing a shawl and standing at the corner of her restaurant. On warm summer nights, the tables outside are in great demand. The bountiful food is served in portions you may struggle to finish, especially their signature dish, *pasta alle fratte,* laced with Parmesan cheese and dotted with fresh tomatoes. Pizzas are on for both lunch and dinner but are not wood-fired (if that matters to you). Fresh fish is a menu mainstay; so is the beefsteak. Comforting homemade desserts such as banana pudding, cheesecake, and apple pie encourage dieting tomorrow, not today. Taste the house wine before you decide on it. Upgrading a notch or two may be in order.

TELEPHONE
06 1583 5775

OPEN
Mon–Tues, Thur–Sun: lunch noon–3 P.M., dinner 6:30 P.M.–midnight

CLOSED
Wed; Aug (dates vary)

RESERVATIONS
Advised for dinner

CREDIT CARDS
AE, DC, MC, V

À LA CARTE
18–22€

FIXED-PRICE MENU
None

BREAD & SERVICE CHARGES
Bread 2€, service discretionary

ENGLISH
Absolutely, and menu in English

CHECCO ER CARETTIERE ($, 77)
Via Benedetta, 10

Checco er Carettiere is a well-known family-run restaurant that deserves its fine reputation. It is a big place, with most of the entryway occupied by the original wagon that the owner's father used to carry the barrels of wine he sold. Beyond this is a large, rustic main dining room festooned with dried herbs, garlic and pepper braids, and signed photos of the great and near-great who have eaten here. Adjacent is the secluded summer terrace, where diners are spared the usual exhaust fumes and noise that come with sidewalk dining. Now in the skillful hands of Stefania, Susy, Laura, and Mira, the daughters of the original owner, it is a great place to go, especially with a voracious appetite. The *antipasto misto fritto romano* is a feast of fried zucchini flowers, artichokes, meat, and rice balls and makes a nice transition to the rest of the meal. You can try *bombolotti,* short pasta with a hearty tomato and bacon sauce, or spaghetti with garlicky shrimp. Carnivores can celebrate with grilled steak, lamb chops, or tender oxtail

TELEPHONE
06 581 7018, 06 580 0985

INTERNET
www.checcoercarettiere.it

OPEN
Mon–Sat: lunch 12:30–3 P.M., dinner 7:30–11:15 P.M.; Sun: lunch 12:30–3 P.M.; bar, *pasticceria*, and *gelateria:* Tues–Sun 7 A.M.–2 A.M.

CLOSED
Sun dinner; July–Aug

RESERVATIONS
Advised

À LA CARTE
40–60€

FIXED-PRICE MENU
None

BREAD & SERVICE CHARGES
Bread 2€, service included

ENGLISH
Yes

stew simmered in a celery broth. Fish fanciers only have to remember what they saw in the iced fish display to know if they want sea bass, turbot, or sole, just to name a few of the seasonal offerings. The ice cream, the zabaglione, and all the cakes are made here.

Down the street at Via Benedetta, 7, is their bar, *pasticceria,* and *gelateria,* which is open every day but Monday. At Via Benedetta, 13, where the grandfather sold wine and his wife labored over steaming pots of robust fare for the local tradespeople, plans are in the works for an *osteria* and a tearoom.

DA GIOVANNI OSTERIA E CUCINA (¢, 71)
Via della Lungara, 41A

TELEPHONE
06 686 1514
OPEN
Mon–Sat: lunch noon–3 P.M., dinner 7:30–11 P.M.
CLOSED
Sun; Aug
RESERVATIONS
Not accepted
CREDIT CARDS
MC, V
À LA CARTE
10–15€
FIXED-PRICE MENU
None
BREAD & SERVICE CHARGES
Bread 0.75€, service included
ENGLISH
Very limited

For local color, Cheap Eats, and few other tourists, check out this hole-in-the-wall on Via della Lungara, which runs along the Tiber River. It is definitely a family-run show. The *padrone,* Giovanni de Blasio, is a neighborhood fixture (his sister runs the *tabaccheria* next door). Before the restaurant opens at noon, grandchildren occupy some of the tables, while their mothers hurry about getting ready and writing out the daily menu.

There are two rooms: The front one squeezes in fifteen tables and is "decorated" with coat hooks, a clock, some dusty wine bottles, and copper pots with dried pasta sticking out of them. The green-and-white tablecloths are covered with butcher paper. The small room in back is where the many regulars come in early to get their favorite table and catch up on local news. For lunch or dinner, you will be almost elbow-to-elbow with your neighbors—a young student couple falling in love, a table full of boisterous workers in paint-spotted overalls downing their fourth glass of house red, or relatives of inmates from the Regina Coeli prison, which is down the street.

No one comes here for inspirational cuisine, but for the kind of simple, satisfying peasant food their grandmothers used to make. Forget the Italian menu posted outside and zero in on the handwritten one; it's a worthwhile struggle to decipher. On Monday, everyone starts with a bowl of homemade egg noodle or chicken soup, and on Tuesday, the bean soup. Thursday, it is gnocchi, and on Saturday, the loyalists come for *agnolotti* (meat- and cheese-stuffed pasta with tomato sauce) or zucchini flowers filled with minced meat. Ambitious portions of roast veal, chicken, fresh fish, and boiled beef follow, with the usual seasonal vegetables and salads available as extras. The dessert choices are narrow, so it is best to stay with the fresh fruit or a slice of the chocolate cake if your sweet tooth insists.

DA LUCIA (81)
Vicolo del Mattonato, 2B

Four generations of the Renato Bizzarri family have been cooking here since 1938. What is their key to continuing success? Dependable meals that remind everyone of slower, less complicated times, when friends and family gathered around a big table eating comfort food *all'italiana*. In places like this, some things never change, mainly because the regulars would rise up in rebellion. So you can count on a short list of pastas highlighted by *spaghetti alla gricia* (tossed with sausage, pecorino cheese, and black pepper); *involtino* (beef roll with peas); beef stew laced with onions; rabbit cooked with a touch of vinegar, white wine, rosemary, and garlic; seasonal vegetables; and without fail, gnocchi on Thursdays and *baccalà* on Fridays. No one skips desserts, because they are all made here: crème caramel, chocolate mousse, *panna cotta*, and on Saturday, tiramisù.

TELEPHONE
06 580 3601

OPEN
Tues–Sun: lunch 12:30–3:30 P.M., dinner 7:30 P.M.–midnight

CLOSED
Mon; 15 days in Aug (dates vary)

RESERVATIONS
Advised

CREDIT CARDS
None

À LA CARTE
22–28€

FIXED-PRICE MENU
None

BREAD & SERVICE CHARGES
Bread 1€, service discretionary

ENGLISH
Yes

DAR POETA (79)
Vicolo del Bologna, 45/46 (near Piazza della Scala)

Take your pick at this pizzeria: crusts are either thin, or thick and puffy. Either way, both are covered with the usual mix of toppings, plus a few offbeat combinations such as *pizza bodrilla* (apples and Grand Marnier) and the calzone filled with Nutella (a chocolate and hazelnut spread) and ricotta cheese and dusted with sugar and cocoa. Open nightly for dinner only, it is perpetually crowded, a good value, and a great pizza eat in Trastevere. It is run by three men and their mother, who makes the desserts. They don't take reservations, so arrive when the doors open or very late. Otherwise, expect to get to know the people standing in line with you.

TELEPHONE
06 588 0516

INTERNET
www.darpoeta.it

OPEN
Daily: dinner 7:30 P.M.–1 A.M.

CLOSED
Never

RESERVATIONS
Not accepted

CREDIT CARDS
AE, DC, MC, V

À LA CARTE
8–20€

FIXED-PRICE MENU
None

BREAD & SERVICE CHARGES
None

ENGLISH
Sometimes

PIZZERIA AI MARMI (¢, 86)
Viale di Trastevere, 53/59

TELEPHONE
06 580 0919
OPEN
Mon–Tues, Thur–Sun: dinner
6:30 P.M.–2:30 A.M.
CLOSED
Wed; Aug 8–28 (dates vary)
RESERVATIONS
Not accepted
CREDIT CARDS
None
À LA CARTE
Pizzas 5–8€, antipasti 4–7€
BREAD & SERVICE CHARGES
None
ENGLISH
Yes, and menu in English

The place may not look like much, but despite the drab interior it is one of the loudest, most crowded, and above all, cheapest pizzerias in Trastevere. If you time it right on a weekend night, you will witness the pizza chefs turning out more than a hundred pizzas per hour to a loyal corps of young-at-heart diners. As you can guess, service is casual, and the tables are smashed together in the interest of squeezing in as many people as possible. If you want some variety with your pizza, there are several very good bean dishes. Try the *fagioli di fiasco* (beans cooked in wine over an open fire) or the white beans with tuna, onions, and cabbage. Here is all the fiber and roughage you will need for a week! Take a pass on the uninspired antipasti and the tired desserts.

RISTORANTE CAMILLO (88)
Largo Alessandro Toja, 2/3

TELEPHONE
06 581 2188
OPEN
Mon–Sat: lunch 12:45–3 P.M.,
dinner 8 P.M.–midnight
CLOSED
Sun; Aug
RESERVATIONS
Advised
CREDIT CARDS
AE, DC, MC, V
À LA CARTE
22–28€
FIXED-PRICE MENU
None
BREAD & SERVICE CHARGES
Bread 1.50€, service included
ENGLISH
Limited, but menu in English

It doesn't get any more local or robust than at this well-loved gathering place situated at the bottom edge of Trastevere, which has been run for years by Camillo Tosti, a big, happy man who greets his guests with fervor. Not to be forgotten is his hardworking wife, who keeps the kitchen humming every day of the week but Sunday. The bright lighting, tables set for from two to twenty (and all filled), and the backslapping good fun everyone seems to be having leave little opportunity for a mood-enhancing romantic evening. Nevermind—make the trek, bring an appetite, and get ready to dig into plenty of Roman soul food. As Camillo says, the starters are simple. "We have fried artichoke and Parma ham, or Parma ham and fried artichoke; take your pick." The platters of pastas are slightly more diverse—based on hefty meat sauces or, when in season, mushrooms or artichokes (again). Massive servings of good-quality meat headline as mains, as well as fresh fish on Tuesday and Friday. I loved the bite-size, crispy-fried lamb chops seasoned with a squirt of lemon and a dash of salt and pepper. Garnishes? Here? Not unless you count fried potatoes or beans dressed in olive oil. I don't know how dessert could be a consideration, but I do like a frothy glass of Camillo's own *limoncello* liqueur to cap this Great Eat in Rome.

TRATTORIA DA AUGUSTO (80)
Piazza de' Renzi, 15

Trattoria da Augusto, a Trastevere fixture, has been serving basic Roman food to legions of budgeteers for decades. The spirited place is run by the late Augusto's wife, Leda, who is in charge of desserts; their daughter, Anna, who cooks; and their son, Sandro. It has no sign outside, absolutely no decor inside, and certainly no pretense anywhere. The menu is handwritten in an Italian script that takes only a little detective work to decode. The locals know it by heart and thrive on the filling and predictable fare—big bowls of lentil soup on Monday, bean or vegetable soup on Wednesday, gnocchi on Thursday, calamari on Tuesday, and *baccalà* every Friday. Everything is washed down with large amounts of the rough house wine, and a good time is had by all.

TELEPHONE
06 580 3798

OPEN
Mon–Fri: lunch 12:30–3 P.M., dinner 8–11 P.M.; Sat: lunch 12:30–3 P.M.

CLOSED
Sat dinner, Sun; Aug

RESERVATIONS
Not accepted

CREDIT CARDS
None

À LA CARTE
12–18€

FIXED-PRICE MENU
None

BREAD & SERVICE CHARGES
Bread 0.80€, service included

ENGLISH
Yes

Gelaterias

FONTE DELLA SALUTE (87)
Via Cardinale Marmaggi, 2/4 (corner of Viale di Trastevere)

If you are in Trastevere, you are probably planning on pizza for dinner. For dessert, I can think of no better choice than a creamy gelato from Fonte della Salute. You can order yours in a cup, but I think the ice cream, especially their "After Eight," a minty rendition of the candy, tastes wonderful in a chocolate-dipped cone. Of course, you can also follow the lead of the gelato-loving Romans around you and gild the lily by asking for *panna* (whipped cream) on top, or any of the other two dozen toppings that range from cornflakes, rice crispies, and crumbled brownies to fruit and candies. Dieters can order frozen yogurt, fruity *sorbettos,* or a soy-based sugar- and milk-free ice cream—and of course, skip the *panna*—but if you do, you will miss the real experience of gelato in Rome.

TELEPHONE
05 589 7471

OPEN
Daily: 10 A.M.–2 A.M., continuous service

CLOSED
Never

CREDIT CARDS
None

PRICES
From 1.70–3.50€

ENGLISH
Depends on server

Pastry Shops and Bakeries

PANIFICIO ARNESE–LA RENELLA (82)
Via del Moro, 15/16

TELEPHONE
06 581 7265

OPEN
Daily: 7 A.M.–11 P.M., Fri–Sat till midnight

CLOSED
Never

CREDIT CARDS
None

PRICES
Bread from 1.10€ per 100g, pizza slices and focaccias 2–4€

ENGLISH
Depends on server

You are going to have to use your nose to find this insider bakery in Trastevere. Even though there is an address, there is no sign outside. As you are walking along Via del Moro, look for number 48, which is across the street from the bakery.

Any bakery that sells one thousand loaves of bread and five hundred pizzas *daily* is clearly a roaring success. The breads and pizzas are baked in a 150-year-old wood-fired oven. When you go, take a number and you will eventually be called to the counter. Waiting a few minutes to be served works in your favor, allowing you time to look and decide what you want—but there is not much time for dallying once your number is up! If you are buying a slice of zucchini and cheese, potato rosemary, or plain tomato pizza to eat here, ask to have it heated; it will then be handed to you wrapped in wax paper and sitting on a tray. Other eat-in choices are big pieces of focaccia bread slit and then filled with tomato, mozzarella, and arugula, and topped with a dash of pure olive oil. They cannot make these wonderful sandwiches fast enough to keep up with demand. Once you have been served, take your tray to a stool at the bar along the wall, buy a soft drink from the machine nearby, and enjoy one of the best Great Eating snacks in Rome.

Trevi Fountain

To ensure a return visit to Rome, Frank Sinatra advised in song that all visitors toss a coin into the Trevi Fountain—that is, of course, if they can get close enough to hit the water. The most famous fountain in Rome seems to be at the top of everyone's list, and it is jam-packed day and night. The fountain, a magnificent white marble rococo of sea horses, craggy rocks, and Tritons, is worthy of the attention and the hundreds of rolls of film used every day by those wishing to preserve their trips in a scrapbook of memories.

Restaurants

AL MORO ($, 44)
Vicolo delle Bollette, 13 (off Piazza dei Crociferi)

It would be easy to miss this quintessential Roman trattoria if you didn't know it was tucked away on a tiny street about a minute away from the swarms of tourists photographing each other by the Trevi Fountain. There is nothing nouvelle here, either on the menu or in the brisk service of the owner (in the blue shirt) or of the corps of waiters. Al Moro is one of Rome's most popular addresses, and it is full every day of the week except for Sunday with regulars and visitors who appreciate the kitchen's time-tested classical Italian dishes. In the early spring, start with an order of some of the best fried artichokes in the city, followed by a wholly satisfying, waist-enhancing dish of tagliatelle with butter, fontina cheese, and truffle cream. Chicken livers with mashed potatoes, roast lamb, veal scaloppine, boiled meats, wonderful fresh fish either grilled, sautéed, or baked, and fried brains for the daring are only a few of the Great Eating second courses. If you are still up for dessert, order the wonderfully sweet profiteroles or *zabaione* with hot chocolate, or fresh fruit *crostata*.

TELEPHONE
06 678 3495, 06 6994 0736

OPEN
Mon–Sat: lunch 1–3:30 P.M., dinner 8–11:30 P.M.

CLOSED
Sun; Aug

RESERVATIONS
Essential

CREDIT CARDS
MC, V

À LA CARTE
40–50€

FIXED-PRICE MENU
None

BREAD & SERVICE CHARGES
Bread 2.50€, service discretionary

ENGLISH
Yes

COLLINE EMILIANE (33)
Via degli Avignonesi, 22

In Rome, as in any world-famous city, quality has its price. To enjoy a fine meal in subtly stylish surroundings during your stay in the Eternal City, follow the lead of savvy Romans and reserve a table at Colline Emiliane.

The decor takes its cue from the countryside, pairing yellow walls with yellow floral tablecloths, and accenting the two rooms with food posters and fruit and vegetable prints. The Bolognese food is hearty and served with style. All of the pastas are made by the owner's wife, and I'm sure you

TELEPHONE
06 481 7538

OPEN
Mon–Thur, Sat–Sun: lunch 12:45–2:45 P.M., dinner 7:45–10:45 P.M.

CLOSED
Fri; Aug

RESERVATIONS
Essential

CREDIT CARDS
MC, V
À LA CARTE
35–40€, house wine included
FIXED-PRICE MENU
None
BREAD & SERVICE CHARGES
Bread 1.50€, service included
ENGLISH
Yes, and menu in English

will agree that they are superb. The springtime *tagliatelle con asparagi e prosciutto* (homemade noodles with asparagus and ham) and the *tortelli di zucca* (pumpkin dumplings) are both worth a trip across town. To go all out, treat yourself to one of their truffle specialties, which range from a salad with truffles to veal and cheese fondue dotted with this epicurian delight. All is fit for a king and priced accordingly. For the *secondi piatti* (main course) stay with any veal preparation or the mixed boiled meats served with green sauce. Don't leave without trying, or at least sharing, the pear tart with raisins and pine nuts, the *zabaione* mousse, or the *budino al cioccolato,* a chocolate custard.

GIOIA MIA (34)
Via degli Avignonesi, 34

TELEPHONE
488 2784
OPEN
Mon–Sat: lunch 12:30–3 P.M.,
dinner 6:30–11:30 P.M.
CLOSED
Sun; Aug
RESERVATIONS
Advised
CREDIT CARDS
AE, DC, MC, V
À LA CARTE
22€, pizza 6–8€
BREAD & SERVICE CHARGES
Bread 1€ per person, 15%
service added
ENGLISH
Yes, and menu in English

Gioia Mia has a well-deserved reputation for consistently good food, service, and prices—as is evident from the tantalizing smells and the always happy crowd. The inside is typical trattoria, with hanging sausages and peppers, bowls of seasonally fresh fruits and vegetables in the window, wines displayed on high shelves, and for fun, a clothesline with baby clothes clipped to it.

Smart diners at both lunch and dinner start light by ordering a vegetable *antipasto misto* and then one of the twenty wood-fired pizzas, ranging from a *margherita* (with tomato sauce, mozzarella, and basil) to the *super televisione,* topped with peas, mushrooms, sausages, and an egg. A number of meat-based main dishes also vie for your attention, and you may be hard-pressed to choose between the beautifully grilled baby lamb chops and the *cuscinetto alla Gioia Mia,* veal and ham wrapped around cheese and served in a white-wine cream sauce topped with peas and mushrooms. Those with trencherman appetites can attack the one-pound *bistecca alla Fiorentina,* an enormous grilled steak that is almost enough for three people.

The two desserts to keep in mind are the *millefoglie della casa* (a flaky pastry layered with thick cream, chocolate, and whipped cream) and the *pera alla Gioia* (a pear cake covered with whipped cream and chocolate). No one said this would be a meal for someone on Weight Watchers!

VINERIA IL CHIANTI (42)
Via del Lavatore, 81/82

TELEPHONE
06 678 7550, 06 679 2470
INTERNET
www.vineriailchianti.com

A stylishly rustic wine bar, Il Chianti celebrates the bounteous food and wine of Tuscany from Monday to Saturday nonstop from noon until the wee hours. Lunch and dinner are both packed with an attractive crowd, who enjoy the well-prepared Tuscan fare. The pretty front terrace is perfect for people-watching or sharing a bottle of wine with a special someone. The house pasta special, made with tomatoes, mushrooms, and pecorino cheese, or the oversized spinach and ricotta ravioli, bursting with the flavor of truffles, will remind you of why you are in Italy. Il Chianti is also popular because you don't have to order a huge meal here. In addition to daily lunch specials, the menu lists a handful of pizzas, some beautiful salads, a selection of *crostini* and cold meat and cheese plates, plus their own warm *torte de mele* with cinnamon-spiked *zabaione* (a warm apple torte). The more formal restaurant next door is under the same ownership, but I think the Great Eats are to be had in this wine bar.

OPEN
Mon–Sat: 12:30 P.M.–2:30 A.M., continuous service

CLOSED
Sun; Aug

RESERVATIONS
Advised

CREDIT CARDS
AE, DC, MC, V

À LA CARTE
20–30€

FIXED-PRICE MENU
None

BREAD & SERVICE CHARGES
Bread 1€, service discretionary

ENGLISH
Yes, and menu in English

Gelaterias

IL GELATO DI SAN CRISPINO (43)
Via della Panetteria, 42 (off Via del Lavatore)

For an unforgettable taste of what gelato connoisseurs consider the absolute best in Rome, come to this *gelateria* not far from the Trevi Fountain. Il Gelato di San Crispino is run by Giuseppe and Pasquale Alongi, who are meticulous about using only the highest-quality ingredients in all of their flavors, which of course they make themselves. Put butterfat grams, cholesterol concerns, and dietary worries aside, if only for a moment, so you can try without guilt their *gelato di San Crispino* (a heavenly combination of heavy cream and honey), zabaglione (a rich mixture of Marsala wine and egg yolks), wild orange, or dark chocolate. Don't ask for a cone—the brothers only serve their manna-from-heaven in cups, because they believe cones interfere with the purity of the ice cream flavors. Fifteen or twenty flavors are available at any one time and can be scooped to go or eaten at one of the tables in back, which is lined with framed rave reviews from around the world.

TELEPHONE
06 697 3924

INTERNET
www.ilgelatodisancrispino.com

OPEN
Mon, Wed–Sun: noon–12:30 A.M. (Fri–Sat till 1:30 A.M.)

CLOSED
Tues; Jan 15–Feb 15

CREDIT CARDS
None

PRICES
Cups 1.70–6.30€

ENGLISH
Yes, and all flavors labeled in English

The Vatican and Piazza Cavour

St. Peter's Basilica, the Sistine Chapel, and the Vatican Museums and Gardens are all within a 108-acre area known as Vatican City in the Vatican State, the world's smallest independent sovereign state. No one leaves Rome without seeing the splendors of St. Peter's Basilica, the world's largest church and the holiest shrine of Roman Catholicism; the Sistine Chapel, with its magnificent Michelangelo ceiling; and one of the world's greatest art collections, housed in the Vatican Museums. The views from the top of the Vatican to the heart of Rome are wonderful. An important side note is that mail sent from Vatican City goes much faster than from any other location in Rome.

Piazza Cavour holds nothing much for a visitor other than its proximity to Castel Sant' Angelo. The Castel was originally built by Emperor Hadrian in A.D. 135 as his tomb, and it was used as a fortress in A.D. 271 during the building of the Aurelian Wall. Now visitors can see a chapel designed by Michelangelo for Pope Leo X, military paraphernalia, beautiful frescoes, and *tromp l'oeil* paintings.

($) indicates a Big Splurge
(¢) indicates a Cheap Eat

Restaurants

DAL TOSCANO (3)
Via Germanico 58/60

Dal Toscano, which specializes in the foods and wines of Tuscany, is truly a Great Eat that is always packed with boisterous, gesticulating Italians, many of whom look like they have been firmly planted at the same tables—eating the same rich food and discussing the same gossip or politics—for years. The restaurant is so popular that reservations are required at least one day in advance. Seating is in a large two-room space dominated by a huge exhibition kitchen and open grill.

I think it is best to get started by ordering the hand-cut prosciutto or a light soup to save room for a bracing second course of veal or beefsteak grilled over the coals. As a garnish, consider forgoing the usual vegetables and ordering the *fagioli toscani all'olio,* white beans cooked in olive oil with a liberal lacing of garlic. They are so creamy and wonderful . . . I dream of having them right this minute. If you add a small salad and a bottle of Chianti Classico, you will indeed be a contented Great Eater. Another strong recommendation is the house dessert, which has been served since the day they opened. It is simply a cream cake with hot chocolate sauce poured over it at the last minute, but it provides the perfect finish for this Great Eat in Rome.

TELEPHONE
06 3972 5717, 06 3972 3373
INTERNET
www.ristorantedaltoscano.it
OPEN
Tues–Sun: lunch 12:30–3 P.M., dinner 8–11 P.M.
CLOSED
Mon; Aug 10–13
RESERVATIONS
Essential, as far in advance as possible
CREDIT CARDS
AE, DC, MC, V
À LA CARTE
30–40€
FIXED-PRICE MENU
None
BREAD & SERVICE CHARGES
Bread 1.50€, 10% service added
ENGLISH
Yes

HOSTARIA DEI BASTIONI (11)
Via Leone IV, 29 (almost to Via Germanico)

Due to the constant influx of tourists to the Vatican, finding a decent meal at a fair price can begin to feel almost like a mission. All Great Eating hope is not lost, however, thanks to the Hostaria dei Bastioni, which is entered through a tiny doorway below street level on the busy Via Leone IV. Inside, the basement dining room is nicely turned out with black and red chairs and tables covered with colorful yellow, green, and rose linen. There is also a sidewalk dining terrace where you can relax in comfort and thank your lucky stars that you are not standing in the queue across the street that wraps around the block, filled with pilgrims waiting to get into the Vatican museums.

The appreciative diners are made up largely of businesspeople, neighborhood regulars, and smart visitors. At this homey, hospitable eatery, you will find moderately priced seafood and a host of other familiar Roman dishes.

TELEPHONE
06 3972 3034
OPEN
Mon–Sat: lunch noon–3 P.M., dinner 7–11:30 P.M.
CLOSED
Sun; July 15–31
RESERVATIONS
Advised for dinner
CREDIT CARDS
AE, DC, MC, V
À LA CARTE
20–25€
FIXED-PRICE MENU
Lunch only: 11€, 3 courses
BREAD & SERVICE CHARGES
Bread 1€, service included
ENGLISH
Yes, and menu in English

The antipasti selection is limited. Just have a peek at the display and see what looks best—it changes constantly—or ask Antonio, the hands-on owner, who never seems to stop meeting, greeting, and serving his guests. You can't go wrong with the house specialty—*fettuccine alla Bastioni,* made with cream, bacon, fresh tomato, and a hint of orange. The risotto with seafood, the veal with potatoes, or the assorted roast meats, also served with potatoes, are safe bets if you do not go for the other house specialty, fish. The house tiramisù or a seasonal fruit are the best endings.

HOSTARIA DINO EXPRESS (¢, 17)
Via Tacito, 80

TELEPHONE
06 361 0305
OPEN
Mon–Sat: lunch 12:45–4 P.M.
CLOSED
Sun; Aug
RESERVATIONS
Not necessary
CREDIT CARDS
None
À LA CARTE
15–18€
FIXED-PRICE MENU
None
BREAD & SERVICE CHARGES
Bread 1€, service included
ENGLISH
Yes, ask for Andrea

If you're hungry, cash strapped, and yearning for home-cooking near the Vatican and Piazza Cavour, this jewel, run by the Marrocus family, is a smart choice. I knew immediately upon seeing the eight-table room and smelling the wonderful aromas floating up from the tiny kitchen in back that I would have my lunch here—and would return as often as possible. The whitewashed, rough stucco walls are hung with wood carvings, braids of garlic, dried herbs, old cooking pans, and pretty baskets. Each day a new handwritten menu on a piece of graph paper with a little drawing in the corner is placed on the tables. This is the place for those who don't mind tackling a serious midday meal, anchored by a filling bowl of gnocchi (Thursday only) or lasagne, followed by roast chicken or pork, lamb meatballs, or rolled beef stuffed and served with peas. Accompany your repast with a glass or two of the house Chianti or Romana Castelli wine. If this is not enough, there is always dessert—meringue cookies with lemon or a *crostata* with jam—and all for a final tab every Great Eater can appreciate. Please note that the higher à la carte price includes both wine and dessert, while the lower price includes water but no wine or dessert.

IL RAGNO D'ORO (4)
Via Silla, 26

TELEPHONE
06 321 12362
OPEN
Mon–Sat: lunch 12:30–
3:30 P.M., dinner 7:30 P.M.–
midnight
CLOSED
Sun; Aug, a few days at
Christmas (dates vary)

The name is just one of those go-figure oddities so common in Rome. The sign in front says, "Ristorante Ragno d'Oro," the name on the menu says, "Il Ragno d'Oro," and on the business card it reads, "Trattoria Pizzeria Ragno d'Oro da Marco e Fabio Formichella." Whatever you call it, this establishment is known by its followers as Da Marco e Fabio Formichella, after the father-and-son team who run it. Because it is far enough from the mainstream tourist beat, it has remained a genuine neighborhood trattoria, catering to regular diners who know that the food, from first to last course, seldom disappoints. The interior has been totally redone (thank goodness!). Gone is the dizzying collection of lighted Greek and Roman busts, mirrors, and paintings, including one of Rosie's Diner and a Hindu god. Now the long dining room is painted a soft yellow, with framed prints of old Roman streets on the walls and an open kitchen in the back.

The food remains true to its origins and continues to offer a bracing blend of Roman favorites. Start by sharing the *antipasto alla Marco e Fabio,* a plate of quickly fried zucchini, salt cod, stuffed olives, and cheese and potato puffs. Lighter eaters may want to start with the *prosciutto e melone* (melon and ham) or *caprese* (tomato, mozzarella, and basil drizzled with olive oil), but frankly, these are not as interesting as the antipasti mix. There are sixteen pastas, ranging from a plain spaghetti with *ragù* to a heady *rigatoni alla grigia,* featuring salty cured bacon, olive oil, and plenty of pecorino cheese, spinach, and ricotta. For the undecided, a sampling of several pastas is another choice. Pizza is available, as well as a full roster of meats, fish (check to be sure it is fresh and not frozen), and vegetable sides. The best dessert is not listed; ask for the dessert *misto,* a large assortment of bite-size pieces of cheesecake, macaroons, various *biscotti,* and shelled nuts. For just the right ending, round out the meal with a frosty shot of *limoncello* liqueur, made by Fabio's mother. It will leave you glad to have found this restaurant, knowing you will receive the same hospitality and good food every time you return.

RESERVATIONS
Not necessary
CREDIT CARDS
AE, DC, MC, V
À LA CARTE
20–30€
FIXED-PRICE MENU
None
BREAD & SERVICE CHARGES
Bread 1€, service discretionary
ENGLISH
Yes

LA CAVA ($, 5)
Via Attilio Regolo, 21

La Cava is a smart, artistically interesting restaurant on a side street within easy walking distance of the Vatican. From the outside, you might wonder what the restaurant actually is. As you approach the corner location, you will see the windows facing the street covered halfway with hundreds of smooth river stones; a heavy metal door opens from the street into a large space with a minimalistic, Zen-inspired decor. River stones line the walls and are stacked in wire grids that act as room dividers. Along one wall, a lighted cubicle artistically houses a single stone. Even the bathroom is unusual, with a white laundry sink dividing the men's and women's sections.

Run by a dynamic duo, Francesco and Silvia, La Cava has been a success from the get-go because the food is as

TELEPHONE
06 8424 2751
OPEN
Mon–Fri: lunch noon–3 P.M., dinner 7:30–11 P.M. (till 11:30 P.M. Fri); Sat: dinner 7:30–11:30 P.M.
CLOSED
Sat lunch, Sun
RESERVATIONS
Advised
CREDIT CARDS
AE, DC, MC, V
À LA CARTE
40–45€

FIXED-PRICE MENU
Lunch buffet: 12€, includes
water and espresso
BREAD & SERVICE CHARGES
No bread charge, service
discretionary
ENGLISH
Yes

bold and imaginative as the surroundings. The market-fresh lunch buffet is a beautiful display of hot and cold vegetables, *bruschettas,* pastas, and one or two meat offerings. This well-priced offer sells out quickly, so go early for the best selection. In addition, there is a seasonal menu loaded with Great Eats, whether you are dining on the light side and ordering just an appetizer, or in for the count for all courses. Start with marinated salmon served with three colorful peppers and a goat cheese canapé, or a plate of grilled vegetables served with a round of *mozzarella di bufala.* I thought the *mezze penne* with a fish ragout and basil was not a pasta I would repeat; however, the ravioli pillows with eggplant and smoked provolone cheese in a bright tomato sauce was one to come back for. I also liked the seared tuna, simply served with a lemon and mint sauce, as well as the beef fillet, served with an interesting side of red turnips. The dessert to have, no matter what, is the illegally rich dark chocolate cake.

L'INSALATA RICCA (¢, 12)
Piazza Risorgimento, 5/6

For a complete description of this restaurant, see page 104. All other information is the same.
TELEPHONE: 06 3973 0387

PIZZA RUSTICA AI GRACCHI (¢, 13)
Via dei Gracchi, 7

TELEPHONE
06 3973 8182
OPEN
Mon–Sat: 10 A.M.–8 P.M.,
continuous service
CLOSED
Sun; Aug 8–31
RESERVATIONS
Not accepted
CREDIT CARDS
None
À LA CARTE
0.60–1.30€ per 100 g
FIXED-PRICE MENU
None
BREAD & SERVICE CHARGES
None
ENGLISH
Depends on server, but
generally very limited

The pizza joint across the street is usually empty, with the waiters standing at the door and watching all the customers crowding into Pizza Rustica ai Gracchi. At this take-out pizza stand, the pizza chefs and ovens work overtime, turning out big trays of lip-smacking pizza as fast as they can sell it. There are thirty to forty pizzas made here on a revolving basis, but the simple *margherita* with tomato and mozzarella is still the best-seller. Also available are rotisserie chicken and soft drinks. The food prices along this strip of real estate near the Vatican tend to reach the outer limits, so it is nice to find a convenient pit stop for refueling, either before or after tackling the Vatican's "D" plan: a five-hour walking tour. When you order, you choose the type and size of your slice from twelve to fifteen varieties, which are then cut and sold by weight. You will probably not snag the one plastic chair, so plan to take this one with you.

TAVERNA ANGELICA ($, 24)
Piazza Amerigo Capponi, 6 (near Piazza delle Vaschette)

No one said this hidden jewel would be easy to find. I still don't quite know how I found it, but I was happy I persevered, asking for directions all along the way. The best time to make this safari is when you want a leisurely Sunday lunch. Their delicious fixed-price Sunday lunch features virtually all of the high-quality dishes that are served for dinner during the rest of the week, and costs half as much. The Asian-inspired interior features pieces of bamboo clumped together, huge wicker umbrella-styled wall lights, and copper artwork hanging on the walls. (The horse saddle dominating one of the front windows seems out of place.) The bare wooden tables are sparsely covered with a runner and nicely set with simple cutlery and glassware. It is a setting that could be anywhere; only the voices around you tell you it's Rome.

When you are seated, a glass of prosecco and an assortment of *bruschetta* arrives in prompt order, allowing you to nibble while looking over the menu. Three of the four starters feature fish. I liked the fresh salmon tartare lightly dressed with a spritz of lemon and a dusting of chives, and the unusual octopus salad, served on a bed of potatoes and accompanied by a rich black-olive sauce. For the first course, the fettuccini with fresh tomatoes, basil, and burrata cheese is a light choice; the puréed barley with seasonal vegetables and the rosemary herbed rabbit are too heavy if you are thinking about having more courses. The energetic second plates star duck breast with orange sauce and carmelized onions, veal osso buco in a white wine sauce, and my favorite—tender baby lamb with a lovely assortment of vegetables. The homemade desserts are irresistible. How could you not try mango Bavarian cream with a bright-green kiwi sauce, soft chocolate cake with a bitter-orange sauce, or fresh dates filled with coffee cream? These are just a few of the dishes awaiting you for Sunday lunch at this Great Eat in Rome.

TELEPHONE
06 687 4514
INTERNET
www.tavernaangelica.it
OPEN
Daily: dinner 7:30–11 P.M.; also Sun lunch: noon–3 P.M.
CLOSED
Aug, a few days at Christmas (dates vary)
RESERVATIONS
Essential for Sunday lunch, advised for dinner
CREDIT CARDS
MC, V
À LA CARTE
40–45€
FIXED-PRICE MENU
Sun lunch: 20€, 4 courses, includes bread, mineral water, wine, and service
BREAD & SERVICE CHARGES
Bread 1€, 10% service added
ENGLISH
Yes, and menu in English

TRATTORIA PIZZERIA LA CARAVELLA (9)
Via degli Scipioni, 32/32b, at the corner of Via Vespasiano

Hearty cooking speaks to us all, and you can always find it at La Caravella, a busy all-purpose neighborhood trattoria with courteous service and a massive menu that includes twenty pizzas. The scope of seasonal specialties, pizzas, and tried-and-true favorites will appeal to everyone from the

TELEPHONE
06 39 726 161
OPEN
Mon–Wed, Fri–Sun: lunch noon–3:30 P.M., dinner 6–11 P.M.
CLOSED
Thur; Jan

RESERVATIONS
Not necessary
À LA CARTE
18–25€
FIXED-PRICE MENU
11€, 3 courses, bread and
service included
BREAD & SERVICE CHARGES
Bread 1€, service included
ENGLISH
Yes

diet-conscious to the diet-allergic. Also very appealing is the wraparound corner terrace, which is filled to capacity during warm weather. The fixed-price menu offers good value and plenty of first- and second-course choices, especially if you are seriously hungry and can polish off lasagne, veal escallops, roast chicken, or fried fish, with a green salad, fried potatoes, and fruit salad for dessert. Bread and service are included; drinks are not.

Gelaterias

GIOVANNI FASSI/PALAZZO DEL FREDDO (10)
Via Vespasiano, 56 a/b/c

For details on this *gelateria,* please see page 152. All other information is the same.

TELEPHONE: 06 3972 5164
OPEN: Tues–Sun: 12:30–8:30 P.M. (Sat till 1:15 A.M.)
CLOSED: Mon; Oct–March 31

Food Shopping in Rome

Gourmet Food and Wine Shops

BUCCONE (6)
Via di Rippeta, 19/20 (Piazza del Popolo)

Buccone has an amazing selection of wines, spirits, liqueurs, olive oils, and balsamic vinegars, and all of these can be shipped to any address on the planet. Please see page 114 for a description of their wine bar and restaurant.

TELEPHONE
06 361 2154
OPEN
Mon–Thur: 9 A.M.–8:30 P.M.;
Fri–Sat: 9 A.M.–midnight
CLOSED
Sun, except in Dec
CREDIT CARDS
AE, DC, MC, V
ENGLISH
Yes

CASTRONI (15)
Via Cola di Rienzo, 196 (The Vatican)

Castroni, with two locations, is Rome's answer to Fauchon in Paris. The stores are a wonderland of regional specialties, plus they offer the largest selection of imported foods in Rome, which they will pack for you but not ship.

TELEPHONE
06 687 4383
INTERNET
www.castronigroup.it

171

OPEN
Mon–Sat: 8 A.M.–8 P.M.
CLOSED
Sun; a few days mid-Aug (dates vary)
CREDIT CARDS
MC, V
ENGLISH
Yes

The prices are on the high side, but if you are having Skippy extra-chunk peanut butter withdrawal pangs or want tacos and refried beans for dinner, here is the place to satisfy your fix.

The second store sells an array of American brands of cake mixes, soups, and cereals . . . even Pop Tarts. Also look for small bottles of olive oil, truffle oil, and different types of dried pastas, which make great gifts to take home to lucky friends. The second location is at Via Ottaviano, 55, at the corner of Via Germanico; tel: 06 3972 3279.

ENOTECA COSTANTINI (18)
Piazza Cavour, 16 (The Vatican)

TELEPHONE
06 321 1502
OPEN
Wine shop: Mon 4:30–8 P.M., Tues–Sat 9 A.M.–1 P.M., 4:30–8 P.M.; wine bar: Mon–Fri 12:30–2:30 P.M., 6–11 P.M., Sat 6–11 P.M.
CLOSED
Sat lunch (wine bar), Sun; Aug
CREDIT CARDS
AE, DC, MC, V
ENGLISH
Yes

If you are a serious wine lover and connoisseur, Enoteca Costantini should be on your priority list of places to visit. The shop is on two levels, the first of which is devoted to an expensive restaurant and a wine bar, where, for a modest outlay, you can happily munch your way through a variety of cheeses and bar snacks while drinking a glass or two of wine. It also features shelf after shelf of distilled spirits, and bins of bargain (and not so bargain) wines. Downstairs on the lower level is where the serious business of wine tasting and wine selling takes place. Four times a year, the family holds wine-tasting seminars here amid the rows of magnificent wines they have been collecting for thirty years. These tastings, conducted in Italian, unfortunately are not for the casual tourist, but for real aficionados who pay around 185€ for seven two-hour "wine-tasting les-sons," where four wines are tasted and discussed. However, anyone can buy their wines, which range from 3€ to the unheard-of price of 40,000€ for an 1894 Brunello.

FRANCHI (16)
Via Cola di Rienzo, 204, at the corner of Via Terenzio (The Vatican)

TELEPHONE
06 686 4576
INTERNET
www.franchigift.com
OPEN
Mon–Sat: 8:15 A.M.–9 P.M.
CLOSED
Sun
CREDIT CARDS
AE, DC, MC, V
ENGLISH
Yes

A rival to nearby Castroni, Franchi has a deli of your dreams, with wonderful antipasti and roast meats for creat-ing gourmet picnics, fresh coffee ground to order at their coffee bar, and an enormous selection of ham, cheeses, and wines from all over Italy.

LA BOTTEGA DEL CIOCCOLATO (117)
Via Leonina, 82 (Colosseum)

Looking for a replica of the Colosseum, the Vatican, or Buddha in white or dark chocolate? Here is your source, an amazing little shop selling all sizes and shapes of chocolate replicas, including Venetian Carnivale masks and Mickey Mouse in white chocolate. A small Colosseum is 12€; a large one will set you back 35€. Everything is made here and can be gift wrapped, and you can also design your own basket of chocolate goodies.

TELEPHONE
06 482 1473
OPEN
Mon–Sat: 9:30 A.M.–7:30 P.M.
CLOSED
Sun; June–Aug, and any time it is too hot to make chocolate
CREDIT CARDS
AE, DC, MC, V
ENGLISH
Limited

TRIMANI (98)
Via Goito, 20 (Train Station)

Trimani has been considered one of Rome's premier wine and liquor shops since it opened in 1821. Naturally, you can buy a vintage *cru* that could cost more than your trip to Rome, but they also stock a good selection of affordable wines, and they ship worldwide. In addition, they offer assorted dry pasta, jams, jellies, honey, dried fruits, and olive oils. To sample a few wines before you buy, go around the corner to their wine bar and restaurant, also called Trimani, at Via Cernaia, 37b (see page 151).

TELEPHONE
06 446 9661
INTERNET
www.trimani.com
OPEN
Mon–Sat: 8:30 A.M.–1:30 P.M., 3:30–8 P.M.
CLOSED
Sun
CREDIT CARDS
AE, DC, MC, V
ENGLISH
Yes

VOLPETTI (91)
Via Marmorata, 47 (Testaccio)

Volpetti is recognized as one of the best *salumeria/* gastronomic shops not only in Rome but in all of Italy. At first glance, you may wonder why, but if you speak with Claudio, who oversees their products, you will understand how they earned a high reputation. Let's start with their cheeses, most of which come from Norica in Umbria and are stored in a climate-controlled cellar. Every day Claudio washes the rinds with whey and turns them, the way his mother did, to keep the cheeses clean and uniform. Claudio is passionate about his cheese and works twelve hours a day. He says, "Cheese is like a child, it changes every day. Climate, terrain, and the hand of man make a cheese. The animal is the means to the cheese, but the land is the source." He can explain the cheeses, tell you what wine and foods to serve with them, offer samples, and put your choices in vacuum packs for the trip home. In addition, Volpetti sells a tremendous variety of meats, breads, aged balsamic vinegars, and interesting salsas. For a real taste of their foods, treat yourself to lunch at their nearby cafeteria-style restaurant, Volpetti Piú (see page 143). If you can't get to Rome, shop at Volpetti online and have your order delivered.

TELEPHONE
06 574 2352
INTERNET
www.volpetti.com; www.fooditaly.com
OPEN
Mon: 8 A.M.–2 P.M., 5–8:15 P.M.; Tues–Sat: 8 A.M.–8 P.M.
CLOSED
Sun
CREDIT CARDS
AE, MC, V
ENGLISH
Ask for Claudio

Grocery Stores and Supermarkets

CONAD AT TERMINI (105)
Forum Termini Mall, Termini Station

OPEN
Daily: 6 A.M.–midnight
CLOSED
Never
CREDIT CARDS
MC, V
ENGLISH
Limited

Located on the lower ground floor of the train station, this lifesaving mini-market is similar to a 7-Eleven, though the convenience comes at a high price.

STANDA/OVIESSE (85)
Viale Trastevere, 60 (Trastevere)

OPEN
Mon–Sat: 8:30 A.M.–8 P.M.; Sun:
9:30 A.M.–1:30 P.M., 4–8 P.M.
CLOSED
Never
CREDIT CARDS
AE, DC, MC, V
ENGLISH
Limited

Standa is a supermarket in the basement of Oviesse, a dime store–quality department store. Both are good if you need a few things quickly, such as toothpaste, another cotton shirt, or a few snacks to take back to your hotel. Most of the produce is prepackaged, but the prices are fair and the grocery selections are outstanding.

NOTE: Two other branches of this supermarket are located in Rome: one is near the Vatican (on Via Cola di Rienzo), and the other is on Viale Regina Margherita, on the outskirts of Rome.

SMA (113)
Piazza Santa Maria Maggiore (Train Station, near Santa Maria Maggiore)

OPEN
Mon–Sat: 9 A.M.–9 P.M.; Sun:
10 A.M.–8:30 P.M.
CLOSED
Major holidays
CREDIT CARDS
AE, DC, MC, V
ENGLISH
Very limited

Located near the Basilica Santa Maria Maggiore, this is Rome's latest answer to one-stop shopping. It looks and feels like a U.S. supermarket and stocks aisle after aisle of everything you could possibly need to outfit a kitchen and begin turning out gourmet Italian meals. Upstairs there is a UPIM department store, with quality on par with Target.

Indoor/Outdoor Markets

Rome has many food markets of all types and sizes. The most central and interesting are listed here. Most districts also have their own local morning food markets, which usually operate from 7 A.M. until around 1:30 to 2 P.M., but it all depends on the seller. If you follow the times given below, you will generally be assured of finding the stands open. Of course, the best selection will not be found five minutes before they are closing up shop for the day. At all of these markets, do not count on much English being spoken, and plan to pay in cash.

CAMPO DE' FIORI (65)
Piazza Campo de' Fiori

OPEN
Mon–Sat: 8 A.M.–1 P.M.

Campo de' Fiori has been a focus of Roman life since the sixteenth century, and it is still one of the most charming squares in the city. Today the colorful outdoor market attracts loads of camera-toting tourists. After the market is over, the square resembles a gigantic trash heap until the garbage troopers come through with their loud, water-spraying machines and scoop most of it up.

MERCATO DEI FIORI
Via Trionfale, 47/49 (northwestern edge of Rome)

OPEN
Tues: 10:30 A.M.–1 P.M.

This is an indoor wholesale flower market with bargain prices that is open to the public on Tuesday morning only.

MERCATO ESQUILINO (114)
Via Principe Amadeo and Via Rascoli
(Train Station)

OPEN
Mon–Sat: 7 A.M.–1:30 P.M.

The old market on the Piazza Vittorio Emanuele has been razed, and the space turned into a park and playground. Cheesy shops still ring the piazza, anchored by the biggest cheap shopping thrill in Rome—Mas, which can best be described as a multilevel flea market for clothing and accessories.

The new market is still big and busy, with stalls selling everything from fish and produce to dairy products and meat, including parts you have never seen before and probably would not want on your plate, ever. The market draws a large ethnic clientele, and as with all markets, quality varies with each stall. My advice is to case the place first, then select the stall that suits you. Watch your money at all times, and especially watch out for gypsies, who cruise through in packs about an hour before the market closes in the afternoon.

PIAZZA DELL' UNITA (14)
Off Via Cola di Rienzo (The Vatican)

OPEN
Mon–Sat: 8 A.M.–7 P.M.

There are wonderful selections, good prices, and underground parking in this indoor market not far from the Vatican.

PIAZZA DI S. COSIMATO (83)
South of Piazza Santa Maria in Trastevere

OPEN
Mon–Sat: 7 A.M.–1 P.M.

S. Cosimato is a smaller market, but one with a good selection.

PIAZZA TESTACCIO (90)
Off Via Aldo Manuzio (Testaccio)

OPEN
Mon–Sat: 8 A.M.–1:30 P.M.

This market is in a working-class neighborhood with prices to match. There are also a few clothing stalls and a lot of shoe stalls.

VIA DELL' ARANCIO (25)
Off Via Tomacelli at the end of Via di Ripetta (Spanish Steps)

OPEN
Mon–Sat: 8 A.M.–1:30 P.M.

This small market in a high-end neighborhood makes up in quality what it lacks in size. The few stalls sell only prime produce. If you keep going back to the same stall, after four or five visits you will be treated like a regular.

VIA MILAZZO (104)
Via Milazzo (near Termini Station)

OPEN
Mon–Sat: 8 A.M.–1 P.M.

This is a very typical neighborhood morning market with excellent produce. An organic seller comes on Wednesdays and Fridays. The bakery on the corner is excellent. The lingerie stall is a throwback to the days when eighteen-hour bras, serious girdles, and garter belts were in vogue. On Mondays there are only a few stalls open.

Venice

Venetians know all too well that they are picturesque; in Venice one never loses the sense that life is being staged for the onlooker.
> —*Jonathan Raban,* Arabia Through the Looking Glass, *1979*

When I went to Venice, my dream became my address.
> —*Marcel Proust, 1906*

Founded more than fifteen hundred years ago on a cluster of mudflats, Venice became Europe's trading post between the East and the West, reaching the height of its power in the fifteenth century. Although it no longer enjoys such elite status, it remains a glorious reflection of its rich past, depending for its income now on the mass of visitors who arrive every year to marvel and experience enchantment.

In Venice, one always has the feeling of being suspended in time. Little has changed over the centuries to diminish the harmony of colors, lights, and sounds that float dreamlike over its canals and lagoons. Composed of more than 100 islets linked together by 354 bridges spanning 177 canals, it is little wonder how easy it is to get lost, even for a native. However, becoming hopelessly lost in the maze of *rios, campos,* and *campiellos* is one of the most pleasurable experiences of a visit to this romantic city on the Adriatic.

Since you cannot drive a car, hop on a bus, or hail a cab, what you will do in Venice is walk, walk, and walk. To save yourself supreme confusion, it is necessary to become familiar with the six districts, or *sestieri,* that make up the city: three per each side of the Grand Canal. They are Cannaregio, Castello, and San Marco to the east, and Dorsoduro, San Polo, and Santa Croce to the west. This is also how the listings in *Great Eats Italy* are organized, followed by restaurants on the outlying islands. Only three bridges cross the Grand Canal: Ponte degli Scalzi (at the train station), Rialto, and Accademia. Addresses are usually given only by the district and number (i.e., Dorsoduro 3437), often omitting the name of the street. All of the listings in the Venice section of *Great Eats Italy* include the name of the street and the number (i.e., Calle dell' Oro, 5678), with restaurants listed by *sestieri* (districts). This will help, but you will still get lost: street names may repeat in more than one district, some buildings have more than one set of numbers, and numbered addresses close to one another sequentially may indicate buildings at opposite ends of the district, since within each district there are some six thousand numbers, with no clear-cut sequence. It is just as bizarre as it sounds and often leads to hair-tearing frustration, especially when you mistakenly try to use logic—or a map.

Though you may be lost, do not panic. Look for the yellow signs posted throughout the city to find the direction you want. For example, look for the sign saying "Rialto," the bridge that connects the San Marco district with San Polo, when you are going to shop at the Rialto Bridge. "Accademia" is the sign to look for if you want to see the Peggy Guggenheim Collection or the Galleria dell' Accademia, which has the most important collection of Venetian art in the world. If you are going back to get to your parked car, watch for signs saying "Piazzale Roma." If your destination is St. Mark's Square, look for signs pointing to San Marco. If you are leaving Venice on the train, go in the direction marked "Ferrovia" (train station). For a definition of Venetian street terms, see page 181.

Venice celebrates a number of holidays (*feste*). The most important is Carnivale, held during the ten days before Lent and ending on Shrove Tuesday with a masked ball for the elite and dancing in St. Mark's Square for the rest of us. Crowds during this time defy description. Unless you enjoy elbow-to-elbow pushing mob scenes and the-sky-is-the-limit prices in hotels and restaurants, it is best to avoid Venice at this time.

If you think food is pricey in Florence and Rome, you have not yet eaten in Venice, where even Italians used to runaway inflation consider dining out expensive. While Venice is a city of romantic enchantment, the high cost of living and the endless flow of tourists keep the prices in the stratosphere. Remember, nothing is produced or grown here—everything is brought in and hand-carried to its destination by foot or by boat. The best word-of-mouth recommendation for a Venetian restaurant is that the prices are not too high. My own feeling is that the short-term visitor should seriously consider casting aside thoughts of great economy and take the philosophical view that he or she may never pass this way again. This is not to say that good-value restaurants do not exist, because I have found many wonderful ones. This is just a warning that you will probably spend more for food in Venice than you want to.

One way to shave food costs is to lunch in a *bacaro* (bar). Most Venetians do, and many order a plate of *cicchetti*: bite-size appetizers similar to Spanish tapas. To go with your plate, have an *ombra,* a glass of dry white wine. Another option is a plump *tramezzino,* a sandwich filled with almost anything you can think of. The cheapest eat will be a picnic you make up yourself from foods bought at a market.

Venetian cuisine is known for its simplicity, and its best dishes often come from the sea, such as *granseole* (spider crabs), *molecche* (soft-shell crabs), *sarde in saor* (sardines marinated in vinegar, onions, raisins, and pine nuts), *bigoli in salsa* (thick, whole-wheat pasta with anchovies and onions), and *seppie in nero* (squid cooked in its own black ink and usually served with pasta or polenta). When ordering at a restaurant, remember that on Sunday and Monday the Rialto fish market is closed, so any fish served on these days will not be fresh that day. Risotto is the favored starch, sauced with delicate seafood or tender seasonal vegetables. Another popular rice dish is *risi e bisi*—a thick, soupy dish of rice, peas, and pea pods. Polenta appears not only with fish but with the famous *fegato alla veneziana,* calves' liver with onions. Pastries and sweets abound. Try the ring-shaped cookies called *bussolai,* which are the specialty of Burano, or the thin, dry oval cookies called *baicoli,* dipped in sweet wine. Certain foods are traditional to eat on certain feast days. During Carnivale you will see small doughnuts known as *frittelle,* which come plain, with fruit (*con frutta*), or with cream (*con crema*). Buy a bagful and don't hesitate to eat them all right away, as they do not keep well. The most popular wines are from nearby Fruili and the neighboring Veneto, especially the white Soave or the red Valpolicella and Bardolino. Prosecco is a light, sparkling wine that is a delicious apéritif. Grappa—strong and fiery (so exercise caution)—is made from plums, grapes, and juniper berries.

While most restaurants in other cities take their annual holidays in either July or August, the most popular months to close in Venice, in addition to July and August, are late November, December, January, and February (until the beginning of Carnivale), when the dampness and all-embracing cold of Venice subside. However, the period between Christmas and New Year's is becoming an increasingly popular time to visit Venice, so to meet the tourist demand, many restaurants will open during this time, then close again until Carnivale.

Because Venice exists primarily for tourists, many waiters and waitresses, and unfortunately restaurant owners as well, have become very jaded about the quality of service they offer. If a place is very busy, often the Venetians get the service and the tourists are ignored, and you can only laugh when an old waiter slides the basket of bread past you down a long table or reaches over your head to serve someone else across the table. In an effort to improve its service image, especially in the better places, a group of independent restaurateurs called Ristoranti della Buona Accoglienza has been formed. This organization pledges a proper price-to-quality ratio, the use of fine products, and exceptional service in an agreeable atmosphere. Most of these restaurants are Big Splurges, but you are virtually guaranteed a wonderful meal. If you have any complaints about the food or service in any of the member restaurants, please call 041 528 5521, or write to them at Casella Postale No. 624, 30100 Venezia, Italy. The members listed in *Great Eats Italy* are:

Ai Gondolieri, page 219
Al Covo, page 199
Al Gatto Nero, page 238
Alle Testiere, page 200
Fiaschetteria Toscana, page 191
Il Nuovo Galeon, page 202
Osteria da Fiore, page 231
Ristorante Riviera, page 225
Vini da Gigio, page 196

Discount Cards

VENICEcard is a one-, three-, or seven-day card giving holders discounts and accesses to many services in Venice. Its main benefit is that it allows holders free access to public transport (i.e., the *vaporettos*) and reduced fare on the Alilaguna boat service from and to the airport. There are two types of cards: orange and blue. The orange card costs twice as much as the blue but offers much more, including free or reduced access to museums, churches, and cultural events, as well as discounts in the carparks near Piazzale Roma, and in bars, restaurants, and shops with the VENICEcard logo. You can reserve a VENICEcard online (www.venicecard.it) or by telephone (39 041 2424). If you reserve and pay in advance online by credit card you get a discount. VENICEcards without advance reservations can be bought from Vela, Apt, and Ava tourist offices, which have booths at Piazzale Roma.

The Rolling VENICEcard is for visitors between 14 and 29 years old. Holders are entitled to discounts at selected hotels, restaurants, museums, and shops, as well as reduced-fare three-day *vaporetto* tickets and 50 percent off concerts at La Fenice. The card can be purchased at any Vela office. There is one at Piazzale Roma, Tel: 041 272 2249 (no credit cards accepted). A central one that accepts MasterCard and Visa is near Piazza San Marco at Calle dei Fuseri, 1810; Tel: 041 272 2310. For further information, consult the Website: www.velaspa.com.

Special Tours and Arrangements

Special Venetian travel tip: Whatever reason takes you to Venice, all I can say is—don't miss Samantha!

For a memorable private tour of Venice and an inside look into how the Venetians live, eat, shop, and play, please call Samantha Durrell, who, while originally from New York, has been a resident of Venice for almost twenty years. Besides being delightful, she knows and understands Venice better than most natives, and seems to know them all. It is clear that everyone adores Samantha, and after one day spent on a tour with her, you will too.

She offers four distinct tours: a culture walk, a photo walk, a sailing excursion through the waterways of Venice, and finally, a food walk—*The Art of Eating Well*. On this walk, Samantha will take you shopping in neighborhood markets for ingredients, then guide you in preparing and eating your Venetian specialty meal in her beautiful home overlooking a picturesque lagoon. Believe me, this will be one *buon appetito* you will never forget.

Culture, photo, and food walks (maximum of four people, at least four hours): $325 for the first 2 people; $60 each additional person; $25 school-age children. Sailing excursion (maximum of three people, about six hours): $600.

Contact information: Venetian Travel Advisory Service, Tel & Fax: 212-873-1964 (New York), 041 523 2379 (Venice).

Venetian Street Terms

calle	main alleyway, often picturesque
campiello	small square
campo	square, usually with a church on it with the same name as the square
corte	courtyard
crosera	crossroads
fondamenta	pavement along a section of water
piscina	former pool that has been filled in
ponte	bridge
ramo	small side street linking two streets
rio	small canal used by gondolas and cargo boats
rio terà	a canal filled in to make a street
riva	a major stretch of pavement along water
ruga/rughetta	main shopping street
salizzada	sometimes spelled *salizada,* the main street of a district
sestiere	district
sottoportico	small alley running beneath a building

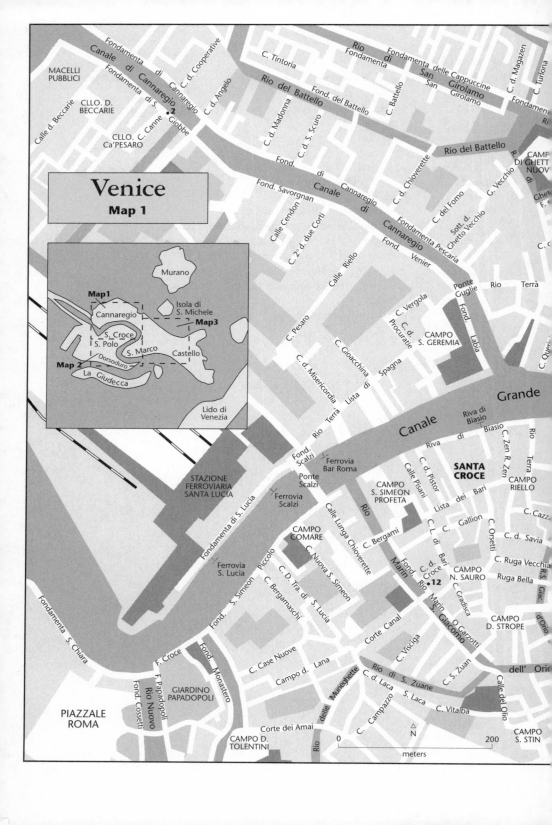

Venice
Map 1

MACELLI
PUBBLICI

CLLO. D.
BECCARIE

Calle d. Beccarie

Fondamenta di Cannaregio

Canale di Cannaregio

Fondamenta di Cannaregio

Fondamenta di S. Giobbe

CLLO. C. Canne
Ca'PESARO

C. d. Cooperative

C. d. Angelo

C. Tintoria

Rio del Battello

Fond. del Battello

C. Battello

Rio Fondamenta

Fondamenta delle Cappuccine

San Girolamo

San Girolamo

C. d. Magazen

Fondament

R.

C. d. Turlona

C. d. Madonna

C. d. S. Scuro

Rio del Battello

C. d. Chioverette

C. del Forno

G. Vecchio

R. d. S.

Sott. d. Ghetto Vecchio

CAMPO
DI GHETT
NUOV

Ghet
F.

C. c

Fond. di Cannaregio

Fond. Savorgnan

Calle Cendon

C. 2° d. due Corti

Fondamenta Pescaria

Fond. Venier

Fondamenta Cannaregio

C. del Forno

Calle Riello

C. Pesaro

Calle Riello

C. Vergola

C. d. Procuratie

Ponte Guglie

Rio Terrà

Fond. Labia

CAMPO
S. GEREMIA

C. Querin

C. c

Murano

Isola di S. Michele

Map1

Cannaregio

Map3

S. Croce
S. Polo

S. Marco

Dorsoduro

Castello

Map 2

La Giudecca

Lido di Venezia

C. Gioacchina

Spagna

C. d. Misericordia

Lista di

Spagna

Rio Terrà

Rio Terrà

Fond. Scalzi

Ferrovia
Bar Roma

Ponte
Scalzi

Ferrovia
Scalzi

Riva di Biasio

Riva di Biasio

Riva

Canale

Grande

C. Zen R. Zen

Rio Terrà

CAMPO
RIELLO

STAZIONE
FERROVIARIA
SANTA LUCIA

Fondamenta di S. Lucia

Ferrovia
S. Lucia

CAMPO
COMARE

Calle Lunga Chioverette

C. Bergami

C. Nuova S. Simeon

Piccolo

C. D. Tra. di S. Lucia

C. Bergamaschi

Fond. S. Simeon

CAMPO
S. SIMEON
PROFETA

Calle Pisani

C. d. Pistor

Rio

Fond. Marin

C. d. Bari Croce

Rio Marin

C. Marin S. Giacomo

Lista dei Bari

C. L. di Bari

Gallion

•12

O Garzotti

C. Gradisca

SANTA
CROCE

C. Cazz

C. Orsetti

C. d. Savia

C. Ruga Vecchia

Ruga Bella

CAMPO
N. SAURO

R.S.

Gra

d'Oria

CAMPO
D. STROPE

dell' Oric

Fondamenta S. Chiara

F. Croce

Fond. Monastero

Fond. Cossetti

Rio Nuovo

Fond. Papadopoli

GIARDINO
PAPADOPOLI

PIAZZALE
ROMA

Corte Canal

C. Case Nuove

Campo d. Lana

Corte dei Amai

CAMPO D.
TOLENTINI

Rio delle Muneghette

C. Campazzo

Rio di S. Zuane

C. d. Laca

S. Laca

C. Visciga

C. S. Zuan

C. Vitalba

Calle del Olio

CAMPO
S. STIN

0   200

meters

△
N

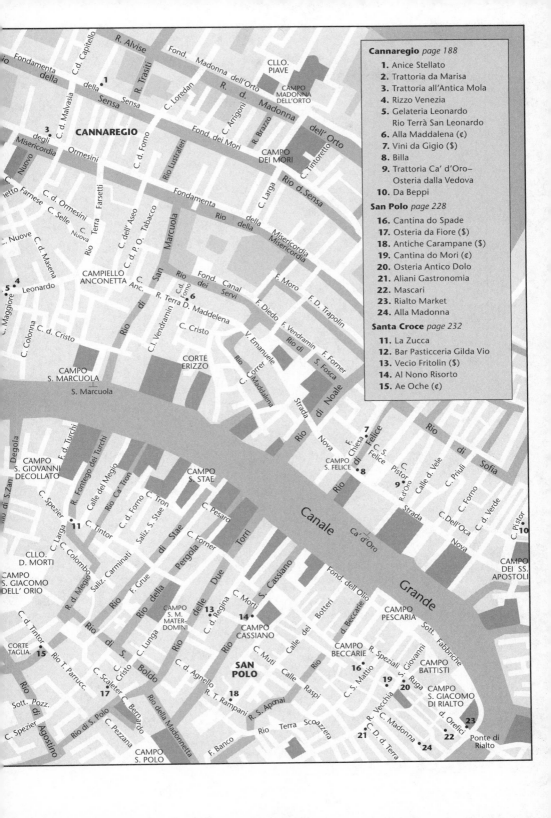

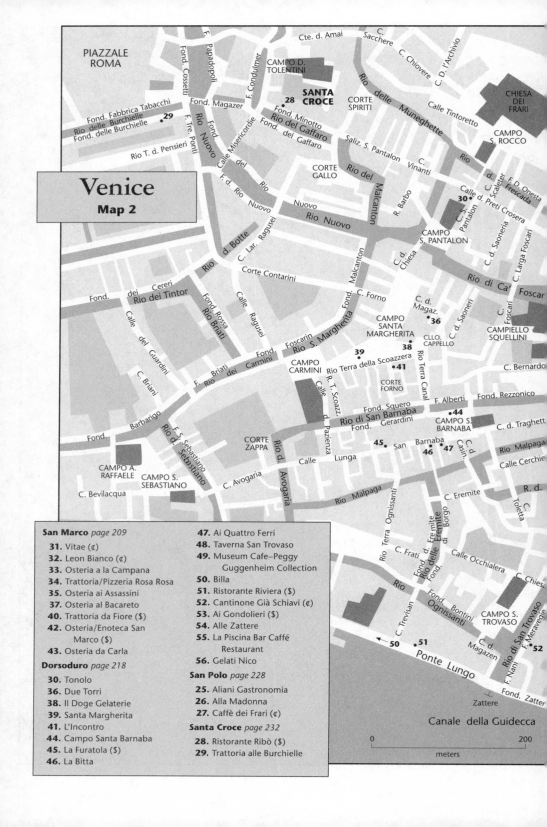

Venice
Map 2

PIAZZALE ROMA

Canale della Guidecca

0   200
                 meters

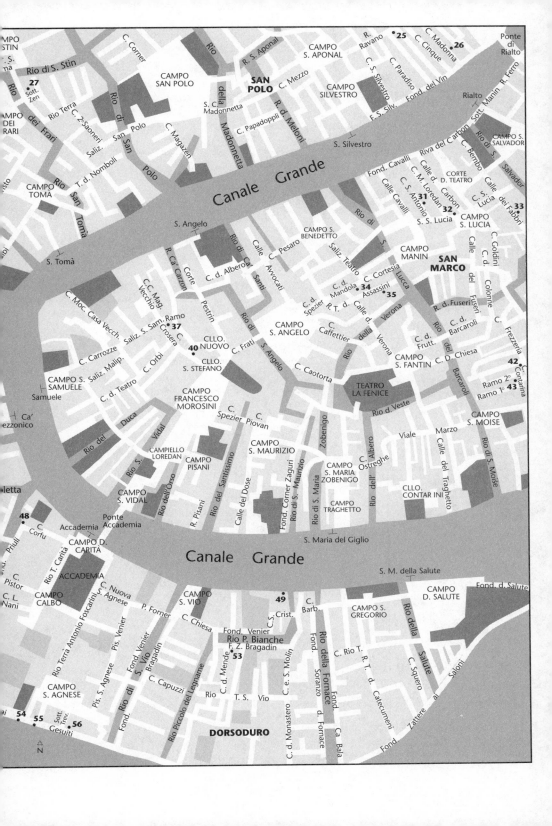

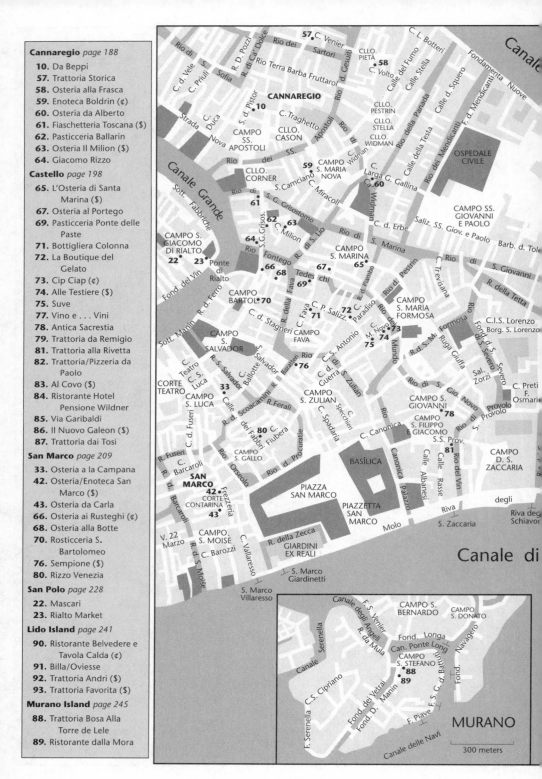

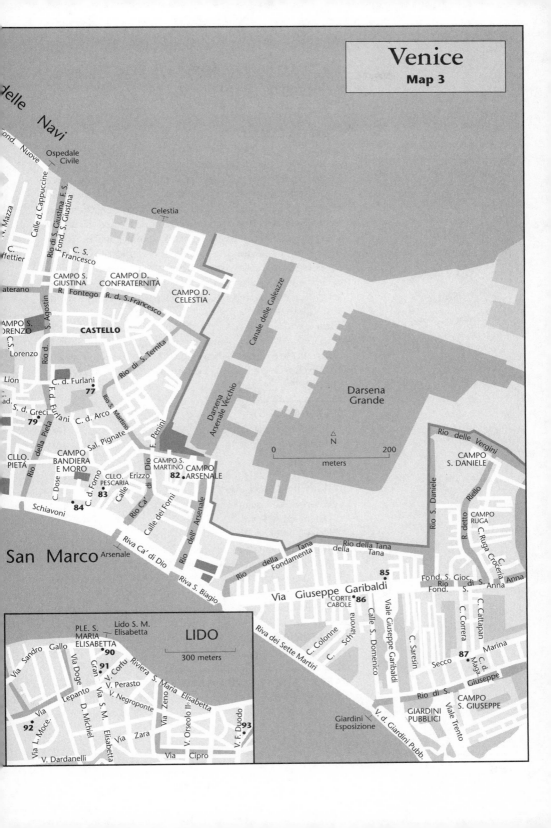

Venice
Map 3

delle Navi

ond. Nuove

Ospedale
Civile

Celestia

C. d. Cappuccine

Calle di S. Giustina F. S.
Fond. S. Giustina

V. Mazza

C.
effettier

aterano

C. S.
Francesco

CAMPO S.
GIUSTINA

CAMPO D.
CONFRATERNITÀ

R. Fontego

R. d. S.Francesco

CAMPO D.
CELESTIA

AMPO S.
ORENZO

CASTELLO

C.S.
Lorenzo

S. Agostin

Rio d.

Rio di S. Ternita

Canale delle Galeazze

Lion

C. d. Furlani

F. P. Furlani

77

S. d. Greci

79

C. della Pietà

C. d. Arco

Rio S. Martino

Sal. Pignate

Darsena
Arsenale Vecchio

Darsena
Grande

Rio delle Vergini

CAMPO
S. DANIELE

CLLO.
PIETÀ

CAMPO
BANDIERA
E MORO

C. Dose

C. d. Forno

CLLO.
PESCARIA

83

Erizzo

Calle

CAMPO S.
MARTINO

82

CAMPO
ARSENALE

F. Penini

Rio Ca' di Dio

Calle dei Forni

Rio dell' Arsenale

0   N   200
         meters

Rio S. Daniele

Riello

R. detto

CAMPO
RUGA

84

Schiavoni

San Marco

Riva Ca' di Dio

Arsenale

Riva S. Biagio

Rio   della   Fondamenta

della

Rio della Tana

Tana

Tana

85

Fond. S. Gioc.
Fond.

Rio
di S. Anna

Anna

C. Ruga Croseria

C. Cattapan

C. Correra

Via Giuseppe Garibaldi

CORTE
CABOLE

86

C. Colonne

Schiavona

C.

Calle S. Domenico

Viale Giuseppe Garibaldi

C. Saresin

Secco

87

C. d.
Maga.

Marina

Giuseppe

Rio di S.

Riva dei Sette Martiri

Giardini
Esposizione

GIARDINI
PUBBLICI

V. d. Giardini Pubb.

CAMPO
S. GIUSEPPE

Viale Trento

PLE. S.
MARIA
ELISABETTA

Lido S. M.
Elisabetta

LIDO

300 meters

Via Sandro Gallo

Via Doge

Gran

90

91

V. Corfu

Riviera S. Maria Elisabetta

D. Michiel

V. Perasto

V. Negroponte

Via Zeno

V. Orseolo II°

Lepanto

Via S. M.

92

Via L. Moce.

Via

Elisabetta

Via   Zara

V. Dardanelli

Via   Cipro

V. F. Duodo

93

Restaurants East of the Grand Canal

Cannaregio

This is the northern, most populated *sestiere,* and the one most visitors see first if they arrive by train. It is also one of the most authentic districts because it does not rely solely on tourism. The area around the train station (*Ferrovia*) is the exception. It is very touristy, and if you don't know where to go, you can easily be overwhelmed by the assault of greasy spoons and questionable hotels. In the center of Cannaregio is the Jewish Quarter, sometimes referred to as the Jewish Ghetto; in fact, *ghetto,* the universal term describing a restricted area for a poor, minority population, is an Italian word. Part of the *sestiere* along the Grand Canal is lined with aging *palazzos,* the most famous of which is Ca' d'Oro, which holds an impressive art collection. In the northern part of the *sestiere* is the Madonna dell'Orto, a Gothic church containing Tintoretto's *Presentation of Mary at the Temple.*

GOURMET FOOD AND WINE SHOPS
Giacomo Rizzo   **250**
Rizzo Venezia   **250**

GROCERY STORES AND SUPERMARKETS
Billa   **251**

OUTDOOR MARKETS
Rio Terrà San Leonardo   **251**

($) indicates a Big Splurge
(¢) indicates a Cheap Eat

Restaurants

ALLA MADDALENA (¢, 6)
Rio Terra della Maddalena, 2348

Where do you go when you find yourself stranded in the dining desert around the train station and do not want to settle for the unappetizing tourist food that is the rule rather than the exception here? One answer is Alla Maddalena, a fine place for a sandwich, a plate of rigatoni, tagliatelle, or the daily hot special. All the food is made fresh daily and in some cases is in limited supply, so when they run out of roast beef or the pasta of the day, you are out of luck. The desserts are brought in, so I recommend going to the *gelateria* across the street and having a scoop or two. At Alla Maddalena, you can enjoy your repast standing at the bar and kibitzing with the friendly bartenders or sitting on a tall stool by the window and watching the foot traffic hustle by.

TELEPHONE
041 720 723

OPEN
Mon–Sat: bar 7:30 A.M.–9 P.M.; hot lunch 12:30–3 P.M.

CLOSED
Sun; Aug

RESERVATIONS
Not accepted

CREDIT CARDS
None

À LA CARTE
Sandwiches from 1.20€, main dishes from 4.50€

FIXED-PRICE MENU
12€, 2 courses, vegetable, water or wine, and coffee

COVER & SERVICE CHARGES
No cover, service included

ENGLISH
Limited; as the barman says, "We don't speak English, only Venetian"

ANICE STELLATO (1)
Fondamenta della Sensa, 3272

Anice Stellato is for the adventurous diner who is not afraid to be way out of the tourist mainstream; here, you will join locals relishing a menu devoted almost entirely to fish and seafood. Frankly, it is not an easy menu, but Alessandro, the friendly owner, is willing to spend time explaining and suggesting dishes. The chef, who happens to be his brother, is reluctant to change, adapt, or make any substitutions to any dish listed. Therefore, the best

TELEPHONE
041 720 7444

OPEN
Wed–Sun: lunch 12:30–2 P.M., dinner 7:30–10 P.M.

CLOSED
Mon–Tues; 1 week Jan & Feb (opens for Carnivale), 3 weeks between Aug & Sept (dates vary)

RESERVATIONS
Essential, at least 1 or 2 days in advance
CREDIT CARDS
MC, V
À LA CARTE
Lunch: 22–25€, dinner 35–40€
FIXED-PRICE MENU
None
COVER & SERVICE CHARGES
Cover 1€, service included
ENGLISH
Yes

approach to this typical Venetian meal is to put yourself in Alessandro's hands for both your food and wine. Unfortunately, the bread is commercially produced, though this means you won't be tempted to fill up on this part of the meal. Desserts tend to be quite sweet, and oddly enough, fresh fruit is not an option. Portions for antipasti, first, and second courses are designed to allow most guests to easily order all three and not feel overwhelmed. For starters, the *antipasto misto* is a seasonal plate that could include poached salmon with sundried tomatoes, fresh anchovies in balsamic vinegar, or *sarde in saor,* pan-fried skate flavored with fresh ginger and tossed with white beans, sautéed red onions, and olives. The first and second choices change daily and are limited to three choices each. On my last visit, the pasta standout was rough-cut spaghetti served with fat crayfish. For the second plate, the seared tuna had enough kick to make it memorable, thanks to the Greek yogurt sauce spiked with onion, mint, and cumin.

Seating is simple—bare tables in two rooms and alongside the canal, set with bistro paper and simple glassware. Because everything served is of such high quality for the price, nabbing one of the tables ahead of the regulars requires reservations a day or two in advance.

DA BEPPI (10)
Salizzada D. Pistor, 4550

TELEPHONE
041 528 5031
OPEN
Mon–Wed, Fri–Sun: lunch noon–3 P.M., dinner 7–11 P.M.
CLOSED
Thur; 1 week at Christmas, Jan–Feb (until Carnivale)
RESERVATIONS
Advised for weekends
CREDIT CARDS
MC, V
À LA CARTE
30–35€
FIXED-PRICE MENU
None
COVER & SERVICE CHARGES
Cover 1.50€, service discretionary
ENGLISH
Yes

One hundred years ago this was a rough-and-ready watering hole for the workers who cleaned the canals. Today only the beamed ceiling remains as a reminder of those rowdy days. Inside this modest little trattoria near Ca' d'Oro are two wood-paneled rooms featuring the usual paintings of Venice. In front is a shaded patio that is perfect for warm-weather dining and people watching. Owned by Delfinia and her son Loris, Da Beppi creates the Venetian homestyle cooking and atmosphere everyone hopes to find.

Always ask about the daily specials, which depend on the season and whatever is fresh at the market. No matter what time of year, you can expect to find *baccalà* (creamed salted cod) with polenta; marinated sardines; liver and onions; and steak either grilled or cooked with garlic, tomatoes, and oregano. The pastas are served in generous portions with a basket of crusty bread on the side to sop up the last drops of sauce. For dessert, hope that Delfinia has made her wonderful homemade chocolate almond cake with creamy chocolate frosting.

ENOTECA BOLDRIN (¢, 59)
Salizzada San Camciano, 5550

In Venice you can spend a whole day getting lost inside the liquid maze of canals and narrow passageways linking one area to another. Adding to the fun are the mystifying maps, which do not necessarily spell the names of the streets the same way you will see them spelled on street corner signs or on business cards—if, in fact, they are even listed. A good case in point is Enoteca Boldrin, located on Salizzada San Camciano, if you go by one map and the restaurant sign, or Salizzada San Canzian if you go by another map. Whichever way you spell the street, the restaurant is located in the same spot, and that, ultimately, is all that matters.

What is the big news about another cafeteria-style lunch? First, this one is a hot ticket for locals, from workmen in overalls to ladies draped in designer duds and gold jewelry. Why? Because the food is always fresh and plentiful, is nicely prepared and displayed, and is a quantum leap above the average deli-style dining that passes for lunch in Venice. There are at least a dozen first- and second-course choices, with an emphasis on fish, pastas (including risotto and lasagne), colorful vegetables, and desserts.

Great Eating, even in a cafeteria, is always better with good wines, and there is no lack of them here—two walls are filled from floor to ceiling with more bottles than anyone cares to tally. At Boldrin, the M.O. is to get your food, pay, then hope you can snag a seat. Seating is along the walls next to the wine shelves, or at the wraparound bar where the dishes and *tramezzini* (sandwiches) are displayed.

TELEPHONE
041 523 7859

OPEN
Daily: 9 A.M.–9 P.M., continuous service

CLOSED
Sun in Jan

RESERVATIONS
Not necessary

CREDIT CARDS
None

À LA CARTE
Sandwiches from 1.50€, hot dishes 6–9€, dessert 2.50€, wines from 2.20€ per glass

FIXED-PRICE MENU
None

COVER & SERVICE CHARGES
None

ENGLISH
Limited, but ordering is as easy as pointing

FIASCHETTERIA TOSCANA ($, 61)
Salizzada San Giovanni Grisostomo, 5719

Fiaschetteria Toscana is the top choice of many Venetians for a celebration meal. In the two pleasant dining rooms, the Murano wall lights and candles cast a soft and romantic aura on the evening and the memorable food. On warm days, the prime seating is on the covered terrace across the street from the restaurant.

Fish plays a starring role in every course, and it is always excellent. The black *tagliolini* with lobster or white *tagliolini* with scampi and zucchini flowers are perfect pasta choices. For the second course, soft-shelled crab is a luxurious dish, the baked eel with bay leaves will please those who love something different, and the baked sea bass with potatoes will satisfy anyone. If you order their signature dish, *frittura della Serenissima*—a mixed fried seafood and

TELEPHONE
041 528 5281

INTERNET
www.fiaschetteriatoscana.it

OPEN
Mon: dinner 7:30–10:30 P.M.; Wed–Sat: lunch 12:30–2:30 P.M., dinner 7:30–10:30 P.M.

CLOSED
Mon lunch, Tues; 1 week after Carnivale, part of July and Aug (dates vary)

RESERVATIONS
Essential

À LA CARTE
50–70€

FIXED-PRICE MENU
None
COVER & SERVICE CHARGES
Both included
ENGLISH
Yes, and menu in English

vegetable platter—you will receive a complimentary plate to commemorate your meal. If fish isn't on your agenda, there are plenty of delightful alternatives, beginning with warm artichoke hearts from Sant' Erasmo; thin, chopped sautéed vegetables; or *risi e bisi,* a traditional Venetian summertime soup made with rice, green peas, and pea pods. The restaurant is also well-known for its *Fiorentina* steaks (Chianina beef), simply grilled and topped with fresh Parmesan cheese and arugula. I think it is important to plan for dessert here, even if you only have room to share a bite or two. I am always torn between the *zabaione* served with crisp *baicoli* cookies (which is made only during the winter), the caramel apple tart with a scoop of vanilla ice cream, or the smooth chocolate mousse with whipped cream. And usually, despite whatever I have promised my dining companion, I am reluctant to share in the end.

NOTE: Fiaschetteria Toscana is a member of Ristoranti della Buona Accoglienza; see page 179 for details.

OSTERIA ALLA FRASCA (58)
Corte della Carità, 5176

TELEPHONE
041 528 5433
OPEN
Wed–Mon: bar 11 A.M.–4 P.M., 5–7 P.M.; hot food 11 A.M.– 4 P.M., 5–11 P.M.
CLOSED
Tues; Aug 15–21, Dec 24–Jan 5
RESERVATIONS
Advised
CREDIT CARDS
MC, V
À LA CARTE
35–45€
FIXED-PRICE MENU
Lunch only: 15€, 2 courses, salad
COVER & SERVICE CHARGES
No cover charge, 10% service added
ENGLISH
Yes

If you have yet to lose yourself in this sinking city's seductive byways, the hunt for this hidden gem is your golden opportunity. Actually, if you follow these directions, it may be disappointingly easy. From Fondamenta Nuove, walk down Calle del Fumo to Calle del Volto, turn right, and Corte della Carità is the second opening on your right; you will see the restaurant at the back of the little square. There is nothing touristy about this Venetian square, where the weekly laundry blows in the breeze and flaps against the aging buildings, window boxes are filled with bright flowers, dogs and children play after school, old ladies gossip, and the men talk politics and sports. For local color, it does not get much better.

The tiny *osteria* itself isn't much to look at, but it does have an interesting history as the storeroom where Tiziano kept his art supplies. All evidence of the artist is long gone, now replaced by a few tables and a menu displayed on an old wine barrel. (Weather permitting, more tables are available outside.) As you can imagine, the food here is comforting rather than trendy, and its mainstay is fish . . . served in soups, with polenta, tossed with tagliolini, grilled, fried, or baked in the oven and served with roasted potatoes. Meat-eating gourmands will be happy digging into the one kilo (2.2 lb.) steak served with either Bernaise sauce or aromatic herbs and balsamic vinegar. The best dessert consists of hard cookies from Burano to dip in sweet wine; this may sound plain, but after a while, you will become addicted to this special Italian finale to your meal.

OSTERIA DA ALBERTO (60)
Calle Largo Giacinto Gallina, 5401

This rustic two-room *osteria* sits alongside a canal, with several tables overlooking the waterway. You might think that the tables on the canal would be the place to sit, and while this might be true late in the evening, at lunch you want to be up front near the bar, where all the action is taking place. This is a place to come for fun, food, and Venetian-style camaraderie. The order of the day should be a plate with assorted *cicchetti,* or the daily hot dishes washed down with ample glasses of the *vino della casa.*

TELEPHONE
041 523 8153

OPEN
Mon–Sat: lunch 10 A.M.–3 P.M., dinner 6–11 P.M.

CLOSED
Sun; Jan 15–22, last 2 weeks of July and 1st week of Aug

RESERVATIONS
Advised for dinner

CREDIT CARDS
MC, V

À LA CARTE
From 1.60€ for *cicchetti;* 2-course meal 20–25€

FIXED-PRICE MENU
None

COVER & SERVICE CHARGES
Cover 1.60€, no service charge

ENGLISH
Yes

OSTERIA IL MILION ($, 63)
Corte al Milion, 5841 (behind San Giovanni Cristomo Church)

The rustic interior is correctly set with pink linens, and at night the protected outdoor terrace is romantically lit. Neighborhood patrons arrive before lunch to have a drink at the bar with owner Roberto Bocus, who has been serving them well for the past three decades. The menu is seasonal, and daily specials are always highlighted. In the spring, start with fresh salmon marinated in orange juice or a delicate spider crab salad. If pasta is on your dining agenda, consider sharing a risotto tossed with scampi and zucchini or, for something heavier, risotto with black cuttlefish sauce. A second plate of broiled monkfish or John Dory *al Milion,* cooked with capers, pickles, tomatoes, and white wine, are both good choices. Add a plate of grilled vegetables or a salad followed by lemon *sorbetto* or fresh strawberries splashed with strawberry wine, and you will have had a Great Eat in Venice.

TELEPHONE
041 522 9302

OPEN
Daily in summer: lunch noon–3 P.M., dinner 6:30–11 P.M.; winter: Mon–Tues, Thur–Sun

CLOSED
Wed in winter; Aug

RESERVATIONS
Advised, especially for dinner

CREDIT CARDS
MC, V

À LA CARTE
49–50€

FIXED-PRICE MENU
None

COVER & SERVICE CHARGES
Cover 3€, 10% service added

ENGLISH
Yes, and menu in English

TRATTORIA ALL'ANTICA MOLA (3)
Fondamenta degli Ormesini, 2800

TELEPHONE
041 717 492
OPEN
Daily: noon–midnight,
continuous service
CLOSED
Aug
RESERVATIONS
Advised
CREDIT CARDS
AE, DC, MC, V
À LA CARTE
20–25€
FIXED-PRICE MENU
None
COVER & SERVICE CHARGES
Cover 1.29€, service included
ENGLISH
Yes (ask for Ricardo)

Venice exists today because of the huge influx of tourists, who spend more than $150 million a year here. So a visitor can easily become a sitting duck for dining rip-offs. With a little extra effort and some ingenuity, however, venturing off the beaten tourist track can yield not only better food but better value. Trattoria all'Antica Mola, located along a canal on the edge of the Jewish Quarter, will give you a decent meal at a fair price, as the many locals filling adjacent tables and enjoying the same can attest. It is an unassuming place, but you will be able to spot it as you approach: just look for the flags flying beside the canal-side tables. The easiest way to find it is to cross the Campo Ghetto Nuovo to Fondamenta degli Ormesini and turn right, or walk along Rio Terrà Farsetti, cross the bridge, and turn left.

Time and tradition stand behind the food and the dowdy atmosphere. Decorated with old copper, postcards from regulars, and signed drawings on napkins, the two rooms are definitely in need of an update, but Franco, the long-standing owner, is certainly not thinking of doing anything like that any time soon. In warm weather, you won't care what the interior looks like, because you will be sitting in the back garden or along the canal. For the most satisfying meal, focus on the simple pastas and second courses based on fish. If you want dessert, try the fruit-topped custard tarts or the orange cake. The house wines are good . . . and cheap. Another bonus is that the food is served continuously from noon to midnight every day.

TRATTORIA CA' D'ORO–OSTERIA DALLA VEDOVA (9)
Calle del Pistor and Ramo Ca' d'Oro, 3912–3952 (off Strada Nova)

TELEPHONE
041 528 5324
OPEN
Mon–Wed, Fri–Sat: lunch
11:30 A.M.–2:30 P.M., dinner
6:30–10:30 P.M.; Sun: dinner
6:30–10:30 P.M.
CLOSED
Sun lunch, Thur; 2 weeks after
Carnivale, July 23–20, Aug
(dates vary)
RESERVATIONS
Not necessary
CREDIT CARDS
None

The name on the business card reads: Trattoria Ca' d'Oro–Osteria dalla Vedova. But on the window it's simply La Vedova, which is how it's known by its devotees. This spot has been in the same family for 135 years, and judging from the inside, little has changed in that time. The two rooms are filled with what looks like original furniture, a marvelous collection of copper pots hanging from the ceiling, and pretty antique lights. Any time you go you will find the brother-and-sister owners, Lorenzo and Mirella, mixing and mingling with an interesting sampling of area regulars, who sit at the plain wooden tables sharing a bottle of *vino rosso* and arguing about Sunday's soccer scores or the latest Italian political scandal.

There is no proper menu, and they do not serve dessert, but this is a good place to keep in mind for a light lunch or dinner. Find out what the chef has prepared for that day—maybe a pasta with fresh clams, or a hearty soup—and add a plate of *cicchetti,* a few chunks of bread, and a sturdy wine, and you will be all set. The service has been known to be cool, but after a few glasses of Tokai, or red wine from Padua, your Italian should improve, and you will feel more welcome.

À LA CARTE
Cicchetti from 1€ at the bar, 1.50€ at a table, 2-course meal 18–25€

FIXED-PRICE MENU
None

COVER & SERVICE CHARGES
Cover 1.50€, service included

ENGLISH
Yes, also French and German

TRATTORIA DA MARISA (2)
Fondamenta San Giobbe, 652

Unless you speak some Italian and can understand—even vaguely— a spoken menu rattled off in a loud voice, Marisa is probably not the Great Eat for you. On the other hand, if you want to rub elbows with a contingent of workers at lunch and with lively locals at night and are willing to eat whatever the cook bought at the market, you will be happy. The best time to go is for lunch on a warm, lazy Sunday, when time is not of the essence—you can sit at one of the canal-side tables and watch the boats float by in this corner of Venice seldom seen by the average visitor. Another reason to aim for a Sunday is because it is the only day the chef *sometimes* makes *zabaione,* which everyone agrees alone makes the trip worthwhile. Other dishes to look forward to are the lusty stews, grilled fish, pasta with duck sauce, and risotto with bone marrow. This last is the house specialty, and unfortunately it makes infrequent appearances. To make your appearance, you can take the number 52 *vaporetto* and get off at Tre Archi.

TELEPHONE
041 720 211

OPEN
Mon, Wed, Sun: lunch 1–2:30 P.M.; Tues, Thur–Sat: lunch 1–2:30 P.M., dinner 8–11 P.M.

CLOSED
Dinner on Mon, Wed & Sun; Aug

RESERVATIONS
Essential

CREDIT CARDS
None

À LA CARTE
26–40€, includes house wine

FIXED-PRICE MENU
None

COVER & SERVICE CHARGES
None

ENGLISH
Very limited

TRATTORIA STORICA (57)
Salizada Seriman, 4858

Every once in a while we need a port in a storm, and this little trattoria is just that. It is not worth a special trip, but if you are in the area—perhaps en route to the boat to Murano—and need a little sustenance, this is an answer. The interior is decidedly simple, accented with the owner's collection of contempory art. Outside is a pleasant wraparound terrace.

The best Great Eating deals are found on the two fixed-price menus. One good thing about these menus, which draw a steady neighborhood clientele, is that the choices change often. The *menù Veneziano* features fish from starter

TELEPHONE
041 528 5266

OPEN
Mon–Sat (sometimes Sun): lunch noon–2:30 P.M., dinner 7–10:30 P.M.

CLOSED
Call for Sun and annual closing times

RESERVATIONS
Advised

CREDIT CARDS
AE, MC, V

À LA CARTE
35–45€
FIXED-PRICE MENU
Menù Fisso: 18€, 2 courses
(meat or fish) and vegetables;
Menù Veneziano: 28€, 2 courses
(all fish), vegetables and salad;
both include cover and
service charges
ENGLISH
Yes, and menu in English

through main course and includes salad and vegetables. The *menù fisso* starts with vegetable soup, offers two fish pastas as well as penne with *radicchio,* and includes a main course of liver with polenta, spicy chicken, or grilled salmon, all garnished with seasonal vegetables. With both of these menus, dessert and drinks are extra, but service and cover charges are included. Because it consists mainly of fresh fish, the à la carte side can creep into the Big Splurge category. As owner Pierantonio said, "We don't buy a lot, but we do buy quality."

NOTE: Please take a minute while you are in this area to visit Chiesa di S. Maria Assunta (Gesuiti), which contains works by Tintoretto. The church is located down the street from the restaurant and is open from 10 A.M. to noon and from 4 to 6 P.M. Mass is at 5:30 P.M.

VINI DA GIGIO ($, 7)
Fondamenta di San Felice, 3628A

TELEPHONE
041 528 5140
INTERNET
www.vinidagigio.com
OPEN
Tues–Sun: lunch noon–2:30 P.M.,
dinner 7:30–10:30 P.M.
CLOSED
Mon; 3 weeks in Jan and Aug
(dates vary)
RESERVATIONS
Advised, at least one day ahead
for dinner
CREDIT CARDS
DC, MC, V
À LA CARTE
40–50€
FIXED-PRICE MENU
None
COVER & SERVICE CHARGES
Both are included
ENGLISH
Yes

You will always dine well at the friendly Vini da Gigio. To be surrounded by fellow travelers, go early for dinner. For a more Venetian dining experience, book a table for 9 P.M. and settle in with the locals. They know a good thing, and they like and respect what the talented kitchen staff can do with the bounty of succulent seafood from the lagoon and produce from the nearby island of San Erasmo. The wine list offers many affordable bottles from the Veneto, as well as a dozen or so interesting grappas. The satisfying food is cooked to order and served by just two waitpersons, who, despite the unfavorable table-to-server ratio, nevertheless manage to be gracious and accommodating. The small, intimate interior has two windows overlooking the San Felice canal and closely placed tables nicely set with white linens.

The menu is seasonal but always features antipasti of both raw and cooked seafood, as well as *sarde in saor* (sardines marinated in vinegar, onions, pine nuts, and raisins) and *baccalà* (whipped cod) with polenta. After this course, you might sample spaghetti with clams or crab, followed by a mixed platter of fried lagoon fish or a thick piece of rare tuna garnished with fresh tomatoes. Meat eaters are not left out—they can start with foie gras or beef *carpaccio* garnished with *rucola* and Parmesan cheese. Pastas might include penne tossed with gorgonzola cheese and pistachios or one of the kitchen's signature dishes—ravioli with *rucola* and a light *zabaione* mousse of *taleggio* cheese. Lamb chops, liver with polenta, osso buco, or a fillet steak follow. Desserts to do penance for on the Stairmaster include a fresh strawberry tart with vanilla sauce, a dark and light chocolate parfait, or almond cake highlighted by eggnog sauce.

Gelaterias

GELATERIA LEONARDO (5)
Rio Terra San Leonardo, 1525 (near Campo San Leonardo)

The strip of real estate leading from the *ferrovia* (train station) on Rio Terra di Spagna across Campo San Geremia and along Rio Terra San Leonardo is full of tourist traps. You really need to be careful to avoid getting soaked by poor-quality restaurants and greedy shopkeepers selling mostly garish junk. Clearly, this is not my favorite Venice neighborhood. However, most visitors travel this corridor at some point, and there are a few redeeming places worthy of a stop. Gelateria Leonardo is one to put on your snacking list if you are in the mood for a *gelato produzione propria*—gelato made in-house and served in cones, cups, and fancy sundaes. For those who are lactose-intolerant, they make soy ice cream.

TELEPHONE
041 710 000

OPEN
Daily: 10 A.M.–midnight, in winter until 8 P.M.

CLOSED
Dec and Jan

CREDIT CARDS
None

PRICES
Cones 0.90–2.30€, cups 1.50–2.50€, *panna* (whipped cream) 0.50€, sundaes and banana splits 3.50–5€

ENGLISH
Depends on server

Pastry Shops and Bakeries

PASTICCERIA BALLARIN (62)
Salizzada San Giovanni Grisostomo, 5794

For some of the best pastries and coffees in this part of town, Venetians pour into this lovely pastry shop, located a minute or two away from the Rialto Bridge. It is always crowded, there is nowhere to sit, and unless you get lucky and claim a corner of the one tall table, you must belly up to the glass countertop to indulge in your sweet. Everything is made here, and they sell out on a daily basis, right down to the last buttery cookie.

TELEPHONE
041 528 5273

OPEN
Daily: 7:15 A.M.–8:15 P.M.

CLOSED
Never

CREDIT CARDS
AE, MC, V

PRICES
Coffees from 0.80€, pastries from 1€

ENGLISH
Enough

Castello

Constituting the eastern portion of Venice, Castello is the largest of the *sestieri* and the only one without real estate along the Grand Canal. The central building is the huge Gothic church of Santi Giovanni e Paolo, with the equestrian monument of Bartholomeo Colleoni by Andrea del Verrocchio. In back of the church is the Ospedale Civile, where the ambulance boats are tied up at the dock alongside the canal, ready to respond to emergencies. Campo Santa Maria Formosa serves as a major crossing point between Piazza San Marco and the Rialto Bridge, and it is an interesting place to sip a cool drink in the afternoon and watch the neighborhood children gather to play while their mamas and nannies gossip and talk. Also in this district is the Arsenale—the shipyards of Venice—and the Riva degli Schiavoni, Venice's premier promenading ground, lined with grand hotels (such as the Danieli) and waves of tourists. Farther east is Rio Terà Garibaldi, the lusty workingman's quarter, and the only large green park in Venice, Giardini, which is where La Biennale, the famous international contemporary art exhibit, is held every two years.

GROCERY STORES AND SUPERMARKETS
Suve   **251**

OUTDOOR MARKETS
Via Garibaldi   **251**

($) indicates a Big Splurge
(¢) indicates a Cheap Eat

Restaurants

AL COVO ($, 83)
Campiello della Pescaria, 3968

The popularity of Al Covo is due to both the excellence of its cuisine, prepared by Cesare, and the warm atmosphere created by his wife, Diane. This dynamic Italian/American couple opened the restaurant in 1987, and the attractive, rough-hewn interior always has fresh flowers adorning the tables, which are formally set with attractive china, heavy cutlery, and gleaming crystal. In the summer, there is a protected terrace with cushioned seating. The prices are definitely not for budgeteers, so please reserve this for a special occasion or a final night in Venice with someone you love.

Service by the English-speaking staff is attentive and helpful. When you are seated, a plate of bite-size appetizers is brought to your table, along with assorted breads served with iced butter curls, a treat found in few other Venetian restaurants. All of the dishes are prepared to order, based on what the market offers each day and what products are in season. No frozen or canned foods are used, and neither are farmed fish. Cesare is justly well known for his imaginative and delicate fresh seafood dishes, which are cooked without the use of butter or other animal fats. All the pastas are made in-house daily, and the tomato sauce is made from a recipe Cesare inherited from his grandmother. In winter an anticipated specialty of the house is roasted local wild duck served with fresh mixed vegetables.

Whenever you eat at Al Covo—and some Great Eats readers have come here once and then eaten nowhere else for the rest of their Venetian stay—you absolutely must try at least one or two of Diane's homemade desserts. If the pear and prune cake with grappa sauce is available, have it for sure. It is so good it was featured in *Gourmet* magazine. The other choices are endless: zabaglione made at your table, bitter chocolate cake with a chocolate and chili

TELEPHONE
041 522 3812

OPEN
Mon–Tues, Fri–Sun: lunch 12:45–2 P.M., dinner 7:30–10 P.M.

CLOSED
Wed–Thur; Jan, 2 weeks in August (call to verify Mon opening)

RESERVATIONS
Essential

CREDIT CARDS
AE, MC, V

À LA CARTE
80–85€

FIXED-PRICE MENU
Two tasting menus: 78€, 10 courses, including dessert or cheese; 64€, 7 courses, including dessert or cheese

COVER & SERVICE CHARGES
No cover charge, service discretionary

ENGLISH
Yes, and menu in English

sauce, walnut cake with caramel sauce spiked with aged rum, and *panna cotta* with dark chocolate sauce. Whatever you order, your meal will be followed by a complimentary dish of nuts, chocolate, and mints as a grand finale.

A word of caution: group dining at Al Covo can present problems. Even though the kitchen is famous for its fish preparations, no fish dishes are available à la carte, and meat dishes are served *only* à la carte. Fish is only available on the two tasting menus, which consist of either seven or ten courses, with no choices for any course. To order a tasting menu, everyone at the table must join in, whether there are two or twenty. I think this is very restrictive, as it means either everyone in your party must agree to eat a seven- or ten-course fish meal, or else everyone must order meat from the à la carte menu, forgoing all fish.

NOTE: Al Covo is a member of the Ristoranti della Buona Accoglienza; see page 179 for details.

Al Covo now also has two nearby apartments available for one-week minimum bookings. Al Covo is one of the most well-known and well-liked restaurants in Venice—and their delightful apartments come just as highly recommended. Email the owner (cesare.benelli@tin.it) for rates and information.

ALLE TESTIERE ($, 74)
Calle del Mondo Novo, 5801 (off Salizzada San Lio)

TELEPHONE
041 522 7220
OPEN
Tues–Sat: lunch noon–2:30 P.M., dinner 7–11 P.M.
CLOSED
Sun–Mon; last week of July and first 3 weeks of Aug, 3 weeks at Christmas
RESERVATIONS
Essential
CREDIT CARDS
MC, V
À LA CARTE
50–60€
FIXED-PRICE MENU
None
COVER & SERVICE CHARGES
None
ENGLISH
Yes

Pssst, over here. Where do the Venetians go for fish? Alle Testiere.

When a place is "found," its name is as closely guarded as insider stock trading information. Such was the case when Alle Testiere opened. Everything about the spot is modest, except the quality of the fish (and, potentially, the size of your check if you are not careful). Seating is on hard bistro chairs around bare tables, and service is quick—they have to turn those tables several times a night to keep out of the red. The menu is short, and fish plays a central role in every dish—it is always fresh, well prepared, and delightful. If it is available, the pan-seared tuna cooked with sesame seeds and a dash of teriyaki, or the tiny scallops quickly cooked with just a touch of mint, are two beautifully prepared and served selections. From a very meager beginning, the restaurant is now the talk of the town; it has, you might say, achieved "blue chip" status as a solid dining investment. An added bonus: The restaurant is completely nonsmoking.

NOTE: Alle Testiere is a member of Ristoranti della Buona Accoglienza (see page 179).

ANTICA SACRESTIA (78)
SS. Filippo e Giacomo, 4442, at the corner of Calle de la Sacresta

Your two teenagers are demanding pizza, your wife wants a vegetarian meal, your mother-in-law thinks pasta and a salad would hit the spot, and you are yearning for ham and eggs (and some relief from negotiating everybody's appetites). No problem: simply head for Antica Sacrestia, about a ten-minute meander from San Marco. As you've already guessed, this all-purpose Great Eat offers something for everyone . . . including some stiff cocktails and (best of all) prices that are easy on your travel budget. Begun hundreds of years ago when the priests of the Church of San Giovanni Novo prepared meals in their kitchen for the poor, over time Antica Sacrestia became famous for its pizza, and it still is. Thirty-eight pizzas are enhanced by a dozen other pizza specialties, four more pizzas feature white cheese and vegetable toppings, and for dessert, there is an orange liqueur–infused pizza as well as those topped with chocolate, bananas, or kiwis. Present owner Pino Calliandro has also added a roster of favorite Venetian dishes designed to meet the tastes of all diners. The five fixed-price menus cover all the bases, from a basic three-course budget meal to two menus dominated by fish, a menu for vegetarians, and a menu described as having *porzioni enormi* (enormous portions) of all the house specialties. If this is not enough of a selection, there are two pages of à la carte menu items: pastas (including macaroni and cheese, crêpes, and a vegetable torte), fifteen fish dishes, as many meat preparations, ten desserts, and, of course, the above-mentioned ham and eggs. If you can't find something to eat at Antica Sacrestia, I give up.

TELEPHONE
041 523 0749

INTERNET
www.anticasacrestia.com

OPEN
Tues–Sun: lunch noon–2:30 P.M., dinner 7–10:30 P.M.

CLOSED
Mon; first week of June, a few days at Christmas

RESERVATIONS
Advised

CREDIT CARDS
MC, V

À LA CARTE
28–40€; pizza from 6–15€

FIXED-PRICE MENU
Menù turistico: 15€, 3 courses; *Vegetariano:* 25€, 3 courses and salad; *Menù Veneziano:* 28€, 3 courses; *Specialissimo di Pesce:* 38€, 3 courses (all fish); *Antica Sacrestia:* 62€, house specialties from appetizer to dessert. All menus include vegetables, dessert, cover and service charges.

COVER & SERVICE CHARGES
Both are included

ENGLISH
Yes, and menu in English

CIP CIAP (¢, 73)
Calle del Mondo Novo, 5799

For some of the best *pizza al taglio di tutti tipi* (pizza slices of all types), a bulging calzone, or an assortment of mini-pizzas to munch on for a quick snack, do not miss this busy little corner establishment off Campo Santa Maria Formosa. This is Italian fast food, and I love it. It was located close to my Venetian flat, and, I will admit, I was a regular customer.

You can eat here if you want to stand along the Calle del Mondo Novo, but it is better to have your slices packaged to go. Everything is sold by weight from 1€ per 100 grams. Dole out the worthwhile 2€ or so per slice of

TELEPHONE
041 523 6621

OPEN
Mon, Wed–Sun: 9 A.M.–9 P.M., continuous service

CLOSED
Tues; 3 weeks in Jan (dates vary)

RESERVATIONS
Not accepted

CREDIT CARDS
None

Pizza slices from 1€ per 100 g;
tortas 1.40€ per 100 g; calzones
from 2.40€ per 100 g; whole
pizzas from 5€

FIXED-PRICE MENU
None

COVER & SERVICE CHARGES
None

ENGLISH
Sometimes

pizza or torte, and a little more for the calzone, take your feast over to the Campo Santa Maria Formosa, and sit on a bench and watch the neighborhood at work and at play. It is a great way to feel Italian and have a satisfying Great Eat in the bargain.

IL NUOVO GALEON ($, 86)
Via Garibaldi, 1308

TELEPHONE
041 520 4656

OPEN
Mon, Wed–Sun: lunch 12:30–2:30 P.M., dinner 7:30–9:30 P.M.

CLOSED
Tues; Jan to Carnivale

RESERVATIONS
Advised

CREDIT CARDS
AE, DC, MC, V

À LA CARTE
45–55€

FIXED-PRICE MENU
Lunch only, 25€, 2 courses, dessert, wine, mineral water, cover and service charge

COVER & SERVICE CHARGES
Cover 3€, 12% service added

ENGLISH
Yes, and menu in English

Via Garibaldi is a wide, bustling street that cuts through the eastern part of Castello. In the morning it is filled with shoppers, and in the evening with locals, strolling down the middle and filling the bars. If you look along the side streets of this neighborhood, you will see bright-red flower boxes at almost every window and laundry lines rustling in the breeze. The whole area is about as local as it gets. Just off Via Garibaldi are the public gardens where La Biennale, the international art exhibit, is held every two years. If you look carefully into the pond surrounding Garibaldi's formidable statue at the entrance to the garden off Via Garibaldi, you will see turtles sunning themselves on the exposed rocks.

So where does everyone eat? Besides bars, there are several choices, but for the best fresh fish, head for Il Nuovo Galeon. The restaurant's seafaring motif extends to the bar, which is an actual boat, and to the back rooms, which have wraparound murals of Venetian waterways. The set menu is a lunchtime Great Eat in that it offers fish for each course and includes wine and dessert. You can start with *spaghetti alle vongole* (with clams) or *baccalà,* then have a mixed fried fish plate or grilled sole, dessert, wine, and mineral water—all for less than just one or two of these courses could cost in the higher rent districts. Going à la carte can stretch your Venetian budget, especially if you order four courses. While there are choices other than fish, both on the set menu and à la carte, the restaurant is best known for fish.

NOTE: Il Nuovo Galeon is a member of Ristoranti della Buona Accoglienza (see page 179).

L'OSTERIA DI SANTA MARINA ($, 65)
Campo Santa Marina, 5911

A meal at Agostino Doria and Danilo Baldan's charming restaurant on the quiet Campo Santa Marina is a feast of extraordinary good cooking featuring superb fresh fish. In fact, I rate it as one of the best restaurants in Venice—one no serious Great Eater should miss. The intimate dining room has a bar to one side and an interesting collection of French black-and-white sketches collected by Danilo's grandfather. The room seats only forty, and an additonal ten or twenty can be served on the covered summer terrace. There is only one seating per mealtime, which encourages guests to relax and linger. The gracious service is always very friendly and helpful, whether guiding you through the seasonal fish-based menu or helping you order just the right bottle of wine to complement your meal.

While you are trying to decide among the many delicious options, a complimentary appetizer is served; perhaps warm baby shrimp lightly tossed with shredded zucchini and resting on a bed of polenta. Accompanying this is a basket of the chef's homemade bread. If you are ordering an antipasto, try the lukewarm spider crab delicately seasoned with a hint of lemon and olive oil, or the boiled octopus with red onion, grated orange peel, and balsamic vinegar—a bold combination of taste and texture that is unusual and very good . . . even if you don't like octopus. The house pastas are simple, the way they should be when starring seafood. The sea bass and shrimp ravioli is a good example, as is the *tagliolini* tossed with spider crab. For a second course, hope that the John Dory fillet with summer vegetables is on the menu. It is an uncomplicated, simply prepared dish that allows the flavor of the fish to shine through. Tuna steak lightly seasoned with rosemary or the richly satisfying soft-shell crabs with fresh artichokes are two more winning main courses. Portions are not overwhelming, so you can safely add a mixed green salad or a plate of lightly grilled vegetables drizzled with extra-virgin olive oil. If you are eyeing the tasting menu, note that it must be ordered by the entire table.

Desserts are, in a word, divine. If chocolate is your passion, don't miss the *tortino al cioccolato*—a rich chocolate pie that is worth every calorie. If you want an even lighter but still sweet ending, order the strawberry *sorbetto* with port wine sauce, or the *semifreddo* iced *zabaione* mousse topped with fresh raspberry and blackberry sauce.

NOTE: The restaurant is open until 11:30 P.M., but the last order is at 9:30 P.M.

TELEPHONE
041 528 5239

INTERNET
www.osteriadisantamarina.it

OPEN
Mon: dinner 7:30–9:30 P.M.;
Tues–Sat: lunch 12:30–2:30 P.M.,
dinner 7:30–9:30 P.M.

CLOSED
Mon lunch, Sun; first 2 weeks
in Aug, Jan 7–Feb 1

RESERVATIONS
Essential

CREDIT CARDS
MC, V

À LA CARTE
50–60€

FIXED-PRICE MENU
Menù degustazione (price per person): 65€, 7 courses, dessert, and cover charge

COVER & SERVICE CHARGES
Cover 3€, service discretionary

ENGLISH
Yes, and menu in English

OSTERIA AL PORTEGO (67)
Calle della Malvasia, 6015, near Campo San Lio

TELEPHONE
041 522 9038
OPEN
Mon–Fri: bar 10:30 A.M.–10 P.M.;
Sat: 8 A.M.–3 P.M.; continuous
service for *cicchetti*; hot food
noon–2 P.M., 7–9 P.M.
CLOSED
Sun
RESERVATIONS
Not necessary
CREDIT CARDS
None
À LA CARTE
Cicchetti from 1.30€, 2-course
meal 20€
FIXED-PRICE MENU
None
COVER & SERVICE CHARGES
None; bread charge 2.10€
ENGLISH
Yes

This small, picturesque place is crowded with copper pots, low beams, barflies, and wine barrels. The affable owners, Carlo, Sebastiano, and Riccardo, welcome everyone to their great Venetian hangout. Here you eat *cicchetti,* fish risotto when it comes out of the kitchen at 1 P.M., or any of the hot specials of the day, neatly written on a piece of olive-brown construction paper. Your wine will be from the Veneto and your check will be a Great Eat buy.

RISTORANTE HOTEL PENSIONE WILDNER (84)
Riva degli Schiavoni, 4161

TELEPHONE
041 522 7463
INTERNET
www.veneziahotels.com
OPEN
Mon, Wed–Sun: 11:30 A.M.–
6:30 P.M., 7–11 P.M., continuous
service
CLOSED
Tues
RESERVATIONS
Preferred for dinner
CREDIT CARDS
AE, DC, MC, V
À LA CARTE
Pizza from 6–11€, 3-course
meal 30–35€
FIXED-PRICE MENU
Seven different 3-course menus,
all 16€; beverage extra
COVER & SERVICE CHARGES
Both included
ENGLISH
Yes, and menu in English

The stretch of pavement facing the beautiful Canal di San Marco that runs along Riva degli Schiavoni from Piazza San Marco to Arsenale is one of the most picturesque tourist trails in Venice, and one that no visitor misses. Because of the throngs of people, the endless shops and carts selling one tacky souvenir after another, and hawkers displaying fake designer handbags, you would think this would be a dining wilderness. And you would be correct, with one exception . . . the Ristorante Wildner. For a hotel dining room, it is exceptional, not only for the service and quality of food, but for the price. All bases are covered by the kitchen, which turns out pizzas from morning to night, seven well-priced fixed-price menus, a cheese plate served with fresh fruit marmalade and honey, and several large salads plus an à la carte menu touching all the Venetian bases from fish and seafood to meat and pastas. The views from the front-row seats across the lagoon are memorable, the service is knowledgeable, and the prices right for most Great Eating budgets.

NOTE: For information about the Hotel Pensione Wildner, see *Great Sleeps Italy.*

TRATTORIA ALLA RIVETTA (81)
Ponte San Provolo, 4625

Trattoria alla Rivetta, squeezed in on the right just before the Ponte San Provolo and off Campo S.S. Filipino e Giancomo, is a genuine alternative to the many touristy alternatives that plague this area of Venice. A good sign, as always, is that the locals eat here in droves, filling every seat in the house almost as soon as it is open. You will see everyone from gondoliers on their breaks grabbing several *cicchetti* at the bar and a glass of *vino della casa* to women out for a gossipy lunch with friends. True, it has been discovered, but that fact has not diminished its authenticity one bit. The menu is printed in English, and the restaurant serves full meals from 10 A.M. to 10 P.M.—two distinct advantages for visitors.

Portions are not for the light eater, and neither is the food. In fact, the bowl of mussels ordered as a first course will be plenty if you add a salad and the fresh bread that comes with every Italian meal. Hungry diners can start with the *tagliolini con granchio,* pasta with fresh crab, or a time-honored spaghetti with meat sauce. The squid cooked in its own ink and served with polenta and the grilled jumbo shrimp are delicious entrées. There is also a full line of meats, including Venetian liver and onions, veal chops, and boiled beef with pesto sauce. Desserts are run-of-the-mill except for the house tiramisù, a heavenly rum-spiked cake layered with triple-cream cheese and dusted with chocolate.

TELEPHONE
041 528 7303

OPEN
Tues–Sun: 10 A.M.–10 P.M., continuous service

CLOSED
Mon; last 2 weeks in July–Aug 25 (dates vary)

RESERVATIONS
Not accepted over five. If you have to wait, *cicchetti* and a glass of wine are sometimes offered

CREDIT CARDS
AE, MC, V

À LA CARTE
30–35€, includes house wine

FIXED-PRICE MENU
None

COVER & SERVICE CHARGES
Cover 1.50€, 12% service added

ENGLISH
Some, and menu in English

TRATTORIA DAI TOSI (87)
Secco Marina, 738

Trattoria dai Tosi occupies small but vibrant quarters that are further from tourist central in spirit than they are in kilometers. Located off Via Garibaldi (take Calle Correra until you get to Secco Marina, turn left, and it will be on the corner of Corte Magazen), about a twenty-minute walk east of Piazza San Marco, this neighborhood gathering place is owned and run by two former waiters at Harry's Bar—Fabio and Paolo, along with their wives, Lorena and Jackie, who share cooking responsibilities. Jackie, Paolo's English wife, did not start out to be a chef. On a lark, she left her native Cornwall at age seventeen and came to the Lido, where she taught pony riding to children and worked her way up, finally becoming well-known as a trainer for top Italian show jumpers. Along the way she met Paolo,

TELEPHONE
041 523 7102

OPEN
Mon–Tues, Thur–Sun; lunch noon–2:30 P.M., dinner 7–10 P.M.

CLOSED
Wed; 2 weeks in mid-August, a few days at Christmas, last week of Jan or 1st week of Feb (dates vary)

RESERVATIONS
Suggested for Sat & Sun

CREDIT CARDS
MC, V

À LA CARTE
Pizza from 5–10€, 3-course meal 27–30€

FIXED-PRICE MENU
None

COVER & SERVICE CHARGES
Cover 1.50€, service included

ENGLISH
Yes

and the rest is history: They married, had two children, and became partners in this restaurant. Pictures of their children hang on the left wall in the room beyond the bar.

At noon, blue-collar workers pour in for Jackie's specials and her *pasta della casa,* an imaginative mix of vegetables, scampi, shrimp, calamari, pepperoni, zucchini, and carrots all tossed with spaghetti and a spoonful of cream. This makes a nice meal, accompanied by one or two crusty rolls, an *insalata mista,* and a glass of the house red wine. If you do go for lunch, be sure to take the time to see the oldest church in Venice, which is quite close by. San Pietro di Castello is open daily from 8 A.M. to noon and 3 to 6 P.M., and on holidays from 8 A.M. to noon and 4:30 to 7:30 P.M.

The kitchen is closed for full dinner meals on Monday, Tuesday, and Thursday nights, but the pizza ovens work overtime, turning out almost fifty varieties of pizzas, ten of which are vegetarian. On these nights, you eat your pizza here or have it packed to go. On Friday, Saturday, and Sunday nights, the kitchen turns out its full menu, which includes pizza. For the best results, my suggestion is to stick with a pizza or Jackie's special pasta.

NOTE: Inexplicably, another place calling itself Trattoria dai Tosi has opened on the opposite corner. It won't take you long to figure out which is which . . . the Great Eat Tosi is the small one with the single lantern outside and the locals spilling out onto the pavement in front on summer evenings or jamming the bar in winter. The new Tosi is the big, boring one with the chef standing in the doorway wondering when he will be busy.

TRATTORIA DA REMIGIO (79)
Salizzada dei Greci, 3416

At Trattoria da Remigio, all your choices are happy ones, whether for your appetizer, pasta, or fish or meat course. For those looking for a lighter meal, they do serve omelettes, which are hard to find in a nice restaurant. For a new twist on an old dish, try the *gnocchi alla pescatora,* potato-based pasta puffs with fish. For best results, always pay close attention to the handwritten daily specials, which offer some of the best shellfish preparations in Venice and at the best prices. Arrive late and you will need a shoehorn to get in. The restaurant enjoys the fiercely devout patronage of Venetians, and they virtually pack it full day and night, so call ahead for a reservation and be on time.

TELEPHONE
041 523 0089

OPEN
Mon: lunch 12:30–2:30 P.M.;
Wed–Sun: lunch 12:30–
2:30 P.M., dinner 7:30–10:30 P.M.

CLOSED
Mon dinner, Tues; Dec 20–
Jan 20, last week of July and
1st week of Aug

RESERVATIONS
Essential

CREDIT CARDS
AE, DC, MC, V

À LA CARTE
35–40€

FIXED-PRICE MENU
None

COVER & SERVICE CHARGES
Cover 2€, 12% service added

ENGLISH
Limited

TRATTORIA/PIZZERIA DA PAOLO (82)
Campo Arsenale, 2389

You could not possibly ask for a better view of the commanding entrance to the Arsenale, the historic twelfth-century shipyard that hundreds of years ago employed 16,000 men, who could assemble a galleon in twenty-four hours. The entire Arsenale covers 318 square meters and is still used by the Italian navy, but it is not open to the general public. Therefore, the stunning view of the lion-guarded entrance you have from a table on the terrace of Paolo's trattoria is about as close as you will get to this important Venetian landmark, unless you ride on the number 1 or 42 *vaporetto,* which cut through the Arsenale.

Besides the location, what does Paolo's have going for it? If you order what they do best, it has a lot going for it. If you stray too far from these items, not so much. In addition, the service can become distracted (and sometimes nonexistent) when it gets very busy. Warnings aside, I still recommend it and suggest you arrive early to get a good seat. And what do they do best? Order their *spaghetti della casa* with tomatoes, clams, mussels, and crayfish, or order a pizza, especially the house pizza, loaded with vegetables, salami, and ham. Ask for a basket of warm pizza bread, drink the house Tokai white wine, take some pictures to show the family back home, and enjoy another lovely day and Great Eat in Venice.

TELEPHONE
041 521 0660

INTERNET
www.dapaoloarsenale.it

OPEN
Tues–Sun: lunch noon–3 P.M.,
dinner 7–10 P.M.

CLOSED
Mon; 2–3 weeks at Christmas
and New Year's, 1st or 2nd
week in Sept

RESERVATIONS
Advised for dinner on weekends

CREDIT CARDS
MC, V

À LA CARTE
Pizza 5–10€, 3-course meal
25–35€

FIXED-PRICE MENU
None

COVER & SERVICE CHARGES
Cover 1€, 12% service added

ENGLISH
Yes

Gelaterias

LA BOUTIQUE DEL GELATO (72)
Salizzada San Lio, 5727

TELEPHONE
041 522 3283
OPEN
Mon–Tues: 10 A.M.–8:30 P.M.;
Wed–Sun: 10 A.M.–midnight
CLOSED
Never
CREDIT CARDS
None
PRICES
Cones or cups 1–3 €, *panna*
(whipped cream) 0.55 €, *frappé*
2–2.30 €
ENGLISH
Yes

Italians know good gelato, and nowhere is it better than here. This *gelateria* is easy to find; just look for the line that weaves down the narrow Salizzada San Lio. The line forms when they open around 10 A.M. and lasts until they close, at midnight Wednesday to Sunday and at 8:30 P.M. on Monday and Tuesday. Run by an energetic duo—Sandra and Silvio Cavaldoro—this tiny operation does an amazing business. They are smart: They offer only a few knockout flavors, sold by the cone or cup or packaged to go. There is no seating at all, and no beverages are available. I passed the shop coming and going to my flat each day, and each time it was all I could do not to stop in for a scoop of *nocciolosa* (a creamy chocolate gelato laced with nuts) or their specialty (and secret recipe), the *millefoglie*. In the summer I look forward to refreshing kiwi, pear, lemon, or strawberry *sorbettos*. Sandra and Silvio both speak English and have friends in San Francisco whom they often visit. If you are anywhere near either of their Venice *gelateria,* please have a scoop or two for me.

Pastry Shops and Bakeries

PASTICCERIA PONTE DELLE PASTE (69)
Ponte delle Paste, 5991, at the end of Calle Carmine, off Salizzada San Lio

TELEPHONE
041 522 2889
OPEN
Daily: 7 A.M.–8:30 P.M.
CLOSED
Never
PRICES
Pastries from 1.10 €, hot and
cold sandwiches 1.60–3.20 €
ENGLISH
Yes, Monica speaks English

Aside from the mouthwatering display of pastries, I like this *pasticceria* because everyone is so friendly and nice. After a few visits in the morning you are treated as a regular. Monica and her staff know everyone, as well as the kind of coffee they prefer; often they have your pastry in hand before you have given your order. Around noon, trays of *tramezzini* (sandwiches), toast with ham and cheese, pizza slices, and salads are served in two tiny tea rooms. All the sugary delights can be packed to go.

San Marco

Piazza San Marco is the heart and soul of Venice and has been since the first rulers built the Doge Palace and St. Mark's Basilica, with its magnificent mosaic-tiled walls, ceilings, and domes. On Sunday evening at 6:45 P.M., the lights are turned on, and a one-hour mass in Latin follows. Often flooded, ringed with outrageously expensive shops and *caffès,* and populated by both people and pigeons, Piazza San Marco is the place every tourist visits and usually spends money. It is also the focus of the Carnivale season leading up to Lent, when crossing the square is virtually impossible due to the masses of costumed posers and revelers. Many of Venice's essential sights are centered around San Marco, as well as posh hotels, shopping streets, and many overpriced restaurants. The don't-miss sights include the Correr Museum, a lovely untouched archaeological museum; the Bridge of Sighs; the gothic San Stefano church; the Palazzo Grassi, the city's most important venue for art shows; and La Fenice Opera, which tragically burned a few years ago but is being reconstructed amid great controversy.

RESTAURANTS

Leon Bianco (¢)	**210**
Osteria ai Assassini	**210**
Osteria ai Rusteghi (¢)	**211**
Osteria a la Campana	**211**
Osteria al Bacareto	**212**
Osteria alla Botte	**212**
Osteria da Carla	**213**
Osteria/Enoteca San Marco ($)	**214**
Rosticceria S. Bartolomeo	**214**
Sempione ($)	**215**
Trattoria da Fiore ($)	**215**
Trattoria/Pizzeria Rosa Rosa	**216**
Vitae (¢)	**217**

GOURMET FOOD AND WINE SHOPS

Rizzo Venezia	**250**

($) indicates a Big Splurge
(¢) indicates a Cheap Eat

Restaurants

LEON BIANCO (¢, 32)
Salizzada San Luca, 4153 (between Campo San Luca and Campo Manin)

TELEPHONE
041 522 1180
OPEN
Mon–Fri: 9 A.M.–6 P.M., hot food noon–2:30 P.M., cicchetti all day
CLOSED
Sat–Sun; Aug
RESERVATIONS
Not accepted
CREDIT CARDS
None
À LA CARTE
Cicchetti from 1.20€, sandwiches from 2.50–5€ hot dishes from 3.60–6€
FIXED-PRICE MENU
None
COVER & SERVICE CHARGES
No cover or service charges
ENGLISH
Limited

When you want a snack or light meal and cannot face another slice of street pizza, try Leon Bianco, the type of place Venetians patronize daily. Terrific *cicchetti* (finger-food snacks) and *tramezzini* (sandwiches) are served throughout the day, and hot food is offered between noon and 2:30 P.M.

Rice or cheese croquettes, grilled shrimp, and roasted vegetables are only a few of the *cicchetti* you can pluck with a toothpick and pop into your mouth. There are always two or three hot dishes, and if you want to sample more than one, they will serve half portions. Every time I am in Venice, I always consider their *tramezzini* some of the best—toasted or plain bread filled with prosciutto, mushrooms, tomatoes, tuna, egg, shrimp, roast beef, or pork. You can rub shoulders standing at the marble counters and bar, or if you want to take a more relaxed approach to your meal, you can sit at a table in back and still not have any cover or service added to your bill. When you are finished eating, be local and take your dishes back up to the bar.

OSTERIA AI ASSASSINI (35)
Rio Terra dei Assassini, 3695

TELEPHONE
041 528 7986
INTERNET
www.osteriaaiassassini.it
OPEN
Mon–Sat: lunch 11:30 A.M.–3 P.M., dinner 6:30 P.M.–midnight
CLOSED
Sun; 2–3 weeks in Aug (dates vary)
RESERVATIONS
Advised
CREDIT CARDS
MC, V
À LA CARTE
25–30€
FIXED-PRICE MENU
None
COVER & SERVICE CHARGES
Cover 2€, service included

For years this was only a place to buy wine by the bottle or case. Then Giuseppe Galardi turned it into an *enoteca* (wine bar), and it has enjoyed popularity with the locals, probably because they are the only ones who can find it.

Actually, finding Rio Terra dei Assassini is not hard, but the fun of the hunt comes when trying to locate the *enoteca* itself—there is no sign or name outside. You must look for the yellow light over the door, which is *sometimes* turned on when the place is open.

Every day the long wooden tables and benches are filled with people having lunch or *cicchetti* while sipping a glass or two of the eighty to ninety varieties of Italian wines available. *Cicchetti,* similar to Spanish tapas, range from a piece of bread with a slice of prosciutto to meatballs, deep-fried veggies, and whipped salt cod. For many, a few *cicchetti* with a glass of nice wine can easily substitute for lunch or be a light supper. The hot special changes daily, featuring a certain dish each day of the week: on Monday it's a dish with white meat of some sort; Tuesday, stew or offal; Wednesday, *bollito,* boiled meat with four or five sauces; Thursday, *baccalà* with polenta; Friday, fish; and Saturday it's whatever the chef feels like cooking. Of course, pasta is served every day, and an impressive number of Italian wines are poured. A favorite dessert is a plate of homemade biscotti to dip in sweet wine.

ENGLISH
Yes

OSTERIA AI RUSTEGHI (¢, 66)
Campiello del Tentor, 5513 (near Campo San Bartolomeo)

Call it tiny. Call it local. Call it clean. But above all, call it good. Tucked away on a little court only a heartbeat from the tourist madhouse on Campo San Bartolomeo, this wine bar is hard to find for the usual befuddled tourists. Roberto runs a tight ship, and hot meals are not part of his program. What *tramezzini* (sandwiches) you see in the glass display case are what you are going to eat, unless you want a mixed green salad. No one speaks much English, but it is a good place to plunge in and practice your Italian, which will improve dramatically after your third *ombra* (glass of wine).

TELEPHONE
041 523 2205

OPEN
Mon–Sat: 10 A.M.–3 P.M., 5:30–9:30 P.M.

CLOSED
Sun; 1 week Aug, 1 week Jan & Feb (dates vary)

RESERVATIONS
Not accepted

CREDIT CARDS
None

À LA CARTE
Sandwiches from 1.10–1.30€

FIXED-PRICE MENU
None

ENGLISH
Very little

OSTERIA A LA CAMPANA (33)
Calle dei Fabbri, 4720

"Where do you go for a good, cheap lunch in this neighborhood?" I asked Nellie, the friendly owner of Locanda Casa Petrarca, a nearby budget hotel (see *Great Sleeps Italy*). "I go to La Campana on Calle dei Fabbri," she said. Once you find it, you, too, will go back to this small, homey place with a dark wood interior that can charitably be called rustic. For the best selection at lunch, get there early, when the *cicchetti* are at their picture-perfect best. You can always find rice balls with a mozzarella cheese pocket inside, tuna or potato puffs, grilled vegetables, frittatas, and chunks of cheese all displayed along a counter.

If you want something more substantial, ask what the chef prepared that morning. There is a posted menu for lunch, but no one bothers looking at it. Fish is the Friday special for both lunch and dinner. On other days look for bean soup, hearty stews, and assorted risottos and pastas. For dinner, the choices are all à la carte and the prices are substantially higher.

TELEPHONE
041 528 5170

OPEN
Mon–Sat: lunch 11:30 A.M.– 3 P.M., dinner 7–10 P.M.

CLOSED
Sun

RESERVATIONS
Not necessary

CREDIT CARDS
AE, MC, V

À LA CARTE
Cicchetti from 1.30€; 2-course lunch 15–20€, including house wine; 3-course dinner 35€

FIXED-PRICE MENU
None

COVER & SERVICE CHARGES
Cover 1.10€ lunch, 2€ dinner; no service charge for either meal

ENGLISH
Yes

OSTERIA AL BACARETO (37)
Salizzada San Samuele, 3447 (at Calle delle Botteghe)

TELEPHONE
041 528 9336
OPEN
Mon–Fri: lunch noon–3 P.M., dinner 7–10 P.M.; Sat: lunch noon–3 P.M.
CLOSED
Sat dinner, Sun; Christmas Day, Easter, Aug
RESERVATIONS
Advised
CREDIT CARDS
AE, MC, V
À LA CARTE
Cicchetti from 1.70€, 3-course meal 25–40€, includes house wine
FIXED-PRICE MENU
None
COVER & SERVICE CHARGES
Cover 1.60€, 10% service added
ENGLISH
Yes, and menu in English

Emilio and his son Adriano told me, "You eat in this restaurant as a family." The house wine is good, the welcome always warm, the other diners interesting, and the prices fair. In short, this is a winner. Everyone seems to know one another at this comfortable family *osteria,* where you may see the neighborhood dogs sitting patiently by the door waiting for their masters to finish eating. At lunch, to feel part of the action, order a plate of *cicchetti* or a sandwich and a glass of the featured wine. Remember, if you stand at the bar to eat, you will save both the cover and the service charges. For dinner, reserve one or more of the sixteen places at any of the outside tables for a ringside seat on the evening *passeggiata.* If you stay with the chef's versions of Venetian dishes, the food will not disappoint. For example, *sarde in saor* (marinated sardines), the *risotti vari* (rice mixed with peas, squid, vegetables, or seafood), and the *bigoli in salsa* (whole-meal pasta with anchovy and onion sauce) are surefire first courses. Move on to the excellent seafood offerings, or liver and onions served with polenta, and close with whatever dessert Mama has made that morning

OSTERIA ALLA BOTTE (68)
Calle della Bissa, 5482 (off Campo San Bartolomeo)

TELEPHONE
Osteria: 041 520 9775; *enoteca:* 041 296 0596
INTERNET
www.osteriaallabotte.it
OPEN
Mon–Wed, Fri–Sun: lunch 10 A.M.–3 P.M., dinner 5:30–11 P.M.
CLOSED
Thur; Aug, a few days at Christmas
RESERVATIONS
Suggested for dinner on weekends
CREDIT CARDS
MC, V
À LA CARTE
Cicchetti from 1.10€, full meal 25–30€
FIXED-PRICE MENU
None
COVER & SERVICE CHARGES
None
ENGLISH
Yes

There must be ten or more *bacari* (wine bars) in a two-minute radius of Alla Botte, each one interesting in its own way and worthy of a few visits until you find the one that suits you. At Botte, you can almost tell the time of day by the type of patrons jamming the bar. On a Sunday morning, it is the place where old men gather to jumpstart the day with a grappa-laced coffee or a couple of straight shots of the potent elixir. During the week, businessfolk and shopkeepers dash in for a quick bite and a glass or two of their favorite *vino.* At lunch you can barely wedge your way in through the hungry throng munching snacks at the bar or downing the daily hot dishes of *pasta e fagoli,* penne with *funghi porcini, bigoli in salsa,* or *baccalà* with polenta in the tiny dining area in back. When it reopens around 6 P.M., the crowd is a young mix, everyone schmoozing, flirting, posing, and preening, whether inside or in the narrow alleyway in front, blocking the entry so it is almost impossible to get in. Later on it calms down and is filled with couples drinking in the bar or having a simple Great Eat in back.

If you like the wine you are drinking, go to their wine shop on Calle della Bissa, 5529, and buy a supply in bottles or have one of the free liter-size plastic bottles filled with local red or white *vini sfusi*. The latter choice will set you back less than 2 or 3€ per plastic bottle . . . and that is a mighty cheap drink of decent wine!

OSTERIA DA CARLA (43)
Corte Contarina, 1535 (off Frezzeria)

Hidden? You bet. Discovered? Yes again, but only by the cognoscenti in this part of Venice, who say, "Let's go to the Carla," and everyone knows exactly what they mean and where it is, even though the sign over the doorway reads "Pietro Panizzolo." In short, if you don't already know about it, you would never find it, and that's the way the locals like it.

I was introduced to the Carla by a Great Eating pal from Florence, who said he had been eating here for years and that I simply had to try it. We arrived late on a Saturday afternoon when the place was almost empty and the staff was preparing to close. It didn't matter—we were welcomed as if we were regulars. We settled in with a plate of assorted sandwiches and shared a bottle of beer. It was a perfect late lunch, and I knew I would come back when it was operating in full force. When I did, several times, I was always amazed. This place is super, and the food is terrific. There is soup in the winter, and always three or four pastas, including a risotto, a meat and a fish dish, fresh vegetables, and homemade tarts. Not ready for a big meal? Then order a sandwich from the bar and sit at one of the tables inside or, on a warm day, snag one of the tables placed in the walkway of the small courtyard on the side. The kitchen is closed from 3 to 6:30 P.M., but during this time the bar is open and you can always get a cold plate.

NOTE: Here's how to find Osteria da Carla coming from Piazza San Marco: Walk out the south exit from the piazza along Salizzada San Moisè and turn right on Frezzeria. The first archway on your left will be Sotoportego e Corte Contarina. This is it; you will see the barrel at the end of the court with a bouquet of fresh flowers sitting on top. *Buon appetito,* and *tante grazie,* Frank.

TELEPHONE
041 523 7855

OPEN
Mon–Sat: bar 7:30 A.M.–11 P.M., lunch noon–3 P.M., dinner 6:30–10:30 P.M.

CLOSED
Sun; 15 days in Jan (dates vary)

RESERVATIONS
Advised for dinner

CREDIT CARDS
MC, V

À LA CARTE
Sandwiches from 1.50€; lunch, 3-course meal, 20–25€; dinner 30–35€

FIXED-PRICE MENU
None

COVER & SERVICE CHARGES
Cover 1.10€, no service charge

ENGLISH
Yes, and menu in English

OSTERIA/ENOTECA SAN MARCO ($, 42)
Calle de Frezzeria, 1610

TELEPHONE
041 528 5242
OPEN
Mon–Sat: bar 10:30 A.M.–
midnight, lunch 12:30–3 P.M.,
cold food 3–7:30 P.M.; dinner
7:30–11 P.M.
CLOSED
Sun; 1 week around Aug 15
RESERVATIONS
Absolutely essential
CREDIT CARDS
MC, V
À LA CARTE
40–50€, includes glass of wine
FIXED-PRICE MENU
None
COVER & SERVICE CHARGES
Cover 2.60€, service
discretionary
ENGLISH
Yes, and menu in English

The Osteria/Enoteca San Marco has it all: stylish clientele enjoying equally stylish food that is prepared with care and attention and presented by a knowledgeable crew of waiters. The brick-walled interior is softened at night by candles glowing on the intimately spaced bare wood tables. Three hundred and sixty wine labels are available, with the emphasis placed strongly on Italian vintages. Fortunately, the waiters are well-versed in the lofty list, enabling them to select just the right one to accompany a meal. And what a meal it will be. The menu changes with the seasons, which keeps the regulars anxiously returning. In fact, this is one of the hottest dining addresses in Venice because it is consistent and always offers good value for the money. For starters it seems impossible to go wrong with the pilgrim scallops nested in arugula and dressed with balsamic vinegar. If you have never tried octopus, here is the perfect chance; order the warm octopus torte for a very different and delicious treatment of this very Venetian dish. The homemade pastas follow the seasons: in late spring, perhaps there will be tagliatelle with artichokes, zucchini flowers, and pecorino cheese, or a lasagne layered with vegetables. If seafood is still on your mind, consider the fresh monkfish on a bed of sautéed zucchini, eggplant, carrots, and a few tomatoes for color, or skewered sesame-crusted king prawns. Osso buco can be a heavy affair, but not here, as the mint-braised veal shanks are served with a colorful array of spring vegetables. Dessert is required eating, especially the warm slice of chocolate cake with vanilla sauce drizzled with bitter chocolate, or the hazelnut ice cream resting on top of a crisp waffle.

NOTE: This is a nonsmoking restaurant.

ROSTICCERIA S. BARTOLOMEO (70)
Calle de la Bissa, 5424/A (on Campo San Bartolomeo, near the Rialto Bridge)

TELEPHONE
041 522 3569
OPEN
Mon: 9 A.M.–4 P.M.; Tues–Sun:
9 A.M.–9:30 P.M., continuous
service
CLOSED
Mon evening
RESERVATIONS
Not accepted
CREDIT CARDS
AE, DC, MC, V

If you are watching your food budget, do not go to the upstairs restaurant here. Instead stay downstairs, go through the self-service line, and take your food to one of the long bar tables by the window, thus avoiding the cover and service charges as well as the higher prices, for almost the same food served in the restaurant.

The ground-floor cafeteria is a popular refueling stop for those who want a proper meal anytime between 9 A.M. and 9:30 P.M. Featured each day, in addition to sandwiches, are salads, pastas, and hot dishes, which include the Venetian specialties of *baccalà alla Vicentina* (salt cod simmered in milk and herbs), deep-fried mozzarella, *seppie con polenta* (squid with polenta), meat or vegetarian lasagne, and all the usual desserts. The bottom line? For around 10 to 18€, you can get a three-course meal and a glass of house wine, which, in Venice, qualifies as a decent eat that won't send budgets (or gourmet expectations) into orbit. Everything you see can be packaged to go.

NOTE: All prices quoted are for cafeteria dining.

À LA CARTE
Sandwiches from 1€, main courses 10€, salads 6–8€

FIXED-PRICE MENU
12–14€, fish, vegetable, and salad; 18€, fried fish, salad, wine, and bread; 18€, one fish-based main course and Tokai wine

COVER & SERVICE CHARGES
None

ENGLISH
Limited, but ordering is easy

SEMPIONE ($, 76)
Ponte Bareteri, 578

The beautiful canal-side setting, attentive service, and tempting Venetian cuisine draw me back to this family-run restaurant time after time, presided over by owner Sra. Santa and her two great waiters, Renato and Danielo. Its privileged location near St. Mark's Square and some of the city's most luxurious shops makes it an ideal stop for a leisurely lunch or dinner. The best tables, naturally, are by the leaded windows overlooking the canal and the gondolas quietly floating by. They cannot be reserved, so arrive a few minutes before the doors open if you want to eat here. The food is simple, with unfussy preparations and a lavish use of olive oil, but no butter, cream, or mushrooms. *Pennette* (small penne) tossed with a well-flavored *amatriciana* sauce of tomatoes and sweet red peppers is a hit. So is the pasta with spider crab and the spaghetti Sempione with prawns, mussels, and octopus. Finish every morsel, but save room for the heaping platter of scampi and squid or the calamari. Meat lovers will be pleased to find liver and onions served with polenta, steaks, veal dishes, and roast chicken. For a pleasant ending, I like to have a bowl of fresh strawberries or a plate of Venetian cookies and dessert wine.

TELEPHONE
041 522 6022

OPEN
Mon, Wed–Sun: lunch 11:45 A.M.–2:45 P.M., dinner 6:45–10:30 P.M.

CLOSED
Tues; Dec–Jan

RESERVATIONS
Only for large parties

CREDIT CARDS
AE, MC, V

À LA CARTE
40–50€

FIXED-PRICE MENU
None

COVER & SERVICE CHARGES
Cover 2€, 12% service added

ENGLISH
Yes, and menu in English

TRATTORIA DA FIORE ($, 40)
Calle delle Botteghe, 3461

Well-run by an organized family team headed by Sergio and his two children, David and Lisa, the Trattoria da Fiore has been a favorite address just off Campiello Santo Stefano for almost twenty-five years. Any time of day you walk by, you will see the loyalists standing around the bar or huddling along the walkway by the open window downing a glass of wine and sampling a bite or two of *cicchetti*. The two inside rooms reflect Sergio's love affair

TELEPHONE
041 523 5310

INTERNET
www.trattoriadafiore.com

OPEN
Mon, Wed–Sun: bar 10 A.M.–10 P.M., lunch noon–3 P.M., dinner 7–10 P.M.

CLOSED
~eeks in Jan

SERVATIONS
~ for dinner

EDIT CARDS
MC, V

À LA CARTE
Cicchetti (at the bar) 1–2€,
3-course meal 48–58€

FIXED-PRICE MENU
None

COVER & SERVICE CHARGES
Cover 2€, service included

ENGLISH
Yes, the family lived in
Australia for five years

with Venice: a miniature gondola crafted by his brother is proudly displayed, as is a *fero* (the metal piece on the front of a gondola that represents the six *sestieri,* or districts, of Venice and the Grand Canal) and numerous paintings of the city. The menu and its portions cater to people with serious appetites. Fish is always featured, but don't worry, there are other possibilities, including a plate of perfectly roasted seasonal vegetables, springtime risotto with fresh peas from Sant' Erasmo, the island in the Venetian lagoon known for growing vegetables, cannelloni with ricotta and spinach, and roast beef with roasted potatoes. If you love chocolate, don't miss their homemade chocolate cake.

TRATTORIA/PIZZERIA ROSA ROSA (34)
Calle della Mandola, 3709

While the trattoria menu lists a range of dishes—such as gnocchi with salmon; tagliatelle with onions, cherry tomatoes, and basil; grilled *scamorza* cheese with vegetables; and a rundown of meats—when you come to Rosa Rosa, think *only* pizza. With the help of his wife, Elisa, Cristiano has run Rosa Rosa since 1985. He specializes in thirty-five thin-crust pies that are not too crisp and offers enough toppings to please just about everyone. If you missed breakfast, order a pizza featuring bacon and eggs. Even more far out is one with horsemeat, and another with goose. Less adventurous is the *San Nicandro,* with tomatoes, mozzarella, goat cheese, olives, onions, and capers. If, after consulting the three pages of options, you still don't see a pizza that pleases you, ask for what you want; they will customize. They also offer a 10 percent discount for *Great Eats Italy* readers who show the book.

TELEPHONE
041 523 4605

OPEN
Mon–Tues, Thur–Sun: lunch
noon–3 P.M., dinner 7–11 P.M.

CLOSED
Wed; Jan 6–Feb 1 (dates vary)

RESERVATIONS
Advised for the outside tables

CREDIT CARDS
AE, MC, V

À LA CARTE
Pizza from 12–20€; 10%
discount for *Great Eats Italy*
readers who show the book

FIXED-PRICE MENU
None

COVER & SERVICE CHARGES
Cover 2€, 12% service added

ENGLISH
Yes

VITAE (¢, 31)
Calle Sant'Antonio, 4118

Vitae has a reputation as a happening place for lunch, which is the only time serious food is served. Later, the action shifts and it becomes the watering hole of the moment for a chic, black-clad crowd, who keep the place jumping until the wee hours. During the peak lunch service, around 1 P.M., an air of organized chaos reigns, so be prepared to hang around the bar until a table clears. Use this time to watch the food being assembled by the hardworking owner and decide what looks best: lasagne, eggplant Parmesan, gnocchi with four cheeses, risotto, raw beef on a bed of arugula, or perhaps a veal or pork dish. The only dessert decision is whether or not you want cream on your bowl of fresh fruit.

NOTE: A second location is near Rialto on Campo Belle Vienna, 222, San Polo.

TELEPHONE
041 520 5205

OPEN
Mon–Fri: bar 9 A.M.–1 A.M., hot lunch 12:30–3 P.M.; Sat: bar 5 P.M.–1 A.M.

CLOSED
Sat lunch, Sun

RESERVATIONS
Not accepted

CREDIT CARDS
None

À LA CARTE
Cicchetti and *tramezzini* from 1€, hot food 6–8€

FIXED-PRICE MENU
None

COVER & SERVICE CHARGES
1€ cover charge at a table, service charge included

ENGLISH
Yes

Restaurants West of the Grand Canal

Dorsoduro

Dorsoduro, which lies between Santa Maria della Salute and the docks of San Nicolò in the southern part of Venice, is known for its beautiful churches, as well as the magnificent art in the Accademia and its contemporary counterpart, the Peggy Guggenheim Collection, the latter beautifully housed in a *palazzo* along the Grand Canal. Dorsoduro is also the center of Venice's university population. Campo Santa Margherita, the heart of the *sestiere,* is one of the city's largest squares and a center of changing local activity. The small morning fish and produce stalls draw the housewives before lunch; in the afternoon the *campo* is filled with children playing; and at night it is a mecca for the under-thirty crowd.

($) indicates a Big Splurge
(¢) indicates a Cheap Eat

Restaurants

AI GONDOLIERI ($, 53)
Rio Terra San Vio, 366

When reserving your table at Ai Gondolieri, ask to be in the main dining room, where the linen-covered tables are set with smart china and crystal, fresh flowers, and glowing candles in the evening. The other narrow room, off the bar, has the same pretty place settings, but the wooden benches along the wall are uncomfortable, and the room serves as a corridor for restaurant patrons coming and going.

The food at Ai Gondolieri is more expensive than some, which is why it should be saved for a Big Splurge. The detailed, creative menu is not translated, but this is not a concern, because the waiters all speak English and willingly explain the dishes. The restaurant is well known for *not* serving fish—instead, arrive for its superb cheese list, truffles from November to January, and homemade pastas, including two risottos served in a hollowed-out loaf of bread. The best buy is definitely the *menù degustazione,* since it includes all of owner Giovanni Trevisan's monthly changing, seasonally inspired dishes from appetizer to dessert. Wine is extra. You may start with three or four antipasti choices such as snails in Burgundy wine sauce, an unusual treatment of polenta cooked with smoky bacon, or a baby artichoke torte. Next will be homemade pasta, perhaps early spring asparagus tossed with buttery egg noodles or tiny ravioli with truffles. The main course might be a tender guinea hen garnished with seasonal vegetables, steak with mushrooms, perfectly roasted pork with horseradish sauce, or fillet of beef in Barola wine sauce served with potato purée. Wrapping it all up is a choice of such luscious homemade desserts as ricotta cheesecake with fresh strawberry sauce or a plate of specially selected cheeses served with fig jam, Corbezzolo honey, fruit and vegetable mustards, and an appropriate wine.

NOTE: The restaurant is a member of Ristoranti della Buona Accoglienza (see page 179). Under the same management is the Museum Cafe at the Peggy Guggenheim Collection (see page 224).

TELEPHONE
041 528 6396

INTERNET
www.aigondolieri.com

OPEN
Daily: lunch noon–3 P.M., dinner 7–10 P.M.

CLOSED
Christmas Day

RESERVATIONS
Advised, especially for dinner and on Sunday

CREDIT CARDS
AE, DC, MC, V

À LA CARTE
60–70€

FIXED-PRICE MENU
58€ (minimum 2 persons), 7 or 8 courses, no choices, includes cover

COVER & SERVICE CHARGES
Cover 4.20€, service discretionary

ENGLISH
Yes

AI QUATTRO FERRI (47)
Calle Lunga San Barnaba, 2754/A

TELEPHONE
041 520 6978

OPEN
Mon–Sat: lunch noon–2:30 P.M.,
dinner 7:30–10:30 P.M.

CLOSED
Sun; July

RESERVATIONS
Not accepted

CREDIT CARDS
None

À LA CARTE
20–25€

FIXED-PRICE MENU
None

COVER & SERVICE CHARGES
1.10€ cover, no service charge

ENGLISH
Limited

You can't beat an order of grilled fish or that old Venetian standby, spaghetti with fresh clams, at this typical spot off of Campo Margherita run by Barbara and Davide. No reservations are taken, so that means come early, when the *piatto del giorno* is usually still available, or be prepared to wait. The market menu changes daily and offers four antipasti, four pastas, six or eight fresh fish choices, but nothing for a carnivore. To compound things for a visitor, English is limited and becomes positively nonexistent when the owners are trying to keep up with the lunch trade. While probably not destination dining for dinner, it is a handy Great Eat for lunch with the locals . . . and at local prices.

ALLE ZATTERE (54)
Rio Terra Foscarini, 795

TELEPHONE
041 520 4224

OPEN
Wed–Mon: lunch noon–3 P.M.,
dinner 7–10 P.M.

CLOSED
Tues; Nov 15–Carnivale

RESERVATIONS
Advised

CREDIT CARDS
MC, V

À LA CARTE
30–35€, pizza 8–12€

FIXED-PRICE MENU
20€, and 28€, both 3 courses
with coffee

COVER & SERVICE CHARGES
Cover 1.50€ for pizza, 2€ all
other orders; 12% service added

ENGLISH
Yes, and menu in English

On a warm summer evening, sitting at a table overlooking the Giudecca Canal and watching the sun set in a crimson sky . . . ah, it just doesn't get much better than this for a night out in Venice. For more than twenty-four years, pizza maker Luigi Vianello has been turning out some of the best crisp pizza in Venice. The quality and freshness of his ingredients is evident, as is the special attention he gives to balancing the traditional pizza ingredients to satisfy even the most demanding pizza fancier. On any given day, at least twenty pizzas are available, from a simple *Margherita* to the *Pizza con Asparagi alla Bismark*, loaded with asparagus, eggs, and ham. If pizza is not on your mind at the moment, there are a host of other choices that cover all the pasta, meat, and fish bases, but for my money, if you come to Alle Zattere, you eat Luigi's pizza.

CANTINONE GIÀ SCHIAVI (¢, 52)
Fondamenta Nani, 992 (on Rio di San Trovaso)

TELEPHONE
041 523 0034

EMAIL
cantinone@mac.com

OPEN
Mon–Sat: bar 8 A.M.–2:30 P.M.,
3:30–8:30 P.M., sandwiches
noon–2:30 P.M.; Sun: 8 A.M.–
2:30 P.M.

Beginning with Giaccomo, three generations of the Schiavi family have kept up a 110-year-old tradition of selling fine wines from this canal-side location. In addition to selling wines by the bottle and case, it has become a favorite local wine bar selling sandwiches and *cicchetti* at lunch. In fact, Alessandra, the wife of the present owner, Lino, makes over three hundred sandwiches a day, which sell out by 2 P.M. Multiply that by the week, month, and year, and not only is it amazingly prolific, it means they have a hit. If you are looking for something unusual to give as a gift, try a bottle of their *Fagolina Bianco* (strawberry wine), which you can sample by the glass and buy by the half-liter.

NOTE: When you arrive, don't be confused by the sign outside that reads, "Vini: Al Bottegon"—you are at the right place.

CLOSED
Sun afternoon; Aug 15–25
RESERVATIONS
Not accepted
CREDIT CARDS
None
À LA CARTE
Cicchetti from 1€, sandwiches from 3€
FIXED-PRICE MENU
None
COVER & SERVICE CHARGES
No cover charge, service included
ENGLISH
Usually

DUE TORRI (36)
Campo Santa Margherita, 3408

On Campo Santa Margherita there are plenty of eating places, but only this one is frequented by the locals, who consider it a genuine kitchen because Venetians cook the food and prepare the pizza. It is clear that none of them ever thumbed through a fat-free cookbook, nor did the owner call in an interior decorator at this unchanging local pit stop where the *cucina casalinga* (home cookin') is as hearty as the characters eating it. This no-frills lunchtime spot with plastic-covered tables is a gathering place for ruddy workers, who prefer to polish off a few glasses of red before digging into their lunch of pasta and fresh fish. Those in a hurry stand at the bar and indulge in the selection of *cicchetti*. In the afternoon, the older men return to play poker and toss down glasses of beer or grappa. On Tuesday, Thurday, and Friday, one of the house specialties, *baccalà,* is available for takeout at 3.80€ per 100 grams. Dinner is served on Friday and Saturday from May until mid-November, and from around May until October, tables are set up outside on the campo.

TELEPHONE
041 523 8126
OPEN
Mon–Sat: bar 7 A.M.–9 P.M., lunch noon–2:30 P.M.; also dinner Fri–Sat May–mid-Nov 7–10 P.M.
CLOSED
Sun; first 3 weeks Aug
RESERVATIONS
Not accepted
CREDIT CARDS
MC, V
À LA CARTE
20–28€
FIXED-PRICE MENU
None
COVER & SERVICE CHARGES
No cover charge, service included
ENGLISH
Yes

LA BITTA (46)
Calle Lunga San Barnaba, 2753

Great Eats await you at La Bitta, a small trattoria with an even smaller walled back garden, which is where everyone wants to sit on a warm Venetian night. La Bitta is unusual in that it *only* serves meat. If you want fish, you can just walk down the street to La Furatola, a longstanding seafood favorite that is run by members of the same family (see page 222).

La Bitta is owned by talented chef Marcellino and his friendly wife, Debora, who competently handles the entire

TELEPHONE
041 523 0531
OPEN
Mon–Sat: dinner 6:30–11 P.M.
CLOSED
Sun
RESERVATIONS
Essential
CREDIT CARDS
None

À LA CARTE
28–35€
FIXED-PRICE MENU
None
ENGLISH
Yes, and menu in English

dining room and terrace by herself. The atmosphere in their rustic restaurant is decidedly unfancy, but the food gets two forks up from everyone who has discovered it. The menu changes almost daily and is based exclusively on fresh, seasonal food. A wonderful beginning in early summer is the salad of raw baby artichokes gently tossed with sharp Parmesan cheese and served on a bed of arugula. Another winner is the smoked beef carpaccio dressed with balsamic vinaigrette. The pastas step out of the ordinary with such choices as penne served with baby asparagus and beets, or remind you how delicious a simple dish of spaghetti tossed with roasted garlic and extra virgin olive oil can be if it is prepared correctly. My dining companion was estatic over his plate of *Fegato di vitello alla Veneziana* (veal liver cooked with onions and served with polenta) and said, "This is as soothing a soul dish as I could hope for. It melts in your mouth like butter, and tastes the way liver should. I wouldn't ever want to order it anywhere else." For dessert, I would never want to order anything but Marcellino's bitter chocolate cake or the fresh pear cake with a butterscotch sauce. The wine list is good, and although it is possible to order a bottle of the house red or white and pay only for what you drink, I suggest consulting Debora, who is a sommelier, for her recommendations on just the right wine to complement your meal. If you order an after-dinner coffee, Debora will prepare it for you on her 1965 Faema (model E-61) espresso machine, a valuable collector's item of which she is very proud.

LA FURATOLA ($, 45)
Calle Lunga San Barnaba, 2869/A

La Furatola is a Venetian landmark famous for serving only seasonally fresh fish. The old-fashioned interior has a singular appeal, especially the collection of black-and-white photographs of old Venice. Diners are seated at pink linen–covered tables decorated simply with a basket of breadsticks. Reservations are absolutely essential for dinner, and if you are thirty minutes late, your table will not be waiting for you.

I recommend starting with an antipasti mix of both warm and cold seafood. It is rich and filling, so if you need to pace yourself, perhaps skip the pasta if you are having a main course, or consider the pasta as your entrée. If you do, the *spaghetti della casa,* topped with a seafood ragout, is wonderful. On Friday, the order of the day is always fish soup, followed by grilled sole, monkfish, sea beam, or

TELEPHONE
041 520 8594
EMAIL
furatola@gpnet.it
OPEN
Mon: dinner 7:30–10:30 P.M.; Tues–Wed, Fri–Sun: lunch 12:30–2:30 P.M., dinner 7:30–10:30 P.M.
CLOSED
Mon lunch, Thur
RESERVATIONS
Advised for lunch, required for dinner (and held only 30 minutes)
CREDIT CARDS
AE, MC, V
À LA CARTE
45–55€

whatever fish is best that day. Salads and vegetables make cameo appearances and are meant to garnish, not inspire. In the winter, zabaglione is the dessert to have; in summer, a glass of sweet wine with assorted dipping cookies is a refreshing finish. The house red or white wine is way above average, but if you are looking to upgrade, the featured Veneto and Friuli wines are also excellent.

If you don't want fish, reserve a table at La Furatola's sister restaurant, La Bitta (see page 221), which is down the street and serves only meat.

LA PISCINA BAR CAFFÈ RESTAURANT (55)
Fondamente Zattere, 782

La Piscina has a magnificent waterside dining terrace on the Fondamenta Zattere overlooking the Guidecca Canal. The inside dining room is just as nice, formally set in a blue-and-white color scheme, with view windows. With a history dating back to the sixteenth century, when the storerooms of lime sellers were here, over time this site has served as the gathering place for many writers and intellectuals, including John Ruskin, who stayed here at the Pensione Calcina in May 1877. As its name suggests, all the dining bases are covered throughout the day. In addition to the restaurant lunch and dinner service, the bar is always open for drinks, sandwiches, snacks, afternoon tea, sweets, and pastries. The Mediterranean cuisine uses only the best seasonal ingredients available, is carefully prepared to each individual order, and is generously served. Everything is made in-house, including the breads and ice creams, and many of the dishes are specifically vegetarian. The wine list is interesting and offers a large choice by both glass and bottle. For a memorable Great Eat in Venice any time of day, I cannot imagine a more delightful choice than La Piscina.

NOTE: La Piscina is part of the Pensione Calcina (see *Great Sleeps Italy* for further details).

L'INCONTRO (41)
Campo Santa Margherita, 3062A (near Ponte dei Pugni across Rio Terà Canal)

L'Incontro is the kind of place you always hope will be just around the corner, and it was for me. The first time I researched Venice for this guide, I lived on Campiello Squiellini, near the Campo Santa Margherita in Dorsoduro. Naturally, I tried every restaurant candidate in the vicinity, and L'Incontro topped my list of favorites. I liked it because it was local and extremely popular; it served

---

FIXED-PRICE MENU
None

COVER & SERVICE CHARGES
Cover 3€, 10% service added

ENGLISH
Yes, and menu in English

TELEPHONE
041 241 3889, 041 520 6466

INTERNET
www.lacalcina.com

OPEN
Mon: dinner 7–10 P.M.; Tues–Sun: lunch noon–2:30 P.M., dinner 7–10 P.M.; bar daily: 11 A.M.–11 P.M.

CLOSED
Mon lunch

RESERVATIONS
Advised, especially for the terrace

CREDIT CARDS
AE, DC, MC, V

À LA CARTE
Sandwiches from 5.50€, salads 10.50€, light meals from 9.50€, 3-course lunch or dinner 35–40€

FIXED-PRICE MENU
None

COVER & SERVICE CHARGES
Cover 2€, service included

ENGLISH
Yes, and menu in English

TELEPHONE
041 522 2404

OPEN
Tues: dinner 7:30–10:30 P.M.; Wed–Sun: lunch 12:30–2:30 P.M., dinner 7:30–10:30 P.M.

CLOSED
Tues lunch, Mon; 2–3 weeks in Jan, 1 week in Aug (dates vary)

RESERVATIONS
Advised
CREDIT CARDS
AE, DC, MC, V
À LA CARTE
30–40€
FIXED-PRICE MENU
None
COVER & SERVICE CHARGES
Cover 2€, 10% service added
ENGLISH
Yes

dependable, well-priced food; and it was, until then, totally undiscovered. During my latest stay in Venice, while working on the fifth edition of this guide, I ate here several times, and I am happy to say I still like the consistency of this restaurant.

The small establishment is composed of two rooms divided by a bar, plus a sidewalk terrace. The low-beamed ceilings, lacy window curtains, flowered tablecloths, baskets on the walls, and strawflower arrangements create a cozy, old-world atmosphere. If you go for dinner, arrive about 8:30 or 9 P.M. to give it a chance to fill up with other diners. When planning your meal, forget the long printed menu and stay strictly with the handwritten daily one, which changes for lunch and dinner. The owner, Paolo, is Sardinian, so the dishes reflect his love for the cooking of this region. The chef does not prepare any fish, concentrating instead on homemade pastas, fresh vegetables, wild game in season, Chianti beef, and grilled, roasted, or stewed veal and pork. The desserts are adequate but not thrilling, so I always pass on the sweet course and walk over to Il Doge Gelaterie (see page 226) for a scoop of my favorite gelato. The house wine is light and refreshing.

NOTE: When I first discovered L'Incontro, there was no sign. Now there is, but that does not mean the place is a snap to locate. It's toward the lower east end of Campo Santa Margherita as you head toward Campo Santa Barnaba and the floating vegetable market. At lunch and dinner, the daily menu is taped to a small window to the left of the door. The restaurant is next to a mask shop. When all else fails, ask a shopkeeper. Everyone knows it.

MUSEUM CAFE–PEGGY GUGGENHEIM COLLECTION (49)
Fondamenta Venier dei Leoni, 707 (follow signs after Ponte Accademia)

TELEPHONE
041 522 8688
EMAIL
muscafe@gpnet.it
OPEN
Mon, Wed–Sun: 10 A.M.–6 P.M.
(until 10 P.M. Sat in summer)
CLOSED
Tues, and whenever the museum is closed
RESERVATIONS
Not necessary
CREDIT CARDS
AE, MC, V

The Museum Cafe is as contemporary and inviting as its coolly elegant surroundings. Peggy Guggenheim was an extraordinary woman who amassed a brilliant collection of twentieth-century surrealist and abstract art. This museum, which was her home on the Grand Canal in Venice until her death in 1979, showcases her private collection of avant-garde paintings and sculpture.

The modern café wraps around a bar, an outside terrace, and several rooms displaying black-and-white photographs of the life of this remarkable and often controversial patron of the arts. The café is run by Giovanni Trevisan, the chef/owner of Ai Gondolieri (see page 219). The menu follows the seasons and offers large salads, pastas, main courses, sandwiches, and desserts. Many of the daily specials and first courses are the same you would have at Ai Gondolieri but for much less investment. You also have the option of ordering a full-scale meal or only a coffee. The café is open whenever the museum is, but to eat here you must buy a ticket to the museum, which is certainly worth it. Guggenheim members receive a 10 percent discount in the café.

À LA CARTE
Sandwiches 5–11€, salads 10–12€, main dishes 11–21€, desserts 6–9€

FIXED-PRICE MENU
None

COVER & SERVICE CHARGES
No cover charge, service discretionary

ENGLISH
Yes, and menu in English

RISTORANTE RIVIERA ($, 51)
Fondamenta delle Zattere Ponte Lungo 1473 (between Calle Trevisan and Calle dei Cartellotti)

The Ristorante Riviera is an unsung find situated on the wide Fondamenta Zattere al Ponte Lungo, facing the Giudecca Canal. It is owned by talented chef Monica and her husband, Luca, who oversees the front part of the restaurant. Since opening a few years ago, they have worked tirelessly, creating a dining experience that locals continually applaud. Fish is Monica's specialty, and she prepares it competently with a light, original touch—but she succeeds equally well with meats. She also takes justifiable pride in her homemade breads and pastas, especially *tagliolini primavera,* a rich pasta loaded with colorful vegetables. In the early summer, when eggplant is at its peak, I like to start with her eggplant Parmigiano. Fish devotees will be impressed with her *delizie dell'Adriatico,* a mixed fish and seafood appetizer, or the unusual scampi and sardines marinated in vinegar, onions, pine nuts, and raisins. Two favorite main courses are the grilled sea bass garnished with zucchini and fennel, and the liver cooked with onions and served with polenta. For dessert, the choice of chocolate lovers is her warm chocolate cake served with vanilla sauce. Otherwise, she does an impressive crêpe Grand Marnier.

NOTE: The restaurant is a member of the Ristoranti della Buona Accoglienza (see page 179).

TELEPHONE
041 522 7621

INTERNET
www.ristoranteriviera.it

OPEN
Tues–Sun: lunch noon–2:30 P.M., dinner 7:30–10 P.M.

CLOSED
Mon; 1 week in mid-Aug, Jan 7–31

RESERVATIONS
Advised

CREDIT CARDS
AE, DC, MC, V

À LA CARTE
45–50€

FIXED-PRICE MENU
None

COVER & SERVICE CHARGES
Cover 4.50€, service included

ENGLISH
Yes

TAVERNA SAN TROVASO (48)
Fondamenta Priuli, 1016

The small and very popular Taverna San Trovaso is the family-run effort of six brothers, one sister, and their assorted spouses and offspring. You must call ahead for reservations and arrive on time if you expect to get a table. Readers of *Great Eats Italy* as well as smart Venetians know and recommend this as a restaurant where a delicious, uncomplicated meal can be had for a moderate price. I have

TELEPHONE
041 520 3703

INTERNET
www.santrovaso.it

OPEN
Tues–Sun: lunch noon–2:50 P.M., dinner 7–9:50 P.M.

CLOSED
Mon; Dec 31–Jan 1, 2nd week of July (dates vary)

RESERVATIONS	Essential
CREDIT CARDS	AE, DC, MC, V
À LA CARTE	30€, pizzas from 7€
FIXED-PRICE MENU	18€, 3 courses
COVER & SERVICE CHARGES	Cover 2€, service discretionary
ENGLISH	Yes, and menu in English

never walked in without having someone walking out say to me, "This is good!" Restful and relaxing it is not, but it is full of happy locals eating well, having a good time, and sounding like it.

The fixed-price *menù turistico* is a Great Eat value and offers enough choices to keep it interesting. The à la carte menu is varied and includes pizza noon and night, so it should appeal to everyone. The servings are tremendous and the wine very good, so it is imperative to arrive hungry and thirsty in order to do justice to it all.

Gelaterias

GELATI NICO (56)
Fondamenta Zattere ai Gesuiti, 922

TELEPHONE
041 522 5293
OPEN
Mon–Wed, Fri–Sun: 6:45 A.M.–
11:30 P.M., continuous service;
Oct–Jan till 10:30 P.M.
CLOSED
Thur; Dec 21–Jan 23
CREDIT CARDS
None
PRICES
Gianduiotto to go 2.30€, at a
table 4€; other ice cream from
3.70€
ENGLISH
Yes

The Zattere, the southernmost promenade in Venice, is popular with families, who like to spend Sunday afternoon strolling along the walkway that borders the Giudecca Canal. Along the way, there are several *gelaterie,* but Nico is far and away the best and most popular. I was first here on a freezing April afternoon during a driving rainstorm, and there were still ten people ahead of me in line waiting to dig into their specialty, *gianduiotto:* a large slice of dense chocolate hazelnut ice cream buried in whipped cream and served in a cup. You can eat here, but Great Eaters will certainly order theirs to go, because then it will cost only 2.30€. Having it served at a tiny table inside or on the deck overlooking the canal sets you back about 4.20€. The same man has been dipping out *gianduiotti* for almost four decades; others have tried to imitate him, but none have ever equaled his version. There are other ice cream treats available, from sundaes to *frappés,* but almost everyone orders the famous *gianduiotto* no matter how many times they've had it before.

IL DOGE GELATERIE (38)
Campo Santa Margherita, 3058/A

TELEPHONE
041 523 4607
OPEN
Daily 10 A.M.–2 A.M.
CLOSED
Never
CREDIT CARDS
None

I must confess: I adore Italian gelato, and nowhere in Venice is it better than at Il Doge Gelaterie, a shrine to this scrumptious treat. All the ice cream is made here, and there are more than thirty superb flavors in the repertoire, including black-and-white coffee, rum, amaretto, *marron glace,* tiramisù, and zabaglione. There are also countless fruit *sorbettos* in summer and, to keep insistent dieters happy, soya gelato made with no sugar, and several no-fat, no-sugar yogurts. The best of these is the milk and honey, which slips down like silk. However, please put your diet on hold, because there are two flavors you positively cannot miss, and they are *panna cotta del Doge,* a custard-based ice cream swirled with ribbons of caramel, and *crema del Doge,* made with candied orange peel and chocolate. Do they sound pedestrian? Let me assure you, after one taste you will agree that they are anything but. Just thinking about them makes me wish I was there right now eating another scoop or two of these celestial creations.

PRICES
Cones or cups 1–3.10€, *panna* (whipped cream) 0.50€, *granitas* (fresh fruit ices) 0.50–2.50€

ENGLISH
Limited

Pastry Shops and Bakeries

TONOLO (30)
Salizzada San Pantalon, 3764

You will undoubtedly be the only tourist when you join the students, blue-haired dowagers, well-dressed business-people, and shopkeepers at Tonolo, the most popular spot in the San Pantalon area to have a cappuccino and pastry. Before arriving, sharpen your elbows and your determination, so you can edge your way to the counter, where the young women miraculously keep straight all the shouted early-morning orders. Open Tuesday to Saturday from 7:45 A.M. until 8:30 P.M. and Sunday from 7:45 A.M. until 1 P.M., this constantly crowded bakery makes some of the best high-calorie treats in Venice, and everyone knows it. There are no tables, so you must eat standing or have your order packaged to go. In the morning, indulge in a fresh cream-filled doughnut, a plain or almond-topped *cornetto* (croissant), raisin pound cake, or a buttery brioche and a frothy cappuccino served in a pretty blue-and-white cup. At lunch, try two or three little pizzas or bite-size *rustici,* little pastries filled with ham, ricotta, or spinach. In the late afternoon, any one of their indulgent pastries or cakes will make you happy you came to Venice.

TELEPHONE
041 523 7209

OPEN
Tues–Sat: 7:45 A.M.–8:30 P.M.; Sun 7:45 A.M.–1 P.M.

CLOSED
Mon; Aug

CREDIT CARDS
None

PRICES
Pastries from 0.85€

ENGLISH
Very limited

San Polo

San Polo occupies a middle section of the Grand Canal and is the smallest of the six *sestieri*. It is named after the ancient church of San Polo, which stands on Campo San Polo, the largest square in Venice after St. Mark's. The Rialto area, once the center of the city's bargaining, buying, and selling, is still famous for its colorful produce and fish markets and the countless tourist stalls that line the Ruga del Orefici. The Rialto Bridge is one of the three that cross the Grand Canal, and it is one of the most photographed sites in Venice. No one should miss the enormous gothic church of the Frari, with three of Venice's best altarpieces (one of these is Titian's *Assumption*), and the Scuola Grande di San Rocco, with its paintings by Tintoretto.

RESTAURANTS

GOURMET FOOD AND WINE SHOPS

OUTDOOR MARKETS

($) indicates a Big Splurge
(¢) indicates a Cheap Eat

Restaurants

ALLA MADONNA (24)
Calle della Madonna, 594

TELEPHONE
041 522 3824

OPEN
Mon–Tues, Thur–Sun: lunch noon–3 P.M., dinner 7–10:30 P.M.

CLOSED
Wed; Aug 1–15, Dec 20–Jan 31

RESERVATIONS
Essential

Alla Madonna is in a pivotal location on a narrow street on the San Polo side of the Rialto Bridge. Almost every guidebook to Venice lists it as one of the restaurants you must visit, and for good reason. The fresh fish is always delicious and reasonable, and the atmosphere is authentic and pleasing. The unadorned tables are filled every day with a mix of chattering Venetians and visitors. If you arrive without reservations, unless you are here the moment lunch or dinner service starts, you can expect to wait up to an hour for a table, so beware. Service by the white-coated waitstaff, some of whom have been on the job since time began, can be brusque, but given the number of tables they have to serve, it is easy to see why patience can run thin during the crunch.

From appetizer to pasta and main course, the star of the show is always fresh fish. Anything else, including the overcooked vegetables, can be disappointing. At the entrance is an iced display of only some of the many delicacies awaiting you. The specialties are seafood risotto, spaghetti with black squid, squid with polenta, fried cuttlefish, a mixed fish fry, and grilled sole.

CREDIT CARDS
AE, MC, V
À LA CARTE
30–35€
FIXED-PRICE MENU
None
COVER & SERVICE CHARGES
Cover 2€, 12% service added
ENGLISH
Yes, and menu in English

ANTICHE CARAMPANE ($, 18)
Rio Terra de le Carampane, 1911 (near Campiello Albrizzi)

Almost everything, from the formal atmosphere to the reliably tasty food, remains unchanged at Antiche Carampane, reported to be one of the oldest taverns in Venice. For a dress-up meal designed to impress your boss, difficult mother-in-law, or important date, this should do very well, provided everyone likes fish, since that is all they serve. To help casual guests not "in the know," a sign posted outside states that they do not serve pizza, lasagne, or pasta with *ragù* sauce, and there is no fixed-price menu. They should add that there is no printed à la carte menu. The food you eat depends on what looked best that day at the Rialto Market. This is an old-school Big Splurge designed for those who prefer tradition over life in the fast lane, and it is the type of destination dining the locals frequent when they want a fine meal.

TELEPHONE
041 524 0165
INTERNET
www.antichecarampane.com
OPEN
Tues–Sat: lunch noon–3:30 P.M., dinner 7–11 P.M.
CLOSED
Mon–Sun; Aug
RESERVATIONS
Advised
CREDIT CARDS
AE, DC, MC, V
À LA CARTE
38–45€
FIXED-PRICE MENU
None
COVER & SERVICE CHARGES
Cover 2€, service discretionary
ENGLISH
Yes

CAFFÈ DEI FRARI (¢, 27)
Fondamenta dei Frari, 2564

At this rambunctious *caffè* near the Campo dei Frari (at the foot of Ponte dei Frari), you will join Venetian students, men quaffing their third glass of Chianti far too early in the day, and elderly women fortifying their trip to the market with a *caffè macchiato* or cappuccino. There is always neighborly service and made-to-order savory sandwiches (with salads added in the summer) served from dawn to dusk by the casual crew. I like to go around noon and order a sandwich filled with slices of *prosciutto crudo*

TELEPHONE
041 524 1877
OPEN
Mon–Sat: 8 A.M.–9 P.M. (till 1 A.M. in summer)
CLOSED
Sun; 1st or last week of Aug
RESERVATIONS
Not accepted
CREDIT CARDS
None

À LA CARTE
Sandwiches from 1.30–3.50€,
salads 6€
FIXED-PRICE MENU
None
COVER & SERVICE CHARGES
Cover 1€ at a table, service
discretionary
ENGLISH
Some

(air-dried salt-cured ham) and thin slices of provolone or *mozzarella di bufala* cheese. For the best people-watching, sit downstairs at one of the six round tables along the padded banquette or, in summer, at one of the tables outside facing the canal. As is the case in all *caffès,* if you sit at these tables, or one upstairs, and order drinks with your sandwich or salad, you will pay an additional charge—here it is 1€—to have the waiter negotiate the narrow stairs with your order or bring it to you outside.

CANTINA DO MORI (¢, 19)
Calle do Mori, 429 (off Ruga Vecchia S. Giovanni)

TELEPHONE
041 522 5401
OPEN
Mon–Sat: 8:30 A.M.–8:30 P.M.
CLOSED
Sun
RESERVATIONS
Not accepted
CREDIT CARDS
None
À LA CARTE
Cicchetti from 1.30–1.89€,
sandwiches from 2.25€
FIXED-PRICE MENU
None
COVER & SERVICE CHARGES
None
ENGLISH
Limited

For a glimpse of where the Rialto Market traders, delivery boys, and local office workers go for wine and camaraderie, look no further than Cantina do Mori, which has a decidedly male-dominated atmosphere. Inside it is long, narrow, and dark, with hanging copper pots and a stand-up bar (there are no tables at all). You will eat great *cicchetti,* platters of local salami and prosciutto, and enormous sandwiches, and drink wines sold by the glass. In existence since 1462, this timeworn *enoteca* is run by Rudi and Gianni, who will be happy to advise you on which wines you should drink with whatever you are eating. For instance, if it is salt cod, it should be a glass of prosecco. With winter sausage and beans, you will need a robust Cabernet.

NOTE: There are no toilets.

CANTINA DO SPADE (16)
Calle do Spade, 860

TELEPHONE
041 521 0574
INTERNET
www.dospadevenezia.it
OPEN
Mon–Tues, Thur–Sun: bar
9:30 A.M.–9:30 P.M., lunch
noon–2:30 P.M., dinner
7–10:30 P.M.
CLOSED
Wed
RESERVATIONS
Advised on weekends
CREDIT CARDS
MC, V
À LA CARTE
Cicchetti 1–2€, full meals
25–35€
FIXED-PRICE MENU
None

One of the top tourist attractions in Venice, the Rialto Market, the old commercial meeting place along the Grand Canal, is a lively and colorful outdoor market for fish and produce, crowded with countless stalls and shouting hawkers selling everything that is seasonally fresh. Housewives and chefs come early each morning for the best selections, and visitors wander through eager to soak up the local color and take advantage of the endless photo opportunities. Surrounding the market is a labyrinth of narrow streets and alleyways lined with bars, tiny cafés, and food shops.

Whenever you are in this area, Cantina do Spade is a good place for a robust lunch or dinner. With a typical Venetian interior displaying an eclectic mix of antiques and kitsch, it is old and well-known, even to Casanova, who drank here. Emilio, the present owner, is a friendly guy who meets and greets all his patrons with the same backslapping welcome and jokes about his well-known "Monica Lewenski" sausage. In addition to a range of other cured meats and *cicchetti,* he offers a core menu, which the regulars ignore completely. They know he shops daily at the Rialto Market, so the *speciali del giorno* are all they zero in on, washed down with glass after glass of the house red or white, poured from a barrel.

COVER & SERVICE CHARGES
Cover 1.50€, no service charge
ENGLISH
Yes, and French and German

OSTARIA ANTICO DOLO (20)
Ruga Vecchia San Giovanni, 778 (often called Ruga Rialto)

For good wine and food near the Rialto Bridge, stop by Antico Dolo, a picture postcard–perfect *osteria* frequented by neighborhood residents. There are only twenty-five places in the two little rooms, decorated with hanging pots and a lazily turning ceiling fan. Yet the size does not seem to deter the faithful, including gondoliers who swear by the chef's lunch dishes of country sausages, hearty seafood pastas, locally caught fish, and tripe with polenta. Designed to get people in and out in a hurry, the lunch menu costs considerably less than dinner, but the quality and preparation are not compromised. At dinner, the fish and meat choices increase, as do the prices. Anytime, there are three dessert choices: homemade tiramisù, ice cream with fresh fruit, or *esse,* the buttery *s*-shaped cookies from Burano for dipping into *vin santo* in the winter or *fragolino* (strawberry wine) in the summer.

TELEPHONE
041 522 6546
INTERNET
www.anticodolo.it
OPEN
Daily in summer: lunch noon–3 P.M., dinner 5:30 P.M.–to last guest; winter Mon, Wed–Sun, same hours
CLOSED
Tues in winter
RESERVATIONS
Essential
CREDIT CARDS
AE, DC, MC, V
À LA CARTE
Lunch 20€, dinner 40–55€
FIXED-PRICE MENU
None
COVER & SERVICE CHARGES
Cover: lunch 2.50€, dinner 3.50€; service included
ENGLISH
Yes

OSTERIA DA FIORE ($, 17)
Calle del Scaleter, 2202

Everyone has a favorite fish restaurant in Venice, and Da Fiore is at the top of many lists. Run by the charming Maurizio Martin, who works in front, and his wife, Mara, who is the capable chef, it has been in operation since 1978. Since that time they have built an enviable reputation for having the best and freshest seasonal seafood available, earning the only Michelin star awarded in Venice in the process. Because of the high demand, reservations are absolutely essential at least two weeks in advance. The well-designed interior is beautiful in its simple elegance, featuring well-spaced tables set with lovely linens, large wineglasses, and shining cutlery. Outside there is a pair of tables on the canal, perfect for a romantic dinner for two. The formally dressed waitstaff are very helpful and

TELEPHONE
041 721 308
INTERNET
www.dafiore.com
OPEN
Tues–Sat: lunch 12:30–2:30 P.M., dinner 7:30–10:30 P.M.
CLOSED
Mon–Sun; Dec 24–Jan 20, Aug
RESERVATIONS
Absolutely essential, as far in advance as possible
CREDIT CARDS
AE, DC, MC, V
À LA CARTE
85–100€

FIXED-PRICE MENU
None
COVER & SERVICE CHARGES
No cover charge, service discretionary
ENGLISH
Yes

will explain the menu and suggest appropriate wines as needed. Please note that meat is not served.

The menu changes daily, but for delicious openers, you can always count on a seafood salad or a delicate fish soup. According to the time of year, you might see imaginative dishes featuring octopus, scallops, or razor clams. Also watch for delicate fried vegetables, light as a feather and not at all greasy. Appetizers might include a very light consommé with scampi and ravioli filled with whitefish, or tuna carpaccio served with capers in Tuscan olive oil. First courses always include a risotto. Be sure to save adequate room for the main courses, which also vary with the season. Look for grilled eel, fillet of striped bass splashed with balsamic vinegar, tuna grilled with rosemary, turbot baked in a potato crust, and soft-shell crab served with polenta. For dessert, the lemon *sorbetto* or the vanilla ice cream with a red wine–soaked pear are light finishes to a lovely meal. This is definitely a Big Splurge, but one that is well worth it.

NOTE: Osteria da Fiore is a member of Ristorante della Buona Accoglienza; see page 179 for details. Da Fiori now has a cooking school that is conducted by Mara Martin in her private Venetian kitchen. For further details, consult their Website.

Santa Croce

In the 1930s, the Fascists built the Piazzale Roma, the gigantic car park just over the bridge from Mestre. Toward the eastern part of the district are weaving walkways that are relatively tourist free. To the west, the area is mainly industrial and geared toward dock and freight operations around the Stazione Marittima. Also here is the Manifattura Tabacci, the oldest industrial building in Venice still used for its original purpose: cigar and cigarette production. Flanking the Grand Canal are fading yet imposing palazzos.

RESTAURANTS

Restaurants

AE OCHE (¢, 15)
Calle del Tintor, 1552A-B

Ae Oche is young, fun, cheap, and good. This popular gathering ground for the Italian fast-food generation is never empty. I have yet to find a way to beat the Sunday crowd of families who arrive for one of the ninety varieties of crisp pizza and calzones. You can dine outside on a little deck, in a tented garden in the back, or at one of the inside booths with bench seats crafted from bed headboards.

Fire-eaters will love pizza No. 15, the *mangiafuoco*, featuring spicy salami, pepperoni, paprika, and tabasco sauce. Tamer taste buds will appreciate No. 30, the *capricciosa*, topped with prosciutto, mushrooms, and artichoke hearts. The *disco volante* (flying saucer), No. 78, made from two pizzas put together sandwich style, is not a stellar choice, and neither is the house wine. You are better off with something from their long international beer list, which offers brews from Australia, Mexico, the United States, and Spain, among others. If pizza is not on your diet, probably one of the sixteen large salads ranging from a basic *insalata mista* to the *Oche*—loaded with tomatoes, artichoke hearts, tuna, pepperoni, mozzarella cheese, asparagus, and black olives—will be. There is also a regular trattoria menu with all the familiar antipasti, pastas, meats, and side dishes. This part of the menu is not the kitchen's strong suit, however, so order these with extreme caution.

NOTE: There are two streets named Calle del Tintor (which is also spelled Tentor). You want the one that leads into Campo San Giacomo dell' Orio.

TELEPHONE
041 524 1161
OPEN
Daily: lunch noon–3 P.M.,
dinner 7 P.M.–midnight
CLOSED
Never
RESERVATIONS
Advised on weekends and holidays
CREDIT CARDS
MC, V
À LA CARTE
Pizza from 4–8€, salads 6–8€, full meal 12–15€
FIXED-PRICE MENU
None
COVER & SERVICE CHARGES
Cover 1.50€, 12% service added
ENGLISH
Yes

AL NONO RISORTO (14)
Sotoportego de Sora Bettina, 2338

The later you go for dinner here the more local it gets, especially on warm evenings, when large families fill the plastic chairs in the big tree-shaded garden outside. At lunch, it is just as full, thanks to the two good-value fixed-price menus. Al Nono Risorto is very informal and not the sort of place to expect heel-clicking service, as overworked

TELEPHONE
041 524 1169
OPEN
Mon–Tues, Thur–Sun: lunch noon–2:30 P.M., dinner 7–10:30 P.M.
CLOSED
Wed

RESERVATIONS
Essential for dinner in the patio

CREDIT CARDS
MC, V

À LA CARTE
30–35€

FIXED-PRICE MENU
Lunch: 14–16€, 2 courses,
bread and cover included

COVER & SERVICE CHARGES
Cover 1.60€, service
discretionary

ENGLISH
Limited

waitresses try valiantly to get to the multitude of tables. To add to the possible frustration, the menu is written in Italian hieroglyphics. Still, this is a locally recommended place to keep in mind for a modestly priced meal not too far from the *ferrovia* (train station) and Piazzale Roma (the carpark area). What is on the menu? Assorted fish antipasti, pastas including the house gnocchi, main courses of *baccalà,* a huge fried-fish platter with polenta, liver and onions, roast chicken with potatoes, and a handful of salads and vegetables. The fare is generously dished out and filling. Desserts are an afterthought; instead, head for a *gelateria.*

LA ZUCCA (11)
Campo San Giacomo dell' Orio, 1762 (by the Ponte del Megio)

TELEPHONE
041 524 1570

OPEN
Mon–Sat: lunch 12:30–2 P.M.,
dinner 7–10:30 P.M.

CLOSED
Sun

RESERVATIONS
Advised for dinner and holidays

CREDIT CARDS
AE, MC, V

À LA CARTE
20–30€

FIXED-PRICE MENU
None

COVER & SERVICE CHARGES
Cover 1.50€, service included

ENGLISH
Yes

Collectors of unusual culinary experiences, take note: This may be your only chance in Venice to sample pumpkin pasta or pumpkin soup, the two tasty treats from which this appealing little trattoria takes its name. Unfortunately, you will have to time your visit in the fall or winter, since these dishes are only available seasonally. The rest of the food on the daily-changing menu shows a degree of originality, as the young and enthusiastic owners strive to please a snappy group of youthful habitués, many of whom are vegetarians who appreciate the chef's interesting way with fresh vegetables for all courses.

Aside from the pumpkin creations, pasta tossed several ways—including with tomato, fresh goat cheese, and black olives—is a first-course front-runner. The mushroom and arugula salad served with fresh shreds of Parmesan cheese, and the potato, zucchini, and mushroom torte with *scamorza* cheese are good lunch choices, while the roast pork, goulash, or rabbit seem more appropriate for dinner. Vegetarians will want to try the side dishes, including carrots cooked with lemon and seasoned with curry, small onions simmered in prosecco wine, or potatoes delicately flavored with lemon and chives. For dessert, the *panna cotta* covered with honey and almonds and the chef's *semifreddo* with *zabaione* sauce display first-class simplicity.

The best seating is outside, overlooking the canal. On cool days, I like to sit toward the back at a window table on the Rio delle Megio canal, rather than up front in the bar and kitchen area, where the shoulder-to-shoulder crowd can get a little loud. When you go, be sure to admire the modern paintings of pumpkins (in every guise imaginable) lining the oak-paneled walls.

RISTORANTE RIBÒ ($, 28)
Fondamenta Minotto, 158

Ribò, on a canal not far from Piazzale Roma and the *ferrovia,* is an upscale choice for a nice meal, especially in the summer, when tables are set in the white-tented garden in back. The light, modern interior, distinguished by a circular bar, gray stone floors, and tree branches espaliered across the ceiling, has a dignified sense of formality to it. The kitchen is unfailingly good, offering the same high-quality food for the two midday fixed-price menus that it does on the à la carte menu, where the prices can move into Big Splurge territory. For lunch, the menus change daily and include two courses with three choices each, vegetables, wine, water, and coffee. At dinner, the lights dim and the candles are lit for fine dining. Both meat and fresh fish are offered, including spider crab or foie gras to start, followed by lobster ravioli in a light asparagus sauce, then perhaps duck breast in a balsamic vinegar sauce or grilled tiger prawns. Braised artichokes, pumpkin and broccoli flan, or sautéed eggplant might be the seasonal garnishes. Finish with a creamy chocolate and amaretto mouse or wild berries and ice cream and you will have enjoyed another Great Eat in Venice.

TELEPHONE
041 524 2486
INTERNET
www.ristoranteribo.com
OPEN
Mon–Tues, Thur–Sun: lunch 12:15–3 P.M., dinner 7:15–10:30 P.M.
CLOSED
Wed; 1–2 weeks in Jan (dates vary)
RESERVATIONS
Advised for dinner
CREDIT CARDS
AE, DC, MC, V
À LA CARTE
50–60€
FIXED-PRICE MENU
Lunch only: 20€, 2 courses, vegetable, wine, water, and coffee
COVER & SERVICE CHARGES
Cover 3€, service discretionary
ENGLISH
Yes, and menu in English

TRATTORIA ALLE BURCHIELLE (29)
Fondamenta Burchielle, 393

Trattoria alle Burchielle was founded on this site in 1503 and is considered one of the oldest trattorias in continuous operation in Venice. Ninety years ago, Bruno Pagin's uncle took charge, and now, under Bruno Pagin and his niece Serena's direction, it is still going strong as a local favorite best known for its treatment of fresh fish. The restaurant is along a pretty canal in a picturesque corner of Venice, not too far from Piazzale Roma. On a summer evening it is wonderful to sit outside and watch the boats drifting by while enjoying textbook examples of traditional Venetian fish preparations.

Noteworthy among the first courses are the seafood lasagne and the spaghetti with whole clams. The most popular main courses are the *sogliola ai ferri* (grilled sole) and the giant prawns in a lemon, garlic, and olive oil marinade. There are a few meat dishes, but they are not the reason to eat here. And the sweets that adorn the pastry cart are not made in-house. A nice change of pace for dessert is a selection of Italian cheeses or sweet cookies dipped in *fragolino* (strawberry) wine. The regular menu is translated

TELEPHONE
041 710 342
OPEN
Tues–Sun: lunch noon–3 P.M., dinner 7–10 P.M.
CLOSED
Mon; Jan–Feb
RESERVATIONS
Advised
CREDIT CARDS
AE, DC, MC, V
À LA CARTE
25–35€
FIXED-PRICE MENU
None
COVER & SERVICE CHARGES
Cover 1€, 10% service added
ENGLISH
Yes, and menu in English

into English but does not include the list of daily specials, so be sure to ask about them.

If you can't manage a full meal, try Grecia e Oriente, their new snack bar on the corner. It serves the usual sandwiches and *cicchetti* until the supply runs out, and around noon it offers a few hot pasta dishes.

VECIO FRITOLIN ($, 13)
Calle della Regina, 2262

TELEPHONE
041 522 2881
INTERNET
www.veciofritolin.it
OPEN
Tues–Sat: lunch noon–2:30 P.M., dinner 7–10:30 P.M.; Sun: lunch noon–2:30 P.M.
CLOSED
Sun dinner, Mon
RESERVATIONS
Essential for dinner
CREDIT CARDS
AE, DC, MC, V
À LA CARTE
40–55€
FIXED-PRICE MENU
None
COVER & SERVICE CHARGES
No cover charge, 10% service added
ENGLISH
Yes, and menu in English

Everything is impressive in this picturesque restaurant—from Irina, the friendly owner, to the cozy, romantic setting and her delicious food. The heavily beamed dining room has well-spaced tables attractively set with red and white tablecloths and tiny lamps. A collection of black-and-white photos of Venice proves that not much has changed in this very old part of the city.

Irina is a hands-on hostess, treating all of her guests with the same gracious respect and always taking time to explain dishes and make adaptations if necessary. The imaginative menu is kept short, and is based on traditional flavors, seasonal ingredients, and careful preparations. Everything is absolutely fresh: no canned or frozen products are used, and all the breads, pastas, and desserts are homemade. Because this is Venice, the emphasis is on fish and seafood, but there is always one meat main course available, and one or two pastas that do not star fish. Two of the best late springtime openers are fat asparagus covered with melted pecorino cheese, or plump scallops with tomato and basil sauce. Pasta with tiger prawns and artichokes, or with gorgonzola cheese and wild arugula, are two dishes you will want again. Local sea bass baked with zucchini and thyme is a deceptively simple yet sophisticated treatment of this popular Venetian fish, and the grilled tuna, served with *misticanza,* a tangy herb salad, is another standout. For dessert, you must sample Irina's satiny crème brûlée or the warm almond cake. There is also a thoughtful wine and cheese selection.

Pastry Shops and Bakeries

BAR PASTICCERIA GILDA VIO (12)
Rio Marin, 784

TELEPHONE
041 718 523
OPEN
Mon–Tues, Thur–Sun: 6:30 A.M.– 8 P.M., continuous service

The Bar Pasticceria Gilda Vio is owned by Gilda Vio, who makes all the divinely sinful pastries and is justifiably proud of the world acclaim her talents have brought her. She is ably assisted behind the counter by her daughter Sonia.

If you have any guilt at all about indulging in these sinful treats, you may be somewhat assuaged to know that all of her products are made using only pure ingredients, without coloring or additives. People in the know beat a daily path to her beautiful shop, which sells some of the best pastries in Venice—and let me assure you, the competition is stiff. Whenever you go, expect a crowd, especially on Sundays around noon, when handsome fathers with young children in tow walk here to purchase dessert for their midday meal. In the morning, order several fruit-filled croissants. Later on, vegetable-based puff pastries, individual pizzas, and sandwiches made on her own bread sell like hotcakes. In the afternoon, stop in for coffee and an airy rum meringue dusted with chocolate , or her famous *crostati di fruita fresca* with fresh whipped cream. You can also pick up a bag of her butter cookies or a box of hand-dipped chocolates for a special treat. Even if you don't buy a thing (a guaranteed impossibility), do go by to admire . . . and to smell.

CLOSED
Wed; Aug, Dec 15–Jan 10

CREDIT CARDS
None

PRICES
Pastries from 0.90€, sandwiches from 1.90€

ENGLISH
Some, and Gilda speaks French

Restaurants on the Islands

Burano Island

Burano is synonymous with lace. The best place to see the real thing is at the school in Piazza Galuppi and its museum and shop. Shops selling more lace than you could ever wash and iron in three lifetimes line the main street, which extends from the exit ramp from the boat dock clear across the island. Buyers along this stretch should beware, however, because most of the work comes straight from Hong Kong or the Philippines. Despite this, the island is a photographer's dream, with brightly colored houses nestled along narrow alleys and walkways. One purchase you can make without worry is a bagful of *bussolai,* the sweet local ring- or S-shaped biscuits that are perfect for dipping in sweet wine. Burano is still a fishing community, and as you walk around the island you will see the boats and nets lining the quays.

TRATTORIA AL GATTO NERO ($)
Via Giudecca, 88

TELEPHONE
041 730 120

INTERNET
www.gattonero.com

OPEN
Tues–Sun: lunch noon–3 P.M., dinner 7:30–9 P.M.

CLOSED
Mon; 7–10 days in Jan, last 10 days of Nov

RESERVATIONS
Absolutely essential, especially on weekends

CREDIT CARDS
AE, DC, MC, V

À LA CARTE
50–60€

FIXED-PRICE MENU
None

COVER & SERVICE CHARGES
Cover 2.10€, service discretionary

ENGLISH
Yes, and menu in English

Most visitors come to Burano for two reasons: to buy the handmade lace and to eat fish. Tourists rarely stray from the Via Baldessare Galuppi, which is lined with shops selling linen and lace and a selection of overpriced eating places featuring greasy fried fish guaranteed to induce acute heartburn. Just beyond all of this is the most attractive part of Burano, blissfully free of fellow travelers. It is here that you will find Al Gatto Nero, widely recognized as the best trattoria on the island, thanks to its charm and character, not to mention its outstanding food, which draws an international clientele.

Owned for the last four decades by Ruggero, the chef, and his son, Massimiliano, the restaurant has two large rooms inside in addition to a covered canal-side terrace for warm-weather dining. One of the more impressive aspects of the service is the unique china, made especially for the restaurant. The large white dishes are ringed with an artist's conception of Burano buildings, and if you look very carefully, you will see the trattoria and Ciccio, their late, gray cat, portrayed in the design. It is the most crowded at lunchtime and on the weekends, when local residents know to let the waiter guide their choices based on the daily specials of fresh fish. There is a menu, but as

Massimiliano says, "We can't put everything we prepare on the menu, or it would be a bible!" You may want to skip the broiled eel but not the fresh prawns, broiled sardines, turbot, or fresh sole. Desserts, even though they are home-made, do not play a starring role, so you can concentrate fully on the rest of the meal. Skip the meat dishes; they are real understudies.

NOTE: Al Gatto Nero is a member of Ristoranti della Buona Accoglienza; see page 179 for further details.

Giudecca Island

Giudecca Island was where the wealthy Renaissance aristocrats built their summer palaces. Michelangelo stayed here when he left Florence in 1529. Today the wealthy hide out at the famed Cipriani Hotel and eat and drink in Harry's Dolce (a slightly less expensive spin-off of Harry's Bar in Venice). There is also a private garden, the Garden of Eden, named after the English gardener who created it, and Andrea Palladio's Church of La Zitelle. The panorama from the *fondamenta* along the water offers a magnificent view of Doge's Palace and the island of San Giorgio Maggiore.

RESTAURANTS

Altanella ($)	**239**
Mistrà	**240**

($) indicates a Big Splurge

Restaurants

ALTANELLA ($)
Calle delle Erbe, 268–270

Altanella has what Italians call a *buona forchetta* ("a good fork") and a *buon bicchiere* ("a good glass"). Buried halfway down a narrow street on Giudecca Island, at Rio de Ponte Lungo, this Stradella family restaurant has been preparing only fish dishes since the turn of the century. It looks undiscovered because there is no sign, only a light outside, but it is firmly on the map. Hemingway was a customer in his day, as was François Mitterand. However, fame has not gone to anyone's head; the food is still marvelous.

During warm weather, reserve a table on the irresistibly romantic terrace overlooking the island's central canal.

TELEPHONE
041 522 7780

OPEN
Wed–Sun: lunch 12:30–2 P.M., dinner 7:30–9 P.M.

CLOSED
Mon–Tues; Jan–Carnivale, Aug 10–20

RESERVATIONS
Essential

CREDIT CARDS
None

À LA CARTE
40–50€ with house wine

FIXED-PRICE MENU
None

COVER & SERVICE CHARGES
Cover 2€, 10% service added

ENGLISH
Yes

Otherwise you can sit at one of the tables inside, where there are pictures of the restaurant in its early days and a photo of the founder over the kitchen door.

There is a menu, but always listen to what's fresh that day. Dishes I look forward to having again are the seafood risotto, the freshly made gnocchi with squid ink and sauced with cuttlefish (a prized recipe of one of the family's grandmothers), mussels and sweet peppers, the grilled sea bream, and the flavorful tuna. The desserts are made here, so be sure to plan on a piece of the lush chocolate cake, the unusual pumpkin cake, or, if you are here at Easter, their special almond cake. In the summer, everyone loves the meringue nest filled with ice cream and the fresh strawberry mousse.

MISTRÀ
Giudecca 212 A

TELEPHONE
041 522 0743

OPEN
Mon: lunch noon–2:30 P.M.;
Wed–Sun: lunch noon–2:30 P.M.
(till 3:30 P.M. Sat–Sun), dinner
7:30–10:30 P.M.

CLOSED
Mon dinner, Tues; Jan

RESERVATIONS
Advised for weekend lunches

CREDIT CARDS
AE, DC, MC, V

À LA CARTE
35–45€

FIXED-PRICE MENU
Mon–Fri, lunch only: 15€,
2 courses

COVER & SERVICE CHARGES
Cover 2.20€, service
discretionary

ENGLISH
Yes

Mistrà is buried deep in a huge boat and marina complex—the Venice Plaza—that few visitors know about, and if they did, they would have a hard time finding it, even during the day—and for sanity's sake, unless you are directionally brave, forget it on a dark winter night. To complicate matters, there is no sign on the restaurant or over the side door, where there is an elevator that will eliminate the forty-four steps up a steep metal staircase you must climb to reach the front door. Whew! Is this place worth the effort? Yes, if you are interested in boat building. There are three gondola makers here, plus countless other workshops all related to the Venetian waters. However, the real reason to make the excursion to Mistrà is the fabulous sweeping view over the lagoon, not to mention the good food and the very favorable lunch prices. At lunch, there is a fixed-price, two-course menu for 15€ geared to the boat workers, so you know it will be hearty, fast, and filling. There are generally several pasta choices and fishy mains. House wine is 9€ for one liter. For dinner (and lunch on the weekends) the food is more complex and expensive. In addition to lobster in your pasta, wild game is available in season, big beefsteaks are tossed on the grill, and apple strudel is served for dessert. The big, bright inside features a water theme with prints and maps of Venice on the walls. It has been owned for several years by Zuchetta, Roberta, and her husband, Alessandro, who is the chef.

NOTE: To get there, take the *vaporetto* from Piazza San Marco to Giudecca and get off at the Redentore stop. Walk along Fondamento San Giacomo to Calle Giacomo and turn left. Go to the end. The restaurant is on your right. It has mercifully posted a few signs and arrows, but if you need help, the locals are very accommodating. Once there, finding the elevator is a real treasure hunt. When you are finally in the midst of the boat-building yard, look for 212 over the door marked C. *Buona Fortuna!*

Lido Island

Early in the 1900s, Lido, which is Italian for "shore," was developed as a Belle Epoque resort. Today it is a playground of twenty thousand inhabitants, with something for everyone's pocketbook and taste. It is known for its stretches of well-kept private beaches and dismal public ones, a gambling casino and film festival, and hotels—both frumpy and flashy. Because Lido has proper roads, a popular activity is to rent a bike and explore the island's neighborhoods, parks, and beachs. Lido comes alive around Easter and closes down by the end of the year.

($) indicates a Big Splurge
(¢) indicates an Cheap Eat

Restaurants

QUATTRO FONTANE ($)
Via Quattro Fontane, 16

Quattro Fontane is one of the most beloved hotels on Lido, because everything about it is designed to encourage guests to enjoy their time here in a pleasing, refined atmosphere. For further information about this lovely location, please see *Great Sleeps Italy*.

TELEPHONE
041 526 0227
INTERNET
www.quattrofontane.com
OPEN
Daily: lunch 12:30–2 P.M., dinner 7:30–10 P.M.

CLOSED
Mid-Nov–April 1
RESERVATIONS
Advised
CREDIT CARDS
AE, DC, MC, V
À LA CARTE
55–65€
FIXED-PRICE MENU
Piccolo Menù Quattro Fontane:
40€, 3 courses, 2–3 choices for
each, includes wine, water, cover
and service charges
COVER & SERVICE CHARGES
Cover 5€, service discretionary
ENGLISH
Yes, and menu in English

The hotel boasts three dining areas, each one very special in its own way. As one guest said to me, "I love the Quattro Fontane, because even though I am Venetian, I feel I am getting away from it all when I come here to eat." In the spring and late fall, meals are served in a baronial dining room dominated by a fifteenth-century stone fireplace, hanging copper pots, globe lights, and varnished red highback ladder chairs positioned around the tables. In the summer, lunches are served outside in the shade of a three-hundred-year-old plane tree, and in the evening you can eat in the magnificent candlelit garden. No matter where you dine, the faultless old-world service is a reminder of a bygone era when dining rooms were fully staffed and the career waiters took their jobs seriously.

There is definitely no staff shortage at Quattro Fontane. Each table is served by a three-person team, who tend to their guests in a polite, hospitable manner. The food is brought to the table on a rolling cart, where the pasta is tossed, the fish deboned, and the meat sliced, then placed on warm plates and served. In the center of the room, the salad fixings are beautifully displayed, as are the tempting selections of homemade desserts, the array of succulent seasonal fruits, and the generous choices of international and Italian cheeses. The fixed-price menu, or *piccolo menù Quattro Fontane,* is an excellent value in that it offers two or three choices for everything from appetizer to dessert and includes a glass of *vino della casa,* mineral water, and the cover and service charges. You might start with a colorful plate of grilled vegetables drizzled with fine olive oil, homemade pasta with clams, or a warming soup. Next, there are garnished fish, meat, and vegetarian main courses, followed by a choice of fresh fruit, pastries, or the housemade ice cream. Otherwise, you can order just the *piatti del giorno* (daily special) or from the full à la carte menu. No matter what you order, the high quality of the food, the careful preparations, and the nice presentations guarantee a Great Eat any time you are fortunate enough to get away from it all at this lovely oasis on Lido.

The hotel is a pleasant fifteen-minute walk from the Santa Maria Elisabetta *vaporetto* stop on Lido. If you are arriving from Venice in the evening, the weather cooperates, and you time your arrival just right, the twelve-minute ride will reward you with a breathtaking sunset over Venice.

RISTORANTE BELVEDERE E TAVOLA CALDA (¢, 90)
Piazzale la Santa Maria Elisabetta, 4

If you are visiting Lido for the day, chances are you will want to eat. Unless you know where to go, most of the food is overpriced tourist pizza or deadly dull and ludicrously expensive hotel dining; there is not much middle ground. Enter the Ristorante Belvedere and its Tavola Calda snack bar next door, which are part of the Hotel Belvedere (see *Great Sleeps Italy*).

Everyone agrees that some of the best food to be had in this tourist mecca is at the Belvedere, right across the street from the Santa Maria Elisabetta *vaporetto* stop. At the restaurant, famished Great Eaters who are staying at the hotel will be eligible to order the *menù per pensioni*, a 20€ value that includes three courses, cover and service charges, but not beverages. Everyone else orders à la carte, but the value for the money is still very good. The food, which features fresh fish with a nod toward several veal and beef selections, is served on a pretty streetside terrace or in air-conditioned comfort in the simple hotel dining room with big picture windows.

Confirmed card-carrying cheap eaters will skip the *ristorante* side completely and head straight for the Tavola Calda, which adjoins it. This is just the answer for the visitor with lots on the agenda who lacks the time, money, or desire for a fancy meal. The same kitchen is used for both places, but the prices here are much lower. Every day there are pastas, roast chicken, fish, and an excellent selection of vegetables, salads, and made-to-order sandwiches. Another benefit is that it is open year-round Tuesday through Sunday, while the hotel restaurant is closed from November to Easter.

TELEPHONE
041 526 0115, 041 526 0164

OPEN
Tues–Sun: lunch noon–2:30 P.M., dinner 7–9:30 P.M.

CLOSED
Mon; Ristorante Belvedere: Nov–April; Tavola Calda: 2 weeks in Nov

RESERVATIONS
Advised for Ristorante, not accepted at Tavola Calda

À LA CARTE
Ristorante, 35–45€; Tavola Calda, sandwiches 1.20–3.10€, salads 2.60–5€, hot meals 8–12€

FIXED-PRICE MENU
Menù per pensioni (hotel guests): 20€, 3 courses, includes cover and service charges

COVER & SERVICE CHARGES
Ristorante, cover charge 2.20€; none in Tavola Calda; service included in both

ENGLISH
Yes, and à la carte menu in English at the Ristorante

TRATTORIA ANDRI ($, 92)
Via Lepanto, 21

Trattoria Andri is housed in a pretty neighborhood just a ten-minute stroll away from the usual tourist track on the island of Lido. Offering ninety places outside on a covered terrace and around fifty more inside the lovely old villa, the trattoria has an open, airy interior, its white walls hung with owner Luca Meneguzzi's modern abstract paintings. Silk flowers adorn each table, and a fresh bouquet brightens up the bar.

Luca's family has been serving Lido residents for more than thirty years, and the best first course is the house specialty: *spaghetti Andri,* featuring fat shrimp. Grilled turbot or fillet of sole sautéed in butter make winning

TELEPHONE
041 526 5482

OPEN
Wed–Sun: lunch noon–3 P.M., dinner 7:30–midnight

CLOSED
Mon–Tues; Jan–Feb or until Carnivale

CREDIT CARDS
MC, V

À LA CARTE
40–45€

FIXED-PRICE MENU
Menù Andri: 60€, 4 courses, dessert, wine, and grappa

main-course selections, as do all the daily specials of seasonal seafood. The seriously hungry will consider the *menù Andri,* a multi-course fish feast featuring numerous selections for each course plus dessert, wine, and grappa. Dessert calls for something light, and the best choice, in my opinion (and in the opinion of a hundred other diners per day), is not listed on the menu and does not have a name. Ask for the *limone digestif*—a frothy, refreshing mix of lemon, ice, sparkling wine, and vodka blended together like a milkshake and served in a champagne flute.

TRATTORIA FAVORITA ($, 93)
Via Francesco Duodo, 33

The regulars at Trattoria Favorita come for the wine and the dependable fish preparations, turned out by a hardworking squad of chefs. I like it because of its location: hidden in a pretty residential district about a twenty-minute walk from the Santa Maria Elisabetta *vaporetto* stop.

Summer seating on the vine-covered terrace is always in demand, but the seats are hard plastic with thin cushions, and not many deals are made or romances begun while sitting here. The inside is more comfortable, as well as air-conditioned, a real bonus during the sizzling Venetian summers. The two large rooms have great atmosphere, featuring heavy beams, a nice collection of country furniture, lots of green plants, and fresh flowers on the formally set tables.

The kitchen does not feature daily specials, concentrating instead on doing a superb job with everything listed on the sensible menu. The emphasis is on fish. In fact, there are only three entrée choices besides fish: steak, liver and onions, and thinly sliced, rosemary-flavored roast beef. The gnocchi with crab is perfect, and so is the spaghetti with fresh clams. Grilled fillet of sole, bass, a mixed grilled fish platter, and turbot make up the bulk of the main courses. Their specialty is San Pietro garnished with seasonal vegetables, and when you order this dish, you will be given a collector's plate to commemorate your meal. The wine list is exceptional, listing only regional wines in all price categories. If something sweet is called for at the end of your meal, sip a *sgroppino*, a vodka-lemon *sorbetto*-prosecco smoothie.

Mazzorbo

The sleepy island of Mazzorbo attracts few tourists, even though it is on the number 12 ferry route from Venice to Torcello and Burano. For a tranquil walk with dynamite views across the lagoon to Venice, get off here, visit the fourteenth-century church of Santa Caterina, and then walk across the wooden bridge that connects Mazzorbo to Burano.

ALLA MADDALENA
Mazzorbo 7/B

Probably the most popular reason to visit this sleepy island in the Venetian lagoon is to have lunch at Alla Maddalena, especially on warm weekends, when the waterside terrace is packed with multi-generational families tucking into course after course of fresh lagoon food. The fixed-price menu includes everything from pasta with clams or red sauce to fried calamari or sole, green salad or fried potatoes, wine, water, coffee, and cookies from Burano. The restaurant has been run by the same family for as many years as anyone cares to remember, has absolutely no decor (unless you count the ice cream dispenser in one corner), and includes a short bar, overseen by a tired woman whose feet probably hurt. The abrupt service follows suit, but the food is dependable, basic, fishy fare that the locals relish.

TELEPHONE
041 730 151

INTERNET
www.paginegialle.it/
trattoriamaddalena

OPEN
Mon–Wed, Fri–Sun: lunch
12:30–3 P.M. (sometimes later)

CLOSED
Thur; Dec 10–Jan 20

RESERVATIONS
Essential on weekends during
warm weather

CREDIT CARDS
MC, V

À LA CARTE
22–28€

FIXED-PRICE MENU
15€, 3 courses, includes wine,
water, coffee, and Burano
cookies

COVER & SERVICE CHARGES
Cover 1€, service discretionary

ENGLISH
Limited

Murano Island

Visitors to Venice make the trip to Murano either to buy glass or to eat fish—or both. Most of the restaurants are closed for dinner, so plan accordingly.

RESTAURANTS

RISTORANTE DALLA MORA (89)
Fondamenta Daniele Manin, 75

TELEPHONE
041 736 344
OPEN
Daily: May–Oct: lunch
11:30 A.M.–5 P.M., dinner
6:30–10 P.M.; Nov–April lunch
11:30 A.M.–5 P.M.
CLOSED
Dinner Nov–April
RESERVATIONS
Essential on weekends
CREDIT CARDS
AE, DC, MC, V
À LA CARTE
30–40€
FIXED-PRICE MENU
Mon–Sat lunch: 13€, 2 courses,
and vegetable, cover and service
included
COVER & SERVICE CHARGES
Cover 1€, 12% service added
ENGLISH
Yes

The best time to experience dalla Mora is on a warm day, and you want to arrive early for lunch and nab one of the canal-side tables, avoiding the six on the side that have no shade. The large interior is attractive and perfectly acceptable, but why not be reminded every minute that you are fortunate enough to be dining in this picturesque part of Venice? The long menu reads well, but concentrate on the fish, which stars in fifteen appetizers, twenty fish-based pastas, and huge platters of fried or grilled fish—be hungry for either of these! Don't worry about dessert; they are the reruns you see everywhere: tiramisù, *panna cotta* with berries, and gelato.

TRATTORIA BUSA ALLA TORRE DA LELE (88)
Campo S. Stefano, 3

TELEPHONE
041 739 662
OPEN
Daily: lunch 11:30 A.M.–3:30 P.M.
CLOSED
Jan 10–30
RESERVATIONS
Advised
CREDIT CARDS
AE, MC, V
À LA CARTE
35–40€
FIXED-PRICE MENU
None
COVER & SERVICE CHARGES
Cover 1.50€, 12% service added
ENGLISH
Yes, and menu in English

Welcome to Lele's trattoria, where knowledgeable Venetians eat when they visit the island of Murano. Lele, a big man with red hair and a twinkle in his eye, is a Murano fixture who meets and greets his guests with great flair. The waiters offer casual service, thus time should not be a top priority on your visit here. There are two rooms inside the building, which dates from 1050 and is the oldest on the island. If weather permits, sit outside and settle in at one of the terrace tables on the *campo* by the clock tower and enjoy a romantic, leisurely lunch, accompanied by a nice bottle of Venetian wine and someone very special . . . and be glad you are not home mowing the lawn or paying bills.

The food probably will not sweep you off your feet, but the kitchen does know how to turn out classic fish dishes with finesse and just the right amount of dash. You will have the best success if you think simple and, as usual, pay close heed to whatever the chef offers for the daily special. The pasta with fresh clams, a brimming fish soup, and *tagliolini* with crab are only a few of the regular first courses, followed by sixteen main courses, all featuring local fish. Desserts are not a priority here.

Sant' Erasmo Island

Sant' Erasmo Island is known as the garden island because it provides many of the best vegetables—particularly artichokes and asparagus—sold at the Rialto Market. Although the island is larger than Venice, its population is sparse. There is one church, one bar, one restaurant, no doctor, no police, no school, and no tourism. You can, however, rent a bicycle and ride around the island, admiring the fields and the peace and quiet of it all. The only boat servicing the island is the No. 13, leaving from Fondamente Nuove. The trip takes about forty-five minutes. If you do make a day of it and bike around the island, make sure you know what time the last boat goes back to Venice, since there are no hotels, either.

CA' VIGNOTTO
Via Forti, 71

Tired of the tourist mob scene in Venice? Yearning for something different, a look at a Venice that the rank-and-file visitor never sees? Are you hungry enough for a meal that never seems to stop? If the answer to these questions is yes, then hop on the *vaporetto* No. 13 from Fondamente Nuove and take the forty-five minute trip to Sant' Erasmo Island, which is light years away from Venice in sophistication and pretense. Whether or not you rent a bicycle to tour the rural island, you can dine at Ca' Vignotto, a pretty farmhouse restaurant that serves only multicourse set meals; Sunday lunch and weekday dinners are the best and most lively times to be here.

The restaurant is about a fifteen-minute walk from the *vaporetto* stop, and finding it is part of the adventure, since of course there are no signs. Here is what to do: Get off the *vaporetto* at La Chiesa, the third stop on Sant' Erasmo. Face the church and take Via dei' Spironi, a dusty road to the left that cuts through fields of whatever vegetable is in season (a cemetery is on your left). Keep going. Be careful not to take the narrow road alongside the church, or you will wind up in someone's backyard, as I did. Stay on Via dei' Spironi until you come to the end, then turn left on Via Forti. The restaurant is on the lefthand side at Via Forti, 71, but the number is nowhere to be seen. Still, at this point you can't miss it: just look for the fountain in the front and the masses of red geraniums in glorious bloom.

Is the food worth this safari? Indeed it is. But be prepared for a huge fish, meat (best in the winter), or vegetarian

TELEPHONE
041 528 5329

OPEN
Mon, Wed–Sun: lunch and dinner by reservation only

CLOSED
Tues; last 3 weeks in Jan

RESERVATIONS
Required

CREDIT CARDS
AE, DC, MC, V

À LA CARTE
None

FIXED-PRICE MENU
25€, includes multiple courses, wine, water, coffee, grappa, cover and service charges

COVER & SERVICE CHARGES
None

ENGLISH
Yes, ask for Rodrigo

meal. The waitstaff troops out course after course in the rustic, barnlike dining room paneled in knotty pine. In April and May you can count on artichokes everywhere: in risotto and pasta and served boiled or fried as side dishes. In June, fresh peas and eggplant are on the menu, as well as fried zucchini flowers—crispy bites of heaven. The meal begins with three appetizers, is followed by three pasta servings, a main course with at least two vegetables, salad, and homemade cake, includes all the red or white wine and mineral water you can drink, and ends with coffee and grappa. If you haven't done the bike trip around the island, maybe now is the time.

NOTE: Bicycle rentals are available at the Capannone boat stop, which is the one before La Chiesa.

Food Shopping in Venice

GOURMET FOOD AND WINE SHOPS

GROCERY STORES AND SUPERMARKETS

OUTDOOR MARKETS

Gourmet Food and Wine Shops

ALIANI GASTRONOMIA (21)
Ruga Vecchia S. Giovanni, 654–655 (main street leading to Rialto Bridge) (San Polo)

For fast, flavorful, and fabulous deli-style takeout, one of the best and most central spots is Aliani Gastronomia, which has been doing business here for over thirty years. The shop offers fresh daily pastas, roast meats, fish on Friday, creamy *baccalà mantecata,* seasonal vegetables, a wide variety of Italian hams and cheeses including *mozzarella di bufala* direct from the producer, and bottles of wine from the Veneto. There is also a good selection of top-quality extra-virgin olive oil and aged balsamic vinegar. Though the deli section is open for business on Monday, hot food is available only from Tuesday to Saturday. On Wednesday afternoon the meat and cheese section is closed.

TELEPHONE
041 522 4913

OPEN
Mon: 8 A.M.–1 P.M.; Tues–Sat: 8 A.M.–1 P.M., 5–7:30 P.M.

CLOSED
Mon afternoon, Sun; 2–3 weeks in Aug (dates vary)

CREDIT CARDS
MC, V

BOTTIGLIERA COLONNA (71)
Calle della Fava, 5595 (Castello)

TELEPHONE
041 528 5137
EMAIL
botcol@libero.it
OPEN
Mon–Sat: 9 A.M.–1 P.M., 4–8 P.M.
CLOSED
Sun; 15 days between Jan & Feb, open for Carnivale
CREDIT CARDS
MC, V

This small shop has a good selection of Italian wines from small producers. They also have a good supply of grappa and speak English.

GIACOMO RIZZO (64)
San Giovanni Grisostomo, 5778 (Cannaregio)

TELEPHONE
041 522 2824
OPEN
Mon–Tues, Thur–Sat: 8:30 A.M.–1 P.M., 3:30–7:30 P.M.; Wed: 8:30 A.M.–1 P.M.
CLOSED
Wed afternoon, Sun; a few days in Aug
CREDIT CARDS
AE, DC, MC, V

One of the best gourmet food shops in Venice is Giacomo Rizzo, which has been dispensing its handmade pastas, balsamic vinegars, truffles, extra-virgin first-pressed olive oils, honeys, spices, herbs, and dried mushrooms since 1905. The dried pastas are made without preservatives or colors, and range from a simple spinach tagliatelle to those flavored with radicchio, smoked salmon, cuttlefish, and beetroot.

MASCARI (22)
Rugha Orefici, 381 (San Polo)

TELEPHONE
041 522 9762
INTERNET
www.imascari.com
OPEN
Mon–Sat: 8 A.M.–1 P.M., 4–7:30 P.M. (also Sun at Christmas)
CLOSED
Sun; Aug 1–17, 2 days at Christmas and New Year's
CREDIT CARDS
None

In the front, it looks like a gourmet grocery store with bags of *funghi porcini*, bottles of specialty olive oils, aged balsamic vinegar, spices, jams, jellies, hard candies galore, and even jars of Dijon mustard. The best part about Mascari is its large Italian wine selection, which is in the back rooms. Ask for Gabriele, one of the sons; he speaks English well and can help you select just what you want. They do not ship.

RIZZO VENEZIA (80)
Calle dei Fabbri, 933/A (San Marco)

TELEPHONE
041 522 3388
INTERNET
www.rizzostore.com
OPEN
Mon–Sat: 9 A.M.–7 P.M.
CLOSED
Sun
CREDIT CARDS
MC, V

Rizzo Venezia is a high-quality gourmet food store with three locations. In addition to their well-known breads and pastries, vast selection of candies, deli section, and fresh ground coffees, they stock all the Italian foods, condiments, and spices you need to set up your own Italian kitchen. The location on Rio Terra San Leandro is the biggest, but the two in San Marco, which are very close to each other, are more central.

There are two other locations: Calle Fiubera, 933 (San Marco) and Rio Terra San Leonardo, 1355 (Cannaregio).

VINO E...VINI (77)
Fondamenta dei Furlani, 3301 (Castello)

Be local and bring your own plastic bottles to fill with table wines dispensed from the tubs here (2–3.20€, depending on type of wine). Or upgrade to one of the best choices of Italian and international wines in Venice. The shop also stocks sixty French champagnes, ninety different grappas, sweet dessert wines, whiskey, olive oils, and balsamic vinegars.

TELEPHONE
041 521 0184
OPEN
Mon–Sat: 9 A.M.–1 P.M., 5–8 P.M.
CLOSED
Sun; 2–3 weeks in Aug (dates vary)
CREDIT CARDS
MC, V

Grocery Stores and Supermarkets

Big supermarkets do not exist in Venice, and most of the so-called supermarkets are well hidden. Hours are usually Monday through Saturday from 8:30 A.M. to 12:30 or 1 P.M. and 3:30 to 7:30 P.M., except Wednesdays, when some may close in the afternoon. Sunday, of course, is a full day of rest.

The largest market is Billa (8), Strada Nova, 3660 (Cannaregio), which has two other locations: Billa (50), Zattere al Ponte Lungo, 1491 (Dorsoduro), and on Lido in the Oviesse department store on Gran Viale Santa Maria Elisabetta. This location has the benefit of being open on Sunday from 9 A.M. to 1 P.M. and 4 to 8 P.M. Smaller markets include Suve (75), on the corner of Salizzada San Lio and Calle Mondo Nuovo, 5812 (Castello). Suve is the most central market, and it has a good meat and cheese selection; it is open nonstop Monday to Saturday from 8:30 A.M. to 7:30 P.M.

Outdoor Markets

Open-air markets selling fruits, vegetables, and flowers are set up in various squares every day but Sunday. They are a colorful part of Venetian life and a window on the ebb and flow of locals and what they are eating. They are all open in the mornings and sometimes in the afternoons. You will find them at Via Garibaldi (85) (Castello), Santa Margherita (39) (Dorsoduro), Rio Terrà San Leonardo (5) (Cannaregio), on a barge off Campo Santa Barnaba (44) (Dorsoduro), and on Lido on Tuesday mornings only. Generally speaking, the hours are Monday to Saturday from 8:30 A.M. to 12:30 P.M., and afternoons (except Wednesday) from 3:30 to 7:30 P.M.

The market to end all markets, however, is the famous Rialto Market (23) (San Polo), which can be found upon crossing the Rialto Bridge. The hawker stalls lining the street leading from the bridge to the market sell everything from T-shirts, masks, jewelry, and glassware to real and fake lace. These sellers are open from around 9 A.M. until 6 P.M. in winter and later in summer. The vegetable market (*erberia*), which is along the Grand Canal, is the best, least expensive, and most picturesque in Venice. It is open only in the morning, Monday to Saturday from 7:30 or 8 A.M. to 1 P.M. Adjoining it is the Rialto fish market (*pescheria*), one of the finest in Europe. Here you will see every known variety of fish and seafood, including some you never knew existed. This is worth a trip, and don't forget your camera. It is open Tuesday to Saturday from 8 A.M. to 1 P.M.

Glossary of Italian Words and Phrases

This glossary is broken down into two sections: The first half gives Italian equivalents for some general words and phrases you might need to use while ordering in a restaurant. The second half gives English translations of Italian words you might find as you read a menu. Many restaurants have menus in English, but invariably they do not include the daily specials, which most often are the best items to order. This glossary is designed to help you make sure there will not be a difference between what you order and what you actually eat.

General Phrases

Hello (telephone)	*Pronto*
Hello/good-bye (familiar)	*Ciao*
Good morning	*Buon giorno*
Good afternoon	*Buon pomeriggio*
Good evening	*Buona sera*
Goodnight	*Buona notte*
Good-bye	*Arrivederci*
Please	*Per favore, Per piacere*
Thank you	*Grazie*
You are welcome	*Prego*
Yes/No	*Si/No*
Excuse me	*Mi scusi*
I am sorry	*Mi dispiace*
I want/I would like . . .	*Desidero, Vorrei . . .*
Do you speak English?	*Parla inglese?*
I don't speak Italian	*Non parlo italiano*
I understand	*Capisco*
I don't understand	*Non capisco*
Where is . . . ?	*Dov'è . . . ?*
Where are the restrooms?	*Dov'è la toilette (per signore {women}, per signori {men})?*
Left	*Sinistra*
Right	*Destra*
Exit	*Uscita*
How much is it?	*Quanto costa?*
A little/A lot	*Poco/Tanto*
More/Less	*Più/Meno*
Enough/Too much	*Abbastanza/Troppo*
Open/Closed	*Aperto/Chiuso*
When does it open?	*Quando apre?*
Please telephone for a taxi	*Per favore, telefoni per un tassi*
No smoking	*Vietato fumare*
I am hungry	*Ho fame*
I am diabetic	*Ho il diabete*
I am on a diet	*Sono a dieta*
I am vegetarian	*Sono vegetariano (a)*

I cannot eat	*Non posso mangiare*
It is hot/cold	*È caldo/freddo*
Please give me . . .	*Per favore, mi dia . . .*

Days of the Week

today	*oggi*
tonight	*stastera*
tomorrow	*domani*
yesterday	*ieri*
morning	*mattina*
afternoon	*pomeriggio*
evening	*sera*
night	*notte*
Monday	*Lunedì*
Tuesday	*Martedì*
Wednesday	*Mercoledì*
Thursday	*Giovedì*
Friday	*Venerdì*
Saturday	*Sabato*
Sunday	*Domenica*

Numbers

1	*uno*
2	*due*
3	*tre*
4	*quattro*
5	*cinque*
6	*sei*
7	*sette*
8	*otto*
9	*nove*
10	*dieci*
11	*undici*
12	*dodici*
13	*tredici*
14	*quattordici*
15	*quindici*
16	*sedici*
17	*diciasette*
18	*diciotto*
19	*diciannove*
20	*venti*
21	*ventuno*
30	*trenta*
40	*quaranta*
50	*cinquanta*
60	*sessanta*
70	*settanta*
80	*ottanta*
90	*novanta*
100	*cento*
1,000	*mille*
2,000	*duemila*

Restaurant Basics

A table (reservation) for ___, please	*Un tavolo (prenotazione) per___persone, per favore*
waiter/waitress	*cameriere/cameriera*
breakfast	*prima colazione*
lunch	*pranzo*
dinner	*cena*
snack	*un spuntino*
takeaway	*da portare via*
The menu, please	*La lista, per favore*
The wine list, please	*La lista dei vini, per favore*
I would like this	*Vorrei questo*
Do you accept credit cards?	*Si accettano le carte de credito?*
The bill, please	*Il conto, per favore*
The bill divided by two	*Uno diviso due*
The bill is not correct	*Il conto non è giusto*
bread/cover charge	*pane e coperto*
service charge	*servizio*
Is the service included?	*Il servizio è incluso?*
Service is included	*Il servizio è compreso/incluso*
appetizers	*antipasti*
first courses	*primi piatti*
second courses	*secondi piatti*
side dishes	*contorni*
dessert	*dolce*
fixed-price menu	*menù turistico/prezzo fisso*
dish (special) of the day	*piatto (speciali) del giorno*
specialty of the house/homemade	*specialità della casa/fatto in casa*
half portion	*una mezza porzione*
in season	*di stagione*
I need a . . .	*Ho bisogno di . . .*
knife	*un cotello*
fork	*una forchetta*
spoon	*un cucchiaio*
cup	*tazza*
plate	*piatto*
chair	*sedia*
highchair	*seggiolino*
table	*tavola*
napkin	*il tovagliolo*
I would like . . .	*Vorrei . . .*
a cup of	*una tazza di*
a glass of	*un bicchiere di*
a bottle of	*una bottiglia di*
a half bottle of	*una mezza bottiglia di*
a carafe of	*una caraffa di*
a liter of	*uno litro di*

Places

alimentari	grocery store
baccaro	Venetian wine bar
caffè	café

drogheria	dried and packaged foods
enoteca	wine shop/bar
gastronomica	grocery store
gelateria	ice cream shop
il forno	bread shop, bakery
latteria	cheese and dairy store
osteria	wine bar
paninoteca	sandwich bar
pasticceria	pastry shop
salumeria	shop for dried, cured meats and cheese
tabaccheria	tobaccanist, a place to get newspapers, bus tickets, lottery tickets, pens, stamps, and so on
tavola calda	cafeteria-style food

Reading the Menu
Cooking Methods

affumicato	smoked
al cartòccio	baked in paper or foil
al dente	firm, not overcooked (as in pasta)
al ferro	grilled without olive oil
al forno	baked
alla brace	barbecued, charcoal grilled
alla griglia/ferri	grilled
allo spiedo	on the spit
al sangue/poco cotto	rare
al vapore/in úmido	steamed/stewed
arrosto	roast
ben cotto	well-done
bollito/lesso	boiled
brasato	braised, cooked in wine
carpaccio	thinly sliced raw meat or fish
cotto	cooked (not raw)
crudo	raw
fritto	fried
griglia	grilled
in bianco	plain; oil or butter on pasta; no tomato sauce on pizza
in brodo	in clear broth
in úmido	poached
involtini	wrapped or rolled
lesso	boiled, steamed
milanese	fried in egg and breadcrumbs
pizzaiola	cooked in tomato sauce
ripieno/farcito/stufato	stuffed
spiedo	spit roasted
stufato	stewed
surgelato	frozen
vapore	steamed

Types of Pasta

agnolotti	similar to ravioli, usually filled with meat
bavette	long, narrow pasta
bigoli	large, whole-wheat pasta (Venice)
bombolotti	short, tube shaped

bucatini	hollow spaghetti
cannelloni	stuffed pasta tubes
capelli d'angelo	angel hair pasta
conchiglie	pasta shells
crespelle	crêpes
farfalle	butterfly-shaped pasta
fettuccine	long, thin flat pasta
fusilli	spiral-shaped pasta
gnocchi	small potato dumplings
lasagne	large, flat noodles layered with ingredients and baked
maccheroni, maccheroncini	macaroni
orecchiette	ear-shaped pasta
paglia e fieno	green and yellow tagliatelle
pappardelle	wide noodles
pasta verde	spinach noodles
pasticcio	baked pasta pie with cheese, vegetables, and meat
penne	narrow, diagonally cut macaroni
ravioli	filled pasta squares
rigatoni	large macaroni
risotto (ai funghi, al zafferano, di zucca)	rice (with mushrooms, saffron, pumpkin)
rotelle	spiral-shaped pasta
tagliatelle	thin, flat egg pasta ribbons
taglierini	thin pasta ribbons
tagliolini	thin, flat noodles
tonnarelli	square-shaped spaghetti
tortelli	ravioli with a filling of potato or spinach and ricotta cheese
tortellini	small meat or cheese-filled pasta dumplings
tortelloni	large tortellini
vermicelli	thin spaghetti
ziti	short, wide, tube-shaped pasta

Pasta Sauces

aglio e olio (e peperoncino)	tossed in garlic and olive oil (and hot peppers)
al burro (e salvia)	with butter (and sage)
al sugo	with puréed tomatoes
amatriciana	bacon or sausage, tomatoes, onion, and hot pepper
arrabbiata	spicy tomato sauce with chilies
astice	lobster sauce
bolognese	meat sauce, usually with tomato
bucaniera	seafood, tomato, garlic, parsley, and oil
cacciatore	tomato, onion, peppers, mushrooms, garlic, herbs, and wine sauce
cacio e pepe	sheep's cheese and ground pepper
carbonara	cream, ham or bacon, egg, and Parmesan cheese
frutta di mare	seafood
funghi	mushroom
gricia	chili, onion, and sausage
matriciana	pork and tomato sauce
norma	tomato, eggplant, and salted ricotta cheese
panna	cream
parmigiano	Parmesan cheese

pesto	ground pine nuts, basil, garlic, and pecorino cheese
pomodoro/pomodoro fresco	tomato sauce/raw tomatoes
puttanesca	tomatoes, capers, red peppers, anchovies, garlic, and oil
quattro formaggi	with four cheeses
ragù	tomato-based meat sauce
sugo (di pomodoro)	puréed tomato sauce
vóngole	clams, tomatoes, and garlic

Pizza

Most pizzerias have dozens of variations on the following basics.

alla Romana	tomato, mozzarella, anchovies
calzone	stuffed pizza
capricciosa	ham, hard-boiled or fried egg, artichokes, and olives
frutti di mare	seafood, usually mussels, prawns, squid, and clams
funghi	mushrooms (from a can unless specifies *funghi freschi*)
margherita	tomato, mozzarella, and basil
marinara	plain tomato sauce, oregano and sometimes anchovies, never cheese
pizza al taglio	slice of pizza
pizza bianca	without tomato
pizza napoletana	thick-crust pizza
pizza romana	thin-crust pizza
pizzelle	small fried pizza with tomato and Parmesan cheese
quattro formaggi	four cheeses
quattro stagioni	literally means "four seasons": mozzarella (winter), artichoke or arugula (spring), fried egg (summer), and mushrooms (fall)
salsiccia	sausage, tomato, and mozzarella

Drinks

acqua	water
acqua di selz	soda water
acqua minerale senza gas/gassata	mineral water, still or gas
aperitivo	before-dinner drink
aranciata, il succo d'arancia	orange drink, orange juice
bicchiere	glass
birra	beer
caffè	coffee
cioccolata calda	hot chocolate
dolce	sweet
ghiaccio (con ghiaccio)	ice (on the rocks)
granita	flavored, iced drink
grappa	potent liquor made from grape mash
Hag	brand name of the most popular decaf coffee; used to mean decaffeinated in general
latte	milk
latte intero/parzialmente scremato/scremato	whole milk, low-fat milk, nonfat milk
limonata	lemonade
limoncello	sweet lemon liqueur, best served ice cold

liquore	liqueur
litro	liter
mezzo litro	half liter
ombra (Venice)	glass of white wine in a bar
prosecco	dry, sparkling white wine
quarto litro	quarter liter
secco	dry
spremuta	fresh fruit juice
spritz al bitter (Venice)	Venetian apéritif: white wine, selzer, dash of bitters (such as Campari), lemon twist
succo (di frutta)	juice (fruit)
tè	tea
tisana	herbal tea
vino (locale, bianco, rosso)	wine (local, white, red)
vin santo	sweet dessert wine
whiskey scozzese, lo scotch	Scotch

Other Menu and Food Terms

A

abbacchio	milk-fed spring lamb
acciughe	anchovies
aceto	vinegar
aceto balsamico	balsamic vinegar
acquacotta	thick vegetable soup, predominantly cabbage, poured over bread
acqua frizzante (naturale)	sparkling water (still)
affettai misti	assorted cold cuts
affettato	sliced
aglio	garlic
agnello; agnellino	lamb; young lamb
agrume	citrus fruit
albicocca	apricot
alici/marinati	fresh anchovies/ marinated
all'alla/alle/allo	in the style of/with
alloro	bay leaf
ananas	pineapple
anatra	duck
aneto	dill
anguilla (Veneziana)	eel (cooked with lemon and tuna)
antipasti misti	assorted appetizers
antipasto	appetizer
aperitivo	apéritif
a piacere	as you like it
aragosta	lobster, crayfish
arancia	orange
arancìno/arancìni	spicy meatball mixed with rice, breaded and fried
arborio	best rice to make risotto
aringa	herring
arista	roast pork
arrosto	roast
arrosto misto	mixed roast meats
asciutto	dry

asparagi	asparagus
assaggi	a series of small portions
assaggio	a taste
astice	crayfish

B

baccalà	dried salt cod, sometimes simmered in milk or fried in batter
baccalà mantecata	creamy cod
baccelli	(fava) beans (Tuscan)
baicoli	thin, Venetian dessert cookie
banane	bananas
barbabietola	beet
basilico	basil
Bel Paese	soft, mild cheese
bieta, bietola	Swiss chard
bigoli in salsa	fat, often whole-wheat spaghetti with anchovies and onion sauce (Venetian specialty)
biscotti	cookies
bistecca	beef steak
bistecca alla fiorentina	T-bone steak, grilled over coals, served very rare
bollito misto (con salsa verde)	mixed boiled meats (with vinegar and parsley sauce)
braciola	steak, chop, slice of meat
branzino	sea bass
bresaola	air-cured beef, thinly sliced
briosca	croissant (also called *cornetto*)
broccoli siciliani	broccoli
broccolo	green cauliflower
brodetto	fish stew
brodo (pastina in brodo)	broth (with pasta pieces)
bruschetta	toasted bread rubbed with raw garlic topped with tomatoes, olive oil, or olive paste
budino di cioccolato	chocolate pudding
bue	beef, ox
burro	butter
bussolài buranèi	doughnut-shaped cookies made on Burano in the round shape of the Island of Burano; the S-shaped versions that portray the Venetian Grand Canal are called *Essi Buranei*

C

cacciagione	game
calamari (calamaretti)	squid (baby squid)
caldo	hot/warm
camomilla	chamomile tea
cannellini	white beans
cannoli (Siciliana)	custard-filled pastry with pieces of candied fruit (pastry shells filled with ricotta cheese and dusted with sugar)
cantuccini	hard almond biscuits to dip in *vin santo*
caparosoli	clams
cape longhe	razor clams
capesante	scallops
caponata	eggplant salad

capperi	capers
capra (capretto)	goat (baby goat)
caprese	fresh tomato, mozzarella, and basil salad
capretto	kid
capriolo	venison
carbonade	beef stewed with red wine
carciofo (alla giudia) (alla romana)	artichoke (deep-fried) (cooked with garlic, parsley and mint)
carne	meat
carote	carrots
carpàccio	thinly sliced raw beef
casalinga	homestyle
cassata	ice cream with candied fruit
castagnaccio	chestnut flour cake
castagne	chestnuts
cavallo	horsemeat
cavolfiore	cauliflower
cavolo (nero)	cabbage (dark)
ceci	chickpeas
cerfoglio	chervil
cernia	grouper
cervello	brains
cervo	venison
cetriolo	cucumber
chianina	Tuscan beef
cicchetti	snacks (Venician)
cicoria	green, leafy vegetable similar to dandelion greens
ciliegia	cherry
cinghiale	wild boar
cioccolata	chocolate
cipolla	onion
coccomero	watermelon
coda di bue alla vaccinara	oxtail stew
coda di rospo	monkfish
congelato	frozen
coniglio	rabbit
contorni	side dishes (vegetables, salads, potatoes)
coperto	cover charge added per person to bill
cornetto	croissant (also called *briosca*)
costoletta	chop or cutlet
cozze	mussels
crema	custard
crespelle	crêpes
crostata	open-faced fruit tart
crostini	toasted bread, topped with grilled cheese spread with pâté
crudo	raw (as in *prosciutto crudo,* raw ham)
cucina	kitchen, cooking
cuore	heart

D

da portare via	to take out
datteri	dates
degustazione	tasting

di stagione	of the season
dolce	dessert

E

erbe	herbs
Essi Buranei	S-shaped butter cookies made in Burano shaped like the Grand Canal in Venice
etto	100 grams (1/4 pound)

F

fagiano	pheasant
fagioli	Tuscan white beans
fagiolini	green string beans
fave	fava (broad) beans
fegatelli	pork livers
fegatini	chicken livers
fegato (alla Veneziana)	calves' liver (with onions)
fettunta	garlic bread with fresh olive oil (Florentine)
fichi	figs
filetto	fillet
finocchio	fennel
fior di latte	mozzarella made from cow's milk
fior di zucca/fiori di zucchino	zucchini flowers stuffed with mozzarella and anchovies, dipped in bread batter and quickly fried
fiorentina	thick, rare Tuscan steak
focaccia	flat bread made with olive oil
folpi/folpeti	baby octopuses
Fontina	delicate, buttery cheese
formaggio	cheese
fragole	strawberries
fragoline	tiny wild strawberries
freddo	cold
frittata	unfolded omelette
frittelle	Venetian fritters made only at Carnivale, filled with raisins or cream
fritto	fried
fritto misto	assorted deep-fried foods (fish, vegetables)
frutta	fruit
frutti di bosco	woodland berries
frutti di mare	shellfish
funghi	mushrooms
funghi porcini	wild boletus mushrooms

G

gamberetti	shrimp, prawns
gelato	ice cream
ghiaccio	ice
gianduiotto	chocolate hazelnut ice cream treat
gnocchi/gnocchetti	small potato dumplings
Gorgonzola	blue-veined cheese
grana	cow's milk cheese similar to Parmesan
granchio/granseola	crab/spider crab
grissini	bread sticks

I

imbottito	stuffed
insalata (di mare)	salad (seafood)
integrale	whole wheat
involtini	stuffed meat or fish rolls

L

lampone	raspberries
lardo	pork fat
latte	milk
lattuga	lettuce
legumi	vegetables
lenticchie	lentils
lepre	wild hare
lesso	boiled
limoncello	lemon liqueur served icy cold
limone (limonata)	lemon (lemonade)
lingua	tongue
lombatine	veal chops
lumache	snails

M

macedonia di frutta	dessert of chopped fresh fruit
maiale, maialino	pork, piglet
mandarino	tangerine
mándorla	almond
manzo	beef
mela	apple
melagrana	pomegranate
melanzane	eggplant
melone	melon
menta	mint
merluzzo	cod
miele	honey
millefoglie	layers of puff pastry filled with custard cream
minestra	soup
minestrone	vegetable soup
misticanza	salad of mixed baby greens and herbs
moleche	deep-fried soft-shelled crabs that are deep fried
more	blackberries
mozzarella di bufala	delicate fresh cheese made from the milk of a water buffalo

N

nazionale	domestic, meaning made in Italy
nervetti	strips of cartilage
noce	walnut
nocciola	hazelnut

O

oca	goose
olio di oliva extravergine	first press, extra-virgin olive oil
olive ascoiane	olives coated with mincemeat and breadcrumbs
ombra	glass of wine (Venetian)
orata	sea bream
osso buco	veal shanks
ostriche	oysters

P

pajata	baby veal intestines
pancetta	spicy, salted bacon
pane (tostato)	bread (toast)
pane e coperto	bread and cover charge
panettone	light yeast cake with candied fruit peel
panforte	cake with dried fruit
panna	cream
panna cotta	vanilla cream pudding
panna (montata)	cream (whipped)
panino	sandwich or roll
panzanella	Tuscan specialty salad made with stale bread, olive oil, tomatoes, and onions
pappa al pomodoro	bread and tomato soup (Florentine)
parmigiano	Parmesan cheese
pasta e ceci	pasta and chickpea soup
pasta e fagioli	pasta and barlotti bean soup
patata	potato
pecorino	sheep's cheese
pepe	black pepper
peperonata	grilled peppers served in olive oil
peperoncini	hot red peppers
peperoni	peppers
pera	pear
pesca/pesche	peach/peaches
pesce	fish
pesce spada	swordfish
piccione	pigeon
pici	thick handmade spaghetti
pignoli	pine nuts
pinzimonio	appetizer of raw vegetables to be dipped in olive oil
piselli	peas
polenta	cornmeal
pólipo/polpo	octopus
pollo	chicken
polpette/polpettini	meatballs
pomodori (ripieni)	tomatoes (stuffed)
pompelmo	grapefruit
porchetta	roast piglet
porcini	cêpe mushrooms
porri	leeks
prezzemolo	parsley
primavera	with spring vegetables
primi piatti	first courses
produzione artiginale, propria	homemade, usually ice cream
prosciutto/con melone	air-dried, salt-cured ham/with melon
prosciutto cotto	cooked prosciutto
prosciutto crudo	raw prosciutto
provolone	smooth cow's milk cheese
prunga	plum
prunga secca	prune

puntarelle	wild chicory greens dressed with oil, vinegar, and mashed anchovies (Roman specialty)
purè di patate	mashed potatoes

R

radicchio (Treviso)	red chicory (a specialty of Treviso)
radice	radish
rape	turnip greens
ravanello	radish
ribollita	bean, bread, cabbage, and vegetable soup (means "reboiled") (Tuscan)
ricci di mare	sea urchins
ricotta	soft, mild white cheese made from cow's or sheep's milk
ripieno	stuffed
risi e bisi	rice and pea soup, sometimes with ham and Parmesan cheese
riso	rice
rognone	kidney
rognoni	kidneys
rombo	turbot
rosmarino	rosemary
rucola, rughetta	arugula

S

sale	salt
salmone	salmon
salsiccia	sausage
saltimbocca	veal rolls with ham, flavored with sage
salumi	cured meats
salvia	sage
San Pietro	John Dory fish
sarda/sardella/sardina	sardine
sarde (in saor)	sardines (marinated in vinegar, onions, pine nuts, and raisins)
scalogno	shallot
scaloppa	thinly sliced meat
scampi	prawns
scoflio	shell and rockfish
secondi piatti	main courses
sedano	celery
semifreddo	soft, frozen, ice cream mousse
senape	mustard
seppie in nero	squid (cuttlefish) cooked in its own ink
servizio	service charge
sfogliatelle	pastry stuffed with ricotta
sformato	soufflé-like vegetable pudding
sogliola	sole
sorbetto	sherbet
spada	swordfish
spezzatino	meat in a casserole, similar to stew
spiedini	spit-roasted kebabs, skewers
spigola	type of sea bass
spinaci	spinach

straccetti	stir-fried strips of veal or beef
stracciatella	broth with egg and Parmesan cheese stirred in at the last minute
straccino	soft cream cheese
surgelato	frozen

T

tacchino	turkey
tartufo	ice cream coated in hard chocolate
tè	tea
tiramisù	rich, creamy dessert made with mascarpone cheese, liqueur, espresso, chocolate, and ladyfingers (means "pick-me-up")
toast	toasted ham and cheese sandwich
tonno	tuna
torrone	nougat
torta	cake/tart/pie
torta della nonna	cake with custard and nuts
torta di mele	apple custard tart
tostato	toasted
tramezzino	sandwich on white bread without the crust (also called *panino*)
trancia	slice
trippa (alla romana)	tripe (in tomato sauce)
trippa e rissa	tripe cooked in broth (Venetian)
trota	trout

U

un etto	100 grams, about 4 ounces
uova	egg
uva	grape
uva secca	raisin

V

verdure (cotte)	green vegetables (cooked)
verza	cabbage (also called *cavolo*)
vitello, vitella, vitellone	veal
vongole	clams

Z

zabaione, zabaglione	custard dessert made to order in a copper pot with beaten egg yolks, sugar, and white or Marsala wine, and served warm
zucca	pumpkin
zucchero	sugar
zuppa	soup
zuppa de pesce	fish soup
zuppa inglese	trifle

Index by City

FLORENCE

BIG SPLURGES

CHEAP EATS

GELATERIAS

PASTRY SHOPS AND BAKERIES

VENICE

BIG SPLURGES

Readers' Comments

In *Great Eats Italy,* I recommend places as they were when I visited them and as this book went to press. I hope they will stay that way, but as seasoned travelers know, there are no guarantees. While every effort has been made to ensure the accuracy of the information presented, the reader must understand that with the passage of time menu selections, ownership, staff and management, opening and closing times, and vacation schedules can change. Therefore, the author and publisher cannot accept responsibility for any changes that occur that result in loss or inconvenience to anyone.

Great Eats Italy is updated and revised on a regular basis. If you find that someplace has changed or make a discovery you want to pass along, please send me a note stating the name and address of the restaurant, the date of your visit, a description of your findings, and any other information you think is necessary. Your comments are extremely important to me. I read every letter I receive and respond to as many as possible. I hope you will take a few minutes to send me an old-fashioned letter, or leave a message on my Website with your comments, tips, new finds, or suggestions for *Great Eats Italy.*

Please send your letters to Sandra A. Gustafson, *Great Eats Italy,* c/o Chronicle Books, 85 Second Street, Sixth Floor, San Francisco, CA 94105, or visit www.greateatsandsleeps.com.